To read stories by Constance Fenimore
Woolson:

"Miss Grief and Other Stories" compiled
by Anne Boyd Rioux

or through HOOPLA downloadable
books "East Angels" and "Anne"

Constance Fenimore Woolson

PORTRAIT OF A LADY NOVELIST

ANNE BOYD RIOUX

W. W. NORTON & COMPANY / NEW YORK / LONDON

INDEPENDENT PUBLISHERS SINCE 1923

Copyright © 2016 by Anne Boyd Rioux

All rights reserved
Printed in the United States of America
First Edition

For information about permission to reproduce selections from this book,
write to Permissions, W. W. Norton & Company, Inc.,
500 Fifth Avenue, New York, NY 10110

For information about special discounts for bulk purchases, please contact
W. W. Norton Special Sales at specialsales@wwnorton.com or 800-233-4830

Manufacturing by RR Donnelley, Harrisonburg, VA
Book design by Brooke Koven
Production manager: Anna Oler

Library of Congress Cataloging-in-Publication Data

Names: Rioux, Anne Boyd, author.
Title: Constance Fenimore Woolson : portrait of a lady novelist / Anne Boyd
Rioux.
Description: First edition. | New York : W. W. Norton & Company, 2016. |
Includes bibliographical references and index.
Identifiers: LCCN 2015036833 | ISBN 9780393245097 (hardcover)
Subjects: LCSH: Woolson, Constance Fenimore, 1840–1894. | Women novelists,
American—19th century—Biography. | Women and literature—United
States—History—19th century.
Classification: LCC PS3363 .R56 2016 | DDC 813/.4—dc23 LC record
available at http://lccn.loc.gov/2015036833

W. W. Norton & Company, Inc.
500 Fifth Avenue, New York, N.Y. 10110
www.wwnorton.com

W. W. Norton & Company Ltd.
Castle House, 75/76 Wells Street, London W1T 3QT

1 2 3 4 5 6 7 8 9 0

To the members of the
Constance Fenimore Woolson Society

Contents

Constance Fenimore Woolson

Portraits

On January 24, 1894, a woman jumps from the third-story window of her Venetian palazzo. She has been ill for almost two weeks but has told none of her family or closest friends, who include the novelist Henry James. Instead, she dies alone, with only a nurse and a doctor at her side, her life of misery and neglect finally over. If only James had loved her, he later thinks, she might not have jumped.

In May 1894 James comes to Venice to help the woman's sister and niece clean out her apartment. He destroys all evidence of their friendship and then rows out into a lagoon with her dresses. He tries to drown them, but they billow up like black balloons that won't be submerged. For years afterward, the woman who wore them haunts the Master's imagination, living on in his fiction. She appears most notably as May Bartram, the self-sacrificing, all-loving, and overlooked friend of the self-absorbed John Marcher in "The Beast in the Jungle."

THESE MURKY vignettes are the extent of what most people know about the American writer Constance Fenimore Woolson, if they know of her at all. Not unlike those ominous, unsinkable dresses, these images continue to crop up in biographies, literary criticism, fiction, and poetry, despite their questionable veracity.[1] Although Woolson was widely considered one of the most accomplished American women writers of the late nineteenth century, what remains in the collective memory are stories of her unrequited love for James and her consequent suicide. These two doubtful details have overshadowed the rest of her daring life, which included travels throughout the U.S. South during Reconstruction, fourteen years of wandering in Europe, an extended trip to Egypt, and a decades-long inquiry into the art of fiction and the pressures of convention on women's lives. Raised to be a traditional wife and mother, Woolson became instead a world traveler and serious writer who sought not only a means of support and celebrity but critical recognition and lasting fame, highly unusual aims for a woman of her time. As a result, the road she chose was at times painful and lonely. But she also possessed a tremendous capacity for joy and a wonderful tenacity in the face of suffering.

Her life story has never been fully or adequately told in large part because it has been eclipsed by James's. Putting Woolson in the center of the frame, however, allows new scenes to emerge, displacing those of third-story windows and ballooning black dresses.

We can see, for instance, a shy, precocious girl, with long curls and pursed lips, watching intently as the grown-ups gathered in the parlor play literary and historical games. She hangs on their every word, her eyes brightening when she hears something that interests her.

In another view, she has grown into a young woman who runs out into the street when she hears the call of a newspaper boy proclaiming the latest headlines of the war. She buys one of the papers and scours it instantly for news of a certain regiment headed by the man she expects to marry, if he returns.

Many years later we see her, dressed smartly but plainly, walking along Manhattan's bustling Fifth Avenue, her keen eyes storing up all she observes of the fashionable elite for the witty, irreverent letters she writes for a newspaper back home.

In another scene, she is walking on top of the seawall that snakes along the shores of St. Augustine, Florida, deep in conversation with the poet and critic Edmund Clarence Stedman. She betrays her feelings with a grateful smile. He is the first man to listen seriously to all of her hopes and plans for her career.

In Florence she stands in one of the side chapels of Santa Croce. At her side the writer and critic Henry James explains the significance of the Giotto murals. Having become quite deaf in adulthood, she watches him intently, reading his lips. She imagines his mystification over her attention and begins to plan a playful story about a man who thinks a woman must want to marry him because she hangs on his every word as he holds forth on Florentine art.

A few years further into the future she sits at a desk in a hotel room in Sorrento, Italy, gazing out across the sapphire Bay of Naples toward smoldering Mount Vesuvius. She has always liked to be up high, where the air is clearest and she feels suspended above life's cares. On her desk is a pile of letters about her first novel, then running serially in *Harper's*, from fellow writers and fans. One, from her publisher, encloses a check doubling her pay. In her excitement she writes to James of her triumph, but she soon regrets it. Her feelings of insecurity, in spite of her novel's great success, overwhelm her.

Many years later, worn out from the cares of housekeeping and the hard labor of writing, she seeks refuge and renewal in Egypt. We can find her on top of a donkey pulled by a young boy through the streets of Cairo in search of as many ornately decorated mosques as she can find. When she arrives at the doorstep of one, the attendant looks at her in shock. No Westerners ever visit, for the mosque is not listed in the guidebooks. But that is why she has come.

There are countless other scenes—some sad, some joyous—that make up the life of a woman hungry for uplifting sights and rich experiences. Her appreciation of the noble and beautiful in life knew no bounds. Yet she also possessed a keen empathy for suffering, so much so that at times it engulfed her. The six novels and dozens of stories she produced were meant to remind readers of their shared humanity and to represent life in all its complexity. She knew, as we must, that no life is without its love and its fury, its awe and its anguish. Hers was no different.

To begin to understand how Woolson ended up dying alone, in the cold street behind her home in Venice, we have to begin by looking at her life through her eyes instead of James's. When we do, we see a life full of heartache, hope, and ambition that started in a conservative era and ended just as the New Woman was being born. We begin to see a powerful writer and conflicted woman who was not simply James's follower but his friend and peer. We also find a woman of great wit and compassion, a woman passionate about art, literature, and love, and a woman at war with herself—in short, a woman as beguiling as any of James's heroines.

If we look at Woolson when she first knew James, in the early 1880s, we see a very different figure than the one of popular imagination. She was more like another James character, Isabel Archer, than May Bartram—more independent than devoted, more self-directed than self-sacrificing. When Woolson first read *The Portrait of a Lady*, a copy of which James sent to her, inscribed, "Constance Fenimore Woolson. / from her friend & servant / Henry James," she felt as if she were looking into a mirror. She had always been, like Isabel, full of ideas of her own and eager to express them. As Isabel first encounters Europe, in the first half of the novel, her great charm is her openness to new sensations, her fondness for her own liberty, and her independent mind. She is unattached and free to make her own way in life. In her twenties, Woolson wrote words that could just as easily have come from the lips of James's character: "[A]lthough I am willing to settle down after thirty years are told, I do not care to be forced into quiescence yet awhile."[2]

Isabel Archer was an exceptional creation because she seemed determined to choose her own path in life. James wrote of her, "She was intelligent and generous; it was a fine free nature; but what was she going to do with herself? This question was irregular, for with most women one had no occasion to ask it. Most women did with themselves nothing at all; they waited, in attitudes more or less gracefully passive, for a man to come that way and furnish them with a destiny. Isabel's originality was that she gave one an impression of having intentions of her own."[3] Woolson, by coming to Europe, free for the first time in her life after her parents' deaths, was charting her own path as well. When James first met her, in the spring of 1880, as he was writing the novel that would become his masterpiece, he saw in his new friend no small portion of the spirit he was trying to capture on the page. No wonder he took time off from his work to show her around the museums and churches of Florence for four weeks.

After reading the novel, Woolson confessed to feeling with Isabel "a perfect sympathy, & comprehension, & a complete acquaintance as it were." She knew Isabel as well as she knew herself. Like her, Woolson did not conform to most men's idea of an agreeable woman. She was too self-contained, in the terminology of the day. Neither possessed the uncomplicated, undiscriminating nature prized in women. They were "idealizing [and] imaginative . . . , sure to be terribly unhappy."[4]

When James first conceived of Isabel, he assumed, as he had about his cousin Minny Temple, on whom she was primarily based, that independence must breed unhappiness. The world was too small for women's expansive minds. Neither Minny nor Isabel would be able to find outlets for their keen observing intellects. James created for Isabel what he imagined Minny's fate might have been, had she not died young: entrapment in a marriage that had seemed as if it would fulfill her greatest desires for mental companionship. In the end, Isabel's husband, Gilbert Osmond, comes to resent his wife "having a mind of her own at all."[5] James was sure that women like Minny and Isabel would find that the world as it existed did not match their aspirations. It was not ready for them.

Woolson agreed. For she didn't believe the world was entirely ready for her either, at least not the woman she wanted to be. Her fiction reflects that belief. It is full of strong, sometimes ambitious women, who, like Isabel, are often caged in the end. In her own life, Woolson clung to the cover of convention, hoping no one would notice how ambitious she really was. She would play the devoted friend to distract James from their obvious rivalry. But she could not hide the fact that she too was intent on making her own destiny. In one important way she was different from Isabel and Minny, however: she lived past the dangerous age of enticement and disillusionment to discover the virtues of independence in her thirties. She had just turned forty when she met James in Florence. She had already chosen her path in life by becoming an author.

James's portrait of Isabel was a bit audacious—"How did you ever dare write a portrait of a lady?" Woolson taunted him.[6] In spite of his boldness, however, he could not imagine the key to Isabel's character that would have allowed her true independence—ambition. He had given her the soul of an artist without the drive or talent to realize it. Her genius, therefore, is channeled into living rather than creating. The man she adores, Osmond, tells her to make her life a work of art, and she allows him to convince her that being his wife will satisfy her desires for beauty and usefulness—for art, in other words. What she doesn't know is that she will become an ornament, a work of art for his consumption alone.

Much of what we think we know of nineteenth-century women's lives comes from men's portraits of them—the fictional as well as the historical—with James's Isabel Archer at or near the head of the list. Woolson, however, was much more than James or even she could imagine on the page: a woman artist as committed to her writing as he was. Imagine Isabel with the ambition of her creator, with the desire not simply to make her life a work of art but to make art from her life. Would it be possible for her to realize her ambitions and satisfy her desires for intellectual and emotional companionship? Could she gain the respect and friendship of her male peers? Could she be happy choosing art over a conventional woman's life? These were the questions at the heart of Woolson's life.

Her life has been called, like Isabel's, tragic. But that is far from the whole story. That she dared to live as only men had previously done—to devote herself to a serious literary career over family and domesticity—makes her courageous, not tragically flawed. How she became one of the first women writers to make such a life for herself, and the particular demons that haunted her along the way—that is the story to be told.

PART ONE

An Education in Womanhood

1840–1869

"For girls . . . their 'land' is their father, or mother, one or both; wherever the father or mother is, that is a daughter's country."

—CONSTANCE FENIMORE WOOLSON

"[T]he war was the heart and spirit of my life."

—CONSTANCE FENIMORE WOOLSON

1

A Daughter's Country

O N MARCH 5, 1840, a healthy, plump little girl was born to
Hannah and Charles Jarvis Woolson in the riverside village
of Claremont, New Hampshire. They named her Constance. Before
they had time to adjust to the fact that yet another girl, their sixth,
had been born to them, the older ones fell ill. Ominous red rashes
spread across their faces, indicating scarlet fever. Connie, as they
called her, was protected by her mother's milk, and Georgiana and
Emma, the oldest, recovered. But five-year-old Ann, four-year-old
Gertrude, and two-year-old Julia did not. They died before Constance was a month old.

The family that remained would soon flee New Hampshire's unfor-
giving winters and the sight of the three tiny headstones in the town
cemetery next to the park. Hannah would never speak of the lost girls,
but Constance knew that her birth had been overshadowed by their
deaths.[1] It is little wonder that for the rest of her life she would look
over her shoulder, expecting her own or someone else's end. In their
letters, she and her family would often qualify their plans with the
phrase "if I live."

Hannah was broken by the sight of her girls' empty beds and discarded playthings. Years later, one of her daughters would explain, "Mother nearly lost her reason. . . . Father often told us children that a 'something' went out of her that week, that was lost forever . . . so that we children did not know what Mother had really been except for a beautiful portrait which Father had had painted of her."[2] It shows a young Hannah with a thoughtful, almost dreamy look in her large, almond-shaped eyes. Constance would never know that calm, innocent gaze. She would know, instead, a worried, watchful mother's eyes.

Many years later Hannah wrote rather coolly about her breakdown after the three little girls' deaths. "My health was so much impaired that it was necessary to leave New England before another winter. We broke up housekeeping," she wrote, using a common expression that conveys something of the devastation she felt. As Clara, the child who

Portrait of Hannah Cooper Pomeroy Woolson,
before the deaths of her children.
(From *Voices Out of the Past*, vol. 1 of *Five Generations (1785–1923)*)

came after Constance, would one day write, "I have always thought the use of 'breaking up' a home so appropriate—to those who feel that it breaks up also a part of the heart that never heals!"[3] This was certainly the case for Hannah, who had not only to pack up her books, silver, mahogany bed, and sewing table, but also to leave her darling little girls lying in the frozen New Hampshire earth.

This was the start of a pattern. When tragedy struck, when life became too hard, the Woolsons moved on. This response to grief became ingrained in their children, most of all Constance, who would spend the majority of her adult life on the move. The Woolsons' home in Claremont was only the first of innumerable homes that would be broken up during her lifetime.

THE WOOLSONS IN CLAREMONT

That first home was a two-story, white, Greek Revival house that her father, Jarvis (he went by his middle name), had built across the street from his parents' house. Claremont's heyday would come and go with the Industrial Revolution. In the 1830s, the water power of the river was only beginning to be harnessed, and the town's prospects remained dim. With the financial crisis of 1837, they all but evaporated. Hannah had no regrets about leaving the sleepy town. She detested the bitter winters and the cold New England stoicism, but Jarvis would always miss the hilly landscape of his youth.[4]

Constance's parents had married on April 26, 1830, having met less than two months earlier at the wedding of Hannah's best friend and cousin, Julia Campbell, and Jarvis's best friend, Levi Turner, an up-and-coming lawyer. Turner had ties in Washington and spent tens of thousands of dollars each year speculating on western lands. Some of his air of promise must have rubbed off on his friend Jarvis, or perhaps Hannah was simply drawn to his sharp wit and affectionate ways, for Jarvis was not a lawyer, businessman, or speculator. His passion was journalism. A more capricious occupation would have been hard to find.

After briefly editing the *Virginia Advocate* in Charlottesville, where a New Englander opposed to slavery had little hope of success, Jarvis worked at the *New England Palladium* in Boston. But in 1833, having already three mouths besides his own to feed, he gave up his dream, moving his growing family back home and joining his father's stove business. His love of the written word—exhibited early when he devoured David Hume's six-volume *History of England* before age eleven—never waned, however. He would bequeath it to Constance, who was his pet and inherited his keen intellect and wit.[5]

After the death of his father in 1837, Jarvis took over the manufacture of the "Woolson Stoves," his father's invention and the most popular stoves in New England. Thomas Woolson left little other legacy. Constance would remember him as "a dreary useless man" who had given himself up to depression. Hannah described him as "a man of great intellectual ability, wonderful inventive powers, curious research into all strange subjects, but very peculiar in his manners, stern and, at times, morose, [making] his younger children very much afraid of him." Much to Jarvis's regret, his father did not come from a noble lineage. When Constance was young, her father spent years searching in vain for an aristocratic Woolson ancestor, finding only a Thomas Woolson who was sentenced in 1685 for peddling liquor without a license. Although she would carry a feeling of social inferiority with her throughout her life, Constance found as much humor as heartbreak in her father's disappointment.[6]

Jarvis's mother, Hannah Peabody Woolson, whose ancestors came over on the *Planter* in 1635, provided the noble ancestry and parental affection in the family. Jarvis took after her, becoming a loving father and grandfather. But Jarvis also inherited his mother's deafness along with his father's tendency toward depression. Unfortunately, Constance also inherited these traits. Jarvis would warn her against succumbing to the darkness that had engulfed his father, but there was little they could do about their acquired deafness. They could both hear as children and developed normal speech patterns, but in their late teenage or early adult years, their hearing began to degenerate and steadily receded throughout their lives, isolating them and exacerbating their depressive tendencies.

Jarvis's worsening hearing may have prevented him from realizing his promise as a journalist or budding industrialist. Hannah's cousin Richard Cooper wrote of him as early as 1831 that his deafness "incapacitates him from those pursuits, by which the majority of our young men rise to commerce and competency."[7] Jarvis never was as devoted to business as were his father, Levi Turner, and most of the men of his class. The only surviving portrait of him, in which he stands stiffly erect, staring directly into the camera with an icy look of confidence, is of a piece with the portraits of nineteenth-century military and business leaders. In life, however, he aspired to neither form of masculine accomplishment. Business was something he had settled for, having been barred from more intellectual pursuits.

Understandably, Constance never liked her father's portrait. It conveyed nothing of his quick wit or lively sense of humor, both of which she also inherited from him. Contrary to the stern image it projects,

Charles Jarvis Woolson.
(From *Voices Out of the Past*, vol. 1 of *Five Generations (1785–1923)*)

he was in fact "something of a wag," responding once to an inquiry about a prospective business associate with the lone fact that he was "a *light-complexioned* young man." Described upon his death by the local paper as "a man of very domestic habits," Jarvis's primary devotion was to his family and to his books. His immense love for his daughters was unclouded by a desire for a boy. He claimed to possess "a strong admir[ation] of the fair sex" and "a pervading desire to render myself agreeable to the younger portion thereof." When his seventh daughter, Clara, many years later became a mother, his affection had a new object in her baby girl. He wrote to Clara on one occasion, "'Gampa' wants to see Baby very bad indeed. He would walk ten miles to play with her half an hour." For Constance, who took after her beloved father in appearance and personality, he was the ideal father.[8]

COOPERSTOWN AND THE COOPERS

The Woolsons' first stop after they left Claremont in the wake of the three girls' deaths was Hannah's birthplace, Cooperstown, New York, on the shores of Lake Otsego. It had been founded in 1786 by her grandfather, the judge and speculator William Cooper. When he moved his family there, to a home still surrounded by wilderness, his wife, Elizabeth, sat in an heirloom Queen Anne chair and refused to budge, according to family legend. In response to his wife's rebellion, William reportedly lifted the chair, with her in it, and placed them both in the wagon, signaling the caravan to begin its journey.[9] This kind of stubborn willfulness cropped up periodically among the Cooper women, and Constance would inherit her fair share of it.

Among the seven Cooper children in that caravan were Hannah's mother, Ann, and the future novelist James Fenimore Cooper, who would make Cooperstown and the region famous in his Leatherstocking novels. Ann and James were born five years apart and after 1820 were the only surviving siblings. James was away in New York and Europe during the years Ann raised her family in Cooperstown. Nonetheless, the bond between the families remained strong despite a rift in the 1820s when Ann and her husband, George Pomeroy, participated in the sale of many of the grand Cooper homes and initiated court proceedings to secure her share of the dwindling Cooper legacy. Unlike her mother, Hannah grew up in genteel poverty with a feeling of beleaguered family honor, which her uncle James redeemed in the early years of her marriage by becoming a famous author. When Constance was born, his prolific career was mostly behind him and he had returned to Cooperstown, restoring the family's home, Otsego Hall, and with it the family's pride.[10]

After the death of the three Woolson girls in Claremont, James urged his niece to come home to Cooperstown. He remembered how her little Annie, who had stayed there the preceding summer, "had made friends of us all," writing to Hannah that "her quiet, affectionate, little ways are often present to my mind when I recall your loss." He encouraged Hannah to turn for consolation to the Almighty, but in the meantime only the love of family and change of scenery could begin to break up the delirium of her grief. "[W]hile you will be just as near the spirits of the little ones here as there," he wrote, "you will be more likely to see them as spirits, than when surrounded by objects familiarly connected with their brief lives. . . . Your friends will prove to you how much they feel for your privations, which are in some degree theirs, and the family tie will be strengthened by the sympathy you will meet."[11] Throughout Constance's life, this tie between the Woolsons and Coopers, especially James's daughters, would remain strong, no matter how far she roamed.

The greatest inheritance Constance received from the Cooper side of the family, however, was the middle name she shared with her great-uncle: Fenimore. While the Cooper name itself was fairly common and locally had fallen from its earlier preeminence, Fenimore retained its luster, which was only burnished by the novelist's worldwide fame.[12]

The Cooper women bestowed on Constance less obvious, but no less important, influences. From them she inherited a contrary mixture of genteel convention and rebelliousness that would define her personality and make her the subtly powerful writer she was to become. Her grandmother, Ann Cooper Pomeroy, hewed closely to a conventional model of reserved womanhood. Her domestic life as Judge Cooper's daughter and then as the wife of the affluent apothecary George Pomeroy fulfilled her every aspiration. She spent her long life in Cooperstown, serving as its chief charitable coordinator and caregiver, attending, it was said, virtually all of its births and deaths. Known as a homebody, Ann is said to have shut herself up in her house when the railroad first arrived in New York, declaring the whole state ruined by its invasion.[13]

Ann's older sister, Hannah (namesake of Constance's mother), was less content with her lot. A spirited young woman who enjoyed society and, in her words, "long, rough walks," she bristled at her domestic and rural isolation in Cooperstown. The future prime minister of the French republic, Charles Maurice de Talleyrand, was charmed by her during his 1795 visit to Cooperstown, extolling her as too refined for her uncultured surroundings. Although her brother James would immortalize her as a paragon of genteel young womanhood in his novel *The Pioneers*, she was in fact independent-minded and skeptical of the role she apparently played to perfection. Marriage seemed to her an intolerable crisis in a woman's life: "It fixes her in a fate of all others the most happy or the most wretched," she wrote in her commonplace book, recognizing the complete submission required of wives. She turned down many proposals, including one from future president William Henry Harrison. Hannah died suddenly at the age of twenty-three when, ignoring her oldest brother's objections, she insisted on riding a new, extraordinarily spirited horse on a twenty-five-mile journey to visit friends. The roads were hilly and rough, and Hannah's horse threw her after being spooked by a dog. She was killed instantly.[14] A considerable portion of her skeptical and restless spirit would find its way into Constance.

As a young woman, Ann's daughter Hannah Pomeroy Woolson possessed some of the daring of her namesake, but it was tempered by a deep attachment to home. Writing when she was almost twenty to her cousin William Cooper, then in Paris with their uncle James, she showed her bold side in a passage about her desire to reclaim for her family the dilapidated ancestral manor: "The present owner [of

Otsego Hall] is a rich and invulnerable hearted old Bachelor. I had the vanity to think at one time, that I might become mistress of the mansion—but he never will be married—for if *I* failed to captivate him, is there any one that can do it[?] Oh certainly not! You may think I have a large portion of *vanity* in my composition, but really, you have no conception how I have improved in all that is beautiful within the last three or four years—and I do think I have but a humble opinion of my own merits."[15]

But in spite of Hannah's vivacity, she was as much of a homebody as her mother. In the same letter she admits that spending the coming winter in the gay society of New York would please her, but she preferred to stay in the relaxed atmosphere of Cooperstown where she felt more at home. She threatened to break out into verse on the subject of her birthplace, blaming heredity for her poetic tendencies.[16] Still, while a young woman proud of her abilities, Hannah was nonetheless fearful of showing them off, an ambivalence she would pass along to her daughters.

Less than two years after writing this letter, Hannah married Jarvis. She gave birth within a year and then had a new baby every year or two thereafter for a decade. The duties of a wife and mother did not come easily to Hannah. She had never been taught the domestic arts; her mother had raised her to rely on servants for most household tasks. But in Claremont, the thrifty wives did all of their own baking, cooking, cleaning, sewing, knitting, and even carding and spinning of wool. Hannah would later write up humorous accounts for her granddaughters of her early mishaps as a housewife. She once mistakenly baked up forty-two perishable mincemeat pies instead of preserving the filling for use throughout the winter. The family got so tired of eating them that she instructed the kitchen girl to dispose of the leftovers after every meal, against the girl's frugal impulses. More seriously, Hannah resented the way she saw wives treated in New England, inwardly rebelling against the "iron rule" of Claremont men who made their wives and daughters prepare breakfast and clean up by candlelight before sunrise.[17]

The Woolson home was presided over by a much gentler patriarch, but still the backbreaking tasks of nineteenth-century housekeeping had to be done. Although Hannah would later have the help of three Irish servants, she put to use the skills she learned from her sister-in-law in Claremont and was by all accounts a consummately domestic woman. She made sure that her own daughters were taught all of the skills they would need as wives and mothers, the only roles she ever imagined they would be called upon to fill.[18]

The gay girl who wrote to her cousin William faded considerably during the Claremont years as Hannah suffered the ill health that childbearing brought. After her third child was born she was so dangerously ill that the baby had to be sent away to a wet nurse. The doctor wasn't sure Hannah would live. This trying period ended "what may be called the youth of our married life," she later recollected. When the loss of the three girls to scarlet fever forever banished her youthful self, she did not retreat from her family, as many grieving mothers did, but was able to overcome her terrible sadness and be a caring, supportive presence in her remaining children's lives. In the evenings, before the children went to bed, they gathered around her, finding a spot on her lap or on the arms of the rocking chair, and listened to her sing English and Scottish ballads, "the toe of her slipper just touching the floor to keep the chair rocking in time."[19]

CLEVELAND

After a brief stay in Cooperstown, Hannah, Jarvis, and baby Connie joined the masses fleeing the depressed East for the promise-laden West. Georgiana and Emma, the two oldest daughters, were left behind with relatives. The heartbroken parents already had been preparing to move for some time. Jarvis's friend Levi Turner had been a key player in the immense land grab that had been taming the upper Midwest frontier and populating it with New England outposts. Levi and others became wealthy seemingly overnight, benefiting from the Indian Removal Act of 1830 and the completion of the Erie Canal.[20]

The financial depression of 1837 had been a major setback for Jarvis, but the plunge in western land values gave him his chance. That year, as the crisis reached its peak, he joined Turner and Hannah's cousin Richard Cooper in search of western land. Jarvis was in for the long haul, rightly assuming that western expansion would continue despite the economic crisis. He made a fateful choice, allowing his "love of picturesque scenery," as Constance later put it, to persuade him to buy lands in Michigan and Milwaukee over Chicago, whose muddy ugliness made him overlook its promising situation. Constance believed that if he had invested a tenth of that money in Chicago lands, he might have become a millionaire.[21] As it was, Jarvis never made a fortune as a speculator, but his investments would provide a modest income well into Constance's adulthood.

Jarvis was not content to simply speculate out west, however. The year before the Woolson girls' deaths, he and Hannah had made an exploratory trip to see where they might want to live. They encountered friends and relatives at nearly every stop. Her cousins in Chicago took her out for a moonlit stroll through the city's sand-covered streets and a sunny drive in the morning to see the vast, grassy prairie. She was impressed but felt this was no place to make a new home.[22]

Their return to the West in 1840 was a mission to find a more suitable residence. They bumped across rutted roads and sailed across Lake Erie, heading again toward that mythical land where the wide-open spaces provided plenty of opportunities to start afresh. When they reached Cleveland, Hannah is reported to have "expressed her first wish: 'I like this place . . . Let's stop travelling and stay.'" The young city had plenty of attractions, including beautiful views of Lake Erie and the fact that the city had been settled by New Englanders, many of whom they knew. Among them were the Turners, who welcomed the family into their home. That first winter was mild enough that Hannah decided they could stay for good. Jarvis retrieved Georgiana and Emma, and the Woolsons started over in a house on Rockwell Street, opposite the post office in the town's center.[23]

The Cleveland they encountered in 1840 looked like a quaint New England village full of green-shuttered white cottages with neat flower gardens. Stores and small manufacturers lined Superior Street, one of the many dirt roads that were dusty in the sunshine and a muddy mess in the rain. As part of the "Western Reserve" of the Connecticut Land Company, Cleveland was a port town that would soon become a railroad hub, but for now shipping determined its fortunes. Lake Erie connected Cleveland to Buffalo and Detroit as well as to the interior of the Great Lakes region, which enterprising men would mine for iron and coal—and which Constance would one day mine for her earliest literary successes. Cleveland held few attractions for a budding writer, however. She would never set a story there. By the time she grew up and started to publish, the city had changed so much she hardly knew it.

Constance not only grew up in Cleveland; she grew up with it. During the years she lived there, from 1840 to the early 1870s, its population rose from 7,000 to 92,000, and it transformed into a bustling manufacturing city. During her youth the Cuyahoga River was bordered with sunny green meadows, and flocks of now-extinct passenger pigeons would occasionally block the sun for most of the day. Just as in Cooper's *The Pioneers*, set decades earlier in Cooperstown, people climbed up to their roofs and, armed with sticks, struck the birds down for food or amusement. But such evidence of nature's abundance would soon fade into memory, and, like her great-uncle, Woolson would fill her fiction with laments for the disappearance of the wilderness. What he had witnessed two generations earlier in the East was repeated in Cleveland. During her teenage years, she and a friend could row up the Cuyahoga River from her father's stove foundry and stop for a picnic along the banks. But before she reached thirty, the river, whose pollution would help spark the twentieth-century environmental movement, caught fire for the first time, its banks crowded with smoke-belching iron mills and oil refineries.[24]

Yet throughout Constance's youth, Cleveland was known as the "Forest City." The residential east side of the city, where she lived, felt like a town surrounded by woods. Elm-lined Euclid Avenue was the city's jewel. During Anthony Trollope's 1861 visit, he lauded the expansive elms that bowed over its homes and sidewalks. Another foreign visitor likened the tree-lined street to "the nave and aisles of a huge cathedral." The Woolsons lived there briefly in a large, two-storied stone house that would be torn down in 1865 to make room for a palatial estate. By then there was a streetcar running down the center of the avenue, which would become known as Millionaire's Row, the affluence of its residents exceeding that of Fifth Avenue's inhabitants in New York. The Woolsons, far from millionaires themselves, moved into a more modest home they called "Cheerful Corner" at Prospect and Perry, just off Euclid.[25]

As their home's proximity to Euclid Avenue suggests, the Woolsons belonged to the city's social elite. But, while the Woolson stove foundry was the first "of importance in Northern Ohio," Jarvis suffered a series of setbacks, including the perfidy of his partner (a brother of Hannah's, who absconded with thousands of dollars), and a fire that destroyed most of his business. He started over with a new partner, creating Woolson & Hitchcock, later Woolson, Hitchcock, & Carter. Still, he never prospered on the scale of the city's other industrialists, such as John D. Rockefeller. Despite bringing the Woolson stove to a brand-new market, one that expanded exponentially during his lifetime, business was fickle. In 1851, Jarvis complained of persistent money problems, explaining, "I have been in such a constant struggle with the world ever since I came west, that I have never had a moment to spend for anything beyond my daily efforts to provide for the large number dependent upon me."[26] It wasn't until the 1860s that Jarvis would be able to provide a comfortable, steady living for his family.

As the daughter of a father who forever felt like an exile from New England, Constance never felt like a "Daughter of Ohio."[27] But growing up among eastern transplants in Cleveland, as it became more and more diverse with Irish and German immigrants, she developed a broader patriotism. There was something about northern Ohio that would produce five U.S. presidents in the last thirty-two years of the nineteenth century and that would also make Woolson a thoroughly American writer, no matter how far away she moved from her Cleveland roots. Ohio was, at the time, the virtual center of the United States and would become a major economic and political force, if never a cultural one.

In Cleveland, Constance grew up among the men of the future—men who would make the coming era the "Gilded Age." The brother of one of her best friends would become a major stakeholder in Standard Oil. Another friend would become one of Hawaii's wealthiest sugar planters. Her nephew would build one of the most ostentatious mansions on Euclid Avenue with the fortune he earned in the coal industry.[28] But the question of what role women would play in shaping the nation's future remained to be answered.

2

Lessons in Literature,
Life, and Death

MOVING WEST provided the opportunity to start over. For Jarvis that meant a new business. For Hannah it meant more children. She got her longest break from childbearing after Constance's birth—three years and nine months. Then she bore another girl on December 20, 1843. Clara would become Constance's closest confidante and rival. Just over a year later, the eighth girl, Ellen Alida, was born, on January 8, 1845. She would soon fall ill. Her first and only year was one of "grief and anguish, in which her lovely little caressing ways were the only cheerfulness in our sorely smitten household," Hannah later wrote. After a long year of worry, Ellen Alida died on January 30.[1] Although Constance had been unaware of her three sisters' deaths in Claremont, this time the five-year-old watched her mother and the baby anxiously, sharing in her parents' fears and torment.

Hannah, nearly thirty-eight years old, gave birth to her last child later that year, on September 7, 1846. What a surprise when this one turned out to be a boy. "In the sultry heat," she wrote, "when flies buzzed and mosquitoes stung, Number Nine arrived—a small, thin boy, who cried so loudly and squared his fists so fiercely in the first moments of existence that the doctor remarked: 'The little chap seems all ready to fight the Battle of Life!'"² The family was elated. They named him Charles Jarvis Woolson Jr., and called him Charlie.

A SERIOUS CHILD

Connie was now six years old and such an inquisitive child that her nickname was "And Why?" Why, she must have wondered, did the birth of a boy cause so much excitement? What made him different and so much more valuable than her and her three sisters? According to Hannah, Charlie showed his family that he was a new sort of being right away: "I could not but notice the difference—throughout his infancy and childhood—between the sisters and this their only brother. He would not be petted, and made a baby of; he would have playthings that made a noise." So Clara remained the indulged baby of the family and probably didn't mind Charlie's arrival.³ Constance, however, seems to have resented it. As she grew older, she noticed the way her mother favored Charlie, despite his shortcomings. A different set of rules and standards applied to him. When she became a writer, she would portray the unconditional love of mothers for their profligate sons. During her youth, she watched resentfully as her mother doted upon the son who could do no wrong.

There is very little documentary evidence of Constance's early years before she began her writing career, but photos and passing comments in scattered sources give us glimpses of her. The earliest surviving photograph of her shows Connie and Clara, about nine and six years old, staring solemnly into the camera. Their hair—Connie's dark and Clara's light brown—is parted down the middle and curled in long ringlets. Clara looks languid, the corners of her mouth turned slightly down, her shoulders slightly drooping, and her hands crossed and relaxed. Connie, on the other hand, sits up straighter and looks serious and resolute, her lips pressed together, her hand clenched. The likeness illustrates perfectly one contemporary's description of her as a "quiet, thoughtful child." Her eyes are intent, as if she is taking in all that she sees, while Clara's are almost blank by comparison. By all accounts, their personalities were quite different. Their paternal grandmother wasn't sure which one she loved best. "When Connie comes before my mind's eye, with her serious, beautiful face, I think she is the one. Then Clara's laughing good-natured face seems to creep in between, as much as to say—'Love *me* as well as Connie!'"[4] The shy, earnest child had already seen too much to be so carefree.

The intensity of Connie's personality, which sometimes peeked through her stoic exterior, was harder to capture in photographs. Her eyes would brighten, betraying her pleasure as she listened quietly to adults' conversations or heard a song she liked. They could flash in anger just as suddenly. According to her niece, she had "a passion-

Constance (l.) and Clara (r.) as children.
(From *Constance Fenimore Woolson*, vol. 2 of *Five Generations (1785–1923)*)

ate and dramatic nature, and a high temper," which as an adult she would manage to hide from nearly everyone outside of her family. She learned early to control it, covering up her feelings not with boisterousness, as some do, but with silence. Her acute sensitivity masqueraded as reticence, which only her closest friends were able to penetrate. An acquaintance of her youth wrote of her, "She talked but little . . . , impressing an observer with the idea that the highways and byways of her thinking were not trodden by every casual acquaintance." Only those who knew her well were familiar with her keen sense of humor and astute observations. One of her most intimate friends would later call her "a most entertaining companion," but few knew the pleasure of her friendship. Her later writings and letters (very few of which have survived from before she turned thirty) are full of a vivacious wit. She felt freer to let out her humor and irreverence on paper. In spite of the many tragedies in her life, she would never lose the ability to laugh at the foibles of others and be amused by life's incongruities.[5]

Her personal reserve also concealed a painfully low self-regard. Clara was the more widely loved, receiving presents from friends and admirers while Constance recalled receiving none. She could not help feeling, as she put it, "un-lovable, and very unattractive."[6] Her excruciating shyness and insecurity, rather than any physical deficiencies, led her to believe she was ugly. She did not struggle under the burden of homeliness; rather, hers was the burden of self-consciousness and self-criticism, which would only intensify as she aged.

Throughout her adult life she would shy away from the camera, even turning her back on it, showing her profile or less to the viewer. However, some photographs taken in her youth and early adulthood reveal her lovely features. In one taken when she was fifteen, she still wore her hair long and parted down the middle, with the long corkscrew curls then fashionable framing her oval face. The three-quarters profile shows a straight, rather small nose and thin but finely shaped lips. She always hated her nose, lamenting that it was too short by nineteenth-century standards, which prized long, classical noses.

Contrary to Constance's low opinion of herself, others thought of her as vibrant and pretty. They most often noted her gracefully straight

Constance at fifteen.
(From *Constance Fenimore Woolson*, vol. 2 of *Five Generations (1785–1923)*)

posture and clear, smooth complexion. Photographs never revealed her animated expressions, her deep blue eyes, the bright tints in her hair, or the rich coloring in her lips. As one acquaintance summed up her appearance, "Miss Woolson is attractive without being beautiful."[7] But she would never accept even that much commendation.

A LITERATE CHILDHOOD

Not surprisingly, for one so insecure, Connie found her closest childhood companions in books. Her family often said that by the age of twelve she had already read everything of significance. That was also the age at which she began her love affair with Dickens, having received from her father a complete collection of his novels, which she read to tatters before she turned twenty. Although she also read history and poetry, her greatest affection was for novels. Besides Dickens, she loved Alexandre Dumas, Charlotte Brontë, George Eliot, and George Sand. She had a strong taste for romantic adventure and stayed up all night reading *The Three Musketeers*. But dearest to her were novels about the struggles of thwarted lives, such as those of Jane Eyre and Maggie Tulliver, young women who, like her, were tormented by the need for self-control and their desire for approval.[8]

However much Constance may have longed to pick up the pen in emulation of her favorite authors, she received mixed signals about what it meant for a girl to have literary aspirations. The Woolson household presented plenty of models and opportunities for girls' writing, but always with an understanding of its inherent limits. Literature and writing were meant to be decidedly domestic affairs.

The parlor of the Woolson home was often filled with family and friends—young and old, male and female—taking part in the creation of music, theatricals, and literature. A large red sofa dominated the room. Comfortable chairs were scattered about, and a piano stood in the corner. White muslin drapes were pushed aside to let in fragrances from the garden. Spread across the floor was a muted, figured carpet, and adorning the gray walls were two vibrant pictures, probably idealized landscapes, and a bookcase full of well-worn books. In the evenings, the Woolsons gathered with friends and visiting family members to play games that tested players' knowledge of history and literature. While too young to play herself, Connie would silently take it all in. Some evenings were spent sharing homemade literary productions. In her most autobiographical novel, *The Old Stone House*, Woolson would portray an "Editor's Sanctum," in which compositions ranging from the serious to the humorous were read aloud, among them a ghost story, a lyric tribute to the month of June, a moving story of a dying soldier, and a humorous poem—one of Woolson's—written in the voice of one of the family's beloved dogs, Pete Trone.[9] Such literary productions provided an evening's entertainment and were not intended to have a life outside of the family circle.

Such was also the case for the writings of the Woolson women, which were associated with familial relationships and domestic tasks. Hannah "used her pen for her children's pleasure in it," a cousin later wrote, perhaps referring to stories and poems she wrote for their amusement. The oldest daughter, Georgiana, enjoyed writing notes in rhyme. One began, "Behold of 'Earth's Apples' I send you a quart / Neither wet nor decayed, but quite a 'good sort.'" Perhaps more important, when they left home their pens traveled with them. Although none of Constance's early journals has survived, those recording Hannah's 1839 trip out west and Georgiana's stay in Marquette, Wisconsin, in 1853, have. Georgiana's journal focused on her close observations of the flora and fauna she saw during her afternoon walks. She also reported on evidence of Indians' continued presence in the region and of earlier habitation by European settlers, as well as the history of nearby Presque Isle.[10] Not surprisingly, Constance's first publications, nearly twenty years later, look very similar. They would be travel essays that began, no doubt, as letters home or journal entries that included numerous historical explanations and observations of the natural world, modes of writing she seems to have learned from her mother's and oldest sister's examples.

Yet while they were content to write for family and friends, very early on Constance displayed a talent that begged for recognition beyond the home. When she was about eight, her long poem titled "Symmes' Hole" impressed her teacher, who called it "a remarkable production, and predicted that [Constance] would excel as a writer."[11] Unfortunately, no one saved the poem. Its subject, at once whimsical and learned, hints at the playful irony that would mark her mature writings. ("Symmes' Hole" refers to John Cleves Symmes's much-ridiculed theory that the North and South Poles were large openings that would lead to the globe's hollow interior, as well as to a popular phrase for lost things, which might be said to have fallen into a Symmes' Hole.)

The encouraging words about Constance's poem may have come from Harriet Grannis, Constance's teacher at her first school, Miss Fuller's, on the Public Square, a rather typical girls' school of the period, which she attended with Georgiana and Emma. Grannis, who happened to be Jarvis's cousin, was an unmarried woman who supported herself by teaching and also had a reputation as a gifted poet. After attending Oberlin, she had published in the *New York Tribune,* the Cleveland *Herald,* and the *Western Literary Messenger.* Unfortunately, no record of Constance's impressions of her teacher remains. But Grannis recalled Constance as "quiet and silent, standing behind my chair while the others were asking the final questions of the day, saying nothing but taking everything in, . . . and gathering for her future work." Connie must also have observed her teacher intently, for Grannis was that rare breed, a woman who wrote for the public. The image did not last long, however. In 1848 she married fellow teacher Oliver Arey and moved to Buffalo, New York, where she edited a children's magazine and in 1855 published a volume of poetry. Its title— *Household Songs and Other Poems*—suggests how Miss Grannis, now Mrs. Arey, presented herself as a model of literary domesticity, even as she ushered her productions into print.[12]

Another female relative also earned a reputation as a writer, making an impression on Constance. Susan Fenimore Cooper, daughter of James, published with her father's recommendation and support her private journal, *Rural Hours,* in 1850. It is one of the earliest pieces of American nature writing, anticipating Thoreau's *Walden* by four years. Constance did not have much contact with Susan until she was beginning her own career, but this example suggested to her how thin a veil separated women's private writings and their sometimes public manifestations.

In spite of such models, however, Constance did not begin to publish her own writings, many of which she surely composed throughout her youth, until she was thirty years old and prodded by the necessity of earning a living. The reasons for her delay are both personal and a product of the times she lived in. Already shy and reticent, Constance was deeply affected by her era's dispiriting attitudes toward women writers. During the 1850s, when she was in her teens and thus most vulnerable to outside perceptions, a widespread and often rancorous debate erupted on the merits of women's authorship. The phenomenal successes of writers such as Harriet Beecher Stowe, Fanny Fern, and Susan Warner—who outsold and outearned their male counterparts by the tens of thousands—provoked many male critics to discourage women from attempting to follow in their footsteps. A characteristic note was struck by the *Putnam's* reviewer who wrote in 1854, "[T]he books of almost all lady authors are readable, just as the conversation of all women is entertaining; the errors, volubility and misconceptions, which we will not tolerate in men, become amusing and entertaining in the case of a lady, or a child." Privately, some men could be even more reproachful. Nathaniel Hawthorne must have dipped his pen in venom when he wrote to his publisher in 1856 that the poet Julia Ward Howe "ought to have been soundly whipped" for publishing her passionate poetry. He even wrote to his own wife, herself a gifted writer, that he thanked God she had "never prostituted [her]self to the public, as . . . a thousand [women] do."[13]

The Woolson household, it seems, was not immune to such prejudice. One measure of its discomfort was scrawled into the family's copy of the first volume of *Harper's New Monthly Magazine*, published in 1850, when Connie was only ten years old. The volume survived repeated moves over the years alongside the family Bible—no doubt because *Harper's* played a central role in Constance's later life as an author. Its significance in the family long before the advent of her career is apparent, however, in its front pages adorned with Jarvis's signature in fancy script and in the children's drawings, colorings, and signatures, some of them dated as late as 1860 and 1864, when the family lived at Cheerful Corner. In the middle of one month's "Literary Notices," Constance carefully wrote her name, perhaps intimating her desire to see it there one day in print. The markings on one page, however, suggest how uneasy the family would feel if the name of one of its female members actually did appear there. The page contains an article about the novelist Jane Porter, in which it is argued that although England has had some accomplished women of which it is proud, no amount of public reputation can make up for what these women have presumably lost in the way of home life and familial love.[14] The portrait of Jane Porter accompanying the article has been overdrawn with a top hat, handlebar moustache, and goatee.

The most likely culprit was Constance's younger brother, Charlie, considering that years later he would express "horror" when his sister published a poem in a magazine promoting women's rights. In one of her earliest writings, Woolson would portray the intolerance of a male relative in *The Old Stone House*, where the oldest boy declares, "I do not think that types adorn a woman's name. A woman ought not to appear 'in the papers' but twice; when she is married, and when she dies." His talented female cousin finds it unfair that an unmarried woman has no "chance of being anybody until she is dead." He assumes she is "shrieking for suffrage," shaming her by equating her aspirations with a desire to participate in the male sphere of politics.[15] The doodling on Jane Porter's portrait sent the same message—to write for publication was to forsake femininity and therefore lovability. Constance would never be able to free herself entirely from the fear of disapproval that accompanied her ambitions.

The introduction of *Harper's* into the family circle was nonetheless a sort of Trojan horse. Over the next decade, the growing number of women's names in its table of contents indicated that women were increasingly expanding their horizons beyond the domestic sphere, planting in young Constance's mind the idea that one day she could do more than simply read *Harper's* and sign her name in its pages.

Her father's views on women's authorship remain a mystery, but his example and training helped to offset Charlie's intolerance. By taking her with him on his travels and teaching her to be someone on whom nothing is lost, he put his daughter on the path toward her eventual literary career. Jarvis preferred to travel by carriage rather than train so that he could pause and look—"he knew every tree and its manner of growth," remembered Constance, who sat beside him on those trips. Along the way, he taught her to observe closely every feature of the landscapes and communities they visited. Their favorite spots were the Zoar settlement in Ohio, an enclave of German separatists in the Tuscawaras Valley, and Mackinac Island on Lake Michigan, where they had a summer cottage from Constance's fifteenth to seventeenth years. There she edited a manuscript newspaper with a male friend, Zephaniah Spalding, the only evidence that remains of her beginning to imagine her literary productions in print. Inspired by local Indian legends, she produced what she thought of as her first piece of original writing, a poem in the vein of Longfellow's epic "Hiawatha." When, after the economic crisis of 1857, the Woolsons had to give up their Mackinac cottage, Constance and her father "went gypsying" throughout Ohio, seeking out the picturesque valleys and villages off the well-worn tracks trod by most tourists.[16] Constance must have been observing and writing all along the way, for so many of her early writings were inspired by these trips.

CHILDHOOD INTERRUPTED

As Jarvis Woolson fed his daughter's desire to travel, he also taught her that new scenery was a powerful tonic. Looking outside of oneself was his most potent remedy for the depression and grief that followed life's inevitable misfortunes, of which the Woolsons had already experienced more than their share. Unfortunately, Constance would need every coping strategy she could acquire during her early adolescence, which was marred by fresh tragedies reminding her of life's frailty.

Emma, the second daughter and most beautiful and musical of the Woolson girls, had an intense, passionate nature that led her at sixteen to fall hopelessly in love with a young minister staying in their home. The Reverend T. Jarvis Carter had come from New York to become rector of Grace Episcopal, a missionary church that sought to bridge the gap between Cleveland's rich and poor. Emma was smitten by his idealism and good looks, her own religious zeal merging with infatuation. Constance, who was only nine, was just as taken with her big sister's suitor. She would later memorialize him in *The Old Stone House* as the young minister John Leslie, "so manly in his goodness, and so frank in his religion."[17]

But Emma and Jarvis Carter's love was ill-fated. He suffered from an unknown and incurable disease, making him only more worthy of worship to Emma. Her parents, however, were terrified at their teen-age daughter's precipitous plunge into a hopeless romance. Seeing only heartache ahead, they sent her back to school in New York, but Emma was so miserable in her exile that they brought her home. As Jarvis Woolson explained to a friend, "It is a hard thing for a Parent, in my opinion, to refuse to consent to a connection which carries with it the best affection, and the happiness, perhaps, of the whole life in this, at best, troublous world."[18]

Emma married Carter on May 7, 1851, at Avon Springs, New York, a resort with mineral springs thought to have the power to cure a multitude of maladies. Marriage and the sulfur waters seemed to improve his condition, and the family began to hope that he could recover. But by July a turn for the worse sent Hannah rushing to New York to assist Emma, whose husband was now surely dying. He did not go quickly. The doctors tried everything they could, all to no avail. Meanwhile Emma nursed him tirelessly, refusing to be relieved of her duty. In August, Georgiana reported that Emma had not had one night's complete rest for twelve weeks.[19] Despite her sleepless care and devotion over the coming months, Carter died in New York on November 15, 1851. His body was brought back to Cleveland and buried under the chancel of Grace Church. His widow was only eighteen years old.

Emma returned to her family with her heart and health broken. It quickly became clear that she nurtured an intense longing to join her husband in heaven. "St." Jarvis Carter, as a typo in a newspaper fittingly dubbed him, seemed to haunt her as she wasted away in the very room he had first occupied in the Woolsons' home. The family had long received alarming reports of ghosts in the room (including several from Carter himself), but Emma "seemed to take pleasure in the thought of spirits coming to her from the unknown world, to which she was so rapidly hastening."[20] Emma died on August 14, 1852, at age nineteen, nine months after her husband. His father, the Reverend Lawson Carter, had moved to Cleveland just in time to preside over the funeral of his daughter-in-law. She was buried with her husband under the altar in Grace Church, which the Woolsons and Carters would thereafter faithfully attend, worshipping each Sunday alongside the graves of Jarvis and Emma.

Although Emma was remembered by her family as having "literally given up her life to her love," she also had a very real illness that took her life and probably her husband's as well. She was described as having died of "quick consumption," and in Constance's first surviving letter, written when she was about twelve years old, she explained that Emma had been "quite sick ever since she came from New York. She took a bad cold and has had some trouble with her lungs." Although Carter's disease was only described as mysterious and baffling in the few letters that have survived, Emma's was surely tuberculosis, then known as consumption, and the likelihood that she contracted it from her dying husband is very high. The disease killed more people than any other in the nineteenth century. It usually claimed its victims, most often women, before they reached the age of thirty. In popular mythology, tuberculosis was the disease of grieving lovers and passionate artists, those of a highly sensitive nature who could not endure the hardships of life.[21] Such was the enduring remembrance of Emma and her husband.

Despite its romantic image, tuberculosis was a brutal disease. It usually began with symptoms similar to a cold and progressed to lingering, harassing coughs, high fevers, throat ulcers, and lung hemorrhages. Suffering at the end was severe. Bodies ravaged by the disease appeared cadaverous, and victims were often suffocated by the blood or mucus they coughed up. At Emma's bedside, Constance would have encountered the sight of gushing blood, the stench of rotting flesh, and the sounds of choking and gagging, all of which she and her family were helpless to stop.[22] The disease's real cause (the tubercle bacillus) would not be discovered until 1882. Until then the disease was presumed to be hereditary. But there was no doubt in the family's mind that Emma's marriage had caused her untimely, horrific death. Constance would never forget the sight of her beautiful, talented sister, so full of life and promise, wasting away. Sadly, it was not long before the oldest sister, Georgiana, also recently married, began to come down with similar symptoms.

At the age of nineteen, Georgiana had married Samuel Livingston Mather on September 24, 1850, scarcely eight months before Emma's doomed marriage. Unlike the later event, it was a happy occasion. At nineteen, Georgiana had chosen a spouse with excellent prospects, "a consummate nineteenth-century capitalist/entrepreneur" who would become one of Cleveland's richest men and a lifelong benefactor of the Woolson family. Georgiana, although reputedly not as attractive as Emma, "possessed a radiant and magnetic personality" that drew people to her, not least her great-uncle James Fenimore Cooper, who had called her "Romping Granite" when she was young because of her boisterous personality and birthplace in the granite state of New Hampshire.[23] The writings Georgiana left behind convey a perceptive, lively, and witty mind. Less than ten months after her marriage, she gave birth to a son, Sam. A second child, Katharine, called Kate, came along two years later. These children would be among their aunt Constance's closest family to the end of her life. Many of her later surviving letters were written to Sam and Kate and convey her gratitude for their emotional and financial support. She, in turn, would help them know a mother they could not remember.

As her second pregnancy had progressed, Georgiana already felt old. A poem she wrote at the time conveys her sense of having lost her youth: ". . . No! my day for long rambles, is over, / For the strength, comes not with the will; / I cough, from the scent of the cloves, / And pant when I climb up a hill! . . ." Georgiana was only twenty-two when she wrote these lines. Two days later, she gave up walking entirely, as she wrote to Samuel in a letter she signed, "Your most affectionate weak wife." She probably never got out of bed after Kate was born. She beckoned Connie and Clara to her side as she lay dying. They said their tearful goodbyes and heard her whisper to Hannah a farewell message for their deaf father: "Tell Father how I have always loved him."[24]

Georgiana died on November 2, 1853, just over a year after Emma's death. Tuberculosis appears to have been the cause. She had complained of coughing and shortness of breath, and symptoms of the disease often worsen after giving birth. Despite these known risks, female consumptives were rarely discouraged from bearing children.[25] Many young women like Georgiana essentially sacrificed themselves in order to bring their children into the world.

Emma and Georgiana's deaths would make Constance enduringly anxious about her own health. Although it appears that no other family members contracted the disease, Constance would for the rest of her life behave as if it were lurking in the shadows waiting to claim her. The fear of consumption and the suggested treatments for it, particularly exercise, fresh air, and travel to warmer climates, shaped her understanding of health for the rest of her life. She would spend much of it chasing the sun and seeking clear air on hilltops.

Above all, the Woolsons learned to behave as if serious illness was inevitable if they were careless about their health. As Constance wrote to Georgiana's son, Sam, over two decades later, "we as a family can not do what many other people can, without breaking down. We cannot go without sleep; we cannot overtax ourselves; we cannot 'overdo' in any way. If we persist either from ignorance or obstinacy, we break down."[26] Having watched Emma and Georgiana succumb to consumption after exhausting themselves, the rest of the family had to be careful of too much mental, physical, and emotional exertion. And having seen her sisters waste away as the disease consumed their flesh, Constance would forever rejoice when she put on weight.

At the age of thirteen, Constance became the oldest daughter, although she had been the sixth born. The responsibility of looking after Clara and Charlie, now nine and seven, fell to her, as would the care of her parents in the coming years. Her mother, in particular, would lean on her. Like that of most married women at the time, Hannah's health had deteriorated rapidly due to the physical toll of childbearing, child rearing, and housework, which kept her inside where, incidentally, the effects of tuberculosis were most pronounced. The surviving accounts of Hannah's illnesses in Jarvis's letters suggest that she suffered from a variety of maladies that worsened as she cared for and lost her children. As early as 1846, he reported that she suffered from "Inflammation upon the Lungs, very severely." In 1850, she had a "Spinal affection . . . wh. affects also the head very disturbingly." Her recurring attacks worsened after Emma's death and would eventually be labeled rheumatism. Looking back, Clara would describe her mother as an "invalid, having been sick a greater part of her life."[27] Hannah would live for many years still, but she increasingly needed others to care for her.

Hannah's invalidism and the deaths of Georgiana and Emma attuned Constance to the ways women gave up their health and even their lives to love and marriage. She understandably harbored complicated feelings about her own romantic prospects, both yearning for and fearing passionate devotion to loved ones. Without such ties, life was hardly worth living. With them, life could also be cut short or, perhaps worse, made unbearable through the deaths of children and one's own broken health.

When Constance began to write, her passionate nature found an outlet in her fiction and poetry, where the themes of love and marriage are prominent. Her sisters' noble sufferings and terrifying sacrifices would become in many ways the great themes of her writing and her life. In herself she would discover the capacity to love as devotedly and selflessly as they had, a prospect both thrilling and frightening. Ever receptive to the wider culture's messages about the all-consuming nature of romantic love—she was too much like the passionate Emma not to be—Constance was also reluctant to give herself away. She would throughout her life feel torn between her desire for love and her fear of its consequences.

FINDING GRACE

The Woolson family coped with their tremendous losses as many families did—by finding strength and community in their church. The Woolsons were Episcopalians and had probably attended Cleveland's Trinity Church, as many of their friends did, until Jarvis Carter entered their lives. Grace Episcopal, the church he and then his father, Lawson, led, became the center of Constance's world as the Woolson and Carter families formed many lasting ties. Jarvis's sister Arabella, six years older than Constance, was soon her closest friend, taking the place of the sisters she had lost. Jarvis's youngest brother, Henry, became a buddy of Charlie's. And the oldest brother, Lawson, became a partner in the Woolson stove business and married Jane Averell, the daughter of one of Hannah's closest friends from Cooperstown, also named Jane. Constance would be very close to Jane Carter, too, and play the role of aunt to her children until the end of her life.

But Grace Church provided much more than an extended family for Constance. It also shaped the fundamental beliefs that would guide her through this life and, she believed, into the next. Grace Church, as part of the High Church movement within the Protestant Episcopal Church (as opposed to the evangelical wing that resented anything redolent of Roman Catholicism), included in its worship traditions from the pre-Reformation Church. These included Gothic architecture, stained-glass windows, elaborate vestments, choral music, candles, flowers, incense, paintings, and Christmas greenery. The High Church movement appealed particularly to Romantic sensibilities that were drawn to forms of worship invoking beauty, passion, and the sublime. Constance, like her father, who would become a churchwarden, was particularly receptive to such an atmosphere. She would for the rest of her life seek out the serene beauty of churches and cathedrals. They would be one of the few constants in her wandering life.

Grace Church's devotion to the beautiful did not blind it to the ugliness of urban life. It was a mission church that offered free seats to the poor and preached equality before God.[28] Its anti-elitism and charitable projects were a strong influence on Constance, whose future writings would often focus on the marginalized and forgotten (albeit without direct reference to religion). God's gifts should be available to all, she believed, not only to those who could afford them.

Constance was strongly attracted to the power of the Church's mission, vestments, and rituals. During her early school years, she at least once delivered a sermon to her classmates on the school steps, with a surplice-like white cloth draped around her.[29] Had she been a boy, she might have carried her childhood performance further and eventually entered the Episcopal priesthood, as did the Carter child closest to her in age, George. The most a girl could do was marry a clergyman, as Arabella would do one day. Ultimately, Constance would have to find other ways to express her faith. It would not be through her writing, however. While many other nineteenth-century women writers used the pen as their pulpit, Constance became a decidedly secular writer, with one notable exception: her first book, *The Old Stone House*, was a children's Sunday school novel, which she wrote for a contest. Although she wrote it under a pseudonym and never acknowledged it, the novel contains many of the beliefs that grew out of her experiences at Grace Church and at her sisters' deathbeds.

The parental figure in the book, the aptly named Aunt Faith, preaches to her young nieces and nephews the necessity of preparing for death. "When I think of our family circle," she tells the youngest child, Grace, "I know that it is possible, I may even say probable that among so many a parting will come before very long." Yet she insists that dying will not be anything "dreadful" but "like going home." Only by submitting to God's will can one be truly ready. He prepares us for the afterlife by purifying us through suffering and loss here on earth. "We must all sometimes be content to give up our wills to the guidance of a Wiser Hand,—be content simply to *trust*," Aunt Faith counsels. The time "will come to you, as sooner or later, it comes to almost all of us."[30]

Woolson's equation of dying with "going home" was not mere sentimental prattle she felt compelled to dish out to her young readers. It was a common component of the Christian faith in antebellum America and one in which she fervently believed. In the coming years, as the scientific thought of the age explained away many of the mysteries of life on earth and many of her contemporaries became agnostics or atheists, she never let go of her "firm and beautiful belief in immortality," as she would later describe it. She clung to it as if to a life preserver in a sea of uncertainty. Referring to the dead, she wrote to her nephew, Sam, "We shall see them again; & they and we shall then be freed forever from all the imperfections & clogs of this lower life." At the age of forty-nine, she still insisted, "I have the firmest faith in another, & brighter existence; to me it is the only solution of the pain

& cruelties, and griefs, of this one."[31] Her belief in an afterlife was the one certainty that would carry her through the troubles that at times left her feeling hopeless.

The lingering image of Emma's and Georgiana's deaths, therefore, was not simply frightening but also inspiring. Theirs were considered "good deaths" because they demonstrated the submission of the individual to God's will. They helped Constance believe that "death was not really death at all."[32] Immortality would be granted to those who believed in it and suffered for it. What she and most American Christians envisioned on the other side was a place where broken families would be reunited and ties shattered on earth would be mended. Death promised the ultimate homecoming.

With heaven described in such ideal terms, many Christians could not help longing for it. Constance was not immune to its siren call, having watched Emma will herself into the next life. In *The Old Stone House*, the Reverend Leslie delivers a sermon admonishing his parishioners to "wait patiently for the Lord in the world in which He has placed [you]." This, admits Leslie, "is sometimes the hardest duty of a long life." Christians must not be so enraptured with thoughts of the next world that they neglect to notice the beauties (and duties) of this one. An early poem of Constance's, based on John 17:15, elaborates this message:

> Not out of the world, dear Father,
>   With duties and vows unfilled,
> With life's earnest labors unfinished,
>   Ambition and passion unstilled;
> Not out of the world, dear Father,
>   Until we have faithfully tried
> To burnish the talent Thou gavest,
>   And again other talents beside . . .
> Not out of the world, good Father,
>   Until we have suffered the loss
> Of self-loving ease and indulgence
>   In willingly bearing the Cross;

> Not out of the world, good Father,
>   Till bowed with humility down,
> The weight of the Cross is forgotten
>   In the golden light of the Crown. . . .[33]

However much her sisters' deaths had encouraged her to look forward to her own, Constance also inherited from her church a fervent appreciation for the beauties of this world that she would carry with her as she explored the natural world in the Great Lakes and the southern United States and, eventually, the man-made wonders of Europe and the Middle East. Her later writings would convey just how much pleasure she derived from this life and how hard she tried to remember the grace of God's gifts in the face of so much loss. But never far from her mind was the idea that death, and those who had gone before, were waiting for her.

3

Turning Points

T HE YEAR after Georgiana died, Constance began the serious studies that would allow her one day to compete on the same intellectual playing field as men. Yet she would always feel that her education had been incomplete, preventing her from being their true equal.

In addition to the reading and presumably writing she did under her father's tutelage, her early formal education had been fairly cursory: first the Episcopalian girls' school Miss Fuller's and then the coeducational private academy Miss Hayden's. At thirteen, Constance had received a comprehensive education alongside boys for one year at a public school named Rockwell. At the end of the year she performed impressively in the public examinations, naming as well as any medical school graduate the parts of the digestive and muscular systems, according to one observer.[1]

At fourteen she began what passed for higher education for girls at the time. If she were a boy, she might have been heading off to college, but such opportunities were scarce for girls. (Nearby Oberlin, which Harriet Grannis had attended, was one of the few exceptions.)

The pioneering phase of women's higher education, from which her mother and older sisters had benefited, had not yet given way to the progressive movement that would create the first large wave of female college graduates in the 1870s and '80s.

In 1823–1824, Hannah had gone to the first institution of higher learning for women in the United States, Emma Willard's Troy Female Seminary. In the late 1840s, Georgiana had gone east to the Albany Female Academy, while Emma went to a school (now unknown) in New York. Such schools professed to prepare young women for motherhood but also taught them to read and think for themselves, training them in the same subjects young men learned at college.[2] Just as Constance turned fourteen, a new school brought such principles to northern Ohio.

A SEPARATE EDUCATION

When the Cleveland Female Seminary opened in 1854, it was housed in a new, poorly heated, three-story brick building on a wooded, seven-acre lot, about two miles southeast of town. There students were trained in the arts of poetry, painting, and music alongside more academic subjects. In her three years there, Constance studied Latin, rhetoric, chemistry, physiology, geometry, algebra, trigonometry, zoology, botany, philosophy, logic, English literature, and the histories of Greece, Rome, and England. The sciences and languages were all taught by male professors recruited from the nearby colleges, while English, history, and math were taught by women. Constance's physiology teacher taught the girls how to dissect a calf and string together a skeleton. Years afterward, Constance still remembered being pursued by a "French Manikin" in her dreams. But she prided herself on having been "medically educated . . . up to a certain point." Her favorite of the male professors—her "demi-god"—was Samuel St. John, former professor of chemistry and geology at Western Reserve College.[3] It is probably due to his instruction and encouragement that natural history in all its forms, but especially botany, would become a lifelong interest of hers.

However progressive Constance's training at the Cleveland Female Seminary, it nonetheless segregated her from young men her age and thus taught her that women's minds and ultimately their lives were intended for a different, lesser purpose, a belief she would have a hard time leaving behind. In later years she would implore that women be educated alongside men, for it was the only way to widen their minds. Women were not mentally inferior, she believed; they had simply been "kept back, and enfeebled, & limited, by ages of ignorance, & almost servitude."[4]

The seminary's most prominent female teacher and its de facto principal, Linda Guilford, lamented that the vast majority of her students would never use their training. As a graduate of Mount Holyoke Female Seminary, the school started by Mary Lyons in 1837 to provide a college-level education for women, she had used her education in the only way available to women of her generation: teaching. Of the typical student at the seminary, she wrote, "When all her powers were stretching into rapid growth, and her mental resources were being developed to fill your own ideal, she left you, and in a few months was a bride." Speaking particularly of young women who married men beneath them, she observed, "The intellect has died of starvation. Worn out with early cares, she is but a wreck." However, Guilford did not suggest any alternatives except for her pupils to attach themselves to more worthy mates. It wasn't until three decades later that she would able to look back and see how some of her former students had used their training to gain meaningful work.[5]

In Constance's case it was Linda Guilford who made such work possible by teaching her how to write well. While outside the snow blew sideways through the wide-open fields and inside the furnace barely warmed the drafty rooms, Constance bent over her desk each week to write her compositions. And each week Miss Guilford patiently corrected her errors in logic and pointed out her faults in style. She was the budding writer's first critic, setting a high mark Constance was anxious to reach. Soon her classmates took notice. One of them later recalled how eagerly "we girls anticipated the Wednesday composition class. I can see the large room now, holding a full circle of intent listeners, while the weekly productions are read, and mark the flush of pleasure on Connie's face as her audience break [*sic*] into open applause after one of her characteristic essays."[6]

Constance made many friends at the seminary who would comprise her social circle during her Cleveland years. No doubt she was a member of the "K.R.T.'s," who read and acted Shakespeare, one of her favorite authors. And she was certainly among the forty students who, after hearing Rev. Ross from New Orleans speak in town about the "Divine Origins of Slavery," held an impromptu assembly. A self-described "red hot abolitionist," she would not have missed this rally against "Southern sentiment and domination." In their leisure time, she and her classmates went for long walks in the Water Cure Woods behind the school, gossiped about the neighboring wealthy bachelor who would provide a perfect match for one of their teachers, and stole freshly baked cherry pies left carelessly on a windowsill to cool.[7]

Although Constance met many amiable girls there, one rose above the rest. She was captivated by Flora Payne, the daughter of Henry B. Payne, former U.S. senator and soon-to-be governor of Ohio. They spent hours together in Flora's room, talking of literature and life, Flora impressing her with her wit and original ideas. Although Flora was two years younger than Constance, she seemed so much more worldly and mature. While the other girls were pretty and smart, Flora was simply brilliant. "[N]o one else approached her," Constance declared many years later.[8]

After their three years together at the Cleveland Female Seminary, both Constance and Flora went east for further education, but their paths diverged widely. Flora went to Cambridge, Massachusetts, and attended the school of Harvard professor Louis Agassiz, a forerunner to Radcliffe College, where many of the students—including Clover Hooper (future wife of Henry Adams) and Ellen Tucker Emerson (daughter of the author)—wondered what they were supposed to do with the Greek, geology, and embryology they learned.[9]

Meanwhile, seventeen-year-old Constance went to New York and attended the French finishing school run by Madame Chegaray. In existence since 1814, the school was steeped in tradition and gentility. Located in Lower Manhattan near Washington Square, it prided itself on educating "only the daughters of the rich and socially prominent," said former student Julia Gardiner, wife of President John Tyler. Although at other modern schools girls might be publicly examined by "bearded professors from boy's colleges," Madame Chegaray's was a relic of a fading age where girls learned "every talent of the agreeable and decorative order," Constance would later write.[10]

The decision to send Constance to Madame Chegaray's, which may have been the school Emma attended, suggests that her parents were not entirely sold on the idea of women's higher education. They wanted their daughter to gain the cultural refinements that the Cleveland Female Seminary had failed to impart. A year of voice lessons, attending the opera, and instruction in French and Italian would make her more attractive to potential suitors than any amount of Latin or calf dissection, especially when she didn't have the fortune Flora had to attract a husband.

Constance felt out of place at Madame Chegaray's. Besides knowing more about geology than Italian opera, she was also one of only three northern girls in an enclave of southern debutantes, and the only westerner. To a "red-hot abolitionist" coming from a school that had been riled by a New Orleans minister's defense of slavery, these new beings were a source of wonder. Their sectionalism intrigued her: while they proudly called themselves "The Daughters of Carolina," she had never thought of herself as a "Daughter of Ohio." Their refinement, from their perfectly curled hair down to the high arches of their feet, awed her. And their dependence on servants mystified her. As they sat in the third-story room they shared, one of the girls would repeatedly call out to the Irish chambermaid to come up and close the door. "Now Kate, why not get up and shut it yourself?" Constance would ask, to which Kate would laugh and answer, "I never thought of it."[11]

This was not only Constance's first encounter with southerners but also with American aristocracy. In an early story she would spoof the way a western girl becomes obsessed with proving her patrician ancestry after attending a fashionable boarding school where the girls wanted to see her family tree and test whether water could run under the arches of her feet. In her novel *Anne*, the title character, also a westerner, is made aware of her "deficiencies in dresses," while her southern classmates wound her with their amused glances. "Girls are not brutal, like boys, but their light wit is pitiless," the narrator observes.[12]

However much the girls at Madame Chegeray's may have wounded her pride, Constance also came to admire them. The enduring result was that she could no longer think of the South simply as the aggressor she had envisioned back in Cleveland. The memory of those girls would stay with her throughout the war and its aftermath, when she would write sympathetically of the losses southerners had endured.

At the end of her year at the school, Constance won top prizes for her compositions. But her first love had always been music, the most passionate of the arts—and the one closest to madness, she would later write. In *Anne*, singing opera music is a powerful outlet for the main character's pent-up emotions, as it was for the adolescent Constance, whose contralto voice thrilled her listeners.[13] In the coming years, however, as her hearing faded, she would have to strain to hear the arias that had so moved her, and she would cease to sing except to herself and select family and friends.

At the end of her finishing year at Madame Chegeray's it was time for eighteen-year-old Constance to put her new charms and talents to use. After attending the graduation in New York, her family outfitted her with a supply of stylish new dresses and took her to visit some of the fashionable resorts along the eastern seaboard where eligible young men abounded. Clara thought of her big sister as "a great belle," but it was also clear that Constance didn't fit in at this veritable marriage market. During their trip, a telling incident occurred. Her mother had persistently warned her, "Connie, do not carry an inkstand up and down stairs as you do—you will some day fall and injure yourself, and spoil one of your pretty new dresses!" One day, as Constance descended the hotel stairs thinking of the writing she was to do on the piazza, she balanced an uncorked bottle of ink atop her limp portfolio. Predictably, she tripped on her voluminous skirts, spilling black ink all over her smart gray dress.[14] There was no surer way to announce to the world her disregard of the courtship rituals in which she was expected to participate.

Behind her family's exasperation at Connie's absentmindedness and destruction of her dress was also a concern that she was in danger of becoming that much-ridiculed figure, a bluestocking. Now that she was grown, her parents had to decide how to handle the fact that she had a distinct inclination and talent for writing. It seems they determined more or less to ignore it, much as they did Clara's acting abilities. One day, when Clara critiqued an incompetent actress's

Constance sometime after her graduation from Madame Chegaray's.
(From *Constance Fenimore Woolson*, vol. 2 of *Five Generations (1785–1923)*)

performance and declared she could have done better, Hannah calmly kept up her mending and said matter-of-factly, "Your father and I knew it long ago—that you could act—but we hoped *you* would not find it out until too late.'"[15] The last thing they wanted was for Clara to become an actress or Connie to become an author. They wanted their daughters to marry, and then it would be too late to be anything else. Sending Constance to Madame Chegaray's was supposed to ensure that she would have the accomplishments to attract a husband and adorn his home. But soon it would be too late even for that.

THUNDERBOLT

Constance returned to Cleveland determined not to marry anytime soon. Five years after her homecoming she wrote to Flora Payne, "[A]lthough I am willing to settle down after thirty years are told, I do not care to be forced into quiescence yet awhile."[16] The intervening years would be consumed by a much larger drama than her own, however.

As the 1860s dawned and sectional discord intensified, Cleveland readied itself to answer the call to war. For years the city had been an abolitionist stronghold, a major stop on the Underground Railroad, and a layover for John Brown's fund-raising tours for his Harper's Ferry raid. In January 1861, the capture of a runaway slave down the street from the Woolsons' home focused national attention on the city and almost catapulted the country into war. A friend of the Woolsons, Judge Rufus Spalding, led the defense team that unsuccessfully tried to free Lucy Bagby. Less than a month later, in the midst of news of the southern secession, president-elect Abraham Lincoln visited Cleveland on his way to Washington, encountering the largest crowds that greeted him on his tour. Constance's father helped plan his reception.[17]

In spite of the tensions that had been mounting for months, news of the beginning of hostilities at Fort Sumter on April 11, 1861, came like a lightning bolt into Constance's life, as it did for so many. The thunder that followed quickly rolled toward Cleveland. As the first regiments to heed the call marched through the city on their way to the nation's capital, every resident seemed to have poured into the streets to see them off. Constance stood among them overcome with emotion. Each departing soldier seemed as though "he had been crowned king" because he was going away "to real battle-fields, where balls would plow through human flesh, and leave agony and death behind."[18] She would never forget their ultimate sacrifice nor the feeling of standing uselessly in the wings while the young men she had grown up with took center stage in the great national drama.

In the coming months and years, many of the men Constance knew went to war, including her future brother-in-law, George Benedict; Flora's brother Oliver; and Arabella's brother George, whose experiences working for the U.S. Sanitary Commission she would use in *The Old Stone House*. (Charlie was too young to go.) But it was her friend Zephaniah Swift Spalding who would come to encompass for her the heroism and tragedy of the war, inspiring intense emotions like no others she had yet experienced. The eldest son of the abolitionist Judge Rufus P. Spalding, Zeph, as he was called, was a friend from Constance's summers on Mackinac Island.[19] He was two years older and had a sister her age who was a classmate at the Cleveland Female Seminary. When exactly Constance fell for him is not clear. But when the war started she already saw a crown, if not a halo, encircling his head.

Zeph was a dashing young man, Germanic in looks, with blond wavy hair, clear blue eyes, prominent cheekbones, a large moustache that curled over his lips, and a long, straight "Greek" nose. Constance would later base many characters on him. In one story she wrote, "He was a marvel of beauty, this young soldier, with his tall, well-knit, graceful form, his wavy golden hair, and blonde mustache sweeping over a mouth of child-like sweetness. He had a cleft in his chin like the young Antinous that he was, while a bold profile and commanding air relieved the otherwise almost too great loveliness of a face which invariably attracted all eyes."[20]

In *The Old Stone House* she had Zeph particularly in mind as she

The only known surviving portrait of Zephaniah Spalding, Constance's wartime beau, probably taken sometime after the Civil War.
(From the collections of Kaua'i Historical Society)

created the character Hugh Warrington. Like Zeph during their last summer on Mackinac Island, Hugh is twenty, has curly hair, is strong and manly, and views the world as his to conquer. His younger cousin Bessie, an artist whose temper and restlessness were based in part on Connie's own personality, looks up to Hugh, idolizing him and envying his independence. Hugh confides in Bessie his plans for his future—to go to New York, work his way up in business, and by forty retire a rich man with leisure to travel the world. "I suppose it sounds conceited," Hugh admits, "but I have unbounded confidence in myself."[21] As did Zeph. Just as Constance had watched the circle of her own life contract upon her return from Madame Chegaray's, Zeph was on his way to conquer the world, beginning with a job as a clerk in New York, just like Hugh. Zeph's life was so full of promise, his physical presence so commanding, his disposition so sunny that Connie could not help but idolize him.

Upon his move to New York, Zeph had joined the Seventh Regiment, a "silk-stocking" militia that had the air of an "exclusive club for New York City's patrician elite." The war now handed these ambitious young men their destinies, and Connie watched eagerly to see what Zeph's would be. Even thirty years later she vividly remembered his father's speech at the public meeting back in Cleveland to send off the local militia. Rufus Spalding roused up the crowd with calls for "every able bodied citizen [to] put on the armor of a soldier." They all wept as he offered his own son in his country's defense, even if it meant he was "brought back to his home on his shield!"[22]

As his father's thundering rhetoric resounded in Clevelanders' ears, Zeph was on his way to Washington with the New York Seventh, outfitted with velvet stools and sandwiches from Delmonico's. Back at home, Constance listened each morning as she awoke for "the distant call of the newsboy far down the street, 'Extra! Extra! All about the last battle!'" For the rest of her life she would remember rushing out into the street for the paper and bringing it home to devour. On the fourth of May a letter from Zeph appeared in the *Cleveland Leader*. He and his comrades knew "that it would be necessary 'to do or die.'" Despite the threats of the "Baltimore Roughs," they made it safely to Washington, where they camped on the marble floors of the House of Representatives. Secretary of State Seward told them they would be "the men who would save the Union."[23] In those first days of the war, they all believed it.

THE ROMANCE AND THE REALITY OF WAR

When the thirty-day enlistment of his regiment was up and it became clear the war would not be over quickly, Zeph came back to Cleveland wearing his uniform. Constance and Flora were caught up in "the glamor that the war threw over the young officers," Constance wrote many years later. Zeph's effect on her must have been something like that of the fictional Lieutenant Maxwell Ruger on the inexperienced teacher Flower Moran in her story "A Flower of the Snow." Ruger looks like Zeph—"a Saxon beauty"—and Flower soon finds herself "ready to plunge with him into those deep shadowed waters of feeling over which society talk usually glides hastily." The narrator expresses how entwined Flower feels with him: "It is but seldom that souls see each other face to face in this world of masks and armor; sometimes there is a glimpse, sometimes a recognition, but instantly the visor is down again, and all is blank. In this case, however, there was no armor, no mask." Amid the high emotions of wartime, Constance's defenses and her fears of acquiescence in marriage crumbled. She and Zeph came to an understanding—they would marry one day, if he survived the war.[24] In the meantime, they most likely kept their engagement a secret.

Zeph wasn't home for long. On August 18, he received a commission as major, third in command, in the Ohio Twenty-Seventh Volunteer Infantry, on a three-year enlistment. Connie, stuck at home, was restless. Many years later she insisted that "the war was the heart and spirit of my life, and everything has seemed tame to me since." But her experiences during those four years have left few traces. No letters from the period survive and only scattered glimpses appear in later letters. We know that she volunteered with the Soldiers' Aid Society of Northern Ohio, collecting supplies for new recruits, singing at fund-raising concerts, and serving as postmistress at the Sanitary Fair, helping to raise money for the society's activities. But as the war dragged on, nursing became Cleveland women's primary task. Constance later wrote, "[S]ometimes a train of cars filled with wounded and dying would halt in the dépôt, and we tried with food, cordials, and fruits to alleviate the sufferings of the men; but some were past help."[25]

Throughout the war, news of Zeph and his regiment appeared regularly in the *Herald* and *Leader* newspapers, which Connie read religiously. The highlight of his service came in October 1862 when he led his regiment to victory in the Battle of Corinth in Mississippi, after which he was promoted to lieutenant colonel. Other news from the front was less stirring. The Ohio Twenty-Seventh spent much of the war on senseless weeks-long marches for which they were poorly outfitted. Zeph's experiences commanding the exhausted regiment, about which he must have written directly to Constance, would later appear in one of her first stories, "A Merry Christmas" (1872). There

Mr. Blunt, a former officer in an Ohio regiment, describes the early part of the war as a "campaign full of the hardship without the glory of war. . . . We marched back and forth hundreds of miles through Tennessee and Kentucky, often traveling in a circle, and retracing our steps of the previous day, burning and rebuilding bridges, collecting supplies, guarding passes, acting as reserves, . . . [and helping] to bury the dead."[26]

Zeph's most harrowing wartime experience also appeared in the story as Blunt describes in detail his capture by Confederates and his detention at a prison that mirrors the one at Cahaba, Alabama, where Zeph was taken. Blunt was confronted by "the gaunt inhabitants. . . . Most of them seemed half crazed; but the saddest spectacles of all were those who sat apart, sternly hopeless, waiting for the deliverance of death." Blunt reflects, "There was one at home who would hear of my capture. Need I say my thoughts were of her?" When a friend plans an escape, Blunt sends with him a note to his beloved. He didn't have long to languish in prison, however. Like his real-life counterpart, he was soon exchanged and allowed to return home.[27]

POSTWAR BLUES

At war's end it wasn't only the hostilities that had suddenly ceased. The excitement and exhilaration that had made the war "the first great event" of Connie's life were also over. The feeling of having truly "lived" was no more. Her friend and publisher J. Henry Harper wrote many years after her death, "The war for the Union was the great romance of her life."[28] His choice of words was more appropriate than he probably knew, for war and love would always be mingled in her memory, each heightening the experience of the other. With the war and the intense emotions it inspired now at an end, Constance and Zeph had to reexamine their wartime commitment to each other.

Zeph's feelings about the war could not have been more different from Connie's. While she tended to romanticize it, he had seen the ugly reality and futility of it. Afterward, he destroyed his uniform and discarded everything that reminded him of his service, refusing to ever talk about the war. He was impatient to get on with his life. In fact, he had done so before the war even ended. In early 1864, he had resigned his commission in the army and become Assistant Special Agent of the Treasury Department in the Military Department of the Cumberland, leasing captured plantations to throngs of northern entrepreneurs hoping to make their fortunes in the fertile cotton fields of the South. There were also many northern officers then involved in the lucrative, illegal trade, and Zeph may have been one of them. He was always "of a speculative nature," Constance later wrote.[29] Before marrying, he would have wanted to secure his fortune, the war having interrupted his upward climb. What he witnessed working for the Treasury Department convinced him that the place to make it was far from Cleveland.

The South had become the nation's new Canaan. Zeph joined thousands of veterans streaming across the Mason-Dixon Line—including two brothers of Henry James and a son of Harriet Beecher Stowe—many of whom were motivated as much by the desire to help the freed slaves as to enrich themselves. Few profited from their ventures, however. In 1867, when the cotton market collapsed and the vast majority of Yankee planters went home deeply in debt, Zeph ventured even farther afield. By December of that year, he had found another Canaan, in faraway Hawaii, where sugar was set to become the new cotton.[30]

Zeph was first sent to Hawaii, then a sovereign kingdom, as a spy by his father's close friend Secretary of State William Seward. He posed as a cotton planter investigating the potential profitability of sugar. Within a year he was appointed the U.S. consul, a post he held until 1869, when he helped form the West Maui Sugar Association. He was finally on his way to striking it rich. By this time, back in Cleveland, Constance already thought of herself as a "spinster."[31]

We can't know exactly how their engagement dissolved—whether she refused Zeph's invitation to join him in Hawaii or he simply prolonged his return to Cleveland for so long that their understanding collapsed on its own. But there is good reason to believe that Con-

stance felt she had made the greatest sacrifice of her life, for the for-
feit of love for duty is one of the major themes of her writings. Her
responsibilities at home had become all-consuming. She was the only
one left to care for her invalid mother as well as her father, whose
health had been deteriorating since the end of the war. Charlie was
in his early twenties and trying to make his way in the world, while
Clara had married and now needed her sister as much as her parents
did. In late 1868, just days before Clara gave birth to her only child, her
house caught fire. She was carried to the Woolsons' home on Prospect
Street and gave birth there, with her mother and sister at her side.
Clara almost didn't survive the ordeal. Indeed, it was Constance, not
the baby's mother, who first beheld the new baby's "wise and scornful"
look upon entering the world.[32] Between her aging parents and the
new mother and baby, Constance would not have felt free to marry
a man who lived thousands of miles away on an island in the Pacific.

Whether or not Constance was the one to break the engagement,
she was devastated to learn that on July 18, 1871, Zeph had married
the sugar heiress Wilhelmina H. Makee. (The couple would one day
inherit her father's substantial holdings, making Zeph one of the
wealthiest men in Hawaii.) The fact that Wilhelmina was nine years
younger than Constance upset her even more. She would never get
over the sting of being supplanted by a virtual child. By then she had
started her literary career, and she soon began to write stories featuring unfaithful, inconstant men who prefer younger, wealthier women.
She gave the name Wilhelmina, an uncommon name at the time, to a
character who lures a man away from the heroine in a story she wrote
in 1871. Three years later, the name of her usurper appeared again in
"Wilhelmina," the story of a young woman who patiently waits for her
fiancé to return from the war only to find out that he has grown away
from her and wishes to marry another.[33]

However, the story that comes closest to portraying the real-life
events and their emotional toll on Constance was never published—
yet it was saved when so many other papers and manuscripts were not.
In "Hepzibah's Story," a New England farm girl waits for her fiancé
through the long years of the war, her heart growing "sore with anx-

ious waiting." Yet even after the war poverty continues to prevent their marrying. Theodore goes west to make a living with his uncle, while she stays home to care for her ailing family. After a few more years and the death of her last family member, she decides to join Theodore, believing her small inheritance will be enough for the farm they always dreamed of. When she arrives, however, she finds him in love with Rose, "a dimpled bright eyed child of sixteen." Hepzibah quickly discovers that during the long wait she has grown old and lost her youthful good looks. In fact, Theodore barely recognizes her at first, but he is prepared to carry through with his promise. Hepzibah gives him up, however, by faking her death in a fire. The story ends with the marriage announcement of Theodore and Rose.[34]

Constance would one day realize that all had turned out for the best. Just months before her death she wrote to her nephew, "I should like to see [Zeph] again. If I could get him alone, I dare say we should have a very friendly and funny talk. But, meanwhile, we should both be inwardly thinking, 'Great heavens—what an escape I had!' It was only the glamor of the war that brought us together."[35] At the time, however, she nursed her despair, writing fictional and poetic accounts of her pain and wreaking her revenge subtly on clueless male characters who foolishly pursue faithless ingenues.

If Constance felt like a failure in what was considered the most important contest of a woman's life, she was also unsure about the desirability of success. She had seen the self-immolating quality of her sister Emma's love and understood marriage as a kind of bondage. In one poem, she portrayed the bride as a "heart-slave for life," and she had one of her heroines beg her would-be lover, "Let me be your servant,—your slave . . . my lord and master, my only, only love!" In nearly all of her novels, Woolson complicated her portraits of marriage, exposing the sacrifices women had to make to secure their husbands' love. Marriage was always a mixture of reward and downfall. Yet she professed to believe that a family of one's own was "the best thing in life . . . the only thing worth living for."[36] She would never get over the feeling that she had not only escaped the repression of marriage but also lost out on possibly the greatest joy in life.

A FATEFUL YEAR

The year before Woolson began her literary career, 1869, was a tumultuous one that would alter her life irrevocably. First, just as it became clear that Zeph was never coming back, Constance lost her two best friends—Flora Payne and Arabella Carter—to marriage. As they became wives, she began to confront what seemed like an empty life before her.

Flora had remained Constance's idol. Not only had she studied with Louis Agassiz, but she had also spent two years during the war traveling with family friends throughout Europe and the Middle East. Constance's envy was intense. She wrote to Flora, who felt as if she were in exile, "I wish I could be in 'exile' too, if I could visit the most beautiful and famous places the world can show! You are the most fortunate young lady I know, and ought to be the happiest." After the war, Flora seemed more committed to her intellectual pursuits than to prospects of marriage. Her friends "thought that she might be a famous musician, a scientist, a linguist, an author, an archaeologist, a translator, an authority on sociological science, so able and acute was her mind, and so thorough and various her training." Nonetheless, she fell in love and became engaged. Constance watched as her intellectual friend was transformed into a precious object to be kept slim, clean, and fair.[37] As the wife of William C. Whitney, future secretary of the navy, Flora would be on display for the rest of her life.

Arabella's marriage was more distressing to Constance, however. Arabella had taken the place of Constance's older sisters, and as Constance settled into her own spinsterhood, she had had Arabella to look up to. Arabella's friendship had provided an alternative to marriage. In 1869 they were thirty-five and twenty-nine and probably imagined they would be spinster aunts together, doting on their nieces and nephews and caring for their aging parents. But now the forty-three-year-old Rev. Alvan Washburn, who had replaced Arabella's father as rector of Grace Church in 1866, had proposed marriage. Arabella did not march calmly toward her fate, however, for reasons unknown. Constance had to convince her to embrace it, using language indicative of her own susceptibility to the romantic ideal: "Why can't you fling all your misgivings to the winds and be simply happy? The glory of your life has come to you. Everything else is trivial compared to it. You and he are really alone in the world together. Two souls that love always are. Do give up your past life and duties and BE HAPPY!"[38]

It wasn't easy for Constance to push her friend down the aisle. "You have been the best friend I ever had," she wrote to Arabella, but "I have felt such a conviction that you would some day lose your interest in me, . . . that I thought best to prepare for the worst." Convinced that her own feelings would never change, she feared that "Mrs. Washburn" would not be the "same friend that 'Belle' has been for so many years." After Arabella married Rev. Washburn and went to Europe on her honeymoon, the two friends remained close for a while. Their paths would diverge widely, though, and twenty years later Constance would complain that Arabella never wrote to her anymore.[39]

As her friends were preparing for their new lives, Constance was forced to face the circumstances that would determine her future as well. Her father's health had been poor for some time due to worries about his business. Then came the shocking death of his partner Lawson Carter, Arabella's brother and the "Carter" in the Woolson, Hitchcock, & Carter stove foundry. On March 31, 1869, Lawson walked into Jarvis's office, asked him to witness his new will, and then went into his own office and shot himself through the heart. Newspaper accounts indicate he had been suffering "severe mental depression, at times approaching mania." He had claimed many times he was "insane."[40] His erratic behavior preceding his death would have been a constant concern for the entire Woolson family, who were close to Lawson, his wife, Jane, and their five children. Constance, in fact, was godmother to their new baby. After Lawson's death, Jane moved to Cooperstown to be near her father, the Woolsons' old friend William Averell, yet Constance's attachment to Jane and her children would never wane.

The summer after Lawson's suicide, Constance's father suffered a severe bout of erysipelas, a bacterial skin infection. When he was able to sit up in bed and appeared to be improving, he sent Constance off to Mackinac Island on July 28 for a break from the cares at home. Her absence left him feeling depressed, but he had wanted her to go for her own sake. She had gone alone, a sign of both her loneliness and her growing independence. It was unusual for a woman to travel solo, but Mackinac felt like her second home. Old friends welcomed her, and she wandered through the aisles of cedar on the hill above town and among the spruce and juniper that covered the rest of the island. She remembered the summers she had spent there with her family and the Spaldings. Every path and rock felt haunted with old associations.[41]

She had only been on the island for a few days, however, when a telegram arrived. Her father had suddenly fallen ill on the fifth of August. There was evidence of typhoid fever, and he was sinking rapidly. Constance caught the first steamer back to Cleveland but did not arrive until midnight on the ninth. Once she reached home, she found the doorbell shrouded in crepe to muffle the bell, and she knew that her father was dead. In fact he had died three days earlier.[42] Neither Connie nor Clara was at his side.

Constance never got over the shock of his death and never forgave herself for not being there to hear his final words and ease his passing. When her nephew, Sam, experienced his own father's death many years later, she wrote to him, "I am thankful for your sakes that you were all with him during the last hours. You are spared the eternal regret that comes, when it has been otherwise. There is something extremely solemn, I think, in the death of a father, or mother; the children are touched to the inmost heart, & it is a moment like no other; face to face we then stand   with the great mystery."[43]

The death of her father left Constance without her anchor. Sixteen years later she wrote, "I have never recovered from the sense of desolation I felt when I lost my father; the world has never been the same to me since, for he made a pet of me." In her fiction, she often portrayed young women who are deeply dependent on their fathers' love and care, much more so than on their mothers, who are often already dead. In one scene where a young woman grieves over her father's dementia, Constance expressed her own feelings about losing her father: "His help, his comprehension, his dear affection and interest had made up all her life, and she did not know how to go on without them, how to live. Never again could she . . . have the exquisite happiness of his perfect sympathy—for he had always understood her, and no one else had. . . . She had cared only for him, she had found all her companionship in him; and now she was left alone."[44]

In many ways, Jarvis Woolson was the love of Constance's life. No man would ever measure up to the perfection of his affection for her. Now, at twenty-nine, she had to learn to live without his devoted love as well as his guidance and protection. His passing left her face-to-face not only with the mystery of death but also with the great question of how her life would go on without him.

PART TWO

An Education in Authorship

1870–1879

"I am just like a prisoner let loose."

—CONSTANCE FENIMORE WOOLSON

"[A]t this late hour I have gotten hold of the pen, and now people must listen to me, occasionally."

—CONSTANCE FENIMORE WOOLSON

4

False Starts

Sometime in the months after Jarvis Woolson's death, Constance walked beneath the overhanging elms along Euclid Avenue on her way downtown to the *Herald* newspaper offices on Bank Street. A portfolio was tucked under her arm. Inside were a historical essay on Mackinac Island, a reminiscence about a visit to Zoar, and a short story about a doomed Indian summer romance at a Zoar-like retreat. Each of these pieces contained a little bit of her father and the trips they took together. On every page were oblique tributes to him, evidence of the gifts he had given her over the years: a historian's reverence for the past, a romantic's adoration of nature unspoiled, and a realist's regard for "strong wood-cuts" over "nondescript scenery."[1] She would show the portfolio to the group of men waiting for her in the *Herald* offices, and they would decide if she could make of herself a writer.

Until now she had shared her writings with only a few carefully chosen friends. They had urged her to exercise her literary talent and even convinced her to allow the *Herald* to publish, anonymously, some of the letters she had written to them while on her summer excursions. But she was alarmed at the idea of seeing her name in print. Fear of failure and of publicity had held her back. Her shyness and low opinion of herself had combined with the lingering feeling that a woman should not dare that way. According to one of Connie's cousins, her father had encouraged her writing while he was still alive, and she deeply regretted that he did not live to see her begin her career. However, without his death and the loss of his income, it is questionable whether she would ever have braved public exposure. In fact, it may have been a fear of disappointing him, should she fail, that prevented her from pursuing publication. Now her friends, including her brother-in-law and his father, part owners of the *Herald* and executors of her father's estate, told her she essentially had no choice. She had to overcome her squeamishness about appearing in print for her own and her mother's sake.[2]

A SERIOUS QUESTION

After Jarvis's death, all his heirs could do was sell his business and some of the land on which the stove foundry was situated for $12,000. There were also the Wisconsin lands, which would continue to earn modestly for many years. But there must also have been debts, for the end result was that Constance and Hannah no longer had enough money to live without constant anxiety. Constance bore the full weight of their financial worries. Charlie had barely left the nest and wasn't making much money. Clara and her husband could help some, but they were not wealthy. The Mathers were, however, and they offered assistance, but Constance would not accept it. At the age of twenty-nine, she was determined to stand on her own.[3]

Thus Constance joined the army of so-called surplus women, who had since the war outnumbered men in many states and had to support themselves. According to an article in *Harper's* magazine, how single women could support themselves had become "a most serious question to society." The typically female occupations of governess, teacher, and seamstress were overcrowded. Constance was certainly well trained for teaching, and her old teacher Linda Guilford, now principal of the Cleveland Academy, would surely have hired her. However, female teachers earned on average only $659 a year, and the uniformly over-worked and underpaid schoolteachers in Woolson's fiction suggest she had little appetite for the profession.[4]

Writing was much more appealing, but also more uncertain. It could be done at home, and the magazines were filled with the names of women who seemed to have made their fortunes—or at least a decent living—at it. However, as the *Harper's* article also pointed out, most who attempted it failed to earn any support at all. Indeed, the literary and journalistic fields had been so glutted with aspiring female writers that the editor of *Harper's* in 1867, replying to someone signing herself "A Weak-Minded Woman," had warned the multi-tudes of women longing to see their names in print to put down their pens. Constance was an avid reader of literary periodicals, including *Harper's*, and very likely read this column, as well as the response from "Another Weak-Minded Woman," who claimed to have been seized by the "*furore scribendi*" to disastrous results, including the neglect of her family. This erstwhile aspirant now took it upon herself to "warn others how straight is the gate and narrow is the way to authorship, and how few there be that find it." She counseled, "Bury pen and paper at once. . . . That way lies madness." The successful writer Eliza-beth Stuart Phelps, who had just published her runaway bestseller *The Gates Ajar*, was hardly more encouraging in her contribution to the discussion, titled "What Shall They Do?" She was grieved "to see in what crowds the women, married and unmarried, flock to the gates of authorship" to be "turn[ed] away in great sad groups, shut out."[5]

In spite of the miserable chances for a young woman from Cleve-land, Ohio, to make a name for herself as a writer, it seemed like Constance's best chance. One reason why was the men waiting for her at the *Herald* offices on Bank Street: family friend George A. Bene-dict, part owner of the newspaper, and his son and partner, George S. Benedict, Clara's husband. Also in attendance was John H. A. Bone, who ran the literary department of the paper and was an experienced author, having published in the *Atlantic Monthly* and elsewhere. The men looked over her portfolio and gave her their verdict: they decided she should make a go of it. Bone knew many of the literary men she would need to approach, including the Harpers, who published a monthly and two weekly magazines, and Oliver Bunce, an editor at *Appletons' Journal*. Bone would write her letters of introduction to each of them. The "weak-minded" women yearning to become authors would have given their eyeteeth for such connections.[6]

Another auspicious circumstance that made Woolson's entrance into the literary world a fait accompli was her middle name. "Fenimore," the name Constance shared with America's first famous novelist, was a marketable commodity, and Bone was eager to capitalize on it. He used her full name in his letters of introduction and suggested that when she talked with prospective editors she mention being a grandniece of James Fenimore Cooper. She was unsure of the propriety of leaning on her Cooper connection and was casting about for a pseudonym. Bone was adamant, however, and she was outnumbered; the three men who held her future in their hands convinced her to brave full exposure. There would be no turning back.[7]

George S. Benedict was soon on his way to New York on business. He brought Constance with him, armed with her portfolio and Bone's letters of introduction. They first visited the Harper & Brothers office on Franklin Square. As she sat in the dusty, cigar-ash-covered office of the editor, Henry Mills Alden, noticing the shelves teeming with stacks of unpublished manuscripts, her heart was in her throat. Although Alden had turned away many a novice author, Constance fared better than she could have hoped. The name "Fenimore" drew his attention, and he was impressed to learn of her connection to the author of *The Last of the Mohicans*. He said he and his colleagues would look at her stories and asked her to return the next day for their decision. When she came back, not only did they want the stories she had given Alden, but they also wanted her to send them everything she wrote. She gratefully agreed. During that first trip to New York, she also met with Bunce at *Appletons'*, who was disappointed the Harpers had gotten her first. He asked her to send him whatever she felt free to submit elsewhere.[8]

From the beginning, she produced more than *Harper's* could publish. Woolson's first two signed publications appeared in July 1870: "The Happy Valley," about Zoar, in *Harper's*, and "The Fairy Island," about Mackinac, in *Putnam's*, a New York magazine to which her great-uncle and her cousin, George Pomeroy Keese, had contributed in the 1850s. Not exactly travel essays, these were whimsical tributes to her two favorite places, both still hidden away from the bustle of the modern world. For the rest of her career she would write about such places, often having to exaggerate their remoteness as the civilized world encroached on them. Four months later, her first short story, "An October Idyl," appeared in *Harper's*. It was oddly unconventional in its portrayal of an illicit flirtation that could not be consummated. Set in a remote Zoar-like village during an Indian summer, the story was the first of many in which Woolson would portray lovers who have found each other beyond the boundaries of an oppressive social world but must resign themselves to lives of duty, "returning to [their] stations in the hard world." After the story's publication, Arabella sent her some criticism, to which Constance responded defensively: "'The October Idyll' was wordy, but I am only feeling my way, now. I shall do better in time, but I never cease to wonder at my success. If you think it is easy to advance, even so short a distance as I have, just try it."[9]

Just as she was launching her career, she and her mother spent the summer in Cooperstown, giving Constance an opportunity to reflect on what she had inherited with her famous middle name. Although her first pieces had appeared under "C. F. Woolson" and "Constance F. Woolson," she soon changed her mind about suppressing the "Fenimore" and even decided to adopt the pseudonym "Constance Fenimore" for a tribute to Cooperstown and her uncle in *Harper's* titled "A Haunted Lake." In the essay she described how "memories of the past" lingered over Otsego Lake and the wild, wooded hills around it. She felt more than a little haunted by the legacy Cooper had left behind: "The air is filled with an unseen presence, and a spirit moves upon the face of the deep. A master mind has hallowed the scene; and as we linger on the pebbly beach the echoes seem to repeat his name over our heads and the waters to murmur at our feet." Although she was drawn to the pioneers and wild frontiers Cooper had so famously portrayed, she was not sure such a heritage was accessible to her as a woman who had grown up in a domesticated Midwest transformed into an industrial center. Nonetheless, she found a model for herself in the kind of writer he had been: "Those authors who write from within, and coin their own brains into words, may go dreamily through the world, their eyes fixed upon vacancy, . . . but the man who takes mankind for his subject, the man who writes to benefit and interest his race, is quick-witted and sharp-sighted, drawing upon his own observations of every-day life." However romantic a writer Cooper may seem to us today, to Woolson he provided a model of the writer interested in keenly observing the "literal truth." In him she found a form of realism that was "far more fascinating . . . than the wildest flights of fancy."[10]

Just as this piece was published, however, Constance had second thoughts about riding on her great-uncle's coattails, deciding to retract her use of "Constance Fenimore" in favor of her "true signature."[11] Yet she still couldn't decide what that should be. In the coming years, she would continue to vacillate between Constance F. Woolson and her full name.

LET LOOSE

Most women writers in the nineteenth century wrote from the vantage point of their homes. Woolson was different. Having trained her eye, as her father had encouraged her, to look out at the world, the impulse to write drove her away from home. Living in Cleveland, she would never amount to much, she believed. She needed a wider field to make her observations of life worth recording. As a single woman, however, her options for roaming were few.

Her brother, Charlie, now nearly twenty-four, was in an entirely different situation. The world lay spread out before him like a smorgasbord. He had only to choose his destination. When he came for a visit to Cooperstown that summer of 1870, he announced that he had been given a position at A. T. Stewart's, one of the largest department stores in the heart of Manhattan's fashionable shopping district. Here was Connie's chance; she could follow her younger brother out into the world. It was decided that as winter approached Hannah would return to Cleveland to live with Clara and George, and Constance would follow Charlie to New York.[12] While he was going there to become a clerk and start his upward climb (as Zeph had done many years before), her prospects were less certain. Moving to New York was simultaneously a step away from her identity as a daughter and a step toward a new identity as a writer that she barely knew how to imagine.

The plan was for Constance to write letters about New York for publication in the *Herald* back in Cleveland. Newspaper writing has always been an important source of income and training for American writers. Woolson's foray into that field would be short, but it was instrumental in helping her develop the critical eye and authoritative voice that would serve her well in her later work. Travel letters were a popular feature in American newspapers throughout the nineteenth century, and many of them were written by women. But it was the opinion columnist—the first was Fanny Fern in the 1850s—who would initiate a new tone for women journalists. During the postwar period witty, sometimes caustic, writers such as Gail Hamilton and Kate Field set the standard. Constance likely knew Field's work, as it often appeared in the *New York Tribune*. Field was the consummate modern woman, roaming widely and living by her pen. Henry James would use her in *The Portrait of a Lady* as the basis for his intrepid female reporter, Henrietta Stackpole, who "smell[s] of the Future—it almost knocks one down!"[13]

Constance would try on a similar literary persona, publishing at least five letters in the *Herald* under headings such as "Gotham. What a Woman Sees and Says," and "Gotham. A Bit of Bright Womanly Gossip." They are long, witty, sometimes chatty, and invariably opinionated. Hiding behind the anonymity of "Our Special Correspondent," she could poke fun at the men's "Manhattan uniform"—incomplete without a "variously shaded brown appendage curving over the upper lip and ferociously waxed at the end"—or marvel at the abundance of fur on the ladies—one "immediately withdraws all he has ever said against our new acquisition, Alaska, where every four-legged animal in the land must have been sacrificed last summer to supply the demand for 'Alaska Sable' now raging in the metropolis." At the venerable St. Paul's, she found fodder for her pen in a name on one of the old memorial tablets: "'Rip Van Dam!' Did anyone ever hear of a more astonishing title? It is of no use to tell that he was a staid, dignified burgher of pious and portly presence. His name is against it, and we will not believe it. No one but a regular rip-and-tear sort of fellow, a very dare-devil, a roistering, rollicking chap, would ever have borne such a name as those three significant mono-syllables, 'Rip Van Dam!'"[14]

Constance found her subjects primarily in the posh part of the city. Her boardinghouse at Broadway and Thirty-Second Street, where Charlie probably also lived, was only a block away from Fifth Avenue and around the corner from the mansions of the Astors, Stewarts, and other upper-crust New Yorkers. Flora Payne Whitney was living comfortably in the new brownstone her father had built for her and her new husband at 74 Park Avenue, three blocks away, where they were rapidly climbing their way up into Mrs. Astor's Four Hundred. Constance was never comfortable around such wealth or ostentation. Walking along Broadway or Fifth Avenue, noting the diamonds, the elaborately braided hair, and long, close-fitting gloves, Constance knew she could never "deceive the cool eye of a city lady who reads you like a book, stamps you as countrified and lets you go."[15]

The real New York she had come to see was to be found in its cultural offerings, reviews of which filled her *Herald* letters. Free of responsibilities for others and free of provincial Cleveland, she was now able to immerse herself in the finest art, music, and theater on offer. She wrote to Arabella that she felt "just like a prisoner let loose." She worried at her excessive fondness for the city's attractions but nonetheless "revel[ed] in the superb orchestras, magnificent architecture, beautiful faces and delicious voices." She felt as if she were at the center of the universe, where "stars of every magnitude have come to shine in the New World."[16]

In the midst of so much culture, her *Herald* letters allowed her to begin to develop the critical opinions that she would hone during her literary career. Her hearing was still strong enough to allow her to make distinctions between the fine performance of the city's premier amateur musical society and the disappointing Italian opera at the French Theatre, where the prima donna's voice was past its prime. Ever a lover of the theater, she relished Joseph Jefferson's performance of Rip Van Winkle and Edwin Booth's of Cardinal Richelieu. She also told her Cleveland readers about the growing fame of their own Clara Morris, who had just made her New York acting debut in a new comedy.[17]

Constance felt sure of herself reviewing music and theater, but art was another matter. Having previously had little exposure to it, she was rather baffled by many of the works in the Academy of Design's new exhibition. For now her taste in literature dictated her expectations from art: she was not so much on the lookout for beauty as for fidelity to reality. She apparently found little of it on display at the exhibition. The most flawed picture to her mind was "The Landing of the Pilgrims," by an artist named Wopper, who, she determined, "certainly omitted the 'A' in [front of] his name." Portraits of the Pilgrims in print or on canvas had been notoriously false, she admitted, but this picture strained all credulity: "One woman . . . is much to be pitied owing to the evident dislocation of her neck and the absence of any spinal column."[18]

As James would later write of Henrietta Stackpole, "the great advantage of being a literary woman was that you could go everywhere and do everything." Constance discovered this for the first time in New York, and forever after in her travels she carried with her the license of being a writer, which gave her the freedom to peer into the places mere tourists avoided. But she also wanted her pen to give her a kind of cover, hiding her from the stares of strangers, allowing her to observe without being observed. This is what prevented her from ever becoming a Kate Field or a Henrietta Stackpole. In later years, after her fame made the *Herald* attach her name to some letters she penned about her travels, she would feel the sting of exposure. She would come to loathe writing newspaper letters. "I do not like to approach so near the public. It is too 'personal' a place for a lady," she decided.[19]

Fiction was a much safer place for a shy woman such as herself, for there she could express her opinions and feelings behind the veil of fictional characters. While in New York, she wrote two stories set at Christmastime that pay tribute to Dickens, who had died earlier that year, and provide glimpses of another New York. One, "A Merry Christmas," featured Zeph's war experience. The other suggests that however much the status of a literary woman freed her from convention, her gender, particularly as an unmarried woman, limited her access to the public world. In "Cicely's Christmas," New York becomes a cruel, inhospitable place for an unchaperoned female of limited means. It is Christmas Day, and a fashionable church is so overcrowded that Cicely can't hear the music or see the service. She is forced to spend an exorbitant sum for a ten-course dinner, only half of which she is able to eat. The men of the city are rude and lascivious, jostling her on a crowded streetcar and ignoring her pleas for directions. At a play, admirers offend her with their advances. When Cicely complains, the usher replies unpityingly, "*[M]ost* ladies has gentlemen with them in such a crowd."[20]

Although we can't assume these were exactly Constance's experiences, the story teems with the loneliness she felt in the bustling city. Despite the presence of Charlie and Flora and a visit from George and Clara, she felt like a "desolate spinster." And although she had met many friendly people in New York, none could make up for the loss of Arabella and her father.[21] After the initial giddiness over her freedom in New York, her sorrow about being all alone in the world had returned with a vengeance.

GONE!

On the morning of February 7, 1871, Constance awoke to a frantic knocking on her door and an urgent voice announcing that a telegram had arrived. The message within informed her that her brother-in-law,

George S. Benedict, Woolson's brother-in-law and adviser. (From *The Benedicts Abroad*, vol. 3 of *Five Generations (1785–1923)*)

George S. Benedict, was presumed dead. She had seen him during one of his business trips to New York and had just kissed him good-bye, on his way back to Clara and the baby. His train to Cleveland had crashed outside of New Hamburg, New York.

Constance packed up her few belongings and caught the first train she could, taking roughly the same route as George's doomed train. She was overcome with grief and terrorized by images of his fiery death. *Harper's Weekly* called the accident "one of the most shocking disasters on record." The train had collided on a bridge at high speed with a car carrying 500 gallons of oil, which had jumped a neighboring track. The subsequent explosion had burned the forward sleeping car, where George had been. He and his fellow passengers must have died instantly. For the rest of her life, Constance would refuse to sleep on trains, insisting on stopping for the night, even when only the humblest accommodations were available. Nearly twenty years later she would write, "I cannot see the curtains of a sleeping car without a sick feeling."[22]

Back in Cleveland, Constance joined her shocked family and community in mourning. She spoke for herself and many others in her poem "In Memoriam. G.S.B. February 6, 1871":

> GONE! But we could not understand,
>   When broken voices said
> That he was gone—we could not feel
>   That GEORGE, our GEORGE, was dead
> Until they brought him home, his hands crossed on his breast . . .

> So young, so beautiful, so strong,
>   So dearly, deeply prized,
> So needed, trusted, leaned upon,
>   So loved, so idolized . . .

> How can we spare thee, GEORGE? How live
>   Through the long dreary hours
> Without thee? . . .

A small service for the family and close friends was held at Clara and George's home. Pallbearers carried the casket to Grace Church, overflowing with mourners, where Arabella's husband, Rev. Washburn, performed the service.[23]

George had become, in her father's absence, Constance's chief adviser and the male relative she relied upon. He was not only her chaperone on her first trip to New York but also her guide to the literary world. He had literally and metaphorically opened to her the doors that remained closed to so many women writers. Who would advise her now? Who would help her negotiate contracts or nudge unresponsive editors who owed her a check? If she were to continue her upward climb, she would have to learn to rise on her own or find another helping hand.

Constance wasn't sure how to look forward. She later reflected, "I was so despondent, and the future looked so dark, yet I wouldn't betray how I felt." That summer came the news of Zeph's marriage as well. In the stories she began to write of young women who found themselves forsaken and alone in the world, suicidal thoughts emerged. In "Hepzibah's Story," the heroine loses all interest in life but can find "no means of dying at hand." Flower, in "The Flower of the Snow," leaves Mackinac Island, murmuring, "Desolation! a land of desolation and death!" As she wanders through a bitter snowstorm that has complicated her departure, a devilish voice whispers temptingly in her ear, "What have *you* to live for? . . . Life will be long and lonely."[24] Constance may have shared her characters' hopelessness, but she had to put on a brave face. Just as she had stepped into her father's shoes, Constance now had to take George's place in Clara's home with the baby Clare ("Plum," they called her) and their dependent mother. The part of herself awakened in New York—the literary woman who roamed and observed—was packed away, for good she feared.

Fortunately, Constance found that she was not as entirely alone in her literary pursuits as she had assumed. George's father, who frequently stopped by Clara's on his way home from work, became her new "mainstay." He helped to sustain her connection to the world of ideas and writing, carrying on long conversations with her about his running of the *Herald* and the latest news. "[H]is encouragement and interest were everything to me," she later explained. "I don't believe I should have gone on if I had not had [him] behind me just at that time." She wrote almost nothing that first year after George's death, publishing a story in *Appletons'*, the essay on Cooper, and the two New York stories, which may have been written earlier. But the worries that always followed a male provider's death brought back the question of how the women left behind would support themselves. Clara had only a small "guardian's allowance" to support Plum. Charlie (according to the city directory) had returned to Cleveland and, boarding elsewhere, was working as a clerk; his salary would barely maintain himself.[25] If the uncertainty of Connie's economic future after her father's death had launched her literary career, the greater uncertainty in the wake of her brother-in-law's death would make her redouble her efforts and question what kind of writer she would be. Would she pursue profit or literary laurels? Was it possible to achieve both?

A DETOUR

During the following year, Constance worked hard, publishing twenty new works, but her earnings were still no better than what a teacher could make, about $700. Even with the income from their father's Wisconsin lands, they could barely get by. Then she read a newspaper announcement: the Boston publisher D. Lothrop was offering a $1,000 prize for the best new story for their "Sunday school series" of pious books for children. Constance was willing to try anything. The deadline was near, so she "shut herself up in her room and wrote as rapidly as possible." Clara, out of desperation over their economic situation, did the same. Within a week, they both had manuscripts to enter into the competition.[26]

The early 1870s were a boom time for children's literature, beginning with the colossal success of Louisa May Alcott's *Little Women* in 1868–1869. As Constance was beginning her career in New York, her old professor Samuel St. John from the Cleveland Female Seminary had visited her and given her "fully an hour's eulogy of Miss Alcott's 'Little Women.'" She liked the book too "but could not place [it] above all else in the world." The new cultural status of children's literature annoyed her, but Alcott and her many imitators had opened up a rich new field, and St. John and others clearly thought this was where women writers could most profitably toil.[27]

The phenomenal success of an old acquaintance from her school days, who published *What Katy Did* in 1872, must have further convinced her to try her hand in the children's market. Susan Coolidge was the pen name of Sarah Woolsey, who was an older sister of a friend from Constance's schooldays. Constance must have noticed how the book reproduced sites and scenes from their childhood. In an early chapter a quiet war is waged between the girls at two neighboring schools—Mrs. Knight's (or Mrs. Day's, which the Woolsey girls attended) and Miss Miller's (or Miss Fuller's, which the Woolson girls attended). Constance was astonished at Sarah Woolsey's success and "a little jealous."

Surely she could do as well, she thought, having herself told stories to her nieces and nephews for so many years.[28]

Hoping to mimic the successes of Alcott and Coolidge, Woolson wrote a book that similarly focuses on a group of children's exploits—inspired by those of the Woolson, Mather, and Carter children—before they learn the important lessons they will need to become adults.[29] Even the Woolson family dogs, Pete Trone, Esq., and Turk, made appearances. She also included a character much in the vein of Jo from *Little Women* and Katy from *What Katy Did*—a wild girl named Bessie who secretly races horses and longs for fame, in her case as an artist.

The Old Stone House won Woolson the coveted prize but not, unfortunately, all of the money promised. The publisher split the award between her and another author. Published in 1873 under the pseudonym Anne March (a tribute to Alcott), the book did not fail, but neither did it prosper. One reviewer, for *The Youth's Companion*, found it "pleasant reading" and noted that it "reminds us of Miss Alcott's 'Little Women.'" The *New York Mail* proclaimed it "a vivacious, wholesome story, whose chief characters are neither prigs nor rowdies, but true girls and boys, romping and laughing and playing tricks, yet having manly and womanly hearts, that may well serve as examples."[30]

Constance, however, was not happy with the results. She would never acknowledge the book, and her authorship of it remained a secret outside of Cleveland until after her death. She had written it too quickly and had to please not only her youthful readers but also a committee of clergyman. She later wrote, "When I had finished and read over the manuscript I was horrified to find it hadn't the orthodox Sunday school tone but was simply a young people's story. I went over it carefully and seasoned it at intervals with the lacking pious condiments." About the same time she wrote a serial for a children's magazine published in Cleveland, which must have been an equally unsatisfying experience, for she quickly gave up writing for children altogether.[31]

Clara, meanwhile, was undeterred by not winning the prize. She sent her manuscript out to other firms and found one willing to publish it, but without payment. *One Year at Our Boarding-School* was barely noticed by reviewers. One complained, rightly, that it read like a diary, concluding, "There is no predominant interest—no grand culmination."[32] If Clara had bested her in marriage, Constance outdid her in the literary sphere. Clara never attempted to publish again. From Constance's letters, it appears that her sister was not particularly supportive of her writing, perhaps out of jealousy. Although the sisters would always be close, Clara would resent Constance's growing devotion to her career.

Fortunately, Clara would soon learn that she and Clare could get by on their own small allowance, with the Benedicts' assistance. Constance was determined to provide for herself and her mother by producing literature she was proud of. She would return to her earlier conviction that although children's literature was worthy of a certain rank, "Shakespeare still existed, and Milton; the great historians, the great essayists, the great writers of fiction." Remarkably, she set her sights on this latter category, to which few women writers—none of them American—had been granted access.[33] Her early successes with the high literary magazines *Harper's* and *Appletons'* had stirred up her long-dormant ambitions. Thus this quiet, thirty-two-year-old woman from Cleveland, who had ventured into the literary arena seeking a means of support, began to hope and work for that most elusive of goals: recognition as a serious artist.

5

Departures

HAVING PUT her experiment with children's literature behind her, Constance was ready to embark on the first major phase of her career. Beginning in the fall of 1873, a veritable flood of the finest stories she had yet written came pouring from her pen. Unfortunately, little evidence remains of how and when she wrote them. During the past few years in Cleveland, she had made brief trips through Detroit and across Lake Huron to Mackinac and down the Ohio River, refreshing her memories of some of her favorite haunts, taking notes along the way. Upon her return, after unpacking and receiving a string of curious visitors wanting to hear about her trips, she settled back down at her desk to fill her blank books with drafts of stories written in pencil.[1] Eventually, neatly written manuscripts of tales set in and around the Great Lakes made their way to editors out east.

The first two—"St. Clair Flats" and "Solomon"—appeared in October 1873. The latter was her first story in the august *Atlantic Monthly*, the home of writing by Emerson, Hawthorne, and other American luminaries. After only three years, she had arrived where a lasting reputation could be made. The papers in Boston, New York, and Cleveland took notice, calling it her "very best literary production" and "quite worthy of the hospitality of the *Atlantic*." It gave her "great pleasure to enter within the 'Atlantic' circle," she wrote to the editor, William Dean Howells, who also hailed from Ohio. In the coming years, whenever her work appeared there, she would feel as if she had been "presented at court." For not only was the *Atlantic* the magazine with the highest literary reputation, but it was also, not coincidentally, "our masculine magazine."[2] There was no doubt that the exclusive sphere it represented was largely a man's world.

About this time Woolson's work became less autobiographical and more self-consciously literary. She had taken, as she told Arabella, "a new departure in my writing. I have gone back to nature and exact reality." This meant breaking not only with children's literature but also with the majority of women's writings, which, she was "sorry to say," were rarely "vigorous and fresh." She had "such a horror of 'pretty,' 'sweet' writing" that she was willing to risk "a style that was ugly and bitter, provided it was also strong."[3] Her ambitions had grown exponentially as she set her sights on realism, a new literary form of which Howells was the primary arbiter.

Woolson told Howells that she had "three models, whose styles I study and admire": George Eliot, Bret Harte, and himself.[4] She may have been trying to flatter the *Atlantic* editor, but her choices exhibit a decided effort to write high literary fiction. Eliot was widely considered the greatest living novelist, while Howells and Harte were both western writers, like herself, who had conquered the eastern literary establishment—Howells by reaching the summit of the *Atlantic Monthly* and Harte by earning an astonishing $10,000 contract from that magazine for one year's output.

Harte's phenomenal success with stories of rough, uncivilized miners and outlaws in California woke Woolson up to the literary marketability of the West. The region she knew best—a Middle West of rapid urban growth and bucolic country towns—was not quite foreign enough to capture readers' imaginations. She could find no inspiration in smoke-covered Cleveland, where in certain parts of town every mouthful of air tasted of petroleum. Instead she looked to the islands dotting the Great Lakes or the rustic logging towns along the shores, wild or frontier places that had disappeared during her lifetime. Readers were captivated by the novelty of her scenes. *Appletons'* called the field of her fiction "a region as fresh and new as any that American literature has touched."[5]

Following in Harte's footsteps, she also peopled these landscapes with male characters fleeing civilization (and the refined women who inhabited it), producing some of her best Great Lakes stories: "St. Clair Flats" (1873), "Peter the Parson" (1874), "The Lady of Little Fishing" (1874), and "Castle Nowhere" (1875). In an unusual move for a woman writer of the time, she often wrote from the male point of view, frequently exposing the limitations of her male characters' ability to understand women's minds and motives. Her male adventurers, eager to lose themselves beyond the frontier and recapture some of the freedom of Natty Bumppo, were also modeled on the men she had known growing up. "[T]he same fellow persistently appears," she explained to Howells, "because that is the kind of young man I have always known." She possessed the same yearning to escape the smoke and social world of Cleveland, but she could follow them only in her imagination. Her female characters who run off to these wild places have been pushed away from a civilization in which men have failed them, such as the religious exile fleeing her husband in "Mission Endeavor" (1876) and the lighthouse keeper Joanna fleeing a broken engagement in "Ballast Island" (1873). The latter is one of her strongest early works, yet Woolson never put it in a collection, perhaps because its portrayal of a woman who finds out her fiancé is in love with another, younger woman reflected her own experiences too closely.[6]

Despite Harte's influence, Woolson insisted she was not imitating him but was only impressed by his style. He was merely "the sensation of the hour; that was all." The most enduring influence on her fiction was George Eliot. Although she would never meet the famous author, she thought of her as a "dear friend," whose death in 1880 would touch her deeply.[7] She saw in Eliot a kindred spirit, particularly in her autobiographical *The Mill on the Floss*, the book Constance often called her favorite. It had been published when Constance was twenty years old, and it reminded her of herself, particularly in Maggie's hunger for intellectual stimulation, her unconditionally loving father who made a pet of her, and her brother, who is granted all the advantages of his sex while Maggie is expected to grow into conventional womanhood. *The Mill on the Floss* had shown Constance the power of literature to make one feel less alone in the world.

Eliot also provided Woolson with a model of the great woman artist. Eliot's aesthetic theories would in many ways inform Woolson's own, producing creative differences with her closest peers, Howells and Henry James, in the coming years. James would not make his presence felt until *Roderick Hudson* in 1875, but Howells had already begun his assault on idealism and romanticism, declaring in *Their Wedding Journey* (1871), "We shall never have a poetry of our own till we get over this absurd reluctance from facts, till we make the ideal embrace and include the real." Woolson did not disagree. She would never think of herself as a romantic or idealistic writer; rather she thought of herself as naturally pessimistic and preoccupied with the real. But she would see limitations in what a critic called Howells's "extreme and almost photographic truth to nature." She believed that writers must possess not only "eyes and ears (occasionally noses); but [also] imagination, or soul." Writers should interpret their characters as they do their mothers, children, or spouses: with intuition and love.[8]

As her contemporary realists increasingly excluded moral and emotional concerns from their definition of literary realism, Woolson adhered to a kind of empathetic realism most famously articulated by Eliot in *Adam Bede* (1859): "[D]o not impose on us any aesthetic rules which shall banish from the region of Art those old women scraping carrots with their work-worn hands. . . . [L]et us always have men ready to give the loving pains of a life to the faithful representing of commonplace things—men who see the beauty in these commonplace things, and delight in showing how the kindly light of heaven falls on them." Eliot wanted to show readers their "fellow mortals" so that they "should tolerate, pity, and love" them.[9]

Woolson found a similar approach in George Sand, a writer she greatly admired but never knew or corresponded with (Sand would die in 1876). While living in New York, Constance had translated Sand's novel *La Mare au Diable* (1846), which she hoped Roberts Brothers would publish. Unfortunately, another translation appeared before hers was ready, so it was never published. The simple peasant tale, Sand wrote in the preface, was a reaction to the new vogue of portraying "poverty as so ugly, so debased, sometimes so immoral and so criminal." The "mission of Art" should instead be "that of inducing people to love the objects of [the artist's] care." Similarly, Woolson, would copy into her notebook two decades later, "Not a single novel or play is considered a masterpiece which fails to arouse sympathy." This concern with human connection was more than aesthetic; it was the foundational ethic of her life. As Clara would write after Constance's death, "She <u>always</u> <u>helped</u> people—knew not only what to say and do—but just how they felt," particularly those "who earned their own livings—oh! how she did admire and like them."[10] Constance's empathy, instilled by her upbringing and religious training at Grace Church, would remain at the center of her life.

In her pursuit of empathetic realism, Woolson helped pioneer a key feature of the local-color literature that would dominate American literature from the late 1870s through the 1890s: the sophisticated, metropolitan narrator visiting remote regions and encountering uneducated, lower-class characters who often speak in dialect. Although many other local-color writers, including Harte, tended to portray their regional characters as comically uncouth, Woolson was more interested in revealing the limitations of her urbane visitors' perception. She portrayed without sentimentality marginal or outcast characters struggling for the same things her readers did: love, dignity, and respect.

Her empathetic aesthetic is apparent in "Solomon," in which the character Erminia says, "In real life we are all masked; but in fiction the author shows faces as they are." "Solomon" portrays an ignorant genius who works in a coal mine to support his disheartened, seemingly shallow wife. He is an untrained artist who has spent his youth trying to capture her beauty on canvas. When a pair of educated women visit the couple, one of them teaches Solomon the techniques of perspective and shadow, allowing him to create a portrait "so noble in its idealized beauty that it might have been a portrait of her glorified face in Paradise."[11] The very next day Solomon dies in an accident at the coal mine. The portrait has accomplished its final work, however, allowing the visitors (and readers) to see the pathetic wife as Solomon had. Woolson had found in a frustrated coal miner/artist and his wife her old women scraping carrots.

THE COMMAND OF THE CRITICS

"Solomon" also introduced a figure that would reappear at key moments in Woolson's career: the failed or frustrated artist. The recurring theme in her fiction of an artist's unfulfilled desires exposed the friction between her own rising ambitions and her ever-present fear of failure. It is not surprising that this theme initially surfaced in Woolson's first story in the *Atlantic*. She knew it would not be easy to court the favor of the male literary elite. When Arabella praised her talent, Constance responded, "You are mistaken, I have but little ability of the kind you mention; all I have is immense perseverance and determination." She compared herself to her favorite dog, who would allow himself to be torn apart before letting go of a mat between his teeth.[12]

The chink in her armor, however, was her immense sensitivity. She often could not sleep after reading her reviews. "[T]hese critics seem to hold my very life in their hands," she later confessed to Howells.[13] She needed to develop a thick skin, particularly as her embrace of realism made her vulnerable to conservative critics' attacks.

The flood of condemnation she received for "Peter the Parson" in September 1874 must have cost her many nights of sleep. *Scribner's* had hesitated publishing it, presumably because of its dark themes. The story of an Episcopal minister sent to save the irredeemable souls in a crude mining town on the shores of Lake Superior offered a bleak view of the fate of idealism. The ignorant miners prefer the bombastic preaching of an evangelist con man over Peter's strict adherence to High Church rituals. Retreating into an ascetic existence, Peter excites suspicion and is ultimately murdered by one of the miners as he attempts to save the thieving evangelist from the mob's retribution. The story's complex portrayal of religious and moral issues—Peter is both misguided and honorable, and his murderer is never brought to justice—made it controversial, especially coming from the pen of a genteel woman. Woolson thought it "the most powerful thing I have written," but many readers balked. One unnamed literary man who wrote to her gave her "up as hopelessly lost . . . into the hard realistic tendencies of the day." Meanwhile, another wrote to her with approbation. She wasn't sure whom to believe. In the face of such censure, however, she insisted "that both in an artistic and truthful-to-life point of view, my ending of the story was better than the conversion of the miners, the plenty to eat and the happy marriage proposed by my critics."[14]

The most virulent attack came from *The Nation*. It called "Peter the Parson" "a story . . . noticeable for the raw coarseness of its assault on the feelings" and found another of Woolson's stories, "The Lady of Little Fishing," about a female missionary who civilizes a camp of hunters and trappers, "wildly improbable." (By contrast, Howells, who had published it in the *Atlantic,* found it full of "dramatic force and skill.") *The Nation*'s critic then launched an offensive on the "band of heart-wrenching female dealers in false feeling" unable to "write a moderate word when the reader's feelings are to be touched." Their "indecent" fiction was no better than that of "the leading graduate of a young ladies' seminary." Such criticism, designed to make women writers feel inferior to their better-educated male peers and unsexed for writing out of their sphere, touched on Woolson's greatest fears. Fortunately, *The Nation* reviewer did not represent the dominant view of the budding writer's merit.[15]

Despite *The Nation*'s peevishness, Woolson's stories gained in reputation and popularity. Early on Mark Twain had noticed the power of her writing, although she would never know that his coauthor Charles Dudley Warner had plagiarized her in an early draft of *The Gilded Age*. Twain told his wife, "[H]e saw it & yet I'm hanged if he didn't hate to lose it because there was a 'nip' & a pungency about that woman's phrases that he hated to lose—& so did I."[16] (Upon Woolson's death, Warner would write one of the most admiring obituaries she received.)

The general reaction to her Great Lakes stories was so favorable that in the fall of 1874 James R. Osgood—former publisher of the *Atlantic Monthly* and Harte's *The Luck of Roaring Camp and Other Stories*—wanted to publish a collection of them. He saw in Woolson a rising star and let her choose what she thought was her best work. She chose "Solomon," "Peter the Parson," "The Lady of Little Fishing," and four other stories, among them what is probably her best early work, "St. Clair Flats." This story, set in Michigan, also plays out the struggle between idealism and realism, this time told through the perspective of a romantic narrator who views the maze-like marshes as "an enchanted land, whose memory haunts me as an idea unwritten, a melody unsung, a picture unpainted, haunts the artist." His cynical companion, with whom he relishes "the wild freedom of the watery waste," contradicts him at every turn, finding no beauty in the land, nor in the prosaic wife of a religious fanatic who lives in the only house on the marsh and takes them in. When the narrator returns, many years later, he discovers that the utilitarian view has triumphed and laments the "unmitigated ugliness" of the canal that has brought commerce to the region and scared off the wildlife and reclusive human inhabitants alike. The subtle biblical symbolism of the story's Edenic setting is overlaid with the realism of women's thwarted lives and the industrial development of the Great Lakes region, making it a prime example, Howells wrote in his review for the *Atlantic*, of "what our strangely varied American real life can do in the way of romance."[17]

For the collection, Osgood also wanted Woolson to write a new story, which would provide the book's title. The ambitious story, "Castle Nowhere," featured another of her male adventurers, Jarvis Waring, who has intentionally lost himself along the wild northern edge of Lake Michigan. There he discovers Old Fog, a man who lures ships to their destruction in order to pilfer goods for his adopted daughter, Silver. Jarvis is horrified by Old Fog but falls in love with the innocent girl and marries her, bringing her out of seclusion. Woolson insisted to

Howells that "the fogs, the islands, . . . the false lights and the wreckers are all from real life," yet the allegorical nature of the story made it the least realistic in the collection. Woolson was uncertain about its obvious romanticism. "I find I cannot go far out of my natural [realistic] style; it makes me feel as though I was telling a thousand lies," she told a friend.[18]

When *Castle Nowhere: Lake-Country Sketches* was published in 1875, a flood of letters told her the title story was the best in the collection, "so much more 'beautiful' than the others." Yet Howells soundly disagreed in his review of the collection, calling it "the least satisfactory of the stories" and asserting that "one is harassed from beginning to end by a disagreeable fantasticality." The rest of his review was very favorable, noting the "high truth to human nature never once weakened by any vagueness of the moral ideal in the author." Yet Constance was stung by the one note of criticism and dashed off a letter to Howells explaining why she had written a more romantic tale. She had heard too many times, "You are too realistic; you have gone after false gods. Give us something ideal, something purely imaginative;—like Undine."[19] So she had, but she swore she would never do so again.

Some readers were uncomfortable with "Castle Nowhere" for another reason, namely its lack of moralizing. Like the murderer in "Peter the Parson," Old Fog was neither condemned nor punished for his crimes. In fact, it appeared to some that his selfless love for Silver was meant to compensate for his deeds. When Arabella expressed her disapproval, Constance insisted upon an artist's prerogative:

> Now just hold your peace about my "want of morality." At least twenty awful letters have I received because I made "Old Fog" say he did not believe in eternal punishment. Is it possible that I am to be held personally responsible for the theology and morality of all my characters? I want you to think of me not as your old friend, when you read my writings, but as a "writer," like anyone else. For instance, take [George Eliot's] "Adam Bede" . . . Would you like to have a friend of yours the author of such a story? Dealing with such subjects [adultery and infanticide]? And yet it was a great

book. . . . The truth is, Belle, whatever one does must be done with one's might and I would rather be strong than beautiful, or even good, provided the "good" must be dull.[20]

Like Eliot, Woolson was faced with her era's insistence that women write from a conventional Christian point of view. She had to assert her right to participate in the decidedly secular movement of literary realism and write with force rather than beauty or moralism.

Overall, the response to *Castle Nowhere: Lake-Country Sketches* was encouraging. *Appletons'* praised Woolson for contributing to American literature "something fresh and vigorous beyond the common." The *New York Tribune* declared she had bested the up-and-coming Henry James "in the use of unhackneyed scenery and incident." Her "positive genius" and "marked power" made the reviewer "ready to offer Miss Woolson glad welcome into the field of letters."[21]

THE ANCIENT CITY

Joining the field of letters had not exempted Constance from the duties of a daughter. Hannah's health still took priority over everything else. During the severest winter Clevelanders had ever known, in 1872–73, Hannah suffered from rheumatism and a painful bout of shingles.[22] Another winter there might kill her. Thus it happened that the one thing keeping Constance at home—caring for her mother— also allowed her finally to leave it, but not for Europe as she most desired. While her brother, Charlie, ventured across the ocean (likely with the Mathers' assistance), Constance prepared to take her mother south.

In November 1873, shortly after the publication of "Solomon" and "St. Clair Flats," Constance, Hannah, Clara, and Plum headed to New York, where they saw Charlie on his return from Europe. (His plan to stay there for some years and pursue business had been interrupted by financial trouble, no doubt caused by the Panic of 1873.) On their way south they stopped in the nation's capital, where they spied President

Grant pacing the White House portico, and then joined the crowds of northern invalids and pleasure-seekers streaming to Florida. The most noticeable change for Hannah as they crossed the Mason-Dixon Line was "the swarms at every station of curious looking negroes." For Constance it was the ubiquitous evidence of the recent war: the shattered, resigned faces, the rows of soldiers' tombstones passing by the train windows, and the names of bloody battles called at each stop. Most troubling were other travelers' casual inquiries about whether she had seen this or that battlefield. She was stunned to discover that the war-scarred South had become a tourist attraction.[23]

Their destination—the coastal town of St. Augustine—was a wholly un-American place that would excite Constance's imagination for many winters to come. Having been enchanted in her youth by the French history of Mackinac Island and the German inhabitants of Zoar, she was now captivated by this former Spanish colony, founded in 1565, forty-two years before Jamestown. It felt like the next best thing to Europe. In the words of Harriet Beecher Stowe, a recent resident, it seemed "as if some little, old, dead-and-alive Spanish town, with its fort and gateway and Moorish bell towers, had broken loose, floated over here, and got stranded on a sand-bank."[24]

The Ancient City, as it was called, was "ancient indeed," Constance wrote home to the *Herald*, "with its Spanish houses, narrow streets, and overhanging balconies." The Woolson women were delighted with the old Spanish fort that dominated the north end of town. It was their "first bona fide ruin [with] dungeons, moat, and draw-bridge." Hannah admired the exotic palms and orange, olive, and guava trees, as well as the dark-eyed inhabitants, descendants of Spaniards and Minorcans. The "Romish Priests with their large hats, and garments as long as a woman's" enhanced the foreign atmosphere.[25]

They found rooms at Mrs. Fatio's boardinghouse, rumored to serve the best meals, on Hospital Street, the oldest street in the United States. The rooms were on the second floor and at night they could hear through their open window the surf striking the seawall two blocks away.[26]

By January, Hannah and Connie were thinking seriously of buying their own small house there. Hannah was so content that Constance, when she wasn't writing, was able to leave her and explore their surroundings. Her glee fairly leaps off the page of a letter to Arabella:

> The life here is so fresh, so new, so full of a certain wild freedom. I walk miles through the hummocks, where it looks as though no one had ever walked before, gathering wild flowers everywhere. . . . Then on other days I take a row boat and go prowling down the inlet into all sorts of creeks that go no one knows where; I wind through dense forest where the trees meet overhead, and the long grey moss brushes my solitary boat as I pass. I go far up the Sebastian River as utterly alone as Robinson Crusoe. I meet alligators, porpoises, pelicans, cranes, and even deer, but not a human soul.

For the first time in her life she felt free to roam without surveillance, unlike in the claustrophobic social world of Cleveland or under the scrutinizing glances of Manhattan socialites.[27]

The study of nature would begin to replace Woolson's love of music as her chief interest outside of literature. She was particularly drawn to ferns, identifying with the "shy little maids who dwell in the woods." Florida had nineteen new species of fern for her to learn and collect. For guidance, she began corresponding with Yale professor and fern specialist Daniel Cady Eaton, sending him specimens for identification. Over the next few years, as her "circle of human friends [grew] narrower," a by-product of her hearing loss, she would become a dedicated botanist.[28]

Woolson had always been very responsive to the natural world, but in her earliest works nature tended to be unpredictable and even deadly, particularly in the form of shipwrecking storms that signified her characters' (and her own) inner turmoil. In Florida, nature both healed and stimulated her in new ways. The tranquility and laziness of St. Augustine and its surroundings were a great comfort after the cares and anxieties of the past few years. During her solitary walks in the sandy forests, she discovered a solace she lovingly described in the poem "Pine-Barrens":

Abroad upon the Barrens the care-worn soul awakens
   From brooding on the long hard paths its weary feet have trod:
How little seem earth's sorrows, how far off the lost to-morrows,
   How broad and free the Barrens lie, how very near to God![29]

It is not too much to say that Woolson was in a sense reborn during her stay in St. Augustine. In her explorations of Florida, she mastered the objectivity necessary for an artist. She felt inspired by Thoreau, whom she references throughout the story "A Voyage to the Unknown River," and Emerson, whose aphorisms she pinned above her desk. Her turn outward is also reminiscent of George Eliot, who combined a love of natural history with her deep affection for the variety of humanity.

The transition Woolson was undergoing materializes in her most autobiographical work of this period: "The Ancient City" (December 1874–January 1875). The thirty-four-year-old author put much of her earlier uncertainty and hopelessness into her characterization of Sara, a magazine writer in her late twenties. She is unusually sensitive, caustic, and isolated, we learn, because of a broken engagement. When her former fiancé, John, shows up in St. Augustine and appears to fall for a young beauty, Sara is so unhappy that she longs for death.

Sara is also the first but not the last of Woolson's failed female artists. Others look down on Sara for being a writer, and the narrator, Aunt Martha, declares, in reference to Sara, "Why is it that women who write generally manage to make themselves disagreeable to all mankind?"[30] Ultimately, a more experienced male writer who arrives in St. Augustine determines that Sara is the type to live poetry rather than write it. A woman who *lives* cannot write, and a woman who writes cannot *live*, an expression of the split that Woolson would feel again and again in her own life. Fortunately for Sara, John proposes to her once again, allowing her to live an ordinary woman's life. For Sara writing has clearly been a replacement for marriage. If Woolson viewed her own writing similarly at first, it was clear that was no longer the case. She was beginning to find ample compensations in the life of a literary spinster.

Woolson's new view of unmarried life emerges in the character of the narrator of "The Ancient City," the forty-year-old Martha. She looks out for Sara because "no one comprehends a girl passing through the shadow-land of doubt and vague questioning that lies beyond youth so well as the old maid who has made the journey herself, and knows of a surety that there is sunshine beyond."[31] Martha is content never to have married and enjoys her freedom to travel. Although not actually a writer, she possesses the gaze of the artist observing the world around her. Martha ventures into the parts of town the other tourists avoid, mirroring Woolson's own tendency to roam beyond the bounds of what is expected of women of her class.

On one excursion outside of St. Augustine's tourist areas, Martha encounters "a dark-eyed, olive-skinned people" who regard her "with calm superiority." Minorcans, she is informed, are descendants of indentured servants brought from the isle of Minorca off the coast of Spain to Florida in 1767, after the British had taken over the colony. The Minorcans mutinied against their oppressors and were given land on which they continued to live. Woolson was fascinated with this community, peopling the margins of her Florida fiction with them and occasionally giving them center stage, as in her fascinating story "Felipa" (1876), where a Minorcan girl who dresses like a boy attracts the attention of a trio of visiting white northerners. Here and elsewhere, Woolson granted her Minorcan characters agency, allowing them to speak back or assert their own value systems. When the artist narrator tells Felipa she can never be as beautiful as Christine, a northern tourist, Felipa turns the mirror back on her, shouting, "You are not pretty either. . . . Look at yourself! look at yourself!" The final line of the story is given not to the narrator and her friends but to Felipa's Minorcan grandfather, who sees what the narrator cannot. While they have dismissed Felipa's powerful feelings, he realizes her great capacity for love, even at eleven years of age.[32]

In "Felipa," Woolson also crossed boundaries of another sort, depicting Felipa's and the female narrator's attraction to the beautiful Christine, complicating notions of women's sexuality at a time well before lesbianism and "Boston marriages" were recognized. In the coming years, Woolson would also portray schoolgirls' crushes on their female teachers in her novel *Anne* and argue in a review that she had herself witnessed "the deepest devotion, in mature, well-educated, and cultivated women, for some other woman whom they adored," although all of those women had since married and put their earlier adoration behind them. It is possible that Constance had herself felt such devotion toward Arabella. Looking back on it now, her feelings seemed remote and no longer possessed the same intensity. Their memory allowed her, however, to recognize in other women their love for each other.[33]

Woolson's time in St. Augustine also exposed her to freed slaves. Her counterpart Martha deliberately seeks them out to see firsthand how they are faring. In spite of other white northerners' claims that they "don't know what to do with [their freedom] yet," Martha notices the freed slaves' defiance and independence. She also visits the schools for freedmen, where the older pupils eagerly learn to read and the younger students "show quick understanding." Woolson would later explore these themes more fully in what remains her most controversial story, "King David" (1878). Just as she refused to condemn Old Fog and the murderer of "Peter the Parson," she did not denounce her lead character, a white teacher who was an abolitionist but is physically repulsed by his black students. Instead of passing judgment herself, Woolson allows one of his pupils to speak on behalf of the freed slaves: "You hab nebber *quite* unnerstan us, sah, nebber quite; an' you can nebber do much fo' us, suh, on 'count ob dat fack."[34] Always an outside observer, Woolson, like Martha, took no overt position on such issues but allowed her characters to assert their own perspectives, thereby conveying her deep respect for those marginalized voices that were otherwise rarely heard. By refusing to state her opinions directly, she split from the moralizing tone of George Eliot and Bret Harte and declared her affiliation with American literary realism.

LITERARY FRIENDSHIPS

In St. Augustine, Woolson also found her first literary friend, Edmund Clarence Stedman, a genial married man in his forties with a prodigious graying beard that he parted down the middle and brushed to each side. Like many of the other northerners, he had come south in search of a cure. His particular ailment was overwork in his job as a Wall Street broker. But it was Stedman's other identity, as one of New York's most prominent critics and poets, that drew Woolson to him. He was, as the poet Harriet Monroe later dubbed him, "the friend and helper of young aspirants."[35]

Stedman met Woolson on March 7, 1874. He showed an interest in her at once. "Rarely have [I] met so gentle, earnest, and brilliant a woman," he wrote to his mother. They talked about poetry, criticism,

Edmund Clarence Stedman, Woolson's most devoted literary friend during the 1870s. (From *Life and Letters of Edmund Clarence Stedman*)

and her career as they walked together in the afternoons along the coquina seawall on St. Augustine's waterfront. Since leaving Cleveland she had been publishing travel essays and poetry and was eager for advice about where her strengths as a writer lay. His first impressions of her were of "a woman gracefully impulsive and independent." He was struck by how "she ignored the formal, fashionable strata of society at St. Augustine" and noticed that under a surface of "inviolable reserve" she had "the gipsy instinct, the love of liberty."[36]

A view of the St. Augustine seawall, along which Woolson and Stedman took long walks and discussed her career.
(From "The Ancient City," *Harper's*)

On her side, Woolson couldn't help noticing how Stedman consistently kept the conversation focused on her. She was, she later told him, "accustomed to the eternal 'I' of all my male friends." She had been the listener for so long that it was a novel experience to be the one commanding attention. "[A]t this late hour I have gotten hold of the pen," she realized, "and <u>now</u> people must listen to <u>me</u>, occasionally."[37] She would look the rest of her life for other men who could listen to her as well as Stedman had.

In "The Ancient City" Stedman appears as Eugenio, "the poet whom poets love." He walks with Sara on the seawall and assesses her writings, leaving her convinced that "[t]here isn't a thing . . . worth the paper it is written on." Nonetheless, he "was generous and kind" and gave her "solid assistance, . . . suggestive hints worth their weight in gold to an isolated beginner like myself," Sara tells Martha. Despite the fact that Woolson had begun to gain the attention of critics (*Castle Nowhere* would come out the next year), she too felt like "an isolated beginner" and solicited Stedman's advice, but his response was nothing like Eugenio's to Sara. He liked "Peter the Parson" and "stir[red] up" his friend Richard Watson Gilder to publish it and another story, "Jeannette," in *Scribner's*. After *The Nation*'s scathing review, she asked him, "I wonder if you meant all you said about the stories." His reassurance then and in the coming years was key to her ability to tune out the critics who seemed to hold her life in their hands. He told her, "[W]hen we find a perfect and dramatic short story which is so rare, we both rejoice and jump for it. The *best* stories since Hawthorne, with American themes and atmosphere, are yours and Bret Harte's."[38]

Stedman also became Woolson's adviser, helping to fill the void left by George Benedict's death. He helped her deal with editors and publishers, beginning with Gilder. In her negotiations with Osgood for the publication of *Castle Nowhere*, Stedman provided continual assistance. When Stedman assumed she had "other advisers," she corrected him. "Whether for good or for ill, the fact remains that I am entirely alone."[39]

On her side, Woolson praised Stedman's writings so often that he apparently tired of her repeated admiration. Her strategy was to approach him as a writer rather than as a man, establishing a nonthreatening, literary intimacy with him. She invited him to "picture" his essays "lying on my toilette-table where I do my most prized reading, and myself poring over your pages the first thing in the morning, and the last at night."[40] She felt safe expressing her infatuation with his words, establishing the ground on which she would later meet other male writers. She formed an intimacy with their works that was unavailable to her on a personal level, as that was the province of wives and male friends.

However, Woolson was not simply the submissive mentee. Although Stedman didn't like her story "Castle Nowhere," she published it anyway. He disapproved of her travel sketches, yet she continued to publish them, telling him, "Well, Mr Stedman, we must all do what we think is best for own selves."[41]

In one important area, Stedman's views were particularly discouraging. Woolson had eagerly devoured his critical essays collected as *Victorian Poets*, published in 1876, sometimes talking back to him in the margins. When she came to the essay on Elizabeth Barrett Browning, she paid close attention to how he treated her compared to the male poets who dominate the collection. She couldn't help noticing a lack of regard that troubled her. She wrote in the margins, "Mr Stedman does not really believe in woman's genius. His disbelief peeps through every line of the criticism below, whose essence is 'She did wonderfully well for a woman'!"[42] With her own ambitions growing, his comments felt somehow directed at herself. It was her first stark realization that the men she looked to for validation—even the most generous, like Stedman—would always view her as their inferior.

When she wrote directly to Stedman, she acquiesced to his view of separate literary spheres for men and women: "I smile a little every time I turn over the 'Victorian' pages to see how nicely you have veiled your entire disbelief in the possibility of true fiery genius in woman. . . . You have no objection to a woman's soaring to lofty heights in the realm of space allotted to her; the only thing you wish understood is that it is in her allotted space, and nobody else's. . . . Well,—I do not quarrel with you about this; and the reason is—that I fully agree with you!"[43] Clearly, she was eager to retain Stedman's friendship and support and therefore wanted to show him that she was not trying to compete with him. Nothing else Woolson ever wrote indicated that she agreed with Stedman about women's inherent inferiority as writers. She would suggest, however, that women were hampered in their ability to ascend to the heights male authors had reached by nature of their upbringing and education.

The subtext for this letter to Stedman can be found in Woolson's own struggles with what she thought of as "the great question" of her own poetic abilities. While Stedman encouraged her in her fiction, he had little to say of her poetry, which she also published prolifically. So she had asked Stedman if he knew a fair critic who would give her an objective opinion of an ambitious verse drama she had written titled *Two Women*. It was about an urban socialite from Washington, D.C., and an Ohio farm girl rushing to the deathbed of the dying soldier they both love. Stedman had recommended his friend the critic R. R. Bowker, who advised Woolson to put *Two Women* in a drawer for a year and read Shelley and Keats.[44]

Bowker's opinion pointed out her deficient knowledge of the English poetic tradition and the lack of polish in her verse. Woolson became convinced that her fault was a certain coarseness. She was trying too hard to counter her impression "that women run too much into mere beauty at the expense of power." As a result, she feared that she had "gone too far the other way; too rude; too abrupt." Then she had read Stedman's *Victorian Poets*. Just as she was noticing how Stedman placed Barrett Browning in a subordinate category, she realized that her ambitions for *Two Women* could not be realized. She would not be able to distinguish herself from most other female poets, who privileged beauty over power, for the simple fact that her work would always be judged the work of a woman. In addition, she realized that she was up against a male tribunal whose training was vastly superior to her own. In the same letter to Stedman in which she addressed his Browning essay, she also mentioned that she had withdrawn *Two Women*, which she had apparently submitted for publication against Bowker's recommendation. However, a year later, the verse drama did appear. The critical reaction confirmed what she had expected. Reviewers were deeply impressed by the emotional power Woolson's poem conveyed but also forthright in their criticism that its versification was "rugged" and "imperfect," with one critic wishing it had been written in her fine prose instead of verse.[45]

Thereafter Woolson published almost no poetry and declined all offers to publish a volume of her verse. By bowing out of the arena of poetry, she not only abstained from direct competition with her closest literary friend and adviser, but she also made a decision to stake her claim in fiction, a genre more hospitable to women and just as significant as poetry, she believed. She roundly disagreed with Stedman's claim in his essay on Barrett Browning that although Sand,

Brontë, and Eliot were her peers, they "have been writers of prose, before whom the poet takes precedence, by inherited and defensible prerogatives." Woolson wrote in the margin: "Not at all."[46]

Another literary friend during these years, the poet Paul Hamilton Hayne, who lived with his wife outside of Augusta, Georgia, would be a lively correspondent for many years, but he looked more to her for advice than she to him. He admired her work greatly, finding it full of "freshness, originality, & real artistic power," as well as "'grit,' vigor, and almost manly verve." He noticed how she had gained access to the premier magazines so quickly and hoped to glean from her any information about how he could do the same.[47]

Hayne was particularly eager to court Howells's attention at the *Atlantic*, which Woolson seemed to have won. She maintained a good working relationship with Howells during these years, but his attack on "Castle Nowhere" suggested he would not be the kind of supportive friend she sought. She agreed with Hayne that Howells was tiresome. In the winter of 1876, she met the *Atlantic*'s publisher, Melancthon Hurd, in St. Augustine. "He has let out that Howells has 'favorites,'" she gossiped to Hayne. "Chief among them at present, Henry James, Jr. I suspect there is a strong current of favoritism up there. As to poetry, I have been told several times that Howells was exceedingly difficult." In her next letter she wrote, "If I please him, I am glad; if I do not please him, I am not in the least dismayed. He is a man of strong and peculiar tastes, and (I fancy) subject to caprices. . . . You never know what he is going to do or say."[48]

THE TRIBE OF UNHAPPY WOMEN WRITERS

Significantly, Woolson did not look to other women writers for friendship or counsel. Her encounters with them tended to make her painfully self-conscious, which may explain why she developed no close ties to any during the early years of her career. She didn't like the feeling that being both woman and writer made her in most people's eyes not only less of a writer but also less of a woman. When Woolson met

Hayne's friend the writer Margaret Junkin Preston, she was pleased to find her "a charming woman; quiet, gentle, and the reverse of the common idea of a 'literary woman.'" But the writer Mary Mapes Dodge, whom she met in New York at the home of Stedman and his wife, excited her anxiety about what it meant to be a woman who was a writer. "Mrs Dodge is 'fine looking,'" she wrote Stedman afterward, "but—anyone would know she was literary. Why must it inevitably be so?—But perhaps it is 'compensation'; as we gain money, or fame, just so surely must we lose that which in our hearts we prize a great deal more." Meanwhile, she imagined "how glad you must be in your inmost soul that your wife was not a writer. How much prettier and lovelier a thousand times over was Mrs Stedman in every motion look and tone than the best we other three could do! What is the reason that if we take up a pen we seem to lose so much in other ways?"[49]

She also met that evening the novelist Elizabeth Stoddard, who was married to the poet Richard Stoddard. Even though Elizabeth had long before given up her a career as a novelist, when Constance later heard she was ill, she couldn't help but reflect, "[W]hy do literary women break down so, and—I do not allude to Mrs Stoddard here of course,—act so? It almost seems as though only the unhappy women took to writing."[50] Such had been her characterization in "The Ancient City" of the disappointed magazine writer Sara. The common perception, Woolson sensed, was that literary women were a despondent, disagreeable bunch, making her eager to disassociate herself from them.

Her encounters in St. Augustine in 1875 with the writer Elizabeth Stuart Phelps again made her anxious about others' perceptions of her as "literary." Phelps was the best-selling author of *The Gates Ajar* (1868) and a regular *Atlantic* contributor. They stayed in the same boarding-house, but Woolson found it impossible to get to know her. Phelps was accompanied by her friend Dr. Mary Briggs, who wore a man's jacket and mystified Woolson's niece. "Mamma, sometimes he wears a skirt, just like a lady," Plum said quizzically, to which Clara could only respond, "Hush." Phelps promoted dress reform, which she hoped would lead to women's mental and social liberation. Her pamphlet

An unusual portrait of Constance in the fashionable dress her mother and sister insisted she wear. (The Western Reserve Historical Society)

What to Wear (1873) advocated the shortening of skirts and the removal of the corset, among other modifications. The point, as Constance saw it, was "to look as man-ish as possible." Meanwhile, she was trying her best to look less "literary." Clara insisted that she wear more attractive dresses, and Hannah wouldn't let Constance wear her glasses because they would "give the finishing touch" to her bookish image.[51]

Yet in spite of the uncertainties of her identity as a woman writer, Woolson was making peace with it. She had long since given up attempting to attract men. "I am as truly out of that kind of talk as a nun," she assured Arabella. "I go about a great deal, but always as an 'observer.'"[52] She felt eminently more at ease watching from the sidelines, storing her impressions for later use.

6

Dark Places

S T. Augustine was paradise, but only during the winter. As the heat and humidity returned, and with it Hannah's old enemy, rheumatism, the Woolson women turned northward, beginning a pattern of wintering in Florida and summering in cooler parts—first in the Upper South, where they could live more cheaply than in the North, and finally in the North with family. Clara often brought her daughter to the Benedicts in Cleveland during the summer, leaving Constance in charge of their mother.

They spent their first summer away from home in Asheville, North Carolina, at that time a remote resort town in the Blue Ridge Mountains, twenty-five miles away from the closest railroad. Hannah's health flourished in the dry, mild climate, and Constance fell in love with the mountains. In the afternoons, she took her microscope and searched for ferns, gathering eleven new species for her collection. What thrilled Constance most was the feeling that Asheville was virtually hidden from the world.[1]

However, the harrowing journey out of town in November dampened her enthusiasm. Sitting on the back of a wagon, they traveled

along the French Broad River on a narrow road cut out of the surrounding rock. They could only see a sliver of blue sky above. Then it
turned dark and a deluge began. Connie moved up to sit next to the
driver and watched as the wheels passed within inches of the edge
of the road that dropped down to surging water below. They never
returned to Asheville after that tormenting ride, but the region lingered long in Constance's imagination as the most beautiful expanse
of wild nature she had ever seen. Twenty years later she would set her
novel *Horace Chase* there and have a character warn its railroad-baron
protagonist, who wants to make a tourist attraction out of the region,
"[W]hen you perceive that your last acre of primitive forest is forever
gone, then you will repent."[2]

Next to wilderness, Constance prized antiquity, an even rarer commodity in the forward-looking United States. She fell in love with
Charleston, South Carolina, where she and Hannah spent parts of the
summer and fall of 1875. She was charmed by the colonial tombstones,
the watchman's cries announcing the time throughout the night, and
the aristocratic inhabitants' stubborn adherence to tradition. She also
noted how little had been done to rebuild Charleston after the war,
making this most aristocratic city also one of the most impoverished
and dilapidated. Constance was fascinated by the skeletal remains of
plantations outside of town, many of them dating to colonial times.
She researched their history at the old Charleston library, discovering
that one of their owners had been a signer of the Declaration of Independence. She also unearthed a lost town, the only vestige of which
was an abandoned church still standing in the middle of the thick
woods that had grown up around it.[3]

LIVING AMONG THE GRAVES

In June 1875, Hannah and Constance left for Cleveland Springs, North
Carolina, a secluded resort two miles from the nearest town. It had
sulfur springs and baths for Hannah and mountains for Constance.
But three weeks of rainy weather brought on Hannah's rheumatism

and drove them on to Virginia. They stopped at Monticello and Charlottesville, then found a wayside cottage in Goshen, about sixty miles west of Charlottesville, where they stayed through August. Day trips to Lexington, where Constance stood for a long time at the grave of her favorite Confederate general, Stonewall Jackson, and The Greenbriar at White Sulphur Springs, the most fashionable of the southern spring resorts, broke up the monotony of their quiet existence in Goshen. Near the end of their stay, they met Clara and Plum at Harper's Ferry, West Virginia, to see the site of John Brown's raid, then went on to Gettysburg, where friends of Constance's had died in battle. The day they spent walking over the grassy mounds of the battlefield was so bright and peaceful she could hardly imagine the horrors that had occurred there. The Harpers offered her a handsome sum to write up her impressions, but she refused. A comment from Clara suggests why: "We could not sleep for nights afterwards, although so long after the Civil War."[4]

The experience of visiting battlegrounds touched Constance deeply. "I always go to see the soldiers' graves," she told Hayne. "I cannot bear to think that they are so soon forgotten; as they are, at the North." She still could not "hear the old war tunes, or pass those soldiers' cemeteries at the South, or see an old flag, without choking up and turning away." The war may have quickly receded from collective memory in the North, but Constance declared she would always be one of the "people who remember." Living in and writing about the South made it difficult to forget. Waking up in the morning, she sometimes thought she still could hear the call of the newspaper boy announcing news of the latest battle.[5]

After their trip to Gettysburg, Hannah returned to Cleveland with Clara, while Constance, against her family's wishes, stayed behind in Goshen. She had much work to do and was convinced that Goshen was the perfect place, with its mountain air and freedom from interruptions, for writing and perhaps even starting her novel. She had her own little cottage away from the hotel. However, life there proved too tranquil. She endured five weeks of cold, rainy weather, with only the mail to break up the dismal evenings. Just as she had in New York, she found the solitary writer's life dispiriting.[6]

On the first of October she met her mother in Baltimore, from which they sailed to Norfolk, Virginia. There they spent one chilly week and then returned to South Carolina, where they stayed at Society Hill and in Charleston until December. Then it was back to St. Augustine, where the abundance of grandees from New York increasingly irritated Constance. She admitted to Stedman that she was "not in very good spirits this winter." It was at this time that she was wrestling with the question of whether to try to publish her long narrative poem *Two Women* and was unsuccessfully trying to begin her novel. In January she gave Hayne the advice she needed: "I beg you to fight against 'Depression,' that evil spirit that haunts all creative minds. Do not let him conquer you. Think of yourself highly, <u>persist</u> in thinking of yourself, as well as you can; be just as 'conceited' as possible. It will buoy you up."[7]

Yet the depression from which Woolson suffered was more deep-seated than a fear of failure might produce or confidence conquer. It was exacerbated by difficult circumstances, but she knew it was much more than situational, admitting, "I think it is constitutional, and I know it is inherited." Today we would likely say that she suffered from clinical depression, an illness typically characterized by recurring periods of very low mood, poor self-esteem, disruption of sleep and appetite, a loss of interest in everyday activities, lack of pleasure, hopelessness, and a longing for death or suicidal thoughts. At the time, when the study of psychology was still in its infancy, depression in women was typically understood as "neurasthenia," a largely female malady that left one feeling "incapable of meeting life," as described by Alice James, sister to Henry James and one of the most famous neurasthenics of the century. While society may have put her in that category, Constance never saw herself as one of that female band of sufferers. Instead, she understood her condition as inherited from her male relatives. To Stedman she explained, "I am overweighted with a sort of depression that comes unexpectedly, and makes everything black. My grandfather gave up to it and was a dreary useless man; my father battled against it all his life, and again and again warned me about it; but I was young then, and only half believed in it. Now, he is gone, and it has come to me. I try to conquer it and sometimes I succeed, sometimes—I do'nt [*sic*]." As a masculine malady, depression was also a way to connect with male peers such as Stedman and Hayne, who spoke of similar afflictions. Later in life, she would connect on like grounds with other men who struggled as she did.[8]

Woolson's depression did not incapacitate her for life. As she explained once to Arabella, "Do'nt fancy I am sad all the time. Oh no. I am much too busy and too full of plans of all kinds. But at times, in spite of all I can do, this deadly enemy of mine creeps in, and once in, he is master." Sometimes her enemy would mysteriously leave on his own. She would once refer to a "ray of light which sometimes comes, so unexpectedly, to cheer one at the darkest hour of gloom," which she thought of as a gift from God. Yet most of the time she viewed herself as a kind of warrior battling with dark spirits, following her father's example. Many years later she would write that "simple courage seems to me to sum up all the virtues of life.—There was an old phrase which my father (a New Englander) sometimes used,—namely 'Keep a stiff upper lip.'"[9] In an era that lacked antidepressants or psychotherapy, "simple courage" was her only real defense against the "evil spirit" that haunted her throughout life.

The condition of the devastated South and its ubiquitous graves and battlefields contributed to the depression she suffered throughout 1875 and 1876. But rather than be overcome by it, she was able to use the empathy she felt toward the ruined region to produce some of her most powerful work. The stories she wrote during this period encapsulate the postwar South like no other stories of the period. Successfully transcending a northerner's perspective, she was able to write about southerners, as a reviewer put it, "[w]ithout blind partisanship." Henry James would write many years later that she had spoken for the voiceless South as "one who evidently did not glance and pass, but lingered and analyzed."[10]

The first of Woolson's southern Reconstruction stories to appear was "Old Gardiston," in the April 1876 issue of *Harper's*. Set in one of the old mansions outside of Charleston, it portrays a proud young woman who defends her country's honor by heaping bitterness upon the occupying soldiers trying to court her. In the end, the impoverished Gardis reluctantly agrees to sell her ancestral home but out of pride still resists the advances of a northern suitor. When the house burns down and she is left with nothing, she finally admits her love for him and surrenders to his embrace. Some critics thought Gardis overdrawn, particularly in her dramatic tendencies, but Woolson insisted her portrait was true to life. She was pleased when the *New York Times* felt she had conveyed "a very touching sympathy for her southern sisters." "Old Gardiston" had clearly hit a nerve, however. One of the Harper brothers happened to be in St. Augustine when it came out and advised her to write no more about the effects of the war and following occupation in the South.[11]

When she received this warning she had just published in *Appletons'* two stories that look back on the war: "Crowder's Cove," about a border-state family's divided loyalties, and "In the Cotton Country," a moving and melancholy story about a once-patrician woman who has lost everything. Another Reconstruction story was already slated for publication in the *Atlantic*. Howells had accepted "Rodman the Keeper" in June of 1875 but had been holding on to it for close to a year.[12] Mr. Harper's warning and the heightened tensions over Reconstruction in the lead-up to the 1876 presidential election suggest why.

Hostility toward the northern occupation was high throughout the South but particularly in still-occupied areas such as South Carolina. From Cooperstown, where she and her mother spent the summer of 1876, Woolson wrote to Stedman, "[W]e are holding on here as long as possible on account of the yellow fever, and the election fever, at the South, the latter disorder I consider the most dangerous; we cannot spend October and November of this year in the interior of South Carolina, as we did last. Should not dare to be there now." She pointed to "[t]he insolence of the blacks and the bitterness of the whites," giving the impression of a volcano about to erupt. That fall riots broke out in Charleston.[13] After the contested presidential election, resulting in the Compromise of 1877 that enacted the withdrawal from the South of the remaining federal troops, the Woolson women avoided South Carolina altogether.

Howells finally published "Rodman the Keeper" in March 1877, placing it as the lead piece in the *Atlantic Monthly*. The story, set in a nameless southern cemetery of northern soldiers, had its germ in Woolson's visit to the Union cemetery in Salisbury, North Carolina, when she was staying in nearby Asheville in 1874. At the time she had written home to the *Cleveland Herald* describing the ex-soldier who kept watch over the graves, the long lines of trenches into which the prisoners had been thrown without record, and the crowds of black people who visited on Decoration Day while their white neighbors stayed away—all elements that reappear in "Rodman." In her letter, she expressed sympathy with both the captives and the Confederates who starved along with their prisoners. In the story, John Rodman, a Union officer who is the keeper of such a cemetery, feels no such sympathy. He hasn't put the war behind him and walks the rows of gravestones, talking to the dead. Yet when a Confederate veteran in the area falls ill, he nurses him, in spite of his partisanship, teaches his former slave to read, and forms an attachment to his cousin, Bettina, who cannot give up her hatred toward those who killed most of her family and ruined her home. The story focuses on Rodman's transformation from keeper of the dead to caretaker of the living, a transformation the whole North is implicitly asked to make, in spite of the South's continued resistance. But Woolson does not end the story with an enforced reconciliation—just simple understanding and respect. Rodman tells Bettina, as she leaves to find work as a teacher, "[D]o not think, dear, that I have not seen—have not understood."[14]

"Rodman the Keeper" was reprinted or noticed in many of the leading papers, and gratifying letters of praise came pouring in. It was recognized in its time as "one of the few artistically perfect tales that the history of the civil war has inspired," in the words of the well-regarded *Christian Union*. If, as Walt Whitman declared, "the real war will never get in the books," Woolson succeeded in capturing the aftermath of the war like no other writer of her generation. The story's popularity "called out a letter from a well known firm," Constance wrote to her nephew, Sam, "asking whether it would not be possible for me to send all I wrote to their house?" They told her she could name her price, but she declined the offer, reluctant to tie herself to the fortunes of one firm. Meanwhile both Osgood and Hurd & Houghton offered to publish another collection of stories, this time focused on the South, but Woolson wanted her next book to be a novel.[15]

Only one more story, "King David," published in April 1878, would address Reconstruction politics with its portrayal of a school for freedmen. It can be read, in fact, as a parable of the failure of the white North to truly care about the plight of freed slaves. The story may have been written earlier, since Woolson had declared as early as April 1876, after the publication of "Old Gardiston," that she was done writing about the South. To Hayne, she wrote, "Do'nt you think that for a red hot abolitionist, Republican and hard-money advocate, I have behaved well down here in Dixie? . . . I have tried to 'put myself in their place,' and at least be fair. Finis! The page is turned. I shall write no more about the South."[16] Although she set more stories there, Woolson was, like the rest of the country, finally ready to look forward.

"SO MUCH FOR MYSELF"

The summer in Cooperstown in 1876 relieved temporarily Constance's feeling of being exiled in the South, reminding her that she could one day, if she wished, have a home there among her mother's family. In addition to her Cooper relatives, Jane Carter and her children welcomed her, as did Arabella, who was visiting them. The two friends walked arm in arm on the hills surrounding placid Lake Otsego, renewing their old intimacy. Taking daily exercise rowing or searching for ferns also seemed to begin to break up Constance's melancholy. By September she was writing to Hayne that she found his interest in Hinduism and longing for unconsciousness troubling, for this world was "a very beautiful and generally speaking a very good sort of world." She couldn't see the dark side of it or want to escape it.[17]

As the leaves began to turn and the Woolsons contemplated their next move, Constance hoped to go to Europe but had to give up her plan again. "So much for myself," she told Stedman.[18] Hannah and Clara wanted to return to St. Augustine, but Constance didn't think she could endure another season among the loquacious society women increasingly abundant there. She made no effort at polite small talk and thus inevitably felt out of place among them, managing to isolate herself by her bluntness. But Hannah and Clara, who thrived in such an atmosphere, outvoted her.

When they arrived in St. Augustine, they found lodgings across the road from the waterfront. Constance's room was on the top floor, from which she could see the fort Castillo de San Marcos, the seawall, Anastasia Island, and, beyond that, the ocean. At night she watched the lighthouse beacon flash through the darkness. All was well until the grandees began to arrive, with their "tiresome atmosphere of gold dust and ancestors." The Astors and Rhinelanders (Edith Wharton's family, although not Wharton herself) were among the exclusive visitors that year. Constance felt like an impostor sailing out on the bay with men who boasted six-figure incomes and always traveled with valets and portable baths. She resented not only their affluence but also the way they scorned Dickens or any author who wrote of the lower classes. "They have only two adjectives, 'nice,' and 'beastly,'" she scoffed. She couldn't help quarreling with them.[19] Her time among the ultrawealthy was not wasted, however; she stored up her observations for use in a novel, if she could ever find the courage and the peace in which to write it.

To make matters worse, upsetting letters from Charlie, then in Chicago, began to arrive. He had completely broken down, physically and mentally, complaining of an intolerable "pain in his head." At the first of the year, he sent frightening telegrams that may have expressed suicidal thoughts. Constance and Clara did everything they could to shield Hannah from the bad news. "Her whole happiness," Constance explained, "even her life I might almost say, depends, and always has depended upon how Charl[ie] is, and how he feels." Hannah was perennially disappointed in him—he rarely wrote to her and couldn't seem to settle down—but he was her only son and apparently her dearest child.[20]

For over two months, Connie and Clara wrote letters back and forth with Charlie, trying to do what they could at such a distance. By the end of February, he had seen Dr. Weber, who was probably their family physician, in Cleveland and appeared to be improving. Constance was sure that his incessant smoking and lack of care for himself had caused the collapse. She firmly believed in her family's constitutional weakness, exposed by the early deaths of Emma and Georgiana.[21] She and Charlie shared another, more virulent, weakness, however, revealed by the psychological aspect of his illness. In Charlie's telegrams and letters, Constance thought she glimpsed her own darkness, although frighteningly amplified. The culprit, Constance believed, was morphine. When Dr. Weber took Charlie off of the drug, which he may have taken for migraines, he began to stabilize.

Charlie likely suffered from manic depression, as suggested by his migraines and erratic moves from one location to another. He frequently tried new ventures when he was up, then abandoned them when he was down, emotionally and economically. When his family reached out to him, he accepted their money but not their closeness. Charlie had never been happy with them, Constance confessed to Sam, so they could not live with him and care for him. She took some of the blame on herself, admitting that her bad temper made her at times impatient with him.[22] Yet Charlie was also fiercely independent and couldn't stand being looked after by his mother and sisters.

As the heat approached in the spring, the Woolson women moved to Yonkers, a bustling town about fifteen miles north of New York City, where Clara had rented a furnished house. They were glad once again to have a semblance of home after so much wandering. Constance's mood had finally improved, she told Stedman: "I am better; in better spirits. I told you I should come out of the shadows in time." The success of "Rodman" the previous spring and Osgood's interest in the novel she wanted to write surely helped. But she had lost more than a year on her novel, "owing to the depressed state of my mind."[23]

Yonkers was certainly no place for her to begin writing it. Despite the presence of family, she complained that she felt "more isolated than ever." She broke up her loneliness with visits to nearby friends she had made in St. Augustine. Eleanor Washington—"the best friend I have ever had," Constance once wrote—lived in Navesink, New Jersey.[24] Her two young sons called Constance "aunt," and her husband and sons would in later years, after Eleanor's death, continue to treat her like family. Another friend, Emily Vernon Clark, whose sister had a home in Yonkers, would become a valued traveling companion in the years ahead. But Constance longed for a visit from Stedman. She was starved for literary companionship.

Woolson was persistent in her pleas for a visit from him that summer. Finally, in September, Stedman came. He brought her a shell necklace and made up for his long absence with his witty conversation. They talked of the novel and whether she should give the southern stories to Osgood, whom she felt had not sufficiently promoted *Castle Nowhere*.[25] After dinner and much conversation, Stedman stayed the night and took the train back to the city in the morning.

As the cold weather returned, Constance wanted to stay in the North, but Hannah's health and comfort took precedence. In mid-December they arrived, with eight trunks full of books, herbariums, and wine, at Hibernia, a plantation near Green Cove Springs, Florida, on the St. John's River about forty miles northwest of St. Augustine. They took rooms in a cottage next to the plantation home-cum-boardinghouse, where they ate their meals. The other residents were sportsmen and families. "Our life will be very different from that at St. Augustine," Hannah wrote to Sam, "but Constance wished an uninterrupted winter of work."[26] At last, Connie had gotten her way. Hibernia was the perfect place to write her novel.

LOOKING INTO CHAOS

Over the next five months, Constance rose early and wrote until the afternoon, when she took her mother for their daily row. Hannah was very good to her during these months, Constance later reflected. She never told her to stop working or urged her to socialize. She kept all of the small details from worrying her daughter, who, when focused on her writing, could get easily agitated. Once, when planning a new story, Constance had told Arabella, "Now I must look into chaos."[27] Trying to delve all alone into the chaos of creativity, as at Goshen, had been a failure. But at Hibernia, with her mother at her side, she found the balance of human connection and peace that she needed to make the words flow.

She also found the courage to push ahead in spite of her fears about her novel's success. "I generally throw half across the room all the new novels of the day," she had told Hayne. "Now these novels the Public like! Moral: will they not be likely to throw mine entirely across the room? I fear so." The criticism she had received for her story "Castle Nowhere" had made her think twice about writing a novel. "For I wo'nt write [the novel] at all unless I write it as I please," she insisted to Stedman. How, she wondered, could she please herself and the general audience who preferred "'pretty and pleasant' stories—not too long"? She imagined, in particular, the women who seemed incapable of feeling deeply and therefore could not "in the least appreciate the tragedy of deep feelings in others." Having been so uncomprehended in life, Woolson wondered how she could expect her novel to be understood. "One would like to plough up such persons and *make* them suffer!" she wrote in her notebooks. "'Pretty and pleasant stories,' indeed!"[28]

Woolson was determined to write much more than a pretty, pleasant story. The summer before she began to write, she had outlined some of her ideas about what made a great novel in reviews for the *Atlantic Monthly*'s "Contributors' Club," a new section of the magazine for which Howells asked her to write. All of the pieces were anonymous, so she felt free to develop her critical principles inconspicuously. In her assessment of Frances Hodgson Burnett's *That Lass O' Lowrie's*, she was particularly drawn to the heroine, Joan, a "grandly-shaped, majestic creature, with her deep inarticulate love." Such a memorable portrait was hard to find in recent literature, she contended. "How few modern novels add distinct personages to the galleries of our memory." Grandcourt from *Daniel Deronda* qualified. Joan likewise "kep[t] standing at the door in a haunting kind of way, and looking in." Woolson also declared that a novel should affect its readers, not merely amuse them. The French writer Victor Cherbuliez's novel *Samuel Brohl et Cie* was "not great," she insisted, because "it does not lift you off your feet, nor send hot chills down your spine, nor call up a tear." In another review, she assessed the novel of analysis "so much in vogue to-day," in which characters "don't *do* anything . . . but . . . *think* a [great] deal." She admitted to being a bit of a traditionalist, preferring a story full of vivid action and dialogue.[29] Nonetheless, the new form would exert considerable influence on her throughout her career. For her first novel, however, she wanted above all a vibrant, memorable heroine to whom something life-altering happened. That would make her readers care, always her primary goal as a writer.

Anne was an ambitious first novel. It is an engrossing book, carrying readers along on a sea of absorbing observations and then sweeping them up in scenes of intense emotion. Its great originality is to be found in what many saw as Woolson's thoroughly American heroine and her loving tribute to Mackinac Island in the opening chapters, which many readers (including Henry James) felt was the novel's strongest section. If she had stopped there, she would have written a regional masterpiece to rival Sarah Orne Jewett's *The Country of the Pointed Firs*. But she was determined not to be one of those writers who could excel on only a small canvas, like Bret Harte or Jewett, whom James would one day damn with faint praise for her "beautiful little quantum of achievement." Instead, Woolson wrote a sprawling Victorian novel, ripe for magazine serialization, that plucked the heroine out of her secluded island home and exposed her to a series of challenges on the road to adulthood, carrying her meanwhile across a good part of the northern United States and introducing her to a considerable cast of well-drawn characters. Ultimately, *Anne* tries to do too much, as many first novels do. Woolson wanted to show what she was capable of in both rural and urban settings, in realism and idealism, in contemplative analysis and suspenseful action. The resulting novel—which progresses from a coming-of-age story to a social novel to a whodunit—was serialized for an unusually long eighteen months in *Harper's* magazine and ended up as a 540-page book.[30]

Despite the vast territory it covered, *Anne* was also a deeply personal novel. Woolson confessed she wrote *Anne* "with all my heart." Like many first novels, it is highly autobiographical. Anne, whose name recalls Woolson's earlier pseudonym Anne March, has strong arms that can row for over an hour and does not conform to "[t]he usual ideal of pretty, slender, unformed maidenhood." Anne grows up on Mackinac Island—the favorite haunt of Constance's youth—as naturally as if she were a wild deer. During the bitter winter, rather than stay inside near the hearth, she runs and sleds with the boys. When she does come in, she brings nature with her, decorating the island church with greenery as Constance had done at Grace Church in Cleveland.[31] Woolson also gave Anne a strong bond with her father as well as the responsibility of having to support other family members when he dies.

At the outset, Anne is innocent and unaware. She has "never analyzed herself" or "lived for herself or in herself." After being thrust into the world to find a way to make a living, she wanders the country from New York to Cleveland to West Virginia, adapting to new circumstances yet remaining the simple island girl. In New York, a wealthy aunt has funded Anne's education at a school modeled on Madame Chegaray's, where she has many of Constance's experiences and feels just as out of place. Woolson also invested Anne with her own feelings of being misunderstood. Her closest friend claims she could not love because her "nature was too calm, too measured." Yet Anne loves deeply and silently, as Constance had. When the man she loves marries another, she is thrust into an existential crisis that is temporarily solved by committing herself to a nun-like existence "of self-abnegation and labor." She teaches school in Cleveland, where her female students idolize her, but she feels empty. When the Civil War erupts, she throws herself into work for the Soldiers' Aid Society and nurses the wounded. Eventually, however, she must confront "the problem of [her] own existence."[32]

Knowing that the vast majority of her audience only read for the love story, as Woolson wrote half-contemptuously in her notebooks, she could not let her heroine find contentment in independence, as she had. So she gave Anne a grand romance, complete with a Byronic lover named Heathcote, in honor of Emily Brontë's Heathcliff. He is also very much like Rochester in *Jane Eyre*, in that he is an arrogant man of wealth and status who has lived a dissipated life. As in Woolson's favorite novels, *The Mill on the Floss* and *Jane Eyre*, Anne is tempted by her lover to fulfill her own selfish desires without regard to duty. Although married to Anne's friend Helen, after having been engaged to her from a young age, Heathcote urges Anne, "Come, let everything go to the winds, as I do, and say you love me; for I know you do." But Anne does not make the same mistake as Maggie Tulliver. Instead, like Jane Eyre, she clings heroically to her sense of what is right and finds her self-respect in silent suffering. Although Woolson would become known for valorizing her heroines' self-abnegation, she never romanticized it. Anne learns that "suffering is just as hard to bear whether one is noble or ignoble, good or bad," that "it is the long monotony of dangerless days that tries the spirit hardest."[33]

From here the novel takes a strange, sudden turn into the territory of a murder mystery. When Helen is found dead and Heathcote is suspected of having killed his wife, Anne turns detective to exonerate him. To many readers the final section of the novel is a jarring development (not unlike that created by the final third of *The Adventures of Huckleberry Finn*, which turns into a farce). However, Woolson's plot device allowed her to grant Anne greater agency and to explore a theme that had surfaced in her own writing career: the publicity of women's private selves. Vividly evoked in a climactic courtroom scene, Anne's confession of her love for Heathcote is read aloud before a crowd of rapacious reporters and onlookers. All eyes are on Anne, surveying her appearance and judging her. This was to Woolson the climax of the book, the moment at which Anne must reveal her deepest, truest self to the world. The scene is a graphic rendering of Woolson's own self-revelation, which she performed over and over again in her writing. It suggests how exposed she felt, putting herself before the public in the form of a semiautobiographical heroine whose emotional life in many ways mirrored her own.

In spite of readers' insistence on a love story, Woolson had no intention of giving her lovers a fairy-tale ending. But her first reader, Hannah, wanted one.[34] Woolson made it quick, ushering Anne to the altar in the final three pages, after Heathcote's name has been cleared by Anne's discovery of Helen's real murderer. By then, Heathcote, like Rochester at the end of *Jane Eyre*, is a weakened and humbled man, having been wounded in the war and freed from jail by Anne's detective work. Although he had earlier often referred to her as a child, he now must recognize her as the capable woman she has become. The real happy ending for Woolson, however, was returning Anne to Mackinac Island. She gave her heroine the home she herself would always yearn for.

The novel finally completed, Woolson wrote to Stedman in May 1878 that she was "'finished' too!" She was exhausted, having worked for nine hours a day for at least a month. She had no idea whether her novel was good, but she had made an honest try of it. Although Osgood was eager to get his hands on it, Woolson's confidence in him had crumbled. She went with the house that had launched her career, Harper & Brothers. Her affection for them would wane, however. Seven months later, in January 1879, she wrote to Stedman, "Do you wonder what has become of my novel? I <u>think</u> you will see it in print during the year. I say no more; although <u>I would like to</u>. You can have no idea how fond I am now of Mr Osgood. I fairly dream of him at night."[35] She would continue to dream for two long years, her manuscript gathering dust, while Harper & Brothers published other novels ahead of hers and she waited to see if she could make her mark as a novelist.

HANNAH'S LAST YEAR

Once done with the first draft, Constance did not have long to enjoy the accomplishment of completing her first serious novel. The manuscript had to be revised and copied, and the heat of a Florida summer was on its way. Hannah wanted to be near Charlie in Chicago but realized that Constance needed fresh air, so they spent the summer in the seaside resort of Narragansett Pier, Rhode Island, where they were joined by the Benedicts, Clara and Plum, in a farmhouse on a hill behind the town. Constance worked hard all day but allowed herself a daily swim.

Soon it was time to chase the sun south again, but Constance and Hannah were tiring of the race. Instead they returned to Yonkers with Clara and Plum. Charlie soon joined them. He was ill, presumably with headaches and depression. Charlie stayed until the first of December, fulfilling Hannah's dream of having all of her living children once more under the same roof. After he left and the Benedicts went back to Cleveland for Christmas, Constance and her mother still did not pack their trunks. Hannah could not see the necessity. She felt "like a child who lives in the present and neither plans for nor cares for the future." The days were bright and very cold, but with the base burner running all day and night, her rheumatism and worrisome cough were kept at bay. When a severe cold snap hit, Constance fell ill, developing a high fever. Hannah had to take care of her delirious daughter on her own. Somehow they muddled through the worst of it, and in mid-January, although Constance could barely stand, they finally sailed south.[36]

An invalid and a convalescent, they were both in need of a cure this time. They returned to the area of Hibernia and Green Cove Springs, famed for its hot sulfur waters. Unfortunately, Hannah found no miracle to help her regain her strength. Her health deteriorated rapidly. Word was sent to Clara, who arrived at their mother's bedside in time to see Hannah take her last, labored breath on February 13, 1879.[37]

Alone with their dead mother and unsure where to turn, Constance and Clara telegraphed the Mathers in Cleveland. "Bring *Mother* here to us" was the reply from their brother-in-law Samuel. Clara later wrote that she and her sister "lived on [that telegram] during that dreadful journey north." The fact that he had simply called her "Mother" instead of "your mother" meant everything to the grieving daughters.[38] When they arrived in Cleveland, Constance's first return in almost seven years, they brought Hannah's body to the Mathers' house and leaned on them through the funeral and for many weeks afterward. The Mathers—Samuel, his two children with Georgiana (Sam and Kate), and Samuel's second wife, Lizzie, who had been a dear friend to Hannah—were now the only family Constance had left besides Charlie, Clara, and Clare.

Although she had often resented the burden of being Hannah's primary caretaker, Constance's reaction to her mother's death was not relief. She had also felt grounded by her responsibility to her; now she felt unmoored. She had lost the one person in the world who both loved and needed her. When her father had died, she hadn't been able to grieve for long because she had new responsibilities. With her mother gone too, the "daughter's country" she had inhabited vanished. At thirty-nine, she was both exile and orphan.

Hannah's death plunged Constance into a deep depression from which Clara despaired of ever retrieving her. Constance would later describe it as a full physical and emotional collapse. Clara whisked her grieving sister away for a change of scenery to Washington, D.C., where Constance wandered almost daily among the white headstones in Arlington Cemetery, as if she herself were no longer among the living. One day she wrote to Stedman, "I am so very desolate without my Mother that I cannot speak of it. The whole world is changed to me. The one person who loved me dearly has gone. Nothing,—nobody,—can ever fill her empty place. <u>She</u> was 'glad['] to go. But <u>I</u> miss her,—miss her. . . . I have got to learn how to live, over again."[39]

In an effort to emerge from the darkness of grief, Constance reached for her lifeline—her pen. One of the first stories she wrote was "Mrs. Edward Pinckney," about a destitute mother trying to raise her children in the absence of a vagrant, alcoholic husband. The story, set in Washington, D.C., near Arlington Cemetery, was a tribute to Hannah's lost hopes for Charlie. In the story, the narrator—a genteel woman who looks out for the family—blames the drunken husband for the wife's woes and is astonished at Mrs. Pinckney's continued devotion to him. The wife explains, "I have loved him deeply, dearly, all my life; and he has been—what you have seen." When he dies, the narrator understands the relief she must feel: "[N]ow she need never be obliged to see his weaknesses and faults, never be forced to witness his failures, but could think of him peacefully as he once was, as he would be again in some future life."⁴⁰ Such was the peace Constance imagined Hannah had attained. Death had delivered her from the sorrow of seeing Charlie fail further in life, and Constance was grateful.

After Washington, Clara and Constance traveled to Cooperstown for the summer, to mourn Hannah's loss among those who had known her longest. Constance's grief only intensified while she was there. She was tormented by recurring thoughts that her hard work on *Anne* had caused her collapse in Yonkers and taxed Hannah's frail health as she nursed her. Jane Carter comforted Constance with the assurance that her care had "prolonged Mother's life for years."⁴¹ That consolation was everything to her during those early months of mourning. But her mother's hometown was a constant reminder of her presence. Like Hannah thirty-nine years earlier, after the deaths of her three young daughters, Constance needed to leave the place of old associations where she could see Hannah at every turn—sitting by the window, playing cards in front of the fire, or laughing at her own memories as Constance rowed her in a boat on Otsego Lake.

Clara watched helplessly as her sister's mental and physical health deteriorated. Just as their father had picked up Hannah after the girls' deaths in 1840 and carried her away from Claremont, so too did Clara need to carry Constance away from Cooperstown and all of the places their mother had lived. The most logical destination was Europe, so Clara booked them passage on a steamer, and Constance finally began to see the void in front of her fill with images of the faraway places she had long dreamed of visiting.

PART THREE

A European Experiment

1879–1886

"[Florence has] taken me pretty well off my feet! Perhaps I ought to add Henry James. He has been perfectly charming to me for the last three weeks."

—CONSTANCE FENIMORE WOOLSON

"I am not strong enough to take much part in Society, or go out much, and do writing-work at the same time. The best of me goes into my writing."

—CONSTANCE FENIMORE WOOLSON

7

The Old World at Last

As the train lurched through the frozen French countryside, a porter came into the train compartment and took from beneath Constance's feet the tin box full of water that was more valuable to her than precious jewels. He would soon return with it full of hot water, but in the meantime she, Clara, and Clare, now twelve, shivered and complained bitterly. They could see nothing out of the frosted windows.

The travelers spent the night in Lyon, where the piles of snow reached their heads, and in the morning boarded another frigid train to Marseille. During the day, the windows began to clear, and the white countryside gradually gave way to fields and vineyards, with châteaux and castles dotting the landscape. Constance began to revive. The next day, she gradually unpeeled the layers of cloaks and wraps that had failed to keep her warm. The tin box was taken away for good. Finally they reached the Riviera and the bluest sea Constance had ever seen.[1]

STARTING OFF

Three weeks earlier, on November 30, 1879, they had stepped off the steamship *Gallia* in Liverpool, England. Constance had no plans to return to the United States. She had always expected that when she finally made it to Europe she would stay indefinitely.[2] The weather may have made her question the longevity of her enthusiasm, however.

Their arrival in Europe had occurred during the worst winter of the century. From Liverpool to London, houses and trees had been coated in ice. They dared spend only ten days in gloomy London, where Constance, despite her fear of the cold, insisted on visiting all of the major tourist sites, from the Houses of Parliament and the Tower of London to Madame Tussaud's, which Clare had longed to see. She found walking the aisles of Westminster Abbey to be one of the greatest pleasures of her life, and pored over the pictures in the National Gallery, instructed by her Baedeker guidebook and catalogs. She was determined to learn to appreciate painting as well as she had music, but she had a long way to go, she realized. Her hearing had become so poor that others referred to her as "deaf," but she had brought with her a new device called an Audiphone that seemed to be working quite well. It resembled a curved fan and was held up to the teeth, creating vibrations that allowed her to hear a delightful Punch and Judy show that she and Clare watched in the street below their windows.[3]

The three had hoped to see Paris, but after a bitterly cold channel crossing they found it virtually shut down and buried under great piles of ice and snow. When they reached the Riviera, they stopped finally at Menton, near the Italian border. The small resort town, a balmy, sunshiny oasis protected from the northerly winds by the Maritime Alps, was a popular wintering place for European aristocrats and invalids. It was, in Constance's eyes, "the 'St. Augustine' of France." She felt a little homesick for Florida, but the foreignness and antiquity of the region delighted her. Her senses feasted on the fragrance of roses, heliotropes, and olive and lemon trees. She relished the castle ruins, Roman aqueducts, picturesque villages that clung to the mountainsides, and the sight of peasant girls in red handkerchiefs.[4] Above all, the bright sun and unmatched blueness of the sea began to rouse her from her long depression.

Somewhere in the middle of the Atlantic Ocean Constance had let the cloak of responsibility fall from her shoulders. While her mother was alive, she had hidden her unconventional identity as an author behind the persona of a devoted daughter. Now she was a writer above all else. She had come to Europe not only to see the sights but also to write.

Her motivation was creative as well as monetary. Clara had been paying a greater share of their expenses so far, but Constance did not intend to rely on her sister's generosity indefinitely. She needed to start earning her own money again if she was going to stay in Europe. Her plan was to settle down for a few months in each place; constant travel and hotels were too expensive, while pensions, or boarding-houses where one stayed on a longer basis, were cheaper. She was earning only about $600 a year at the time so had to economize as much as possible.[5]

In Menton she set to work, writing an essay on the region for *Harper's*, a story for *Lippincott's*, and the beginning of a "novelette"— she was not ready to tackle another long project. While *Anne* had come out of her own struggles, this short novel would be devoted to her mother's memory and the complications of older women's lives after marriage, childbearing, and widowhood. Inspired by the Alps, she looked back to the summer of 1874 in Asheville and set her novel high up in the Carolina peaks. But she would not complete *For the Major* for two years. The memories were still too fresh.

Constance worked every day until one in the afternoon, sitting at a desk that looked out on the Mediterranean. Four and a half hours wasn't nearly enough, she wrote to her nephew, Sam, but "Clara looks so tragic if I attempt anything more." Clara had adopted a motherly role with her sister, whose health and mental state remained fragile one year after their mother's death. Thoughts of her mother invariably brought on tears. Recalling Hannah's concerns for Charlie, Constance wrote to him dutifully, but she did not hear anything in return. He had begun his life over again, this time in California. Finally, after having written him six letters, she received a response. Depressed and suffering from headaches again, he had checked himself into a hospital. Constance could not sleep for thinking of his pain and their mother's old worries, which now seem to have passed to her.[6]

Clara insisted on pulling Connie away from her writing table. They joined excursions to nearby castles and ruins, riding up into the mountains on donkeys that, to Constance's mind, were "the most ridiculous animals in the world; and the man who rides him next." They picnicked in town plazas and lunched in country inns, enjoying the local wine, which was stronger than they thought and made them a rather merry group.[7]

In spite of the scenery and libations, Constance's health and mood seemed to improve only marginally during their four-month stay on the Riviera. Although the sun shone brightly, Menton was not as

A view of Menton, France, where Constance's spirits began to revive.
(From "At Mentone," in *Mentone, Cairo, and Corfu*)

warm as Florida. It remained cold in the shade, and the rooms were not heated. While she worked at her desk, the temperature inside could be fifty-four degrees. It might as well be snowing outside, she complained. She still felt rather weak and "obliged to exercise the greatest care, lest I break down again." She also had a persistent cough and felt rather lonely, she admitted, despite the presence of her sister and niece. Clara worried over her and had become, in their mother's absence, her main emotional outlet, but they were temperamentally quite different—Clara extroverted and Connie introverted. She felt a greater kinship with Clare, who reminded her of herself at that age. She had the same reserve and acute sensitivity. "She and I are great 'cronies,'" she would later explain. "[We] talk long hours together with the greatest mental satisfaction. We are thoroughly 'simpatica.'"[8]

"'MISS GRIEF'"

Teetering on the edge of mental and physical well-being, Woolson wrote that winter her most powerful and provocative story, "'Miss Grief,'" which would be published in *Lippincott's* in May 1880. Set in a vaguely described Rome, which she would not visit for over a year, the story exists in a kind of limbo—somewhere between America and Europe and between her life as a daughter and her independent existence as a writer. Into the main character, Aaronna Moncrief, whom the unnamed male narrator insists on calling "Miss Grief," Woolson channeled her grief over her mother's loss and her anxieties about fully embracing the identity of an ambitious author.

Aaronna Moncrief is a writer struggling to gain the attention of the male literary elite. She approaches the narrator, who is a successful male writer, for his assessment of her work, hoping that he will ultimately help her to publish it. Arriving on his doorstep dressed all in black, as if she is in mourning, she appears to be on the verge of death herself. At first, the narrator calls her "eccentric and unconventional" and views her as having "sacrificed her womanly claims by her persistent attacks upon my door." He thinks she wants to sell him something, but when he learns that she is a writer, he exclaims, "An authoress! This is worse than old lace." She also appears to him "shabby, unattractive, and more than middle-aged" and thus undeserving of (or simply uninterested in) men's attention. Woolson thus emphasized that Aaronna approached the male writer as a peer and not as a potential romantic object. Only after having discovered Aaronna's "divine spark of genius" does he begin to respect her.[9]

Later, when she tells the narrator she would have killed herself had he failed to acknowledge the value of her writings, he is shocked by her sensationalism. But she explains, "I should have destroyed only this poor tenement of clay."[10] It was easy for Woolson, who believed that the next world was a peaceful place, to understand Aaronna's disregard for her earthly existence. She has been living only for her work and the hope of seeing its worth recognized.

Ultimately the narrator is unable to help Aaronna publish her work. It is inherently flawed in vaguely specified ways, and when he tries to improve it for her, he finds it is no longer any good. What had made her writings so strong is precisely what makes them unacceptable to a wider audience, or at least to the male editors who act as the gatekeepers to the literary world. Aaronna, meanwhile, is starving, literally and figuratively. On her deathbed, she requests that the narrator bury her writings with her, except for the drama "Armor," which he has told her, falsely, will be published. After her death he keeps it as a reminder of his own good fortune as an author. Capable of seeing in her what others cannot, he is moved by the pathos of her failure. She, however, dies happy, knowing that he at least has recognized her power as a writer.

No other story by a nineteenth-century American woman so powerfully dramatizes the yearning for literary recognition and the insurmountable obstacles women faced in pursuit of it. (The most comparable work thematically is Elizabeth Barrett Browning's novel in verse, *Aurora Leigh*.) In spite of its bleakness, however, Woolson's story portrays the possibility of a sensitive individual overcoming his prejudice toward an "authoress" and appreciating the merit of her work, even if it does not conform to the standard expectations for polite literature. The surprise of the story isn't so much the woman writer's failure and death—Madame de Staël had long before established that theme in her novel *Corinne*. Nor is it the failure of women, in particular, to see the value in another woman's work. The narrator's fiancée, a conventional woman named Isabel Abercrombie, sees Aaronna's poems as the product of a disturbed mind. Rather, the surprise is the male writer's acknowledgment of her unconventional genius. That others cannot recognize it makes his understanding all the more valuable.

Yet the story remains a powerful indictment of the male literary elite. Although Aaronna never voices resentment for the neglect she has endured, her aunt, who has accompanied her to Europe, vents her spleen most emphatically, charging male authors not merely with neglect but also with theft. "YOU literary men," she shouts at the narrator, "shall not rack and stab her any more on *this* earth. . . . Vampires! you take her ideas and fatten on them, and leave her to starve."[11] The critics seem to suck the life out of Aaronna, flourishing while she wastes away. Aaronna's fate was not Woolson's, but these lines convey some of her own anger. Although she had climbed quite high in the six years since the prizewinning *The Old Stone House*, she still felt as if her efforts had been more arduous than others'.

In her letters to Hayne, who seemed to think of her as the golden writer of the moment, she repeatedly referred to herself as an "outside barbarian" and "Philistine." She belonged to no literary community, she insisted. But she was keenly aware that close-knit literary fraternities existed, particularly in Boston and New York. As she had told Hayne, she had learned that William Dean Howells had favorites he promoted at the *Atlantic*. During the two years he had held on to "Rodman the Keeper"—time when she therefore felt unable to submit additional work to that magazine—he was publishing some of his favorites at a rapid rate. At the top of the list was Henry James, who had two serialized novels and a story published in the *Atlantic* during those same two years. Howells was enamored. "In richness of expression and splendor of literary performance, we may . . . find none greater than [James]," he gushed.[12]

Many have noted superficial similarities between James and the privileged male writer in Woolson's story—both wrote "delightful little studies of society," took Balzac as a model, wrote stories featuring antiquities, have inherited money, and have achieved a certain critical and popular success. She had not met James when she wrote the story but had heard much about him not only from the literary columns of the leading periodicals but also from his friend John Hay, whom she had met in Cleveland in the months after her mother's death.[13]

Hay was a former secretary to Abraham Lincoln and a literary man, a fellow member of the *Atlantic*'s "Contributors' Club." He was well known for his dialect poetry, set in the rural Illinois of his childhood, as well as his essays on Spain, published in the *Atlantic* and collected as *Castilian Days* in 1871. He would soon write a wildly popular novel attacking labor, *The Bread-Winners*, published in 1883, and coauthor the ten-volume biography of Abraham Lincoln, published in 1890, that would establish the president's legacy as we know it today. By the time Woolson sailed for Europe, Hay had become assistant secretary of state, and he would two decades later serve as secretary of state under Presidents McKinley and Theodore Roosevelt.

John Hay—former secretary to Lincoln, statesman, editor, and writer—became a close friend and adviser to Woolson. Photograph circa 1870. (Courtesy of Special Collections, Fine Arts Library, Harvard University)

Hay had surely approached Woolson during her stay in Cleveland after hearing about her from their mutual friend, Stedman. Hay had married the Cleveland heiress Clara Stone, whose younger sister, Flora, was being courted by Constance's nephew, Sam. They would, in fact, soon marry, making Hay and Woolson relatives of sorts by marriage. It seems likely that when they met Hay and Woolson discussed his friend Henry James, about whom she was already curious. Hay had known James since 1875, when he helped him become the Paris correspondent to the *New York Tribune*, where Hay was an editorial writer. He was perhaps James's greatest supporter next to Howells, coming to his defense in the *Atlantic*'s "Contributors' Club" when the expatriate author came under attack for his provocative yet wildly popular story "Daisy Miller."[14] Hay certainly encouraged Woolson to meet James while in Europe, and the ease with which she had gained Hay's friendship must have lessened her fears about how men of letters regarded her. In fact, Hay quickly became an ardent supporter of hers, rivaling Stedman in his praise and advice.

APPROACHING MR. JAMES

When Woolson left for Europe, she had in her trunks a letter of introduction for her and Clara to Henry James from his cousin, Henrietta Pell-Clarke, whom they had met in Cooperstown the previous summer. They had knocked on his door together during their brief stay in London only to find out that James was in Paris. They planned to approach him there but had fled too quickly.[15]

It might seem bold on Woolson's part to seek out the writer who would one day become known as "the Master." However, it was common for European-bound Americans to seek out prominent authors, as James himself had done when he first emigrated. One of his visits was to George Eliot, on whose door he knocked in 1869. In Woolson's case, with a proper letter of introduction and female relatives in tow, she could approach a celebrated writer without raising eyebrows.

Nonetheless, the act was a departure for Constance, who four years earlier had claimed, "[I]f there is anything I dread it is a new acquaintance. I evade, and avoid, and back away from everybody."[16] But Henry James was different. Not only was she willing to make the advance, but she also rather openly alluded to him in "'Miss Grief.'" On its surface, the story suggests she was nervous about how he would perceive her as a literary woman. More than that, though, it hints at the mutual recognition she hoped for.

In "'Miss Grief'" Woolson imagined a stark contrast between the two writers. Aaronna tells the narrator, "You were young—strong—rich—praised—loved—successful: all that I was not. I wanted to look at you—and imagine how it would feel. You had success—but I had the greater power."[17] His work is sophisticated and much sought after, but he has been playing it safe. Aaronna thinks he is capable of much more based on one particular work of his, which she recites. He realizes that it was his favorite and most ambitious writing, which the public had ignored. Aaronna's work, on the other hand, is daring, aimed at something beyond temporary applause, but it lacks the refinement and polish that would make it palatable. Both writers are, in a sense, incomplete. She may possess the greater power, but he has qualities that have ensured his greater success.

The writings of Woolson and James had been discussed in similar terms by reviewers, and although she sharpened the contrast for a greater effect in the story, it seems she had particular reviews of their work in mind when she wrote "'Miss Grief.'" On her side, it was a review she had saved of *Two Women* that appeared in *Appletons'*. It was at once the most favorable and most critical review she ever received. Although it did not mean the death of her career, as the critics' judgment of Aaronna's writing does, it contributed to the end of Woolson's career as a poet and seems to have lingered long in her mind as a definitive judgment of her writing.

The review contained extremely high praise, finding in the verse drama as well as her Great Lakes stories "a strength such as has not informed any woman's writing, that we remember in some years of American magazine literature; and a force and freshness that has belonged to few men in that time." (Aaronna's work is also deemed by the male judges to have "force" and "power," two words that were routinely used to describe Woolson's own writings.) Yet the reviewer determined that the flaws of *Two Women* emanated not from "insufficient culture," a possibility he first considered, but from the artist's impulse to disdain convention and let the "force of feeling . . . cover up the awkward phrase, the prosaic allusion." He suspected that Woolson "will not polish or elaborate but will let her thought, where it spoke out strongly, stand in its first crude expression rather than weakening it by change." Woolson had told Stedman's friend R. R. Bowker as much, claiming she was unable to revise her poetry, although she took great pains with her prose. (Aaronna also says she cannot see how to improve her own writing.)[18] What is lacking, ultimately, is control. Although she possessed the artist's instincts in great measure, he believed she was unable to refine her work into highly polished art.

Bowker's advice about *Two Women* had been to put the poem in a drawer and read Keats and Shelley, advice that was not dissimilar to what Emily Dickinson famously heard from the critic Thomas Wentworth Higginson, who, interestingly, had sought out Woolson after reading *Two Women*. Although not nearly as experimental as Dickinson's radical verse, *Two Women* contained a similarly raw power. But power and originality were not enough to gain the favor of the male literary elite, which Dickinson renounced and Woolson continued to seek. Her problem, she realized, was that while force of feeling mattered more to her than refinement, the critics did not agree. ("To me originality and force are everything," the narrator tells Aaronna, "but the world at large will not overlook as I do your absolutely barbarous shortcomings on account of them.")[19]

While Woolson wrestled with the critical judgment of her work, Henry James seemed to be receiving never-ending accolades. She later told him as much: "I do'nt think you appreciated, over there among the chimney-pots, the laudation your books received in America, as they came out one by one. (We little fish did! We little fish became worn to skeletons owing to the constant admonitions we received to regard the beauty, the grace, the incomparable perfections of all sorts & kinds of the proud salmon of the pond.[)]" She didn't hide from him the jealousy she had felt—"we ended by hating that salmon"—but she certainly overstated the unanimity of his critical success. Although he was widely regarded as one of America's most accomplished story writers, when his novel *The Europeans* was published at the end of 1878, the reviews were mixed. Some critics had grown weary of his style and sounded a note that was in many ways the reverse of the message Woolson had received with the publication of *Two Women*. For instance, Richard Grant White wrote in the *North American Review* that James's novels exhibited great skill but lacked "vital force in their personages. . . . His men and women, although they talk exceedingly well, are bloodless." As a result, his work demonstrated "great half-exercised powers." In this formulation, he is just as incomplete an artist as the male narrator of "'Miss Grief,'" who admires the "originality and force" of Aaronna's writings precisely because he doesn't possess them "to any marked degree" himself.[20]

When Woolson registered her own opinion of *The Europeans* in the *Atlantic*'s "Contributors' Club," she wasn't as hard on James, but she did have her criticisms. Approaching his novel as a fellow writer, she had some advice for a peer she respected but thought could develop his art further. She deemed *The Europeans* "his best work so far" but found "his peculiar style of mere hints . . . better adapted to a short story . . . than to the broader limits of a novel, where we are accustomed to more explanation and detail." In *The Europeans* he had "advanced in his art," she wrote almost facetiously, to the point where "there is absolutely no action at all." What is left is "contrast of character, and conversation," so she proceeded to evaluate the novel on those terms, judging most of his characters either shadowy failures or unfairly ridiculed for their earnestness or lack of beauty. Thus, she more or less agreed with White and those who viewed his characterization as wanting. Yet she also agreed with those, like Howells, who found his style delightful and at times perfect.[21]

As her review appeared, so did a number of other quite negative ones, inspiring Woolson to pick up her pen again, this time in defense of James. In her second review in the "Contributors' Club," published the same month that her mother died, she wrote, "It is certainly evident that [James] has not the genuine story-telling gift, the power of inventing a story interesting for its own sake. His talent lies in another field, that of keen observation and fine discrimination of character, which he portrays with a subtle and delicate touch. It is unreasonable, I think, to complain of a writer for not being something else than he is. . . . Let us do without a story in Mr. James's novels, and enjoy instead something certainly as admirable in its way." Observing the "refined skill" with which he presented his contrasting characters on every page was "pleasure sufficient." Although she clearly preferred a dynamic plot and worried that the novel of analysis threatened to crowd out the novel of action, she admired James's style and was broad-minded in her appreciation of writing different from her own. Like James in his later essay "The Art of Fiction," she "grant[ed] the artist his subject, his idea, what the French call his *donnée*."[22]

Woolson's first review of *The Europeans* suggested that she felt James had far to go to perfect his art—to marry, in a sense, his best qualities as a writer with those she possessed. She, on her side, would have to effect a similar feat in order to become a more complete artist. But in "'Miss Grief'" she suggested that the male writer's faults were more readily overlooked. For he possessed privileges—a superior education, social distinction, and fraternity—from which she was excluded. While Woolson had anonymously joined the "Contributors' Club" in the pages of the *Atlantic*, James belonged to a real club of literary men who supported each other in and out of print. More than that, though, she seemed to feel that her gender contributed to the flaws pointed out by critics. Although the *Two Women* reviewer never directly associated her writings' faults with being female, the correlation was nonetheless implied. Her lack of control over the emotional force of her writing could be construed as a feminine trait. She had all along preferred strength over beauty in an attempt to overcome the association of her writing with what was deemed an inferior category of women's literature. After the publication of *Two Women*, she had begun to wonder if it was simply instinctive for a woman to value a work's emotional power over—or at least alongside—its formal finish. As White's review of *The Europeans* suggests, however, some men shared her preferences.

The goal, as she then saw it, was to strike a balance between feeling and form. She would spend the rest of her career more or less working toward that goal. In the meantime, "'Miss Grief'" also suggests that she may have hoped James would likewise see the value of seeking a middle ground between the two poles. She was eager to find a new literary friend, someone as helpful and encouraging as Stedman had been, yet someone as committed to the literary art of fiction as she was. This time she wasn't in search of a mentor. James had much to teach her, she felt, but she had plenty to offer as well.

A FLORENTINE EXPERIMENT

After four months of soaking up the sun in Menton, Woolson and the Benedicts packed up their trunks and made their way to Florence, where they arrived on March 18, 1880. From that date Constance would finally begin to live again. She could not escape the past completely, as she told Sam: "I find that . . . the skies change when we cross the sea, but not our own minds; they remain the same. And if we were anxious there, we are anxious here. Pictures and Campanile cannot change that!" However, she had begun, as she wrote in a poem about Menton, to leave behind "[t]he care and sorrow, / Sad memory's haunting pain that would not cease." Charlie's latest letters from California showed him coming out of his depression and making plans for the future, soothing her worry. Slowly, she allowed Florence's glorious sites to fill her mind. She began to gush in her letters: "[H]ere I have attained that old-world feeling I used to dream about, a sort of enthusiasm made up of history, mythology, old churches, pictures, statues, vineyards, the Italian sky, . . . the whole thing having I think taken me pretty well off my feet!"[23]

For the next two and a half months, Constance, her sister, and her niece made their home at the exclusive Casa Molini pension on the banks of the Arno near the Carraja Bridge. The courtyard below Constance's window was pleasantly adorned with statues of ancient gods and goddesses, but the labyrinthine interior of the former Medici palace, carved up to house sixty or more guests, had a rather "slip-shod air" with its worn rugs and battered furniture. The clientele was exclusive—no other Americans, mostly English, several of them titled. And fortunately it was cheaper than their lodgings in Menton.[24]

Constance spent her first month in Florence writing all morning and visiting churches in the afternoons with John Ruskin's *Mornings in Florence* as her guide. She was determined to learn all she could about European art, attempting to rectify what she considered a serious deficiency in her knowledge. Hours were devoted to the chapels at Santa Croce, in particular, as she patiently tried to see what he found to admire in "the hideous wooden Byzantine style, . . . Cimabue, Giotto and the rest."[25] She found Ruskin helpful but rather pedantic. Fortunately she would soon have a much more agreeable guide.

Henry James must have been visiting one of his English friends at the Casa Molini when Constance and Clara met him.[26] It seems Clara and Plum quickly excused themselves, having so many other acquaintances in Florence, leaving the two writers to head out on their own.

James had planned to work on *The Portrait of a Lady*, which was to begin serialization in the *Atlantic Monthly* in August, but on April 18 he asked Howells, his friend and editor, for a two-month extension. He had found Italy "fertile in pretexts for one's haunting its lovely sights and scenes rather than one's writing-table." One of those pretexts was Woolson, an independent-minded American woman seeing those sights for the first time. She reminded him too much of his heroine Isabel Archer to forgo the chance to tour Florence with her.[27]

On the third of May James wrote to his aunt, Catharine Walsh, "This morning I took an American authoress [on] a drive—Constance Fenimore Woolson, whose productions you may know, though I don't & who was presented to me (by letter) by Henrietta Temple. Constance is old-maidish, deaf, & 'intense'; but a good little woman & a perfect lady." He had the week before written to his sister, Alice, in much less flattering terms, describing Woolson as "amiable, but deaf" and as having been "pursuing me through Europe with a letter of introduction." Her deafness was a source of some amusement—

she "asks me questions about my works to which she can't hear the answers," he told his sometimes caustic sister, who could be jealous of her brother's female friends.[28] Yet, whatever his initial impressions of Woolson, it is clear that he quickly grew fond of her.

James called at the Casa Molini often. Woolson couldn't help noticing that despite his "many acquaintances in Florence . . . he found time to come in the mornings and take me out; sometimes to the galleries or churches, and sometimes just for a walk in the beautiful green Cascine." Walking beside her, hearing her impressions, seeing everything through her fresh eyes allowed James to ignore the "detested fellow sight-seer[s]" who crowded Florence with their Baedekers in hand. He waxed poetic about the Raphaels and Michelangelos to which he had grown so accustomed, and Woolson enjoyed having a guide who was so knowledgeable about art.[29]

She thought he had peculiar tastes, however, and often did not agree with him. About Michelangelo's statues in the New Sacristy of the San Lorenzo Basilica, they held widely divergent views. He thought the reclining nude figures Night and Day, Dusk and Dawn admirable, but she found them "distracted." Her opinion apparently struck him speechless, and he wandered off to examine another artwork. She confessed to a friend back in Cleveland that she could not judge the much-revered statues because she was so unacquainted with the human form. Their blank faces, however, dismayed her. By contrast, the statue of a clothed Lorenzo Medici moved her deeply, particularly the face: "The whole expression of the figure is musing and sad, but it is the sadness of the strongest kind of a human mind,— almost the sadness of a God. He seems omniscient. To my idea, he seems to represent the whole human race; remembering all the past; conscious of all the future; and <u>waiting</u>. Nothing in the way of marble has ever impressed me so much, and I only wish it was where I could step in and look at it every day." She was determined to learn to appreciate art, but even after James's tutelage she felt she had a long way to go. "Some day you will see it," James told her as she confessed her continued confusion over what he saw in Giotto. "May be," she admitted, but she wasn't sure.[30]

James felt remarkably at ease with Woolson and seemed to enjoy having an admirer. He had been recently in Naples, where he had decided once and for all to distance himself from his friend Paul Zhukovsky, who had been an ardent disciple until he decided to take up with Richard Wagner and his wife. Woolson's attention must have helped to heal that emotional breach. He was also relieved to discover that Woolson was nothing like other women writers he had met. She was less forward and obtrusive than the "literary spinster, sailing-into-your-intimacy-American-hotel-piazza type" whom he had previously regretted encountering. James quickly abandoned his usual reserve. While others could find him formal and somber, Woolson thought him "a delightful companion." In fact, it was not only Florence that had swept her off her feet. "Perhaps I ought to add <u>Henry James</u>," she wrote. "He has been perfectly charming to me for the last three weeks."[31]

If she did not conform to his expectations for women writers, he was an equally novel type to her: a cosmopolitan, Europeanized American man who represented the authority not of money or physical power, as the men back home did, but the authority of culture, which earned her esteem much more readily. She must have been disappointed that he did not know her writings and had apparently never heard her name before. The mutual understanding she had envisioned in "'Miss Grief'" was not to be, at least not yet. But she found instead an immensely interesting figure whom she began to observe carefully, watching his lips closely to catch each word and storing up impressions to imagine how she could adapt him to the page.

The thirty-seven-year-old James, three years her junior, was nothing like Stedman, who had been so full of questions about her work and gave offers of advice. He reminded her somewhat of John Hay in bearing, although taller and broader. Portraits from the period show that he wore a thick beard and that his close-cut dark brown hair had receded significantly, revealing a high, rounded forehead. Constance thought his profile very fine. His penetrating light-gray eyes also gave him a commanding appearance, although she noticed how he erased all expression from them. He stammered a bit, but his voice was sonorous, the kind Woolson could hear better than others. His manner

Woolson observed Henry James closely upon their first meeting in
Florence. Portrait by Abbott Handerson Thayer, 1881.
(Collection of the American Academy of Arts and Letters, New York City)

was rather English, "extremely unpretending and unobtrusive." He
could seem cool and detached and then suddenly surprise you with a
keen observation.[32]

For three or four weeks during the spring of 1880 in Florence, the
two authors were intrigued but not quite sure what to make of each
other. Woolson's story "A Florentine Experiment"—about an American man and woman meeting in Florence, carefully negotiating the
boundaries of their relationship, and trying unsuccessfully to read each
other—captures the pleasures and tensions of their initial meeting.

Upon Trafford Morgan's and Margaret Stowe's first meeting, she thinks him not especially handsome and too cynical; he thinks her too dark for his taste and too ironical. Margaret has read Trafford's writing before—in this case, an ardent love letter to her friend Beatrice, whose beauty has led many men to profess love to her, while she skates easily over the feelings of others. When Margaret discovers he is the author of the letter, she begins to study him, searching for signs of the man who was capable of such deep feelings. Trafford is startled by Margaret's sudden attention and assumes she must have designs upon him, but he "did not think it probable . . . being that he was neither an Apollo, an Endymion, nor a military man." Indeed, "[s]he showed no sign of having troublesomely impulsive feelings." So he decides she must be playing some sort of game, perhaps trying to make someone else jealous.[33]

Margaret and Trafford visit together the places Woolson and James did: the Academy, the Pitti Palace, and the monastery of San Marco. They voice the opinions and preferences of Woolson and James as well—she is partial to the beauty of nature; he prefers the human beauty of art; she loves walking in the cloisters; he waxes poetic on the virtues of Giotto and Botticelli. He tries to lure her into a flirtation, but she does not follow him. When Trafford pierces the façade of their friendship by confessing his love for another, Margaret fumes that she had no genuine interest in him but has only been conducting an "experiment" to see if she could forget her love for a man who had recently married another, knowing that Trafford was unlikely to be affected because he was deeply in love with her friend.

The following spring, Trafford returns to Florence and decides to conduct a similar experiment with Margaret to see if he can get over Beatrice, who has become engaged to another man. At the end of the season, Margaret meets Trafford in the Boboli Gardens to learn the result of his experiment. Professing "satisfied contentment" but not love, he nonetheless asks her to marry him. She is puzzled. "You do not love me; I am not beautiful; I have no fortune. What, then, do you gain?" He confesses that he would gain "the greatest gift that can be given to a man on this earth, a gift I long for,—a wife who really and deeply loves me." She erupts with resentment: "I was but waiting for this. . . . With the deeply-rooted egotism of a man you believe that I love you." She says she had allowed his experiment to proceed, hoping she would get this chance to enact her "revenge" by proving him wrong.[34] Woolson knew only too well that a single woman approaching a man was assumed to be after the offer of his hand in marriage. In "'Miss Grief'" the message was subtle; here it is more direct.

Whether or not Woolson was conducting an emotional experiment of her own—perhaps trying to distract herself from her grief by interesting herself in art and Henry James—she was most certainly conducting a literary experiment in writing this story. She had taken a departure by penning a slice of society life heavy on dialogue and light on plot. She had heard so often that this sort of writing "is much the most 'refined,' 'superior,' 'cultivated' style. And that my own [writing] needs just what that style excels in.—I have been told . . . that there should be next to no 'plot'; that the 'manner' should be more than the 'matter'; and that the best 'art' left a certain vagueness over all the details. I have been especially warned against anything that looked 'dramatic.'"[35] In other words, she had been expressly told that she should write more like James.

Woolson continued the experiment by sending the story to Howells at the *Atlantic* to see if he would take the bait. He did, eagerly, declaring it "an immense advance in manner and arrangement over anything you have hitherto written." With this story, she gained the approbation of the highest rung of the male literary elite by writing in the style it preferred. But she was not pleased with Howells's enthusiastic response, which she found rather "depressing." It made her doubt herself and worry all the more about her novel, *Anne*, scheduled to finally appear in two months. How would Howells, James, and the admirers of this mannered style respond to the work into which she had poured so much of herself and her literary ambitions? She admired "the skill displayed" in James's work and enjoyed reading it, but she also believed "there are other ways of writing," and substance would always be more important than style, "though the skies fall."[36]

Fiction should appeal first and foremost to the heart and the soul, she felt, and only secondly to the head and the ear. Dramatic power and emotional response would always be to her the most vital elements of literature, making her a bit of an outsider in an era that was growing increasingly distrustful of literature that made one feel. But for now Woolson was happy to know that she still had allies, chief among them Henry Mills Alden, editor of *Harper's* magazine. She sent him "A Florentine Experiment" for his opinion and was relieved to find that he agreed with her. Alden encouraged her to go back to her own style, and she would for the most part, although she also could not ignore the growing fame of James's and Howells's writings.[37]

With "A Florentine Experiment" Woolson had also issued James a challenge. He may have read it, as it appeared in the *Atlantic* in October 1880, one month before the first installment of his new novel, *The Portrait of a Lady*. It showed him that Woolson could meet him on his own turf—in his magazine and in his style—and that she could scrutinize him carefully. Surely he recognized aspects of himself in Trafford, perhaps also Trafford's most conspicuous quality: his egotism. Woolson wrote to her nephew, Sam, that she thought "men like 'Trafford' generally <u>are</u> conceited. But that is not the worst of it; the worst is that they are generally, also, so charming (in other ways) that one has to accept the 'conceit' to get the rest!"[38]

Such was her initial reading of James. Beneath the gallantly amiable surface she detected a well of certainty and self-importance that would make it difficult, she saw, to gain his esteem. She would have to tread carefully around his ego (which was actually more fragile than she at first realized). But she was willing to accept this blemish to enjoy the more delightful parts of his personality. That James was equally charmed and intrigued by Woolson is evidenced by the steady growth of their friendship over the next few years. In his eyes, however, she was still not much more than an interesting, independent, genteel American woman with decided opinions and a keen wit. She would play the part for now.

8

The Artist's Life

Having left Florence the first week of June, Constance and the Benedicts meandered through Venice, Milan, and Como before heading to the cool Swiss Alps for the summer. Traveling the St. Gotthard Pass by stagecoach was a dizzying experience, trekking up the precipice-hugging road and then racing down the other side of the Alps until they reached Lucerne.[1]

When they arrived, letters from Charlie and the Mathers were waiting for them. Charlie, then working in an office in Los Angeles, was hoping to buy some land in Riverside, and Constance was willing to give him five hundred dollars for it, if he would settle down and regain his health. She was finally regaining hers and was happy to report to her brother-in-law that she was growing fat on the alpine milk. She also wasn't getting much exercise. No one would hike with her into the mountains, so she stayed close to her pension, finishing "A Florentine Experiment" and "The Old Palace Keeper," also set in Florence.[2]

One day a package arrived from James in London. Constance was surprised to find inside it a recent issue of the *Spectator*, the most influential of the elite London weeklies, containing a review of her just-released collection of stories, *Rodman the Keeper: Southern Sketches.* The review lauded her "quite remarkable power" and called for the book to be published in England. She had never, as she wrote to Sam, "received attention in a paper of that stamp."[3] James must have been rather surprised himself to stumble across the review. If he had thought his new friend a rather obscure writer, the *Spectator* corrected his mistake. It was the first of many such items he would send Woolson over the years—books, magazines, or clippings that he thought would interest her.

Meanwhile, Woolson's literary reputation was soaring back at home with the publication of *Rodman the Keeper* by D. Appleton & Company. In addition to the title story, the collection included "Felipa," "Old Gardiston," "In the Cotton Country," and "King David," as well as an Asheville story, "Up in the Blue Ridge," and a South Carolina story, "'Bro.'" There were also three more Florida stories: "Miss Elisabetha" (about the northern guardian of a Spanish orphan who tries unsuccessfully to import civilization to a Florida backwater), "Sister St. Luke" (the story of a timid nun who is nursed back to health by northern visitors and daringly rescues them from a tornado before happily returning to her repressive convent), and "The South Devil" (a highly evocative portrayal of a Florida swamp that is both sublime and deadly, luring a musician in search of its harmonies to his death).

The assessment of the nation's literary authorities was that these stories deserved a lasting place in American literature. Her achievement, wrote a critic in *Appletons' Journal*, was to "illustrate the possibilities of American life for artistic treatment with a fullness and success scarcely attained in our literature otherwise." The Boston *Literary World* admired "the artist's power—that virile force, that artistic completeness . . . which makes her place secure as one of the most vigorous woman writers of this country." Meanwhile, *Harper's* declared that Woolson had earned the name of "a conscientious and true artist" by not "sacrificing vigor or originality to mere finish."[4]

The one negative voice came from the *Atlantic Monthly*, where Howells oversaw the publication of a highly dismissive review by

James's old friend Thomas Sergeant Perry. It could only have deepened Woolson's distrust of Howells. Perry accused her of imitating "poor novels" rather than illustrating "real life," as well as making use of "melodramatic devices."⁵ Her response has not survived, but she wrote to the reviewers at the *New York Times* and *Scribner's* to defend her portraits of southerners and thank them for their praise of her stories' realism. If she couldn't have the full support of the *Atlantic*, she was glad to have it in other powerful quarters.

A ROMAN WINTER AND SPRING

After a fall spent in Geneva, where Constance took a break from writing and immersed herself in the eighteenth-century writers who had lived on Lake Leman—from Goethe to Madame de Staël—she began to plan her return to Italy. "I must have my three months in Rome," she told Sam. Two difficulties presented themselves: the Roman fever (malaria) and the need for a travel companion, since Clara had taken Plum to Paris for schooling. Constance was still too new to Europe and too concerned about propriety to travel alone. Luckily, an old friend from St. Augustine, the older, wealthier Emily Vernon Clark, was on hand. Emily was "a cultivated, congenial, easy-going person [who] is fond of the things I am fond of," Constance explained to Sam. For instance, she liked "to discuss a book threadbare" as much as Constance did.⁶

In January 1881, when she finally arrived in Rome with Emily and three of Emily's female relatives, the incessant rain could not dampen her excitement "to be really in the old walls at last!" Having dreamed about and longed for the Italian capital since she was a child, she could hardly sleep the first night. After the weather cleared, she began her explorations of the Vatican and St. Peter's, the Borghese Gardens, the Forum, and the Capitoline Museum. She found the ancient statues the most moving, then the solemn ruins and the vast Campagna. Rome was enchanting; her situation as part of a group, however, was not. Constance resented not being able to do as she liked without comment or opposition. She felt her time tampered with and swore she would never travel with a party again, regardless of propriety.[7]

Clara and Clare arrived in Rome for Carnival season in March. Amid the festivities the sisters had some serious conversations about the future. It was time for the Benedicts to return to Cleveland. Constance had no intention of joining them. She still longed for leisurely visits to England and Venice.

By April Constance found herself, to her delight, alone in Rome. Her first act was to escape the crowded, high-priced hotels. She found a fifth-floor apartment with access to the roof where there was a garden of lemon trees and she could look over the rooftops and bell towers as far as the green Campagna. When she tired of writing in her parlor, she wrote up there, savoring the Roman sunlight.[8]

Her first experience of independent living in Europe was a great success. She wrote sometimes for seven hours a day, made her own breakfast of coffee and boiled eggs and at five o'clock, religiously, a pot of tea. A cook made her a simple lunch and dinner, which she preferred to the abundant meals with endless courses served at hotels. When she wasn't writing she was hunting down the city's treasures. Very soon she had "'gone over' body and soul, to Rome!" She devoted herself to studying the ancient ruins, temples, and statues, filling the margins and blank pages of her Baedeker with quotes from Byron, Hawthorne, Dickens, and William Wetmore Story. She took long walks in search of ruins, lingering at the temples in the Forum and climbing the hills outside of town to the Raphael-designed Villa Madama full of frescoes on its crumbling ceilings and walls. She studied the pictures at the Doria Gallery and roamed through the streets, admiring the Italian soldiers on every corner and deciding that "the prettiest product of modern Italy, is a young Italian officer." Stopping regularly at the Pantheon on her walks, she one day glimpsed Queen Margherita inside, kneeling in prayer.[9]

Woolson also made a special visit to the graves of Keats and Shelley at the Protestant Cemetery, that serene spot about which Shelley had written, "It might make one in love with death, to think that one should be buried in so sweet a place." She admired the violets blooming on Keats's grave and the pyramid of Caius Cestius, built ca. 12 B.C., which "bring[s] the past very near us."[10]

Although she mostly avoided the expatriate society of Rome, Constance also made friends with two new families whom she would in future meet often on her travels: that of Richard Henry Dana, the author of *Two Years Before the Mast*, and that of U.S. Navy Lieutenant Commander Caspar Goodrich, whose wife was a niece of her old St. Augustine friend Eleanor Washington. Constance avoided larger parties, where it was difficult for her to hear, but once made an exception for a reception at the home of the U.S. minister to Italy, George Perkins Marsh. Much more to her taste was a tête-à-tête with Henry James, whose two-week visit in Rome included at least one call to her "sky-parlor," where they shared some gossip and a pot of tea. They had much to discuss, including his novel in progress, *The Portrait of a Lady*. He told her he was unsure about his characters Madame Merle and Gilbert Osmond, who had just been introduced in that month's *Atlantic Monthly*. Woolson could only listen to his concerns. She didn't have access to American magazines when she was traveling.[11]

As April waned and the summer heat approached, Constance showed no inclination to leave the Eternal City. She paid little heed to warnings about the Roman fever that carried off many northern visitors. Once May arrived, and the tourists made their exodus, she was delighted to find that Rome was "no longer like a great fair for strangers." Gone were the booths hawking souvenirs. She could linger in the Forum and the Coliseum and lean against the stones warmed by the sun. Her experience coincided perfectly with that of Isabel Archer, who happened to be visiting Rome for the first time in that month's installment of *The Portrait of a Lady* and found May "the most precious month of all to the true Rome-lover."[12]

Woolson stubbornly stayed in Rome until the fourth of June, "reducing everybody at home to serious preparations for [her] funeral." Her subsequent fear of Roman fever would, in fact, prevent her from ever returning to the Eternal City. However, she would always remember Rome as her "true home."[13] Had she been able to take up a permanent residence there, she might have been spared a good deal of the wandering that would characterize the rest of her life.

THE RUIN OF WOMEN ARTISTS

After Rome, Constance journeyed to a town in the Swiss Alps that was off the map for most American tourists—Engelberg, in a small, mountain-rimmed valley at 3,500 feet. She felt entirely hidden there. She took her meals in her room, avoided all acquaintance, and was content in her solitude. As mountaineers passed her window each morning on their way to the alpine passes, she settled in for a long day of work. It was likely there that she completed two long stories, almost novellas, portraying the demise of women artists. Both contain James-like characters who convince women to give up their art and marry them instead. While some of his biographers have seen in these stories indications of Woolson's secret love for James, more probably they suggest—insofar as they may hint at her own feelings— that she viewed any possible relationship with him as destructive to her art. The women in these stories submit to marriages only after losing their financial independence and their faith in their creative power. Most disturbingly, the James-like critics have convinced them that women cannot be great artists. Despite the stories' devastating themes, however, they also show Woolson at the top of her game. Wrestling with the crisis of confidence that followed her encounters with James, she nonetheless exhibited tremendous mastery over her art, suggesting a wealth of emotion boiling under the surface of finely wrought prose.

The first of these stories, "The Street of the Hyacinth," is set in Rome and was probably begun while she was still there. It is redolent of the awe and humility Woolson felt in the presence of so much ancient history and art. Interestingly, however, her main character, the naïve westerner Ettie Macks, at first feels no such humility. She arrives in Rome sure of her ability to realize her dreams of becoming an artist. Although she calls to mind the female artists in James's *Roderick Hudson* and Hawthorne's *The Marble Faun*, Ettie does not merely copy the great works, as they did, but has great ambitions of creating a masterpiece herself, believing in her peculiarly American way that "things that had once been done could . . . be done again."[14]

As in "'Miss Grief,'" Ettie has sought out the opinion of a male authority, the art critic Raymond Noel. Having read all of his essays on art, she has come to Rome expressly to find him. Viewed as a prodigy in her hometown, Ettie attended four years of a western female seminary, where she took art lessons and was hailed as a genius. However, a teacher from New York has told her to read Noel's essays, presumably to show her that she knows little of the Western tradition of art. As Noel seemed to think studying the old masters the only way to learn about art, she has come to Rome to study them with him. He tries to avoid her, especially after he judges her paintings very poor, but Ettie is determined and finally manages to corner him at the Doria Gallery. He shows her all the finest pictures, speaking to her as if "to an intelligent child," and is amused by her opinions of the paintings, which she finds dull, ugly, and meaningless.[15]

Meanwhile, an English art teacher has taken her up, believing that her crude work shows promise and that she would benefit from rigorous training. But he falls in love with her and does not press the importance of technique and execution, leaving her convinced that originality, her strength, is more important. When Noel realizes that she has not advanced in her art studies, he gives her a pile of books by authorities on Western art that are meant to show her how little she knows of the field in which she has hoped to excel. Eventually Ettie discovers her ignorance and mocks herself: "The Western girl, the girl from Tuscolee! The girl who thought she could paint, and could not!" She abandons her art, becoming a teacher and a dutiful daughter to her invalid mother. After Ettie suffers a series of misfortunes and rising debts, Noel comes to admire her and proposes. She refuses, admitting that she loves him but does not "respect . . . or admire" him. He humbles himself for the rest of the story and eventually convinces her to marry him when the street she lives in is scheduled to be demolished. For Ettie, marrying him "was a great downfall, of course," Noel admits, but her aspirations had been too high.[16]

"The Street of the Hyacinth" would appear the following year in *The Century* alongside Howells's novel *A Modern Instance*, making it quite possible that James read the story. If so, he may have recognized aspects of himself in Raymond Noel, such as his polished amiability, popularity in society, and wide knowledge of art. Although Woolson warned her old friend Stedman not to look for actual people in her stories, least of all this one—"Real persons are seldom usable"— James is unmistakably portrayed, perhaps even caricatured.[17] However, twenty-two-year-old Ettie Macks bears little resemblance to Constance beyond her interest in Noel's (James's) opinions of art and her devotion to her invalid mother. What has gone unnoticed by those who read this story and others as thinly veiled wish fulfillments is how Woolson gave her Jamesian characters love interests decidedly different from herself. They are all much younger and, she would have thought, prettier. They are marriageable, in short, a category from which she had long since excluded herself. James, however, was still considered a quite eligible bachelor, and he continued to fend off curiosity about his marriage prospects, including from Woolson. She would soon write to him about the "sweet young American wife I want you to have—whom you <u>must</u> have,—even if only (as you horribly write) as a 'last resort.'" She had picked a woman out for him in New York and was disappointed when he told her he met there "no one in particular." James was adamant, as he told his friend Grace Norton, that he "was unlikely ever to marry."[18]

The second woman-artist story Woolson completed that summer in Engelberg was "At the Château of Corinne." It begins rather lightly with a group of Americans enjoying their leisure in a villa on Lake Leman near Geneva but turns serious when the heroine, Katharine Winthrop, reveals that she is a poet. While she looks back nostalgically on the eighteenth century when men and women seemed to be intellectual equals in the idyllic retreat of Lake Leman, the contrarian hero, John Ford, paints another picture: Madame de Staël, who had sought out the intellectual companionship of Goethe and Schiller, was an egotist who should have waited for them to approach her. As it was, "[t]hey confessed to each other . . . the deep relief they felt when that gifted woman departed."[19]

Constance's fascination with Madame de Staël during the previous summer in Geneva had inspired her to write a story updating the themes of de Staël's famous novel *Corinne*, a female *Künstlerroman* in which the heroine chooses art over the man she adores because love "absorb[s] every other interest and every other idea." Corinne later explains, "Talent requires inner independence that true love never allows." Yet she still yearns for love, so much so that when her beloved marries her docile, talentless half-sister, she wastes away and dies.[20] *Corinne*, published in 1807, created the mystique of the female genius whose gifts marginalize her in life and in love. Generations of women—from Margaret Fuller, who was called the "American Corinne" in the 1840s, on down to Constance's time—wrestled with Corinne's myth. Woolson many times portrayed the idea that a woman could either pour her deepest feelings onto the page or invest them in marriage and domesticity, but not both.

"At the Château of Corinne" is not about the struggle to become an artist, as "'Miss Grief'" and "Street" were. Katharine Winthrop is already an accomplished poet who has published a long poem that received high praise, although it was published anonymously. Katharine seems to be on the verge of crowning her literary success with the love of a man, Lorimer Percival, also a poet, who honors the legacy of de Staël and presumably admires Katharine's work. However, she discovers he was primarily attracted to her fortune and, predictably, has married a simple, beautiful young girl who knows nothing of poetry.

The climax of the story takes place earlier, however, at de Staël's home, Coppet, where Katharine reveals to Ford that she is the author of the widely admired poem, which he has read, and demands to know his opinion of it. Having already scorned the very idea of a woman of genius, he proceeds to tell her what other men won't, because they are too polite: "[I]ts rhythm was crude and unmelodious; its coloring was exaggerated," and its logic was weak. All of this was foreseeable, however, because "[w]e do not expect great poems from women any more than we expect great pictures; we do not expect strong logic any more than we expect brawny muscle. A woman's poetry is subjective." Most unforgivable, however, was

> a certain sort of daring. . . . For a woman should not dare in that way. Thinking to soar, she inevitably descends. Her mental realm is not the same as that of man; lower, on the same level, or far above, it is at least different. And to see her leave it, and come in all her white purity, which must inevitably be soiled, to the garish arena where men are contending, . . . this indeed is a painful sight. Every honest man feels like going to her, poor mistaken sibyl that she is, closing her lips with gentle hand, and leading her away to some far spot among the quiet fields, where she can learn her error, and begin her life anew.

Such opinions appear to be what Woolson sensed lurking behind James's courteous demeanor. For Ford is another of Woolson's Jamesian characters. Although he is neither writer nor critic, the description of him is remarkably like James: Ford also has gray eyes "without much expression" and closely cut brown hair. His manner is "quiet, and quite without pretension," and he is shy, somewhat cynical, and opinionated.[21]

What exactly James said or did to indicate that he held views such as Ford's is unknown. None of his letters to Woolson have survived. But his fundamental disregard for women writers is clear enough in his early reviews. As in Stedman's essay on Elizabeth Barrett Browning, his disbelief in woman's genius was apparent. In one review he wrote, George Eliot possessed "the exquisitely good taste on a small scale, the absence of taste on a large, . . . the unbroken current of feeling, and, we may add, of expression, which distinguish the feminine mind." In another, he wondered why George Sand's novels were less worth rereading than those of other highly accomplished writers. "Is this because after all she was a woman," he asked, "and the laxity of the feminine intellect could not fail to claim its part in her?"[22] Woolson may have already been aware of such views before she met him, but "Street" and "Château" suggest that as she came to know him better, she detected a generally patronizing attitude toward all women writers that more or less crushed her hopes of eliciting from him the respect Aaronna receives from the Jamesian narrator in "'Miss Grief.'"

However much she may have resisted the common perception of a fundamental difference between the male and the female mind, she couldn't help believing it herself. Not long after finishing "Château" she wrote to James, "A woman, after all, can never be a complete artist."[23] She was referring to George Eliot's choice to kill off the odious Grandcourt in *Daniel Deronda*, while James had let the equally loathsome Osmond live, as he would have in real life. She suggests that women cannot but be ruled by their emotions when they write. They lack the cool detachment that art requires. She may not have been referring to herself, however, for she was adamant that realism must trump moral concerns in her own art.

At the end of "Château," Katharine is terribly silent. We do not hear her voice at all. She has promised never to write again, to be instead a dependent, obedient "true woman" in exchange for Ford's hand. The story makes clear how far from beguiling the prospect of marriage was to an independent woman with talent and ambition. Life without art and self-reliance would be, as it seemingly is for Katharine, a kind of death. Marriage is even less of a happy ending here than it was in "Street." Ford may go down on his knees and get misty-eyed, but he rules her and silences her in the end.

When "Château" was done, Woolson sent it to *Harper's*, but they declined to publish it, most likely because *Anne* was just then running in the magazine. So she would lay it away in a trunk for six years before she sent it back to *Harper's*, who then gratefully accepted it. By then, the sting of Ford's and James's derision had lessened.

TRIUMPHS AND TRIALS OF *ANNE*

Just as Woolson was writing her troubling stories about women artists and writers, she was, ironically, also enjoying the greatest success of her career. After a summer of excellent reviews for *Rodman the Keeper*, *Anne* had begun its run in *Harper's* in December 1880. The editors had held it for so long because they wanted it to premiere simultaneously in America and in the first issue of the new English edition of the magazine. (James's *Washington Square* was completing its run.)

From its first appearance, *Anne* was a hit. *The Critic* announced that it was "attracting flattering attention both in this country and in England," adding that "[t]he development of a genuinely American novelist is a matter of no little interest."[24] The public's fascination would only grow over the eighteen months it took for the novel to run its course.

Woolson didn't know how well *Anne* was doing. No one sent her reviews, she complained. But the English and American readers she encountered on her travels gave her very positive reports. By the spring of 1882, fan letters were arriving in every post. They found her in Sorrento, where she spent another reclusive winter in a room overlooking the Bay of Naples with the smoke of Mt. Vesuvius in the distance.

During her stay in Sorrento, a letter arrived from Harper & Brothers that most writers can only dream of. Inside was a thousand-dollar check, doubling her pay for the serialization of *Anne*, along with a contract to publish it as a book. In a handwritten clause, the firm claimed the right of first refusal on all of her future writing.[25] Harper & Brothers had from the outset of her career desired an exclusive relationship with her, but now they were ready to make a serious commitment. And she was ready to accept their offer. From here on she would publish all of her stories, essays, and books with them. They would, in turn, promote her works and reputation as one of their own.

When she sat down to write to James shortly after receiving the good news, she couldn't help but share it. Just as quickly she regretted it. His response has not survived, but it stung her so deeply that months later she was still upset with herself for having mentioned the bonus and the offer. Her apology conveys how much his judgment of women writers had gotten under her skin:

> All the money that I have received, or shall receive, from my long novel, does not equal probably the half of the sum you received for

your first, or shortest. It is quite right that it should be so. And, even if a story of mine should have a large "popular" sale (which I do not expect), that could not alter the fact that the utmost best of my work cannot touch the hem of your first or poorest. My work is coarse beside yours. Of entirely another grade. The two should not be mentioned on the same day. Do pray believe how acutely I know this. If I feel anything in the world with earnestness it is the beauty of your writings, & any little thing I may say about my own comes from entirely another stratum; & is said because I live so alone, as regards to my writing, that sometimes when writing to you, or speaking to you—out it comes before I know it.[26]

Underneath the pleading tone is an unmistakable note of fear—fear that she had jeopardized their friendship, and that in exposing her ambitions she had become the object of his ridicule. The episode actually tells us as much about James as it does about Woolson. Unwittingly, she had touched a nerve. Although she thought him supremely confident, impervious to criticism or fear, he was actually deeply afraid of critical and commercial failure, as his biographers have documented. The two writers would in time share their fears with each other, but at this early date she read his response as a sign of his disdain rather than his jealousy.

In fact, Woolson was winning the implicit contest between them for readers, which her thousand-dollar bonus signified. Indeed, while *The Portrait of a Lady* was read by 12,000 readers in the *Atlantic Monthly*, *Anne* had run almost simultaneously in the more popular *Harper's* to a circulation of 100,000. And while *Portrait* would go on to sell 6,000 copies in book form, more than any of James's previous novels (or any afterward, as it would turn out), *Anne* would sell nearly ten times that—57,000 copies.[27]

Woolson's letters to James about *Portrait*, while they reflect her sincere respect for his achievement, were also meant to distract him from her novel's greater success. She paid keen attention to *Portrait*'s reviews, noting the new tone the critics took toward him. No longer the young writer showing so much promise, nor the presumptuous author of *Hawthorne* who had to be put in his place, he had arrived. She dismissed the negative tone of many reviewers, questioning their powers of perception. (The *Literary World* called it a "cruel book in its dissection of character," and *The Critic* complained, "There is not a single character in the book to whom we grow enthusiastically attached.") Woolson revealed herself to be an astute reader, able to appreciate what the narrow-minded critics could not. Her own view was that *Portrait* was "the finest novel you have written." His portrayal of Isabel, with whom she felt "so much in sympathy," had particularly impressed her, as did the final scene, in which Isabel is subjected to a passionate kiss from her longtime suitor. It had a "force (which real life does contain, I think)—a force which you have rather held back," she told him.[28]

Yet Woolson didn't simply flatter James. She corrected what she saw as some minor missteps but particularly complained that he did not allow the reader to "see, with any distinctness, whether Isabel really loved Osmond." It is simply "left to the imagination of the reader," she wrote, "as things easily to be supplied,—according to the time-honored method of Mr Henry James."[29] Writing to him as a reader, she nonetheless nudged him in the direction of her own writing. But by hiding her ambitions from him, she was also allowing him to look past her, to see in her primarily a reflection of his own great desire for fame and recognition, and to assume her ambitions were all for him. In the coming years, as he confronted fears of failure and irrelevance, he would come to rely quite heavily on that reflection, on her interest and admiration.

If the critics had taken a new tone with James, they did so with Woolson as well when *Anne* was published in book form seven months after *Portrait*, in July 1882. Sam sent her *The Century*'s review, which was representative in its judgment that "the opening chapters are the freshest and most charming" as compared to the off-key murder trial in the last third; however, looked at as a whole, the novel marked a new level of achievement for American novelists. The review's concluding lines heralded Woolson's arrival in the ranks she had longed to join: "Sometimes one is ready to say that a fragment, and not an inferior fragment, of the mantle of George Eliot is resting on her capable shoulders."[30] (Eliot had died just as *Anne* was beginning its serialization.)

The overall tone of most of the reviews was that a major American writer had arrived on the transatlantic literary scene. The *Atlantic*, no longer under Howells's editorship, began its review with the belief that *Anne* could be one of the works that fifty years hence would have "an enduring fame . . . in the succession of literature." *The Californian* summed up, "We observe from the reviews that Miss Woolson's novel has brought to the front again the undying hope and expectation of the Great American Novel." Others called *Anne* a work of "genius" and the product of a "master hand." One paper called it "one of the strongest and most perfectly finished American novels ever written."[31]

Some critics positioned Woolson as America's foremost female author. According to the *New York Tribune*, *Anne* "proves the author's right to stand without question at the head of American women novelists." Others let her lay claim to the wider world of writers, ranking her next to or just below Howells and James. One magazine believed her promise was so great she would not "always rank after these two." *The Century* wrote the following year that Woolson had a great "chance of becoming our best novelist" because she had "something of the analytic touch" as well as the "power of passion."[32]

In England, where disapproval of the analytical novel was intense, *Anne's* compromise between plot-driven and character-driven works did not go unnoticed. The London *Academy* declared, "We venture to say that *Anne* is one of the most remarkable works of fiction that have appeared for many years. It is remarkable for its own sake—for animation of plot and character; and it is remarkable as holding a place midway between the old American novel of incident and the modern American novel of analysis."[33]

Sadly, Woolson remained largely unaware of critics' assessments. Although the Harpers apprised her of their general tone and signed her to an exclusive contract as a result, *The Century* review that Sam sent to her was apparently the only one she saw. Knowing in more detail the overall estimation of her accomplishment could have helped to ameliorate the inferiority complex her friendship with James had inspired. James, it seems, expressed little or no interest in *Anne* at the time. The following year, Constance wrote to him of a friend of his who had read her novel and wanted to meet her, adding, "'Anne' is a book I once wrote."[34]

James may not have noticed her triumph, but his magazine did. Even before the reviews of *Anne* had begun to appear, the *Atlantic Monthly*'s new editor, Thomas Bailey Aldrich, requested a serial from Woolson.[35] She was flattered, but her new agreement with Harper & Brothers prohibited it. It was a sure sign that she had arrived.

It is probably no coincidence that Aldrich was a friend of Constance's old supporter Stedman, who still expressed interest in her career. If her new friend had failed her, her old one did not. He wrote to her later that year,

> *Of course* I read "Anne" seriatim—you never write a line that I do not read at once. You could not have felt more concerned than myself in its quality, in its reception. All in all, I considered it a beautiful work—an epochal stage in your career as a creative writer. . . . [A]s a first novel, 'Anne' is a noble effort, confirming me in my early belief that you can and will produce masterpieces, and become our foremost writer of imaginative prose.[36]

In addition to bolstering her ambitions, Stedman also approved of her literary methods, advising her to remain committed to the course she was on:

> You are now *sure* of your audience; take your time, do *not* over-work, do not strain your eyes, do not be afraid to lie "fallow" for long periods—meditating great rather than *many* novels. You have only yourself to maintain, and have not ___'s [probably Howells's] excuse for bringing out a new book every half-year. Your imagination is more *creative* than Howells's or James's—follow your own

vent, give us life and passion and color, and do not, like them, overdo your "analysis" and "subtilties" [*sic*]. Their novels are clever, dexterous; let yours be free, imaginative, dramatic, human, and not without poetic elevation.[37]

This letter is one of the very few Woolson received that survived her many years of traveling. It must have been tremendously important to her, a talisman she could turn to at times of doubt, when she began to question her own literary instincts.

It was only a few months later, in fact, that Woolson exhibited more confidence when she wrote to James with advice for his future work. She boldly suggested that he "give us a woman for whom we can feel a real love . . . let her love, and let us see that she does; do not leave it merely implied. In brief, let us care for her, & even greatly. . . . Believe me, it is the touchstone to sympathy. . . . This is all commonplace enough no doubt; this desire in the reader to be stirred; to be worked upon; to care. But I only ask you to do it once."[38] The challenge she had implicitly made in "'Miss Grief'" was now explicit. Behind it lay the continued hope that he would care for her writing. But she would have to keep assuring him that his work inhabited a realm far above hers.

THE MASKS WOMEN WORE

Constance's independent life as an artist abroad very nearly came to an abrupt end as the summer of 1882 approached. Alone in Sorrento, she fell ill with fever and an irritating cough, losing much of the sixteen pounds she had so proudly gained over the previous year. "To be ill alone in a foreign land is a dreary experience," she wrote to James. "And it seemed to me as I lay feverish & coughing, that I must go home; go home, get my precious books, & little household gods together, a dog or two, & never stir again."[39] This was her first experience of illness in exile, and it scared her.

Solitude was necessary for her work. It suited her so long as she could take meals in her room and have scenic vistas to contemplate and lovely landscapes to explore. But illness had turned her idyll into a nightmare. With no "home" to return to and the Benedicts on their way back to Europe, Constance repaired to Florence, where she found a British doctor to help her recover. After her convalescence, she joined Clara and Plum for the summer in the German spa town Baden-Baden. Constance admired the nearby forests but instead of exploring them went into her vortex again, writing her next long work.

The Harpers were eager for a new serial to begin in November, so Constance dusted off *For the Major*, which she had begun in Menton over two years before. It took six weeks of ten-hour days and a further two weeks of thirteen-hour days to finish it. As her arm ached up to the shoulder, she remembered bitterly James's comment in Florence that he never copied, and she was overcome with "despair," she told him, "that, added to your other perfections, was the gift of writing as you do, at the first draft!" Of course this wasn't the whole truth—the manuscript of *The Portrait of a Lady* was written at least twice, but his comment increased her perception of a great chasm between them.[40]

A rift was growing between Constance and her sister as well. As Clara later remembered it, every evening she had to coax her sister out of her room so she could stretch her legs, hear the band music in the park, and observe the promenade of the fashionable tourists. Constance was quite aware of Clara's displeasure at "my being shut up in my own rooms, invisible until evening. . . . She greatly detests all my mss. & has already presented me with a new dress and round-hat, so that I shall not look too 'literary.'"[41] Constance resented more than ever having to play the part of someone she was not—a fashionable, conventional woman. As it happened, the masks women had to wear were at the heart of the book she was writing as well.

For the Major was not a long work. It came to less than half the length of *Anne*, but it took just as long to write. The pace of Woolson's writing was slowing down as she worked harder to achieve formal perfection. It is perhaps not surprising that she drew her ambitions in a bit with *For the Major*. It was not a novel, she insisted, but simply a modest portrait of village life, probably too quiet to become a popular success. She hardly expected the critics to pay any attention to it. Yet she felt she had achieved in it a higher level of artistry than in *Anne*.[42]

For the Major has been considered by some to be Woolson's best book and has evoked comparisons to Jane Austen. It does in fact more closely resemble Austen's finely detailed work than the broader, more ambitious novels of Eliot and the Brontës that had inspired *Anne*. With a few exceptions (the *Atlantic* and the *Nation*), the critics agreed that the work was superior to her first novel. *For the Major* was viewed as more artistically complete. "Nothing could be more conscious, finished, modern, than this work," asserted the *Overland Monthly*. The "fine precision" of the language was reminiscent of Henry James. Many continued to compare her to George Eliot. The *Boston Globe* asserted that *For the Major* was a "work of genius" and that "of all American writers of fiction, Miss Woolson may easily become the novelist laureate," a line the Harpers would quote in advertisements for the rest of her career. The *New York Times* called her "the most promising of our women novelists." As Woolson had predicted, however, *For the Major* was not a popular book. It sold only a tenth as well as *Anne*—under 6,000 copies.[43]

For the Major is in some ways a perfect local-color novel in its depiction of the peculiarities of a small, isolated mountain community near Asheville. The novella is a sensitive, economic rendering of village life and one woman's poignant struggle to keep her age and experience hidden from her husband. Madam Carroll has dyed her hair, worn makeup, and pretended to be a young woman not for her own sake but for that of her husband, Major Carroll, who is growing senile. As Madam Carroll explains, she allowed the Major to think her young and ignorant of the world to win his love. As time passed she wondered, "[W]ould he continue to love me if he should know that instead of being the youthful little woman barely twenty-three, I was over thirty-five? that instead of being inexperienced, unacquainted with the dark side of life, I knew all, had been through all?" At the time of their meeting, she had been a destitute woman whose husband had killed a man and fled with their son. When the major appeared and loved her for her "little doll-like face and curls," she gratefully accepted his offer of marriage, believing her husband and son to have died during the attempt to capture them. Thereafter she maintained the façade out of love for the major, she claims, although certainly also out of fear of losing him.[44]

The crisis in the story comes when her son, who has survived and grown into adulthood, comes to her, penniless and dying. She does all in her power to care for him secretly. The real revelation comes near the end when, after the major no longer recognizes his wife, she is finally able to give up her performance. She stops curling her hair and pulls it back to reveal the crow's feet around her eyes and the tiny wrinkles crisscrossing her face. She stops wearing pink-bowed gowns and dons plain black dresses. She also stops affecting "all the changing inflections and gestures, the pretty little manner and attitudes" that had made her seem the ideal southern lady.[45] She can now, with relief, simply be herself.

Read in light of the stories Woolson had written in the preceding two years, *For the Major* provides a rather startling exposé of the duplicities that marriage demanded of women. In Woolson's fiction, women realize that they must play the roles men want to see them in, if they are to win men's affection. Katharine Winthrop in "Château" states this explicitly when she taunts John Ford, telling him that she "had only to pretend a little, to pretend to be the acquiescent creature you admire, and I could have turned you round my little finger."[46]

Although Woolson began *For the Major* while still mourning the loss of her mother, when she came to complete the novel two and a half years later, the masks she adopted in her own friendship with James must have occurred to her as well. The letters she wrote to him in the first three years of their friendship suggest in a myriad of ways that she was diminishing herself for him—repeatedly referring to her work as "small" or "little"—just as Isabel Archer did when she first met Osmond: "She had effaced herself when he first knew her; she made herself small, pretending there was less of her than there really was."[47] Isabel regrets her unwitting deception, for when Osmond finds out how big her ideas and sense of self are, he hates her for it. Woolson had to wonder what would happen if she allowed James to see all of her.

Above all, she worried that he would ridicule or rebuff her the way he had other women writers. "[Y]ou do not want to know the little literary women," she told him. "Only the great ones—like George Eliot." Where did that leave her? She tried to assure him that she did "not come in as a literary woman at all." Instead, she wanted him to think of her "as a sort of—of admiring aunt," despite being only three years older. Her hesitation conveys her uncertainty about how to define their relationship. He had been extremely kind to her in Florence, had singled her out for a private visit in Rome when he avoided meeting another woman writer, and had become a rather faithful correspondent, sending her his photo and a copy of *Portrait* inscribed "Constance Fenimore Woolson from her friend and servant. Henry James."[48] But she doubted his ability to accept both the woman and the writer.

Was writing a small novel as her follow-up to *Anne* also a way of making herself appear less ambitious and therefore more acceptable? Perhaps. Her choice of an American setting—which she would use for the rest of her novels, although she continued to live in Europe—was a result of seeing the old scenes in her memory more vividly than the new ones in Europe, she once claimed. But it may also have been a way of bowing out of competition with James in the field of the international novel and asserting her own identity as a quintessentially American writer. By claiming a separate sphere in which to pursue her ambitions, she could keep them alive.

9

The Expatriate's Life

ONE DAY in the summer of 1882, Constance came upon a beaver
in the Dresden Zoological Gardens who had pulled together
a few branches in a futile attempt to make a dam. She stopped and
stared at him for a while. He reminded her very much of herself—an
American exile yearning for home and rather pathetically attempting to re-create it. "I suppose there never was a woman so ill-fitted
to do without a home as I am," she wrote to Henry James. "I am
constantly trying to make temporary homes out of the impossible
rooms at hotels & pensions."[1] Her wandering life had become its own
kind of cage.

As the Benedicts planned their return to the United States, there
was some talk of Constance returning as well. Instead, she accompanied them only as far as London. With their departure began a new
period in her life. After so much time alone in Rome, Engelberg, and
Sorrento, she entered more fully into expatriate society. "Everybody
I knew, or have ever heard of, seems to be [in London] now!" she
declared to Sam.[2] John and Clara Hay, William Dean Howells and
his wife, as well as various friends from Cleveland were all in town.

When everyone left for the winter, Constance followed the Hays to Paris, where James had just arrived from the countryside. Constance found "a quiet little place" where she could take meals in her own parlor. It was her first real glimpse of Paris, and although the weather was dreary, she enjoyed herself immensely.[3] Whatever time she spent with James appears to have been brief. However, the trip was memorable for another reason. It was her first encounter with Hay's close friend, the American geologist Clarence King.

By all accounts, everyone—from miners to royalty—fell under King's spell. He was often described in superlatives. James called him "the most delightful man in the world," and Hay dubbed him an "exquisite wit, . . . one of the greatest savants of his time."[4] King's book *Mountaineering in the Sierra Nevada*, published in 1872, combined the soul of a poet with the bravado of a mountain climber and made him a national icon. He was the first director of the U.S. Geological Survey and the foremost explorer of the mountainous West. (He named Mount Whitney, the highest peak in the continental United States.) King was strikingly handsome as well, with a brown beard, close-cut hair, and sharp hazel eyes. He was not tall—only five feet six—but had a commanding presence.

Woolson shared many mutual friends with King, among them Hay, Howells, Stedman, and James. Hay hoped to find the inveterate bachelor a wife and appears to have set his hopes on Woolson. They certainly had a lot in common: a fondness for grand mountains and wild places, a love of rowing, a peripatetic lifestyle, a preference for realism in literature and art, and, sadly, struggles with depression. Constance, however, wasn't King's type. He was notorious for pursuing women untainted by education or the trappings of Western civilization, such as the barmaids of London or the native women of Hawaii. He once wrote, "Woman, I am ashamed to say, I like best in the primitive state. Paradise, for me, is still a garden and a primaeval woman." He would soon secretly marry an African-American woman and have a family with her, a fact his friends did not learn about until after his death.[5]

Constance met King in Paris one December evening and would

many years later remember him as "one of the most agreeable men I have ever known." He was "exquisitely <u>kind</u>," she recalled. "He took me to the Comedie Francaise, with the Hays, & his sister, & I was much touched by his thoughtfulness." Constance loved the theater, but it made her uncomfortable. She could find herself stranded on an island of silence as the audience erupted in laughter. King, with his characteristic attentiveness, sat next to her and repeated the actors' words. After that night, Hay wrote to his friend Henry Adams that Woolson, "that very clever person, to whom men are a vain show— loved [King] at sight and talks of nothing else."[6] She had joined the band of the smitten.

King had promised to take Woolson to the Louvre, but she lost sight of him. Her feelings were "divided between liking and disappointment."[7] King no doubt reminded Woolson of Zeph Spalding and the adventuring male characters in her stories of the 1870s. He was a bracing wind all the way from the mythical American West. She would soon find herself caught up in a much stronger current, however.

THE WHIRL OF SOCIETY

After Paris, Constance returned to Florence and her old pension, the Casa Molini. Settling again into her writing routine and taking most of her meals in her room, she felt "at home." She declined most invitations. She didn't feel "strong enough to take much part in Society, or go out much, and do writing-work at the same time," so she saved the "best" of herself for her writing.[8]

Her peaceful seclusion did not last, however, due to the arrival of William Dean Howells and his family. Whatever reservations she had about Howells were put aside as she came to know him well for the first time. As one of America's foremost novelists, Howells received many invitations and was pursued mercilessly by the city's "lion-hunters." Soon the invitations started arriving for Woolson as well. She later explained to James, with her tendency to trivialize, "The same fate that

William Dean Howells, novelist and editor of the *Atlantic Monthly*. Woolson became close to him and his family during their visit to Italy in 1882–83. Photograph circa 1880. (Courtesy of Special Collections, Fine Arts Library, Harvard University)

befell the great masculine Lion, befell the very little feminine one— though on a <u>much</u> smaller scale."[9]

Before long, Woolson's days were full of visits and parties. She had so many friends in town and made so many new acquaintances that she set her own day to accept calls. Besides Howells and his wife and daughter, with whom she became very friendly, there were also the Hays, King's sister, and her old friends from Rome, Lieutenant Commander Caspar Goodrich and his wife, who asked Constance to be godmother to their new son, Wolseley. He was a nice boy, she told Sam, but she regretted "wandering about the world, standing godmother to strange children" when Sam had a new baby in Cleveland.[10]

Florentine society was also full of expatriate artists and writers whom Woolson befriended. There was Violet Paget (pen name Vernon Lee), whom James thought "a most astounding female" with "a prodigious cerebration," and her friend, the poet Agnes Mary Robinson. She also befriended Mrs. Launt Thompson, a writer and the wife of an American sculptor, and Eleanor Poynter, an English novelist and sister of the painter Sir Edward Poynter. Woolson was particularly fond of Miss Poynter, finding her "very quiet" and "appreciative." Most of society overwhelmed her, however, generally reminding her of a "picture of wraiths & shades being swept round in a great, misty, crowded circle, by some bewildering & never-ceasing wind."[11]

Constance was more at home with a group of men and women she met three times a week for six-to-eight-mile hikes in the hills surrounding Florence. On one of those hills, Bellosguardo, Constance met Miss Louisa Greenough (a sister of the sculptor Horatio), who lived next to friends of Henry James in the Villa Castellani, the model for Osmond's home in *The Portrait of a Lady*. Astonishingly, Louisa Greenough, born around 1809, had known James Fenimore Cooper during his brief residence in a neighboring villa in the 1820s and was delighted to meet his relation. Frequent invitations addressed to Miss Fenimore Woolson made their way down the hill.[12]

However much Constance complained about Florentine "society," it was not entirely disagreeable to her. She found that her age and occupation as a writer made her much respected, a rather novel experience for her. Women seemingly past their prime were not "shelved" as they were at home but were "important, considered." Society, however, threatened to consume all of her time. She simply could not "be going out to lunches, & dinners, and evening-companies" and continue her writing.[13] The "best" of herself was being siphoned off gradually but surely.

In the spring, Constance fled to Venice, where she was sure to have "no 'calls.'" Although Howells and his family were also there and the dinner parties continued, she considered the smaller Venetian society much more manageable than that in Florence. Ever since a brief visit to Venice in 1881, she had longed to return. She had discovered then that "the perfection of earthly motion is a gondola" and decided that the "Floating City" was her ideal place.[14]

Woolson found rooms in the Palazzo Gritti-Swift, just above the English art historian John Addington Symonds, where she could see from her arched windows the busy Grand Canal, the Church of Santa Maria della Salute, the pink-hued campanile of San Giorgio, and the boats docked at the Riva Degli Schiavone. In the late afternoons she floated on the canals or enjoyed losing her way in the winding streets. She was starting to wonder, she wrote to James, "whether the end of the riddle of my existence may not be, after all, to live here, & die here."[15]

Shortly after she arrived in Venice, she received a letter from James, who had gone to America after the death of his father. "[Y]ou have added much to the pleasure of my summer by writing as you have," she replied. He had envisioned between them more talks "against an Italian church-wall," but she asked him to leave out such images in the future, complaining that "there has never been but that one short time (three years ago—in Florence) when you seem disposed for that sort of thing. How many times have I seen you, in the long months that make up three long years?" He had as yet no plans for a return to Europe. He asked her to give him "'a picture'—to keep [him] 'going.'"[16]

She happily obliged, setting in front of him sumptuous visions of Venice and then inviting him mentally into her apartment, where she would make him a cup of weak tea, as he liked it, and invite him to sit on the plush sofa from which he could see out beyond the Grand Canal to the lagoon. She offered him her "infinite" "charity," as he had called it. She preferred to name it "gratitude," not for him personally, but for his writings, which "voice for me—as nothing else ever has—my own feelings; those that are so deep—so a part of me, that I can not express them, & do not try to." She was reminded of how Hay had said in Florence that wherever his friend King was, "there is my true country, my real home." She had said the same thing once to Stedman about Rome. If she could not have a literal home, she found it instead in James's books, in which she felt her innermost self uncannily reflected. A few lines later, she implicitly contrasted herself to the wives of their friends Hay and Howells. Mrs. Hay, James had complained, "expressed herself with a singular lack of cultivation." Now Constance commented on how Mrs. Howells was consumed by "[s]mall feminine malice, & everlasting little jealousies."[17] Constance was a very different sort of woman, she subtly conveyed to him, one who could appreciate his work and enter into his plans for future writing with full comprehension.

This letter also suggests a growing appreciation for James the man. She admired his decision to remain in America after his father's death for the sake of his sister, who was "now, save for you, left alone." Such a gesture meant a lot to her, also single and alone in the world. "That you are doing this only confirmed my idea of you—that you are, really, the kindest hearted man I know,—though this is not, perhaps, the outside opinion about you." He was starting to look less like the self-centered author she had first glimpsed. The two letters Woolson wrote to James during her stay in Venice clearly show her venturing into a deeper intimacy, one that the tone of his letter from America had called forth. Although the common perception of James is that he was reserved and aloof, in reality he could be very warm and affectionate. Clearly he had swept away the embarrassment Woolson felt over telling him of her success with *Anne*. Her last letter to him from Venice concludes, "The lagoons, the Piazzetta, & the little still canals all send their love to you. They wish you were here. And so do I."[18]

As the summer approached and the visitors began to pack their bags, Constance wrote in Winnie Howells's autograph book "[Venice] is my 'Xanadu.'—But not for always; Xanadu never lasts, you know!"[19] She stayed on until the seventh of July, leaving finally after a slight illness made her seek out cooler climes and fresher air. Her final weeks in Venice were also tainted by the recent death of her godson, Wolseley Goodrich, whose parents had been staying there as well. Her story "In Venice," published the year before, had presciently portrayed a child's death in the water city. As magically beautiful as Venice was, for Woolson it was already associated with death.

SUFFERING SO PITEOUS

After leaving Venice, Constance made her way first to Engelberg and then back to Baden-Baden, where she met her old friend Jane Carter and her children, Mary, Grace, and Averell. Constance was delighted to renew their old closeness. Mary was now twenty-one, Grace nineteen, and Averell, another godson to Constance, fourteen. Jane had brought her children to Europe in the hopes of breaking off Mary's engagement to a man who reminded Jane of her own ill-fated marriage to Lawson Carter, which had ended with his suicide in 1869. Constance became quite attached to the emotionally fragile Mary, perhaps recognizing some of her own moodiness and sensitivity in her. After the family left Baden-Baden, Constance wrote to Mary of the final gaieties of "the season," recalling all they had done together: the musical evenings, races, walks up the hills to the ruins of Hohenbaden Castle, and royalty-watching.[20]

Constance was virtually alone in Baden-Baden when news arrived of a family tragedy. Her brother Charlie had died on August 20, 1883, in Los Angeles. According to county records, the cause of death was "suicide by poison."[21] Constance collapsed from the shock.

Charlie had seemed to be doing better. Afraid of another breakdown from working too hard in a cramped office, he had bought some farmland the year before with the help of the Mathers and possibly Connie and Clara. At the beginning of 1883, Constance reported that Charlie had been writing to her regularly. He was disheartened by the dreary winter, and she was concerned about how well the farm would do in the next season.[22] But there was no cause for alarm. When summer came, he sank further, despite the California sunshine and promise of the coming harvest.

This time Charlie did not reach out to Constance. Instead, he kept "a sort of diary" over the summer. It appears that as he prepared to take his life, he mailed it to her. Charlie's diary, she told Sam, "showed suffering so piteous that it broke my heart. I cannot imagine any suffering greater than his was, at the last."[23] After reading the diary, she destroyed it, as he had wished. But his agony imprinted itself on her mind. It would find its way at times into her writing, mingling with her own silent suffering.

The revelation of Charlie's torment and suicide plunged Constance into her first deep depression since her mother's death. She told Sam she had never suffered so much in her life. Charlie's death so far away had made her "perfectly desolate, &, for a time, it seemed to me that I

The only known photograph of Charlie Woolson. His death shortly before his thirty-seventh birthday was devastating to Constance. (The Western Reserve Historical Society)

cd. not rally from the depression it caused; & that it was hardly worth while to try." Physically, she was also suffering from a series of painful ailments. She could hear her father's voice telling her to "[k]eep a stiff upper lip." Over time it began to drown out Charlie's final cries. But it would take months for her to regain courage enough to face even the simplest of tasks.[24]

After being paralyzed for weeks, unsure where to go next, she decided on London, arriving in October and planning to stay through the winter. She had long been drawn to its culture, history, literature, and landscape and had hoped she could spend part of every year there while she was abroad. But everyone seems to have discouraged her, worried that the dark, foggy days and cold, damp weather would be detrimental to her health and emotional state. Only Jane Carter was supportive, advising her to give it a try.[25]

To her delight, London was warmer than Menton had been and the houses more properly heated. She enjoyed the homey comforts of England. And the darkness didn't bother her; it was cold she feared.

She was lucky. According to James, it was the "most beautiful winter I have known in England—fogless and frostless." In the middle of January, the temperature rose into the fifties.[26]

James had returned to London on the first of September, and his presence was probably another reason Woolson chose London. She had glimpsed a tenderness in his last letters and probably wondered if he could be a harbor in her emotional storm. There was no other friend in Europe just then she could turn to. She would not only give London a try, but James as well.

Seeing the crisis she was in, he did not turn away. In fact, during the eight months she lived in London, the two friends saw each other often and began what would be one of the closest relationships for either of them outside of their families. So close was it that they would one day decide to destroy their letters to each other, hers from Venice being the last to have survived. We can only piece their friendship together now from fragmented, often veiled references in their letters to others.

James told his good friend Lizzie Boott that if she came to London he could "make a place" for her, "in spite of the fact that Costanza has just arrived," suggesting Constance occupied the principal place just then. Later that winter James wrote to Howells of Woolson, whom he claimed to see "at discreet intervals": "She is a very intelligent woman, and understands when she is spoken to; a peculiarity I prize, as I find it more and more rare." Only a few weeks earlier, Woolson had indicated to Sam that James visited her "now & then," while her neighbor noted to John Hay that James came "frequently" to call on her.[27]

Her neighbors were French Ensor Chadwick, naval attaché for the American Legation in London, and his wife, whom Constance had met in Florence (they were friends of the Hays and Goodriches). They had found her an apartment below theirs in Sloane Street, South Kensington, and were "kindness itself," Constance informed Sam. "They have done everything they cd. think of to add to my comfort & keep me from too much loneliness."[28]

Unfortunately, though, it seems the Chadwicks were not able to help her recover from her depression. As she explained to Hay, whose health had also not been good, Chadwick was "one of the best fellows in the world," but he couldn't understand the kind of grief and illness she and Hay endured. "I really think that he believes I cd. have got better sooner, if I had only tried!" she complained. Hay understood, however, "the illness that hangs on, & baffles effort, & takes the heart out of a man." Just as she had with Paul Hamilton Hayne many years before, she now found a companion in her depression, but Hay was far away. James was nearer and had a good deal of experience with depression, having witnessed his brother William's battle with it in 1869–1870. He was no stranger to depressive episodes and was experiencing his own "pronounced state of melancholy" that winter after the deaths of his father and good friend Ivan Turgenev, the Russian writer.[29] His younger brother Wilky, who, like Charlie, had failed to fulfill his early promise, was also declining rapidly.

A letter James wrote a few months later to his friend Grace Norton indicates how much he understood the kind of psychic crisis Constance was experiencing. He told Grace, "You are not isolated, verily, in such states of feeling as this—that is, in the sense that you appear to make all the misery of mankind your own." Like Constance, Grace was prone to absorb the suffering of others and question the value of a life so filled with pain. In response, James was determined to speak "with the voice of stoicism." Even in the absence of religious faith, he believed, "we can go on living for the reason that (always of course up to a certain point) life is the most valuable thing we know anything about and it is therefore presumptively a great mistake to surrender it while there is any yet left in the cup." He had faith ultimately in the "illimitable power" of human consciousness. He begged Grace to "remember that every life is a special problem which is not yours but another's, and content yourself with the terrible algebra of your own. Don't melt too much into the universe, but be as solid and dense and fixed as you can. . . . Sorrow comes in great waves . . . and we know that if it is strong we are stronger, inasmuch as it passes and we remain."[30]

Far from the uncomprehending admonition simply to get well that Chadwick had offered Woolson, James's advice acknowledged the depth of his friend's pain. So must he have conveyed to Woolson a solidarity in suffering that would have been immensely comforting at a time when she felt alone in the world. It was precisely what she needed to separate herself from Charlie's troubles and find purpose again in her work—that "illimitable power" of consciousness that was the province of the writer. Yet, in her writing as well as in her life, she found it hard to let the troubles of others wash over her.

By January Constance told Sam, "I have conquered, & got a firm hold of myself again." She had fought her way back to "the interest I was full of last summer" and "the habit of daily work." When Hay came over in May, he was pleased to report to his brother-in-law Sam that he and Constance had had many talks and that she was "busily engaged upon her new novel with all the energy of recovered health and spirits." She relished the opportunity to discuss literature with Hay and welcomed him to the band of novelists. His anonymous novel *The Bread-Winners*, his first, had just finished its run in *The Century*. She had written to him in January, "I am terribly alone in my literary work. There seems to be no one for me to turn to. It is true that there are only two or three to whom I wd. turn!"[31] James would soon become one.

Less than a month later, James indicated that he was reading her work, writing to Howells that he was "the only English novelist I read (except Miss Woolson)." James was used to telling his novelist friends what he thought of their work. Many of them trembled to hear his opinions—"I am afraid I have a certain reputation for being censorious and cynical," he wrote to the writer Mrs. Humphry Ward.[32] Woolson, however, had often asked for frank criticism and found few who would provide it. Constructive criticism encouraged her to aim ever higher, as the *Appletons'* review of *Two Women* had done. It is probably no coincidence that she began to write the most ambitious novel of her career as James began to read her work.

During Hay's visit in May, Woolson saw him often and finally had the chance to ask his advice on publishing matters. He urged her to request more money for the serial rights of her new novel, but she wasn't sure she would dare to. King was also in London and had been for months. Woolson was disappointed he had not called on her.

Finally he did. "One visit was all I required to revert comfortably to my old opinion of him,—which was superlative," she told Hay. But one visit was all she would have. She felt as if he had "dropped" her, she complained to Hay, who "comforted [her] by the disclosure that he had dropped, in the same easy way, two Duchesses and the Prince of Wales."[33]

During the spring, when she wasn't writing she "prowl[ed] about this dear, dusky old town." She found all of the sites associated with Thackeray and Dickens and enjoyed the galleries.[34] In June, the Benedicts returned, this time with Kate Mather. Constance secured rooms on Portman Square near Hyde Park and found herself surrounded by young women—not only her two nieces, but also the Carter girls, Mary and Grace (with their mother, Jane), as well as Mary's friend, Daisy, whose real name was Juliette Gordon Low (the future founder of the Girl Scouts).

In July, while the others went to Germany, Constance moved just outside of London to Hampstead, a lovely, hilly town where she could enjoy cooler weather and get some work done high above the London smoke and smog. James visited her often there and wrote to Lizzie Boott that Woolson was "a most excellent reasonable woman, . . . I like and esteem her exceedingly." He was impressed to find her so "absorbed in her work."[35]

Her stay in Hampstead was short, however. Her rooms were too small and damp, so she went back to London, where the summer heat soon overwhelmed her. James was in Dover just then, finding the quiet conducive to work. Constance decided to pack her bags and head for the white cliffs as well.[36] This was the first of their many secret rendezvous. Neither mentioned the presence of the other in their letters. Unmarried as they both were, such meetings could invite scandal. Although James had come to Dover to work, he apparently didn't mind having the hardworking Woolson there as well. They both understood that the other needed time to write and thus were settling into an easy companionship.

Near the end of September, as James resettled in London, Woolson moved to the town of Salisbury, where she spent two blissful, solitary months finishing her new novel. Her time there was one of her happiest abroad. She had always "dream[ed] of spending a few weeks in an English Cathedral town." Her landlord, one of the pulpit vergers, secured her a seat in the thirteenth-century cathedral's choir. She often stayed after services to let the great organ's rumbling tones wash over her.[37]

Her mornings were spent hard at work in her rooms, which looked out over the garden and a beamed house "as old as Shakespeare's time." In the afternoons, she walked into the countryside in search of Norman or medieval churches. On her way home in the cool evenings, she enjoyed spying through glowing windows the cozy scenes of clergymen and their families busy with their tea.[38] Then she happily returned to her rooms for her own tea and read or wrote letters by gaslight.

On September 29, James came down from London, the first time he made a special trip to see her. The pair hired a carriage to take them to Stonehenge. Buffeted by a cold wind, they wandered underneath the towering stones in silence. On the way back to Salisbury, their carriage pulled off into a ditch, where they cowered for half an hour while the wind roared overhead. Back in her lodgings the two dined and then went to a local theater for a rendition of Richard Sheridan's society farce *A School for Scandal.*[39]

EAST ANGELS

In January 1885, Woolson's new novel began to appear in *Harper's* magazine, running concurrently with Howells's *Indian Summer.* She resented the fact, fearing his work would overshadow hers. *East Angels* was her longest novel at six hundred pages. It was, in fact, the longest novel published in *Harper's* thirty-five-year history. Her decision to write a long work was motivated in part by economic need. It was becoming clear that she would have to produce a long novel every two to three years to support herself sufficiently. Her royalties in 1883 had been over $2,000 (nearly $50,000 in today's money). By 1885, they were only $200 (about $5,000 today). Taking Hay's advice, she had asked for a raise for the serialization of *East Angels*, requesting $3,500 (today, $87,500). The Harpers accepted her terms.[40]

If Woolson had put all of her youthful self into *Anne*, she put all of her adult ambitions into *East Angels*. It is her most fully executed realist novel in its analysis of character and motivation. In *East Angels*, she tested her interest in the analytical novel. Some have noted this novel's affinity to James's works, despite its exotic Florida setting, and seen it as an answer to *The Portrait of a Lady*.[41] Woolson had also drawn from one of his greatest influences, Ivan Turgenev, whose works she had grown to love. She learned from him, as James had, to let her plot grow organically from her characters. In writing *East Angels*, she wasn't so much choosing sides in the literary debates then raging as she was experimenting with how far she could take the analytical mode. The result is a work that deserves to be read alongside James's *Portrait*.

The plot is easily told: a group of northerners settles near St. Augustine, and two of them—Margaret Harold and Evert Winthrop—fall in love. However, Margaret is married to Evert's cousin, who has abandoned her, and she will not divorce him. James heartily approved of the work, writing, "[W]hat is most substantial to me in the book is the writer's . . . general attitude of watching life, waiting upon it, and trying to catch it in the fact. . . . [A]rtistically, she has had a fruitful instinct in seeing the novel as a picture of the actual, of the characteristic—a study of human types and passions, of the evolution of personal relations." While James had brilliantly dissected his characters' consciousness, Woolson was after their hearts as well, believing the drama of inner life incomplete without a close examination of characters' emotional states. She was, in a way, applying the new analytical method to the timeless themes of literature, those of the Greeks, Shakespeare, and the Romantics. After a long period in which the genuine expression of emotion had been highly valued, however, the late nineteenth century was becoming increasingly suspicious of it, even demanding its suppression. As the novelist Frances Hodgson Burnett put it in in 1883, "There is a fashion in emotions as in everything else. . . . And sentiment is 'out'" as is "grief." On the other hand, "making light of things" was in.[42] *East Angels*, like so much of Woolson's fiction, charts this transition from a Romantic world of feelings to a modern world of restraint. The shift away from the direct examination of emotions would in fact become central to the invention of modern literature, which would, following particularly in James's footsteps, concern itself with inner consciousness.

Woolson had reproved James for not showing readers whether his heroines truly loved. There had been no evidence in Isabel of the kind of "heart-breaking, insupportable, killing grief" that surely would have followed her discovery of Osmond's perfidy, had she loved him. Almost as if Woolson were showing James how it could be done, she proceeded to portray, with the methods of a realist, the "killing grief" of a woman who loves deeply but silently. Much of the pathos of *East Angels* derives from the way its heroine, Margaret Harold, must constantly repress her emotions, as her era demands. What others perceive as Margaret's coldness and self-righteousness is really a desperate attempt to maintain self-control. "We go through life," she tells the younger Garda, "more than half of us—women, I mean—obliged always to conceal our real feelings."[43] While Garda refuses to guard her feelings, Margaret hides her face whenever she is near Evert Winthrop. She escapes his presence as quickly as she can. Like her creator, she seeks out solitude, particularly in nature, as the only safe place where she can drop her mask and allow her face to express the feelings within.

Whether or not Margaret is right to hide her feelings and then to refuse to act on them when Winthrop forces them out of her is not the point of the book (although this would be the point on which critics fixated). The point is simply for the reader to understand Margaret and to empathize with her. While to other characters she is so "good," particularly when she chooses to stay with her negligent, philandering husband, Woolson shows us the great strain and almost superhuman effort that goes into her self-sacrifice, exposing the costs of women's inability to reveal their true selves. Once, near the end, Margaret expresses bitterness about repressing her feelings. She challenges Winthrop, who is trying to lure her away: "You talk about freedom . . . what do *you* know of slavery? That is what I have been for years—

a slave. Oh, to be somewhere! . . . *anywhere* where I can breathe and think as I please—as I really am! Do you want me to die without ever having been myself—my real self—for even one day?" Winthrop later asks her, "[D]o you wish to die without ever having lived?" He offers her love and life, but Margaret steadfastly refuses, viewing divorce as a great wrong (as Isabel Archer had). In the struggle between Winthrop and Margaret, he threatens to force her acquiescence by overpowering her, but she looks at him, her eyes "full of an indomitable refusal," and tells him, "I shall never yield."[44] Maintaining her self-control is the only way she can maintain her self-worth.

Writing *East Angels* drained Woolson physically and emotionally. After the serial version was finished, she wrote to Hay, "[O]ne novel takes <u>my</u> entire strength, & robs me of almost life itself! I am months-recovering." Her writing process was remarkably arduous. She first wrote a detailed version of the entire plot, then a thorough description of each character, and finally exhaustive accounts of each scene with numerous pages of conversation, much of which never made it into the final book. In fact, all of this prewriting was many times longer than the actual book. To transform it into a coherent novel, she had to piece together the various parts, condense scenes and dialogue, and make them fit into the prescribed space allotted in each issue of the magazine. All of this could take up to two years. As she later explained to her niece Kate, "I don't suppose any of you realize the amount of time and thought I give to each page of my novels; every character, every <u>word</u> of speech, and of description is thought of, literally, for years before it is written out for the final time. I do it over and over; and read it aloud to myself; and lie awake and think of it all night. It takes such entire possession of me that when, at last, a book is done, I am pretty nearly done myself."[45]

Throughout the lengthy, painstaking process, she also poured her emotional life into her work. "Nothing is true or effective which is not drawn from the heart or experience of the writer," she wrote in a journal she titled "Mottoes, Maxims, & Reflections." When asked to respond to a debate about whether or not writers must be moved to tears in order to similarly move their readers, Woolson responded affirmatively, citing "the account of the way George Eliot's books 'ploughed into her' [and] the description of Tourguenieff . . . as pale, feverish, so changed that he looked like a dying man, because the personages of one of his tales had taken such possession of him that he was unable to sleep."[46]

While she was writing *East Angels*, a pitiful tone entered into her letters, not unlike Winthrop's words to Margaret during one of their final meetings: we "have nothing—[we] are parched and lonely and starved." In the summer that she began working on the book, she claimed to be "mournful, and lonely." In January, as she returned to work after her illness, she was again "lonely, & not much entertained with the spectacle of daily life." Despite the visits of Clara, her two nieces, and the Carters, she felt increasingly as if her circle of family and friends was narrowing.[47] She openly envied those with spouses and children and began portraying herself as starved for affection and human interest. It was as if Margaret's fate and her own were entwined.

Writing *East Angels* had also made Woolson homesick for Florida. She declared to Hay, "[T]here is not a twig, or flower, described in 'East Angels' that is not literally 'from life.'" She would move back tomorrow if she could get a small house in St. Augustine.[48] When the widower of her old St. Augustine friend Mrs. Washington told her he was saving six acres twenty miles south of the city for her, she called it "East Angels" and began making vague plans to build a cottage and retire there in ten years or so.

The publication of *George Eliot's Life as Related in Her Letters and Journals*, which Woolson read not long after she finished *East Angels*, revived her feelings of loneliness and resentment toward those who basked in an atmosphere of love and devotion. While in London she had learned all about Eliot and Lewes's marriage in practice if not in fact (he was unable to divorce his wife) and her feelings about her old idol had changed. She did not begrudge Eliot the right to live with Lewes, but she was clearly jealous of the steadfast love they shared: "[S]he had one of the easiest, most indulged and 'petted' lives that I have ever known or heard of. . . . True, she earned the money for two, and she worked very hard. But how many, many women would be glad to do the same through all of their lives if their reward was such a devoted love as that!" What Woolson objected to was "that after getting and having to the full all she craved, then she began to pose as a teacher for others! She began to preach the virtues she had not for one moment practised in her own life."[49] Woolson could not be accused of any such hypocrisy. She practiced the virtue of self-renunciation as vigorously as Margaret Harold did. And she feared she would one day die, like Margaret, without having fully lived.

MEETING ALICE

After a dismally cold winter in Vienna with the Benedicts, Constance returned to England, moving this time to the Isle of Wight. She was relieved to be back in England, but a week after her arrival she was struck with a "troublesome affection of the nerve of the spine" that she blamed on writing too much. She could not use her hands at all. She became anxious and depressed and confessed to Mary Carter that she broke down and cried at times.[50]

Woolson had this photograph taken while she was staying in Leamington and unable to write. (The Western Reserve Historical Society)

The saline baths of Leamington, where she soon moved with Clara and Clare, relieved her pain, but she still could not write much. The three made excursions in the vicinity to places like Stratford-upon-Avon and Oxford, with which she immediately fell in love. After her sister and niece sailed home in September, Constance occupied herself by strolling through the lush gardens of nearby Warwick Castle and reading English memoirs and biographies. England felt like home, yet she was thoroughly worn out and irritable. Finally she consulted Dr. Eardley Wilmot, whose treatment, which probably utilized the Leamington spa waters, enabled her to start writing again.[51] She was desperate to get back to work; the Harpers were awaiting the book revisions of *East Angels*.

Although Woolson had earlier planned to spend the winter in Venice or Florence, she headed to London, returning to her old lodgings in Portman Square. James may have suggested the move. He was a mile away in Piccadilly. He gave her a copy of *The Bostonians* that winter and introduced her to his sister, Alice, and her companion, Katharine Loring, who lived five minutes from him.[52] For years Alice had struggled to maintain her mental and physical health. She had stayed at asylums, received electrotherapy treatments, sought out renowned doctors in New York, and traveled to Europe in hopes of improving her condition. With both parents now dead and Henry and Katharine devoted to her care, she made a new home for herself, primarily in London and later in Leamington.

The apparent cause of Alice's suffering was the struggle between her fierce will and the great effort to suppress her intense feelings, the precise conflict Woolson had described in her character Margaret Harold, who also fell ill when her emotions got the better of her. Alice thought of herself as "an emotional volcano within, with the outward reverberation of a mouse and the physical significance of a chip of lead pencil." Her oldest brother, William, called her "bottled lightning."[53] Alice and Constance were in some ways twins under the skin. The great difference between them was that Constance had found a vocation and an outlet for her emotions, while Alice was effectively

Alice James, Henry James's sister, whom Woolson came to know in London, during the winter of 1885–86. (Correspondence and Journals of Henry James Jr. and Other Family Papers, MS Am 1094 [2247, f.44.4], by permission of the Houghton Library, Harvard University)

silenced by her overbearing father and highly accomplished two older brothers. In 1889, three years after meeting Constance, Alice would begin to find her voice by writing the diary that would be her life's great work.

In the winter of 1885–1886 Constance quickly became "[o]ne of Alice's preferred new friends." However, they were also rivals for Henry's attention. Alice's jealousy toward her brothers' female friends could be severe. When William announced his engagement in 1878, Alice took to her bed for months, "on the verge of insanity and suicide," as her father put it. In the case of Henry's relationship with Constance, Alice complained to family members of his "flirting" and "galavanting [*sic*]" with her. In the years ahead, Constance would be careful to downplay the closeness of her relationship with Henry. In one letter, the only one she wrote to Alice that has survived (and only in fragments), she makes sure to point out that the letter she has just received from Henry, who was ill in Venice, was only "a few scribbled lines," lest Alice feel aggrieved at not having heard from him herself.[54] Nonetheless, frequent notes were exchanged between the two friends in the coming years, and Woolson would also develop a warm relationship with Katharine Loring.

That winter, the day after Christmas, Woolson received a note from Henry James informing her of the death of Clover Adams, wife of Henry Adams and close friend of the Hays. She had been a witty, intelligent woman—a "perfect Voltaire in petticoats," in James's words—who had found few opportunities for intellectual stimulation. Upon hearing the news, Woolson immediately wrote to the Hays, describing Clover's death as "sudden." Although the exact cause of her death was a well-guarded secret, James learned of it afterward and surely passed the news on to Constance. Clover had swallowed photo-processing chemicals, unable to recover from the death of her father and, as James said, "succumb[ing] to hereditary melancholy."[55] It must have reminded Woolson of her brother's suicide. It was also another instance of the "killing griefs" that could rob one of the will to live.

The winter was inauspicious in other ways as well. London was experiencing rampant unemployment that led to riots. One day in February, Woolson was caught up in a mob making its way down Piccadilly. She escaped unharmed, but the unrest lasted for days. In the dark, cold days of winter, "'Babylon' seemed doomed."[56]

Nonetheless she lingered into the spring to finish the book revisions of *East Angels*, allowing herself to spread out beyond the confinements of its serialized form and perfecting its language. The magazine version of her novels never satisfied her. Only as a book could the novel be realized as she had imagined it. When she finally finished, at the beginning of April, with her eyes, hand, and back completely worn out, she departed for Florence, the city of rebirth.

PART FOUR

The Bellosguardo Years

1886–1889

"And now, for the moment, the wheel seems to have turned round completely. . . . After seventeen years of wandering, I have at last a home of my own. . . . I am supremely happy."

—CONSTANCE FENIMORE WOOLSON

"I was prepared to like [Henry James] from Miss Woolson's description of him and his great kindness and attention to her when she was ill."

—FRANCES HODGSON BURNETT

10

Home Found

WHEN WOOLSON returned to Italy in April 1886, she put the exhausting work on the book revisions of *East Angels* behind her. As her train made its way out of the snow-covered mountains of Switzerland and into Italy, she felt her old longing for life in all of its vividness return. The soothing greenery she had left behind in England could not compete with the visual symphony of painted houses and blue sky that serenaded her in Italy. Stopping for two days in Venice and floating in a gondola along the Grand Canal, she "felt compensated for all [her] years of toil."[1]

Her respite was short-lived, however. As soon as she arrived in Florence at her old pension, the Casa Molini, she was greeted with a telegram from Harper & Brothers, telling her that the manuscript she had so carefully prepared was feared lost. The ship carrying it, the *Oregon*, had collided with another vessel. Without even unpacking her trunks, she wrote nonstop for two weeks, fourteen hours a day. When she finally finished the new manuscript and mailed it, she received a cable telling her that the original had survived after all. Nonetheless, after all the extra work, she felt like a hostage set free. But if she had been exhausted before, she was on the verge of collapse now.[2]

The writer's cramp that had stymied her progress on the book in England was now plaguing her right arm and back. Some writers hired others to help them with their manuscripts. James had a "typewriter"—a person, not a machine—who typed clean copies of his works. However, Woolson, ever careful of her finances, was working entirely on her own, writing each copy by hand.[3] The excessive exertion was beginning to cripple her.

Fortunately, she found relief in Florence, under the care of a new physician, an American named William Wilberforce Baldwin, whom she had first met in Venice in 1883. Over the next two decades, as his fame grew, he would count among his patients Edith Wharton, J. P. Morgan, William Waldorf Astor, Queen Victoria and her daughter Mary, as well as Henry, William, and Alice James. Baldwin would also become one of Woolson's closest friends in Europe. His first treatment involved electrotherapy, which helped. Unfortunately, the relief would last only as long as her respite from writing did. Perhaps more important, she had finally found a doctor who seemed to intuit what she needed after two years of what she felt were incompetent English doctors. Baldwin was famous for empathizing with his patients and listening undividedly to them. He diagnosed the whole patient and understood that not all physical ailments had a tangible cause. He would confirm for Woolson what she had known all along—that the body and the mind were inextricably linked.[4] He would one day become an important ally in her battles against depression. For now he was also a valuable friend who loved to talk about literature as well as medicine.

Free of work, Woolson revisited "one by one, and at [her] leisure, all [her] favorite pictures, statues, churches, and places." She was "such an old resident" of Florence now that she didn't even need her Baedeker.[5] She tried to avoid Florentine society this time around, but she didn't have her writing as an excuse for refusing invitations. Instead, she begged off for health reasons and often stayed in her rooms, reading Tolstoy and Dostoevsky, newly available in French translations.

A COMMUNITY OF ARTISTS

James was worried that Woolson's return to Italy would increase her isolation. Although she knew many people from her earlier stay in Florence, he was aware that her deafness made socializing awkward for her. She needed a good friend, like him, who would sit with her and talk into her ear trumpet, which made conversation easier. He had just the man for her, someone who needed her as much as she needed him—his dear old friend Francis Boott, an American composer who had lived in the Villa Castellani on the hill of Bellosguardo, outside of Florence, for nearly forty years. James had known Boott and his daughter, Lizzie, since his post–Civil War years in Newport. Their close filial relationship inspired his creation of the bond between Osmond and Pansy in *The Portrait of a Lady*. By introducing Woolson to the Bootts, James was also providing a companion for Boott to help fill the void left by his daughter's recent marriage.

In May, James sent off the letter that would change the lives of his two lonely friends: "I wonder, my dear good Francis, whether you will do me rather a favour," he began. "My excellent and amiable friend Constance Fenimore Woolson is in Florence, and I want to pay her your compliment and administer to her some social comfort." Aware that a bachelor introducing an unmarried woman to a widower could be interpreted as having an ulterior motive, he clarified: "though she has not made any sort of request of me touching this proposal (by which I don't mean that I want you to 'propose' to her, either for me or for yourself), I am sure the sight of you would give her joy. She is a deaf and *méticuleuse* old maid—but she is also an excellent and sympathetic being. If Lizzie could take a look at her and attract her to the villa I should be very glad."[6] With this simple letter began the happiest period of Woolson's life since her childhood home had broken up after her father's death. The family to which James introduced her would fulfill her need for connection and companionship more fully than her relationship with James, whom she saw only at random intervals.

Her friendship with them would also cement the two writers' bond through these mutual friends.

The fatherly Francis Boott appears to have called at the Casa Molini as soon as he received James's letter, and shortly afterward Woolson made the trip up to the Villa Castellani, where she also met Lizzie and her new husband, Frank Duveneck, both of whom were artists. The three were so taken with Woolson that they encouraged her to sublease an apartment in the villa, below Miss Louisa Greenough (related to Francis through marriage), whom she knew well from her earlier stay in Florence. Woolson wasn't sure she measured up to the current tenant's idea for a suitable replacement. She tried her best to fit in. "How I wore my best clothes every day; spoke in a whisper; held myself in as 'distinguished' a manner as I could; & pretended that I had 6 or 8 villas at home," she wrote to Sam. Fortunately, she "'passed,' & got in!" Woolson thrilled at the thought of living across the courtyard from her new friends. She envisioned them painting in their garden and herself writing in her own, with the heavenly view laid out below her.[7]

Woolson moved into her new apartment in September, after spending the hot summer months in Geneva, where she barely touched her pen and rested as completely as she could. At the Villa Castellani, she continued to recuperate, writing very few letters. In the evenings, she opened up the doors to the garden, allowing the strong fragrance from the abundance of flowers to fill the room. By the light of the moon she could see the outline of the Villa Montauto's crenellated tower. Hawthorne had stayed there in 1858, and now, during the day, she could watch its shadow move across her garden. She was so delighted with her new residence that she feared "it was almost wickedness!"[8]

Woolson was so content, in fact, that she didn't want to leave Bellosguardo when her sublease expired on January 1. It seemed like fate when she heard that the second floor of the nearby Villa Brichieri would become available in December. Although she had been perennially wary of settling down anywhere, due to the expense and responsibilities of keeping a home, it seemed as if the perfect situation had presented itself. The comparatively small villa stood perched at the brow of the hill, looking down on the domes and campaniles of Florence. For five hundred dollars a year, she could have nine partially furnished rooms and a terrace with a view that took her breath away. To Woolson, for whom a beautiful view was "everything," this was paradise.[9]

The Villa Brichieri was only about two hundred years old, so it didn't boast a chapel, a ghost, or the mysteriously expansive underground cellars and tunnels of the five-hundred-year-old Villa Castellani. But she could manage the expense, she thought. After selling the last of her father's lands in Wisconsin for $1,000, she had given the money to Samuel Mather to invest for her at 6 to 7 percent. She had hoped to hang on to the land and sell it someday for enough money to buy a home in Florida, but her dreams were shattered by the reality of the slow real estate market. By selling, she could take the interest she earned to help finance a home in Italy. She signed a lease on the Villa Brichieri for a year, with an option to renew under the same terms. She

Villa Brichieri, on the hill of Bellosguardo overlooking Florence, where Woolson finally found a home. (Photograph by the author)

hoped to be able to write a new novel there. "I am looking forward to a year of great tranquility, comfort, & hard work," she wrote to Sam. "Heretofore I have often had the last named, without the other two."[10]

The hill of Bellosguardo was a retreat from the world, far enough from Florence that she could avoid its social whirl, high enough that she could breathe the fresh air and find peace in the vast open space before her. After nearly seven years in Europe, she had finally found a home, but she insisted it would be temporary. Further into the future, she looked forward to returning to Florida and settling into the cottage of her dreams.[11]

On Bellosguardo, the circle of artists she formed with the composer Francis Boott and his daughter and son-in-law, the newlywed painters, was not complete without the person who had brought them all together. James, who had been promising a visit throughout the fall, finally said he would come in December. Woolson's lease on her new villa would begin then, but she had the apartment in the Villa Castellani until the end of the year. She wrote to him with a splendid idea—he could take over the lease on her new villa for the first month and have an excellent, quiet place to work. That the Villa Brichieri was so close—a short walk down the hill—made the situation even better. James was adamant that he wanted rest and time to write during his visit. He asked Boott and the Duvenecks not to *"breathe a word of my advent"* because he had no intention of seeing anyone but them and "Fenimore," as he began referring to her when writing to Francis and Lizzie. He wanted Woolson to remain similarly discreet, which she was more than happy to do. She liked being of use, smoothing the way for him to work, while she herself was still recuperating from her novel and writing at a more leisurely pace. He was struck by Woolson's "immense power of devotion (to H.J.!)," he told Lizzie. To Francis he wrote, "It is very good of you to offer to put in *wood*, but I have an idea that Fenimore, whose devotion—like my appreciation of it—is *sans bornes*, has stacked me up a pile with her own hands."[12]

Woolson had not seen James since her departure from London in early April and was eager to see him, but he now had a serious rival for her attention. As he wrote to Boott in November, she was "very difficult to interest," but it was "plain from her letters that <u>you</u> have achieved that secret!" James had at first joked that in asking Boott to meet her he wasn't intending a romantic interest. Three months later, however, he seemed to encourage the prospect, imagining Woolson at Geneva (where she had gone for a few weeks before taking up residence at the Villa Castellani) "in a balcony of the Hôtel National, hanging over the lake and thinking of—you!" He teased Boott in November, after she had moved in, that he had heard from Lizzie and Woolson he was once "again the ornament of Bellosguardo." As James's arrival neared, he expected to hear even more about Woolson's fondness for Boott. Having bored Boott talking about James, she would soon proceed to "bore *me* with *you!*"[13]

Boott was by all accounts a charming man. Photographs show him to be tall and strikingly handsome, with thick white hair and beard. Years later Woolson wrote to him, "Have you ever stopped to count over your blessings (as the Methodists say) of always having been a

Francis Boott became Woolson's closest friend, next to James. (Correspondence and Journals of Henry James Jr. and Other Family Papers, MS Am 1094 [2245, f.5.2], by permission of the Houghton Library, Harvard University)

handsome man, & being one still? Supposing you had had a snub nose? Or thin hair, dull eyes, and a yellow complexion? Wouldn't each day have been much harder?" He was also a sharp dresser. None of her other male friends "approached you in coats & ties," she told him.[14]

Francis Boott, at seventy three, was twenty-seven years her senior. Being with him must have reminded Woolson of the peace and security she had felt with her father. After seeing Boott again, Henry thought him an "old, old man" whose teeth had gone, along with his occupation in life, which had been looking after his daughter. But Woolson saw him as a handsome, considerate man who respected her not only as a genteel spinster but, more important, as an intelligent woman and writer. Having nurtured his daughter's art career for many years, Francis understood a woman's commitment to art in a way few men of his era did. Her later letters to him indicate that he read her stories and novels carefully, showing an interest in how she created them.[15]

It is easy to see from those letters that during the three years Woolson lived at Bellosguardo she grew very attached to him. Although a romance was not out of the question, it was unlikely, considering their age difference, making him a safer object of her affection than James would have been. He was also more available. A third wheel now that his daughter had married, Boott needed a companion, and Woolson liked feeling needed. He kept a respectful distance, however, understanding that her work came first. He wrote her a poem about her name, playing on the confusion many people had between her and her great-uncle James Fenimore Cooper, but stressing the "worldwide fame" she had already achieved.[16] She had come into his life as a respected writer and he wouldn't forget that, however much she fulfilled his need for feminine attention.

THE BOOTTS

Francis Boott was a cultured gentleman in the old-fashioned sense, a Boston Brahmin who had inherited money from his family's cotton mills in Lowell, Massachusetts, but chose to dedicate himself to a life filled with beauty and the arts rather than business. His insatiable yearning for music, theater, and opera went unfulfilled in New England, so after his wife's death in 1847, when Lizzie was eighteen months old, he brought her to Europe (with her nurse) and devoted himself to his musical studies and his daughter's education. Soon father and daughter moved into the Villa Castellani. His friends in Italy included the artist William Wetmore Story and the writers Nathaniel Hawthorne, James Russell Lowell, and Robert and Elizabeth Barrett Browning. Francis set their poems to music, and Lizzie sketched their portraits.[17]

Lizzie's upbringing as a model jeune fille made her one of the most accomplished young women of her day. She could sing, play the piano, speak Italian and French fluently, read German, and, most important to her, draw and paint. Art was her passion, and her father fostered it in every way he could. When her father brought her home to New England after the Civil War (she was nineteen), she awed her Brahmin cousins and the James family with the extent of her knowledge and refinement. William James wrote to a friend, "I never realized before how much a good education . . . added to the charms of a woman." He concluded that his friend should come quickly and meet her "for you know those first class young spinsters do not always keep forever."[18] Lizzie, however, did not marry then. Instead, she pursued her study of art, for which, William noticed, she had a great talent.

But the shy, serious, and almost impossibly refined woman did fall in love. Like many other female art students of the period, she fell for one of her teachers. Frank Duveneck was a rough bohemian from Kentucky who had many admirers among his pupils. Her father strenuously objected to her marrying a penniless artist who, he assumed, was primarily interested in her money, of which there was a considerable amount. Lizzie also feared what marriage would mean to her career. So she broke off her engagement and moved with her father to the United States, where, from 1881 to 1885, she established a successful career.[19]

Finally, however, Lizzie's desires for a family of her own overrode her fears about losing her career, and she was able to negotiate a com-

Lizzie Boott, who had devoted her life to her art, had recently married when Woolson met her. (Correspondence and Journals of Henry James Jr. and Other Family Papers, MS Am 1094 [2245, f.4.1], by permission of the Houghton Library, Harvard University)

promise whereby father, daughter, and husband would live together at the Villa Castellani. She had come to feel that art was no longer fulfilling enough on its own. "I crave human interests in life," she wrote to a friend, seeking approval for what everyone thought was a disastrous decision. "The abstract ones of art are not enough for me." When they married in Paris on March 25, 1886 (a little more than two months before Woolson met them), Lizzie and Frank both signaled their intent to continue their careers, listing their occupations on their marriage certificate as "artiste, peintre."[20]

Their union interested Woolson immensely. Lizzie was nearly forty, only six years younger than she was. By waiting to fulfill her desire for a home and family and putting her art (and her father) first for so many years, Lizzie had found a new solution to the age-old problem of combining love and art—a very modern one, in fact. In none of Woolson's stories about women writers and artists had she been able to imagine a woman who chooses art over love or who puts love on hold while she develops her talent. For her the identities of wife and artist were incompatible. Yet Lizzie was trying to be both. More than that, she was soon expecting a child. She was conducting a grand experiment that few women before her had attempted, and Woolson had a front-row seat to the drama.

Woolson was also fascinated by the other half of this couple. Her niece later wrote that she was "very attracted to Duveneck—both as an artist and as a man." Woolson herself later told Boott, "I am an old lady now, & so I can say that I admire F.D. very much." She was drawn to his "beautiful & powerful" pictures and enjoyed watching him at work. (James had been enamored of Duveneck's art ever since he first saw it in Boston in 1875 and called him an "unsuspected

The wedding photograph of Frank and Elizabeth (Lizzie) Boott Duveneck, in 1886. Their union of art and love was of great interest to Woolson. (Courtesy of the Kenton County Public Library)

genius" in his review for *The Nation*.) Duveneck invited Woolson into his studio several times. She feasted her eyes on his murky, realistic paintings, which had recently given way to brighter canvases and subjects, perhaps under Lizzie's French-trained influence.[21]

Duveneck reminded Woolson of the men she had known growing up in Ohio. He hailed from Covington, Kentucky, just across the river from Cincinnati, where he spent much of his youth. He looked something like her Civil War beau, Zeph Spalding, with thick golden hair and a full moustache. His rugged western manliness had not been entirely smoothed over by his years of rubbing elbows with the cultured aristocracy of Germany and Italy. She could see what drew the refined Lizzie to him, although no else could. He was bold, "a bluff and hearty, no-nonsense man, a bit of a bully boy . . . and every bit a man's man." Unsurprisingly, James—his opposite—was dubious about the match: "[H]e is illiterate, ignorant and not a gentleman (though an excellent fellow, kindly, simple etc.)." He was mystified by Lizzie's willingness to give "away her independence and her freedom" for someone so uncouth. However, he admitted, "she is forty years old, and she has the right."[22]

Constance, on the other hand, fully understood not only why Lizzie had married but the choice she had made for a spouse. In fact, the irresistible love between the two members of this odd couple would inspire a new theme in her fiction in the coming years as she portrayed refined women falling for rough men in spite of their better judgment and often in opposition to uncomprehending family members. In a way, Constance lived vicariously through Lizzie, who seemed to incite equal parts jealousy and admiration in her. Although little is known about their friendship, it seems they became fast friends, no doubt because Constance sympathized with Lizzie's choice when, it seems, everyone else was against her.

By the time Constance came to live at the Villa Castellani, Lizzie's pregnancy was already in its third trimester. It was clear to Constance that Lizzie was among the happiest women she had ever met. Lizzie came to her apartment for tea and conversation, and Constance often visited their studio. She was even inspired to pick up a brush and try her hand at painting as well. She had long wished to take some art lessons—"Since music and so many other enjoyments have been taken from me, it would perhaps be wise to extend the horizon a little on a side still open," she wrote once—and it appears Frank and Lizzie fulfilled her wish.[23]

When James arrived at the Villa Brichieri just up the road on December 8, the Boott-Duvenecks had already decamped to Florence, where Lizzie soon would give birth. The Duvenecks asked Constance to be the baby's godmother, making her a de facto member of the fam-

Drawing of Woolson from Lizzie Duveneck's sketchbook.
(Courtesy of the Duveneck family)

Henry James
From a Drawing by John S. Sargent, R.A.
1886.

Henry James, drawn by John Singer Sargent in 1886,
the year of his first visit to Woolson's villa.
(From *The Letters of Henry James*, by Percy Lubbock)

ily. (A painter friend of Duveneck's was chosen as the godfather.) So
not only did Constance have a new home, but she also had a new family of sorts. After the baby's birth on December 18 and the mother's
recovery, their close-knit community would resume at Bellosguardo.
In the meantime, James and Woolson had the hill to themselves for
three weeks.

Up-close portrait of Woolson from Lizzie Duveneck's sketchbook.
(Courtesy of the Duveneck family)

AN INTERLUDE WITH JAMES

In December, while Henry James took up residence at the Villa Brichieri only a few steps from Woolson at the Villa Castellani, the two
writers enjoyed their mutual solitude and got down to work. James
insisted that he had come there to hide out and return to some writing
commitments from which he had long been distracted by moving into
a new apartment in London, helping his sister, Alice, relocate into
new lodgings not far from his, and completing two novels (*The Bostonians* and *The Princess Casamassima*). James presented Woolson with a

three-volume set of the latter, which he inscribed, "To his Padrona / Constance Fenimore Woolson, / her faithful tenant & friend / Henry James / Bellosguardo, December 1886."[24]

One of his writing tasks was an essay on his friend "Fenimore" for *Harper's Weekly*, so he set to reading her works on hand, which included all of her books except *Castle Nowhere: Lake-Country Sketches*. He seems to have enjoyed the task. Writing to his brother William and his wife two days before Christmas, he referred to Woolson as "my old and excellent friend . . . the gifted authoress." It seems he didn't mind telling them she was nearby while the Bootts were in town. To their mutual friend John Hay he wrote that she was not five minutes away, "and I see her every day or two—indeed often dine with her," and in one of her letters, she indicated that she "saw him daily." James also told Hay that he looked forward to the many "quiet, sunny, spacious hours for work" Woolson would have in her new home after the first of January, "a prospect, on her part, in which I take an interest, in view of the great merit & progress of her last book," *East Angels*.[25]

During their many talks that month, they surely discussed her novel, which had been published the previous summer, while she was in Geneva. *East Angels* sold twice as many copies as *For the Major* but only a fifth as many as *Anne* (about 10,500 copies).[26] Its reviews had been mixed. One particular review wounded her deeply.

William Dean Howells had disparaged *East Angels* in the "Editor's Study" column in *Harper's*, the first time that magazine published a negative review of her work. After his return from Europe, Howells had moved to New York and taken up with *Harper's*, publishing his novels there and writing the new editorial column on literary matters. From that position of authority, which he would use famously in the coming years to make his case for American realism, he condemned Woolson's portrait of the self-sacrificing Margaret Harold. Although Howells found the rest of *East Angels* full of "excellence" and "mastery," Margaret was, in his view, "too much." She "ought to console such of her sex as have heart-hungered for grand and perfect women in fiction perhaps ever since George Eliot drew Romola," he quipped. But to the male reader craving realistic fiction, Margaret strained credulity.[27]

Woolson didn't mind so much that Howells didn't believe in Margaret, which she had expected. In fact, she had ceased to care for his literary judgments, she told Hay, ever since he had maligned Balzac's *Père Goriot*, which she considered a work of genius. But "his writing as he has done, ex cathedra as it were,—from the literary chair of the magazine in which the story appeared,—strikes me as unfriendly," she wrote to Hay. "[F]or the ordinary reader will not discriminate,—will not notice that it is Howells in his own person who is speaking; the ordinary reader will suppose that the magazine is coming out with a condemnation of its own contributor."[28]

Woolson's strong bond with the Harpers seemed threatened by Howells's animosity. He had been an early mentor to her but was never entirely supportive. Whenever and wherever he saw strains of idealism in her work (as in Margaret), he let her know that he didn't approve. She had tried hard to please him for many years but decided she was done. She didn't need his approval anymore. However, now that he was writing a column for *Harper's*, his views would continue to matter. (In the long run, they would matter a lot. As his biographers indicate, his column would almost single-handedly "creat[e] a canon of late-nineteenth-century literature.") The publisher, Joseph Harper, wrote her two letters, reassuring her of her high value to them and removing any feeling of betrayal.[29] In fact, it is quite possible that the assignment for James to write a profile of her for *Harper's Weekly* was in direct response to the Howells blunder. She would never forgive Howells and no longer counted him as a friend. But James could help heal the wound Howells had caused and repair the breach with the Harpers.

Howells had not been alone in attacking Woolson about her character Margaret. In fact, a debate over Margaret's decision not to leave her philandering husband raged for months in the American press, from which Woolson was largely insulated. Some reviewers agreed with Howells in finding Margaret too good to be true—not even human, said one critic—while others insisted on her veracity. The

Christian Union instead attacked Howells as one who "cannot believe in any one who occupies a higher spiritual plane than that, say, of Bartley Hubbard or Silas Lapham [two of his most famous protagonists]. . . . [A] character like that of Margaret Harold is quite beyond his grasp." But the religious press was generally uncomfortable with what they saw as the novel's godlessness. Some reviewers complained that *East Angels* actually created an atmosphere in which readers found themselves rooting for "wrong," namely that Margaret and Winthrop would find a way to be together. "Young girls read her novels," one wrote, and are led into "dangerous sympathy with temptation." Woolson had come up against the problem faced by Howells and James as well—how to write serious fiction that did not corrupt the innocence of young girls. As Howells would ask three years later in his "Editor's Study" column, "In what fatal hour did the Young Girl arise and seal the lips of fiction?"[30]

On the subject of *East Angels'* artistic merits, reviewers also disagreed. The *New York Times* applauded it as "the work of a most accomplished artist," and *The Literary World* thought it her best work, full of the fine workmanship of *For the Major* and "a remarkable power of observation that we are always conscious of" in her work. *The Independent* captured the book's essential accomplishment: "The art with which Miss Woolson has, as it were, suppressed Mrs. Harold, hidden her resolution, her passion, her sensibility, and kept her subordinate, to bring her forward at length as the great creation and study of the book—this is masterly." Other critics, however, felt she had ventured too far into the territory of the analytical novel, sounding a note similar to that taken in response to James's fiction. *East Angels* was "singularly lacking in the definiteness of plot which should characterize so long a story" and was flooded with "minute and painstaking character studies." The "effect on the reader" was "drowsiness," the perennially ill-disposed *Nation* grumbled. Despite having seen such great promise in *Anne*, Horace Scudder at the *Atlantic* had found it little realized in *For the Major* and even less fulfilled in *East Angels*. Why could she not use her considerable "power," he asked, "in some swiftly accomplished tale, where the quickness of movement will save her from undue subtlety of motive?"[31] Yet James was on her side at last, and so she weathered the American criticism, resting secure in his high opinion of her.

AURORA LEIGH'S VIEW

As the new year arrived, James went down to join Boott and the Duvenecks in Florence, leaving Woolson to take possession of her new villa. The Villa Brichieri was not perfect—it was rough and rather empty feeling—but it more than fulfilled her desire for a home of her own. It was the first place she had settled into since her father had died seventeen years earlier. She could not contain her joy. She was "so tired of a wandering life" that she quickly decided the villa was "the greatest success" of her life. Her high spirits overflowed. After "seventeen years of wandering" and "much sorrow; & pain; & toil," she had found "peace & joy unlimited." "[T]he wheel seems to have turned round completely," she wrote to Stedman. She was "supremely happy."[32]

Woolson was convinced she had "as lovely a view as the world contains." Rather than try to describe its beauty, she told her correspondents to take out their copies of Elizabeth Barrett Browning's *Aurora Leigh* and turn to the following passage:

> I found a house, at Florence, on the hill
> Of Bellosguardo. 'Tis a tower that keeps
> A post of double-observation o'er
> The valley of Arno (holding as a hand
> The outspread city) straight toward Fiesole
> And Mount Morello and the setting sun,—
> The Vallombrosan mountains to the right,
>
> . . .
>
> No sun could die, nor yet be born, unseen
> By dwellers at my villa: morn and eve
> Were magnified before us in the pure
> Illimitable space and pause of sky.[33]

How fitting that one of the earliest nineteenth-century works to confront the difficulty for women of combining romantic relationships with a commitment to the creation of literary art should be set, in part, at Woolson's new villa. In these surroundings, Woolson would again contemplate the mystery of so many women's lives—how to love and maintain a separate identity—all the while enjoying periods of her own perfect solitude.

Her writing room, where she spent the majority of her solitary hours, was the "the best place I have ever had for working," she wrote to Sam.[34] A cook and a maid—Angelo and Assunta—made the villa less lonely. Angelo was a wonder. He could prepare anything she wanted and serve it perfectly. He was over fifty and practically "a Yankee," able to make repairs throughout the house. She paid him ten dollars a month and was thought generous. The elderly Assunta kissed her hand each morning and at night before going to bed. "All goes like clockwork," she was happy to say, "and I have no care at all."[35]

The view today from Woolson's terrace at the Villa Brichieri, Bellosguardo, outside of Florence, Italy. (Photograph by the author)

But she could not feel entirely settled. She was an American, she told herself. Italy was not her home. The Bootts had all of their lives felt torn between the blissful Bellosguardo and their family back in Boston. Woolson drew a clear line in her mind between "home" and Europe, longing to settle finally in St. Augustine. Her dream would be complete, she told Mary Carter, with a summer cottage near Mary's new home outside Cooperstown.[36]

Moving back to the United States would be much more expensive than staying in Italy, however. She would have to save up for it. And a new, sparsely furnished home in Italy that required her to buy carpets, stoves, curtains, furniture, linens, and flatware was not getting her any closer to her goal. The initial outlay after moving into the Villa Brichieri had left her feeling rather poor, in fact, so she asked Sam to wire her some of her savings. She knew he would not approve of her drawing on her reserves, "[b]ut if you could know, Sam, the intense pleasure & comfort this delightful home is to me—you would, I think, agree with me in feeling that it was a wise step. Every morning as I look at the beautiful view while dressing, I thank God for the delight of it. . . . [E]very day I am more content than I was the day before." She would not return to Florida, she insisted, until she could afford her own home there. Now that she had one abroad, she realized how essential it was. Her health, and her ability to keep writing, depended upon it.[37]

11

Confrère

W HEN JAMES'S essay "Miss Woolson" appeared in the February 12, 1887, issue of *Harper's Weekly*, a full-page, folio-sized portrait of Woolson graced the cover of the magazine. It marked the culmination of years of worry over the idea of her portrait appearing in print. In Florence in 1883, Mrs. Howells had urged her to allow her brother, the sculptor Larkin Goldsmith Mead, to make a medallion portrait of her to complete his set of famous authors, comprising Howells, James, and Hay. Woolson expressed to both James and Hay her feelings on the subject: "I do not at all think that because a woman happens to write a little, her face, or her personality in any way, becomes the property of the public."[1]

Mrs. Howells argued that "[w]hen the Harpers want your portrait, to put in the magazine—as of course they <u>will</u>—it will be <u>all</u> <u>ready</u>." When Mead also suggested that portraits of American authors belonged on the Washington Monument, then nearing completion in the nation's capital, Woolson felt as if she were living "a sort of night-mare."[2]

In late 1885, when the Harpers first asked for her portrait, she turned to Hay: "As you may imagine, it is a pang to every nerve in my body, to be produced in public in that way; they say that I should not be able to suppress a likeness altogether, since there is a fancy at present for bringing out 'series' of 'authors' likenesses;' & a photograph of some sort is sure to be obtained of everybody, somewhere; & the thing done whether the victim likes it or not. Therefore how much better to have a good likeness brought out in a proper place. Such is the argument." Woolson knew the craze for writers' photographs well because she had participated in it herself, as a consumer. Her collection included a portrait of Stedman cut from a magazine and a velvet triptych frame containing a poetical Hay, a smiling Howells, and a cynical James. But, she felt, "there's no 'proper place' for an ugly woman!"[3]

When her portrait first appeared in *Harper's*, in the March 1886 issue, she was happy to report that it looked nothing like her. Another representation that didn't look much like her—more like a boy than a grown woman—was a bust created after an 1887 illness in which she had lost much of her hair. She wrote at length about it to her nephew: "Sam, do'nt you think you could lend me your nose? Richard Greenough, the Sculptor, who has been here [at Bellosguardo] lately (he lives in Rome) has formally asked permission to 'do' my head,—again reducing me to the embarrassed & vexed state of mind which the subject of 'a likeness' always produces. Why have'nt I a nose? It would be such a pleasure to decline modestly; & then be <u>forced</u> into consenting; & then have a lovely bust in marble to send you. Your [step]mother, now, might lend me <u>her</u> profile. I have declined Mr Greenough's proposal—with thanks. I shall never sit to anyone—painter, sculptor, or photographer, again."[4] But the requests kept coming, and she was unable to hold them off.

Used to expressing her deepest feelings behind the mask of fiction, Woolson had erroneously believed that she could simply remain hidden. She desired fame for her writings but not celebrity for herself. It had come to her nonetheless. She was now, as a Cleveland paper remarked, "the world's property."[5] She could, however, as the Harpers

Portrait of Woolson used for the etching in *Harper's Weekly*, February 12, 1887, which took up the entire folio-sized cover of the paper. (Correspondence and Journals of Henry James Jr. and Other Family Papers, MS Am 1094 [2245, f.58], by permission of the Houghton Library, Harvard University)

suggested, control her image, limiting, in effect, the public's access to it. The portrait that accompanied James's essay about her was a calculated attempt to satisfy the public's cravings and thwart them at the same time. Rather than allow readers full access to her face, she deliberately turned away from the camera. Her body faces the viewer partially, but her head looks away. Her eyes are downcast, as if she has only reluctantly submitted to the intrusion. Her hair is pulled back into a braided coil. Her curls have been tamed, cut short and tightly framing her face. A neckband hides her throat, and a delicate lace cape conceals her bust. It is hard to imagine a more conservative portrait of the woman author. Look at me if you will, it seems to say to the viewer, but you will see only what I am prepared to reveal. Not coincidentally, the accompanying essay by Henry James sends substantially the same message.

JAMES'S "MISS WOOLSON"

In writing his essay "Miss Woolson," James confronted the many complications of Woolson's personal and public lives, not to mention his relationship with her.[6] He would have to figure out a way to do her justice as the private woman he had come to know and as the author who had become the "world's property." It was also a test of their friendship, for he had picked up the critic's pen, which, as Woolson knew well, could draw blood.

Author interviews and profiles had become incredibly popular in Britain and America, and it was inevitable that the Harpers would want one of the widely admired Woolson. Surely the Harpers asked James to write it because he had recently written two similar essays for *Harper's Weekly*: one of his friend Howells and another of the artist Edwin A. Abbey, both accompanied by portraits.[7] Considering how nearby Woolson was when he wrote the essay, she must have approved of the plan. Unfortunately, her feelings about the piece and the additional publicity it would thrust upon her have not survived. She probably accepted that someone would write a profile of her eventually and it was better to control the circumstances under which it was produced.

But could she? Although it was her friend who was writing the essay, she must also have feared his underlying disdain for women writers. He would, in fact, a few short weeks after penning the essay, write in his notebook venomously about the "scribbling, publishing, indiscreet, newspaperized American girl," whose desire for publicity was "one of the most striking signs of our times."[8] Woolson's withdrawal from public notoriety preserved her status as a proper woman, however. Surely she could trust James to treat her with more respect than he did the "newspaperized American girl." But she still had cause for worry.

While his essay on Howells had begun quite conventionally with biographical details about the author, his essay on Woolson began much differently, indicating how foremost it was in his mind that he was writing about a woman. After a paragraph on the prominence of women in current literature, which says nothing about his proposed subject, he then erects a protective screen around her:

> The work of Miss Constance Fenimore Woolson is an excellent example of the way the door stands open between the personal life of American women and the immeasurable world of print. . . . [Her work] breathes a spirit singularly and essentially conservative—the sort of spirit which . . . seem[s] most to oppose itself to the introduction into the feminine lot of new and complicating elements. . . . [I]t would never occur to her to lend her voice for the plea for further exposure—for a revolution which should place her sex in the thick of the struggle for power. Such is the turn of mind of the author . . . and if it has not prevented her from writing books, from competing for the literary laurel, this is proof of the strength of the current which to-day carries both sexes alike to that mode of expression.

At the end of the essay, he reiterates that her works "all have the stamp . . . of the author's conservative feeling, the implication that for her the life of a woman is essentially an affair of private relations."[9]

On the one hand, James was trying to preserve her privacy by telling readers she desired no "exposure." On the other, he thrust her into the fray of "competing [with men] for the literary laurel," hardly a "conservative" act. James seems to be taking his cues from Woolson herself, seeking a compromise between the private woman he knew and the artist her writings had revealed her to be. It was a conundrum neither could easily solve. His essay suggests he supported her determination to maintain a conservative identity as a woman while she also adopted a fairly radical conception of herself as a serious author.

In fact, the only way she could make the assertiveness of her bid for recognition palatable was to hide it behind an image of herself as a private, traditional woman.

Under pressure to include some biographical details about his subject, James mentions a few, pretending to be simply an interested reader rather than someone who actually knows her. In his essay on Howells, he hadn't mentioned their relationship either because he wanted to distance himself from his friend's critical views, namely an adulatory essay on James that had drawn intense criticism.[10] James also had to distance himself from Woolson, but for different reasons. Their friendship was known to a few friends and relations but it was not something either wanted publicized. To avoid the scandal that could ensue if their closeness became the topic of public discussion, James kept "Miss Woolson" at arm's length.

Applying his own dictum that "[t]he artist's life is his work, and this is the place to observe him," most of the essay concerns itself with her writings. Considering that most criticism on women writers focused inordinately on the author's personal life, his focus on her work suggests his great respect. "Miss Woolson" does, in fact, contain some very high praise. He found her southern stories "the fruit of a remarkable minuteness of observation and tenderness of feeling" and thought *East Angels* "represent[ed] a long stride in her talent," predicting that "if her talent is capable, in another novel, of making an advance equal to that represented by this work in relation to its predecessors, she will have made a substantial contribution to our new literature."[11]

Perhaps most important to Woolson, he was loyal to her in his lengthy defense of her portrayal of Margaret Thorne in *East Angels*. Some small criticisms creep in, and although he could be accused of some "enigmatic doublespeak," he was much kinder to her than he was to Howells. James came close to the heart of her work (and life) when he noted that she was "fond of irretrievable personal failures, of people who have had to give up even the memory of happiness, who love and suffer in silence, and minister in secret to those who look over their heads. She is interested in secret histories, in the 'inner life' of the weak, the superfluous, the disappointed, the bereaved, the unmarried."[12]

Woolson must have been pleased with the essay. James had protected her privacy, taken her side against Howells, and given her some of the highest praise he had granted any woman writer.

UNDER THE SAME ROOF

In the early spring of 1887, not long after the publication of "Miss Woolson," James fell seriously ill in Venice. After much worry over his strange symptoms, he discovered that he had jaundice. Woolson was alarmed and wrote him letters of consolation and advice. She worried she had intruded herself, but he sent her a message through Boott: "Tell Fenimore I forgive her—but only an angel would. She will understand." As James's sister Alice explained to her sister-in-law back in the United States, "I hear from him & from an outside source [Woolson] that the attack is a *light* one." But Woolson must have known how serious it was. James would later say that his health "was more acutely deranged in Venice than it had been since my youthful years." Alice was relieved to learn that he had "Miss Woolson in the background at Bellosguardo upon whom he is going to fall back when he is able to travel to Florence."[13] Woolson had offered him the apartment below hers, where he could recuperate far from the cold air of Venice and avoid the social obligations of Florence.

James arrived in the middle of April. Dr. Baldwin, Woolson's friend and doctor, met him at the train station and escorted him to Bellosguardo. James's health and good spirits revived quickly. He planned to stay until the first of June so that he could fully recover. Unlike his previous stay, this time he was Woolson's guest. He planned to "lead a life of seclusion and finish some work," he told one friend whose lunch invitation he declined. James was busy writing "The Aspern Papers," a story about an eager biographer who insinuates himself into the lives of two unmarried women—an elderly aunt and her middle-aged niece—in Venice. The narrator hopes the aunt will die and leave him her love letters from a famous writer whose memory he has cultivated. James's return to the Villa Brichieri may have recalled to him the voracious appetite of the public for authors' lives, an appetite he had attempted to both satisfy and thwart in "Miss Woolson." The story's theme of a secret relationship, the evidence of which is burned in the end, may also have been inspired by the deepening friendship between the two writers, which they increasingly desired to keep to themselves.[14]

During James's six-week stay, he and Woolson would determine once and for all the nature of their relationship. Were they companions, bachelor and spinster, who could conceivably take the next step toward romance? Or were they writers, that breed apart, who could live outside of the conventional arrangements between men and women? Woolson may have wanted to remain a "proper woman," but her friendship with James was charting new territory that her mother and sisters would not have dared to enter. And he was certainly as conservative as she in his desire to conceal his private life.

Only a few people knew of their living arrangements—Boott, the Duvenecks, Baldwin, and possibly Alice. James wrote of his new situation to his sister-in-law but made no mention of Woolson. Woolson's letters to her nephew, Sam, make no reference to her tenant. Instead, she focuses on her contentment with her new home. "I am so happy here, Sam, that . . . it is pathetic—almost. The old Auntie enjoys, like a child, her own cups & saucers, & chairs & tables. The view is a constant <u>Paradise</u> to me." James, below her, wrote the very next day in similar tones. "I sit here making love to Italy," he told a friend in London. "At this divine moment she is perfectly irresistible." He attributed his bliss to his surroundings, the "supercelestial" Villa Brichieri, and the new flowers of spring. "There is nothing personal or literary in the air," he insisted. "The only intelligent person in the place [Florence] is [the writer] Violet Paget." To Katherine de Kay Bronson, a widow and close friend of the late Robert Browning, who lived in Venice, he casually mentioned that he had met one of her kinswomen who "appeared here yesterday punctually to call on my neighbor Miss Woolson, on whom I was also calling."[15]

Although they were living under the same roof, they were in separate apartments with separate entrances, so their afternoons together

Henry James stayed in the downstairs apartment of Woolson's villa for
six weeks in 1887, visiting with her daily. Photograph from 1890.
(Correspondence and Journals of Henry James Jr and Other Family
Papers, MS Am 1094 [2246, f.33], by permission of the Houghton
Library, Harvard University)

were essentially visits. His account to his brother William indicates
that he wrote all day in his quiet rooms and then went down to Florence every evening for dinner.[16] To William's wife, Alice, he wrote
that he had his own cook. However, he and Woolson must have
shared Angelo, who surely prepared meals for two when James was
in the house. Undoubtedly they had many meals together, as they had
the previous December when he was living nearby.

The two were hardly alone on their hilltop, however. Francis, Lizzie, Frank, and the baby were again in residence at the Villa Castellani. A constant stream of visitors from Florence kept Woolson very busy, as she complained in letters. She had limited social calls to one day a week and did not return them, assuming that people came as much for recreation and the view as to see her. In April and May, while James was living downstairs, every American in Italy seemed to be in town for the series of fetes leading up to the unveiling of the Duomo's new façade.

As the event neared, the city was bursting with excitement about "the processions, the fireworks & illuminations, regattas, tournaments, races, etc." Woolson thought that up on her hill she could stay above the fray, but her position perched above the city proved to be the best place to watch the fireworks. For five evenings in a row she had guests to entertain. As they were English, she had to serve tea and discuss the Royal Society for the Prevention of Cruelty to Animals, their dearest project. Woolson felt as if she were the abused animal in the scenario, especially when they waited in vain night after night for the promised pyrotechnics. Finally, the night of the illumination arrived. All of Florence "blazed with light," and "the tower of the Palazzo Vecchio, the Dome of the Cathedral, & all the spires & campaniles were outlined in lines of glittering stars." The hills all around glowed with bonfires.[17]

Sitting outside during the cool nights took its toll, however, and soon Woolson fell ill. Dr. Baldwin made a house call, and James repaid her kindness by helping to care for her. This isn't the picture usually drawn of their friendship, in which her devotion to him is often portrayed as one-sided. However, Woolson later told the English-American writer Frances Hodgson Burnett, the author of *Little Lord Fauntleroy*, about James's "great kindness and attention to her when she was ill." When Burnett later met him, she "found him all that [Woolson] described, most gentlemanly, kind and attentive—a charming man, indeed."[18] The two friends probably never knew of Burnett's disclosure of their intimacy to a newspaper reporter in Richfield, New York. They would have been horrified if they had.

Beyond such glimpses, however, their friendship during these years is a virtual blank. Not only did they conceal their proximity to others, they also at some point, probably around this time, made a pact to burn their letters to each other. Some have assumed that James was eager to destroy the secrets he shared with her and that he may have even desired to erase her from his life. Many have also suspected that James and Woolson wished to thwart future biographers. But just as likely, the agreement was intended to maintain their privacy in the present. Letters were often read aloud to friends and family or sent on to others for their enjoyment. James's and Woolson's agreement would make their correspondence a private affair. He made no such agreement with anyone else—not even the two other women who were among his closest friends over the years, Grace Norton and Edith Wharton. When Norton once chastised him for reading portions of her letters aloud to others, he responded, "It is indeed, I think, of the very essence of a good letter to be shown,—it is wasted if it be kept for one." By the same token, she was free to share his letters with others.[19] While Norton could not convince him of the necessity of keeping their correspondence an intimate affair, Woolson could and did.

On her side, the pact to burn letters was not unique, so it was probably her idea. She had a similar arrangement with her sister Clara, whose daughter suggested many years later that the two writers' agreement to destroy their correspondence was the result of their wish to "write freely." Clara once noted, "Connie always wrote me when she was going to use me as a 'safety valve,' and pour out to me what *at that moment* was overpowering her." Constance, who guarded herself so carefully, seems to have grown comfortable revealing private aspects of herself to Henry. The mask she wore for the rest of the world had slipped. "Though I pass for a constantly-smiling, ever-pleased person, [m]y smile is the basest hypocrisy," she had earlier told him.[20] What a relief it was to be able to be herself, as her character Margaret Harold never could.

The Constance revealed in the letters that do survive could be frustrated at times and even admit to feeling depressed, but she was mostly chatty, witty, and earnestly observant. It is only from her niece Clare that we know another side of her. As Clare later wrote, "My aunt had a passionate and dramatic nature, and a high temper." This was the Constance who hid behind the smiling façade. Clare continued, "But she was extremely gracious and a wonderful friend. I don't think that Cousin Henry had those characteristics—he had intellect, humour and an extraordinarily fine perception of other people's feelings and ideas." Their personalities complemented each other. Henry offered her his comprehension, which she returned, along with her devotion.[21]

What the two writers felt for each other was undoubtedly a kind of love, but one not sanctioned by their era. They had certainly been very fond of each other from the beginning. But after their frequent meetings in London in 1883 and James's subsequent visits to her elsewhere in England, the affinity between them had flourished. In Italy, not only did they enjoy each other's company, but they also discovered that they could rely on each other at their most vulnerable times, when they were ill, essentially taking the place of faraway relatives. After living together at the Villa Brichieri, Constance began to call him "Harry."[22] Only his family and old friends from America called him that. Perhaps he also started calling her "Connie," as all of her family did.

During this time they were also drawn together by their mutual friends Francis Boott and his daughter, Lizzie. While Henry was staying with Constance, he too became a part of the quasi-family she had joined. Her great affection for Francis undoubtedly lessened Henry's fears that she may have been growing exclusively attached to him. He must have felt more comfortable accepting her hospitality and allowing her to approach him more closely now that it was clear her affection was not for him alone. He could show an even greater interest in her without fearing that she might misinterpret his attention as romantic. Whether or not she ever knew that James was sexually attracted to men, as most critics today believe he was, she certainly understood the boundaries of their relationship.

Although Henry was closer to Constance than anyone else outside of his family, he still raised emotional barriers. He always put his writing above his relationships. His amanuensis, Theodora Bosanquet, would write much later, "He loved his friends, but he was condemned by the law of his being to keep clear of any really entangling net of human affection and exaction. His contacts had to be subordinate, or indeed ancillary, to the vocation he had followed with a single passion." In the coming years, James would write a series of stories that solidified that commitment as he also struggled to make sense of his intimacy with Woolson. She would accept it more easily for what it was—a bond of minds and hearts. The outer limits of their alliance were taking shape but perhaps not yet set. They would arrange visits whenever they could, but they would not marry, they would not live in the same apartment, and they would not have a physical relationship. But there was also a lot of gray area for the two dedicated writers to navigate up to those limits. Woolson must have seen what Edith Wharton would later recognize: he was "a solitary who could not live alone." Wharton perceived "a deep central loneliness" as well as "a deep craving for recognition" in him.[23] Not coincidentally, Woolson possessed those qualities as well. She and James were drawn to each other as two isolated, ambitious souls who feared being completely alone in the world. They both knew there was someone within reach (if only by letter or occasionally by train) who understood their need for connection *and* solitude.

James recognized that Woolson was as devoted to her work as he was to his. Living below her apartment, he was aware of her steady work habits and admired her for them. Sometime in 1887 he gave her a volume of Shelley's poetry inscribed to "Constance Woolson / from her friend and confrère." With the French word *confrère*—colleague or comrade, the root of which is Latin for "brother"—he acknowledged her as a companion in the writing life and as a would-be sibling. Theirs was a chosen kinship. They both knew by now that the other would never marry. Marriage was, however, the only model they had for close relationships between men and women, and families were defined by blood. So they had to forge a new way to think about their intimacy. In later years Clare referred to him as "Cousin Henry," signifying that he was viewed as a member of the family.[24] To think of him as an uncle would have been to insinuate a marital relationship with her aunt. "Cousin," however, kept the connection familial but vague.

Constance and Henry's time together at Bellosguardo ended in the middle of May, earlier than James had at first projected. Alice needed him back in London now that Katharine Loring was preparing to return to her family. Much as Alice and Katharine had created an extrafamilial, extramarital bond that was as close as, if not closer, than those they shared with their blood relatives, so too had Henry and Constance. Although they would never again live under the same roof, their relationship would remain strong for the rest of her life.

BETRAYING MISS WOOLSON

Despite their greater intimacy, however, the tensions between the two as writers remained. They resurfaced when, after James's return to England, he put together a new volume of critical essays, titled *Partial Portraits*, for which he decided to revise "Miss Woolson." He cut out the biographical paragraph (perhaps at her request) but also added some new criticisms of *East Angels*. Woolson always said she wanted candid assessments of her work, but these were hardly the constructive kind.

In his revised version of the essay, which would appear in May 1888, James portrays Woolson as merely a woman writer, who is inherently incapable of writing to the same standard as men. In the new version, he opens with a fuller discussion of the prevalence of women writers: "Flooded as we have been in these latter days with copious discussion as to the admission of women to various offices, colleges, functions, and privileges, singularly little attention has been paid, by themselves at least, to the fact that in one highly important department of human affairs their cause is already gained—gained in such a way as to deprive them largely of their ground, formerly so substantial, for complaining of the intolerance of man." Woolson's story "At the Château of Corrine" certainly had complained of just that. (The story was finally published in October 1887.) To her, men's contempt toward women such as herself had not dissipated, merely gone underground. As Ford tells Katharine Winthrop, men only pretended to appreciate women writers. James insisted, in a new passage added to the essay, "In America, in England, today, it is no longer a question of their admission into the world of literature: they are there in force; they have been admitted, with all the honors, on a perfectly equal footing. In America, at least, one feels tempted at moments to exclaim that they are in themselves the world of literature."[25] Surely he overstates his case.

The real betrayal of his friend (much more serious than calling her "conservative" or belittling her portrayal of men's continued intolerance toward women writers) came in a new paragraph, in which he now delineated *East Angels'* "defects." The most serious was a direct result of the author's gender. "[I]t is characteristic of the feminine, as distinguished from the masculine hand," James wrote, "that in any portrait of a corner of human affairs the particular effect produced in *East Angels*, that of what we used to call the love-story, will be the dominant one. . . . In novels by men other things are there to a greater or less degree, [but] in women's, when they are of the category to which I allude, there are not but that one."[26] While love was not a particularly important subject for men, women seemed incapable of writing about anything else. James's criticism brings to mind that of John Ford toward Katherine Winthrop's poetry. Whether or not James read the story, he fulfilled Woolson's prediction that underneath the polite criticism lingered a deep-seated distaste for women acting on their literary ambitions.

Having worked so long for acceptance by male critics and peers, Woolson was probably disappointed but not surprised by James's condescension. But considering that *East Angels* was in part a response to *The Portrait of a Lady*—which is almost entirely preoccupied with the question of marriage, although less so with love (for which she had criticized him)—she must have been stung by his comments. She had specifically faulted him for not showing his characters in love. Now he criticized her for showing little else, an unfair assessment, really, given the novel's considerable attention to its Florida setting and analysis of character and social relations. The love story is never the sole theme of her novels.

Woolson would have her revenge, but privately. She had recently written in her notebooks, "If a man is a critic like Lang, or Birrell, he will never appreciate or care for a love story. . . . But in spite of these gentlemen the great fact remains that nine-tenths of the great mass of readers care *only* for the love story." Sometime around the time of James's *Partial Portraits* essay, she also wrote out the idea for a tale, never written, of the female writer's victory over the pompous male critics, not unlike the James-like characters in some of her stories:

> The case of Mrs. B., unable to read any tongue but her own, and having read herself but very little even in her own language—but who yet can produce works that touch all hearts—carry people away. A man of real critical talent (like [Matthew] Arnold) and the widest culture, thrown with such a gifted ignoramus. His wonder. At first, he simply despises her. But when he sees and hears the great admiration her works excite, he is stupefied. He follows her about, and listens to her. She betrays her ignorance every time she opens her mouth. Yet she produces the creations that are utterly beyond *him.* Possibly he tries—having made vast preparations. And while he is studying and preparing, *she* has done it![27]

Woolson was no "ignoramus," although she felt that her education had inadequately prepared her to compete with the likes of Arnold or James. Her fantasy of the success of Mrs. B. stupefying the male critics certainly had a personal element to it. She also understood that the fact of her success with the public remained a thorn in James's side. What she didn't add to her idea for this story is the envious male critic disparaging the woman writer's works in print, reasserting his authority over the field of literature, as James had done.

After Woolson's death, James would read her notebooks, even borrowing a story idea from them.[28] So he likely read about Mrs. B. Did he see a shadow of himself and Woolson there? If so, her triumph came too late. Still, she must have taken pride in the fact that she was the only living American author (and the only American besides Emerson) included in *Partial Portraits*. Howells, her chief adversary, was left out entirely.

12

Arcadia Lost

DURING HER first year at Bellosguardo, Woolson's health prevented her from beginning her new novel. She complained that her right arm was seriously damaged from too much writing. At times, it seemed as if the muscles and nerves held "a witches' dance together" that sent her to bed incapacitated. Electrotherapy had helped, but picking up the pen could bring back the pain. After recovering from her cold in May, during the Duomo unveiling, she tentatively resumed work. But upon returning from Geneva, where she spent the hottest weeks of the summer, she found herself virtually unable to walk and, after many months of immobility, decided that sitting at a desk for long hours was the culprit. From then on she always wrote at a stand-up desk, sometimes for ten or more hours a day when working on a deadline.[1]

During the long periods when she could not write, she read voraciously. Many of her surviving books are marked "Florence, 1887." She carried on conversations with authors in the margins, a compensation for the actual discussions she could no longer hear. She chided Augustine Birrell for arguing in *Obiter Dicta* that a man could be respected even if he were "untruthful, unfaithful, unkind," so long as he wasn't a drunk. "But these are just the things drunkards do!" she protested in the margin. *Obiter Dicta* was a gift from James, who understood her frustration at not being able to write. He also sent her Shelley's poems, a novel by the English writer Margaret Louisa Woods, and a set of Emerson's works. That year she also read Thoreau and Turgenev. Every evening, as the sun set, she took a book of John Hay's poems out onto the terrace, settled into her large Vienna rocking chair, and read until dark, when she put down her book and watched the great expanse of stars overhead. Then she went inside, prepared for bed, and read a few poems by Matthew Arnold before falling asleep. "They are somewhat melancholy," she admitted to Hay. "But I am melancholy, too."[2]

Woolson's blue moods were not helped by the fact that Boott was in Boston that summer. He was feeling "very supererogatory since Lizzie's marriage," James informed his sister-in-law, and probably even more so now that the baby had been born. Lizzie and Frank remained at the Villa Castellani, happier than ever "and more and more Bohemian." James reported that little Francis, named after his grandfather, had "quite overtaken himself and is enormous, promising."[3]

Woolson visited her godson and his contented parents often. She sat with them in the garden of the Villa Castellani and "talked till Frank said his brain whirled," Lizzie wrote to her father in Boston. On that lovely July evening, Woolson was "very nice & very amusing," relating how Boott had absentmindedly returned to her books that she had given him, even after writing his name in them. On the evenings she spent alone, Woolson sat in her red salon at the piano and played tunes by her now favorite composer, Francis Boott, straining to hear "a little ghostly echo of the music which once was the best thing in life."[4]

In November, after Boott's return from the United States, the entire family moved to Paris for the winter. Woolson missed them deeply and eagerly awaited their return. In the meantime, she enjoyed the company of a number of women writers, including her old Florentine friend, the novelist Eleanor Poynter; Rhoda Broughton, an English novelist and friend of James; Miss Horner, one of the sister coauthors of the guidebook *Walks in Florence*, who lived nearby and had become "one of [her] particular friends"; and Frances Hodgson Burnett. During Burnett's earlier career, before *Little Lord Fauntleroy* had made her a famous children's author, Woolson had given one of her adult novels a largely favorable review in the *Atlantic*'s "Contributors' Club." Burnett came on Tuesday afternoons, when Woolson received visitors, but stayed long after everyone else had left. Burnett found Woolson "delightful—that best and dearest type of American women—sweet and sincere and deliciously amusing." They would talk in front of the fire until the sun went down. As they commiserated over the strain of writing, Burnett told Woolson she was often confined to bed for six months after each novel, her mind and speech confused, making Woolson feel that her troubles with her arm paled in comparison.[5]

By January 1888 Woolson was finally feeling better, and she began to write her new novel in earnest. She couldn't put the Harpers off much longer. James complained to Lizzie that "Fenimore appears to be really better of her dreary autumn illness & to be driving the pen for the public benefit, or [so] I judge—for she doesn't drive it for mine. I have heard she is not ill, but I haven't heard much more."[6] At the same time she was warning other correspondents that she wouldn't be able to write many letters in the coming year. In fact, there are no surviving letters from February to August. But there was also another reason for her silence.

THE END OF A DREAM

Near the end of March, an urgent message from Paris arrived announcing Lizzie's sudden death. Although Frank had thrived among his old artist friends in Paris, she had struggled to maintain a household, care for a teething baby, manage her husband's career, and serve as his model, standing hours every day for a portrait that was to be exhibited at the Salon in May. She worked in watercolors, an easier medium to manage than oils with her busy life, producing a large painting of the Villa Castellani that would also be shown at the Salon. But before she could enjoy her success, in the midst of a severe, snowy winter, Lizzie contracted pneumonia and declined rapidly. She died on March 23.[7]

Woolson's initial reaction to the news has not survived, but it must have been, as James's was, "unspeakable shock." "I shall miss her greatly," he wrote to a mutual friend. "She was a dear little quiet, gentle, intelligent laborious lady. And the future looks dark for poor F.B." James was particularly worried about how father and husband would manage, "those two poor uncongenial men [now] tied together by that helpless baby." Boott and Duveneck brought the fifteen-month-old boy back to Bellosguardo, where Woolson was waiting for them, ready to "hold out her hand . . . in all sorts of soothing ways," as James imagined in a letter to Boott. James regretted that he could not be there as well and had to content himself with Woolson's description of the funeral: "Many people and mountains of flowers. Boott absolutely calm—& Duveneck sobbing."[8]

As distressed as Woolson must have been, she quickly became the grief-stricken Boott's main emotional support. According to her niece, he veritably clung to her. He came to the Villa Brichieri almost every night, believing that Woolson had the power to draw Lizzie's spirit nearer. Months later Woolson was still dispensing comfort to him, writing in September, "In all your grief and loneliness it must still be a pleasure to you to remember how happy her life was during those last 2 yrs; a woman understands a woman & I think she was one of the happiest wives I have ever known. Her whole life was unusually happy,—first with you,—& then with you & her husband."[9]

Boott and James blamed Lizzie's death on her marriage to Duveneck, convinced that Lizzie "had undertaken an effort beyond her strength, that she staggered under it and was broken down by it."[10] Woolson didn't blame Frank for loving her. Lizzie's brave attempt to combine love and art had been a beacon in the midst of her own darkness. When Lizzie died, Woolson's fragile faith in happiness flickered out. Yet as long as Duveneck, Boott, and her godson needed her, she put on a brave face.

The motherless baby particularly needed a new mother. As godmother, Woolson could have been the one to step in, and she may have wanted to. Her later letters to Boott show how deeply attached she was to the child, and in her new novel, an unmarried woman seeks to adopt her young nephew, possessing a profound yearning to become the child's mother. But Woolson could not properly replace the baby Francis's mother without becoming an actual member of the family. The proposal James had joked about to Boott two years earlier may have recurred to the grieving grandfather, but he did not act on it. He decided to bring his namesake to his relatives back in Massachusetts. Duveneck agreed, and preparations were made to sail in August. Thus the family Woolson had joined was no more.

During the depressing task of packing up the apartment in the Villa Castellani, in which Francis and his daughter had lived off and on for nearly forty years, Woolson assisted in every way she could. She stored much of the furniture in the Villa Brichieri, along with paintings and treasures the Bootts had accumulated over the years. Duveneck left her many mementoes, including a chair that had belonged to Elizabeth Barrett Browning. He also gave her a lovely etching he had done of Venice.[11] By August, nothing remained of her friends but the objects they had left behind. Woolson couldn't help feeling like another remnant of their abandoned life.

It was at this point that her correspondence with Boott began. It would carry on to the end of her life. Although she always addressed him as "Mr. Boott," the letters were quite personal, relating her moods and struggles in a way no other surviving letters do. She didn't take on the role of daughter or female companion, worrying over his health or advising him. She was simply herself. In every letter she mentioned her godson, sending him gifts and asking for a new picture. Her desire for news of "Baby" was insatiable. She often mentioned how much she missed them all. In the first letter, dated August 7, she confessed that she didn't look toward the Villa Castellani anymore "because it makes me too sad—the closed silent house." The baby's chair stood "desolately under the carved table." She had intended to put it away in a trunk but now thought of making a new cover for it and leaving it out to keep his memory fresh.[12]

In subtle ways, Woolson also conveyed her deep affection for Boott and intimated that she considered the age difference between them trivial. In her first letter she enclosed a cartoon about a duchess who had married a much younger man and mentioned similar famous examples, including a baroness who shocked English society when she married her nearly thirty-years-younger secretary. These examples implied that only when the woman was older were such relationships fodder for the newspapers. In later years, she protested his talk of "going" and insisted, "I shall very likely go before you do."[13]

She was not shy of telling Boott how bereft she was of his companionship: "I had a lonely (that is not LOVELY; but LONELY) turkey last Sunday, with your excellent & highly-prized cranberries." Everywhere she looked were reminders of him: "I read your books; & write at your table; & sit in your chairs; I admire your marbles & bronzes, & your hanging lamp." She installed his bedroom furniture in the ground-floor apartment of the Villa Brichieri to "be ready for you, when you come over to pay me a visit." In the meantime, she had the key to his garden and walked in it often. As she read the books he had left behind, she enjoyed discovering his comments. "I sit & laugh," she told him. "Irving's 'Washington,' emended by you, is as good as 'Punch.'"[14]

If Boott seems like a ghost in these letters, Lizzie was even more literally haunting her. Woolson went to the cemetery every week with fresh flowers for her grave. She assured Boott, "I still think constantly of Lizzie; often she seems very near. I fancy it will be so as long as I live here, so near her old home, & with so many of her possessions about me; I like to think so. She was always sweet & serene to me in life. And she remains the same in death."[15] By communing with the only other member of their charmed circle who remained, if only in spirit, she held on to their Bellosguardo past.

Meanwhile, Woolson's new serial novel was due to the Harpers in October. James wrote to Dr. Baldwin, "I take for granted she is overworking—but her powers to keep that up have long mystified me." There may be some jealousy in his mystification, but there was also genuine, if ominous, concern. "Every thing beyond three hours a day (with continuity) in the sort of work she does is a nail in her coffin—

but she appears to desire that her coffin shall have many! Please don't repeat this to her—I have bored her half to death with my warnings." In fact, Woolson was working at her stand-up desk from about seven in the morning until seven at night with only a half hour's break at noon. Her work was once again taking complete possession of her.[16]

RENDEZVOUS IN GENEVA

James said he still hoped to return to Bellosguardo often, presumably to visit Woolson, but he was "literally *afraid*" of confronting the ghosts of the past there. He also told Boott that he found himself tied to England because of his sister, whom he visited regularly in Leamington. By the fall, however, Alice had improved enough that he could plan a short trip. He left London rather suddenly, having told Alice of his plans only a few days before. He apparently revealed to no one where he was really going—to Geneva to meet Woolson, who was taking a much-needed break after sending her novel off to New York. One of the few surviving clues of their rendezvous is a copy of his recently published *The Aspern Papers, Louisa Pallant, The Modern Warning*, inscribed, "Constance Fenimore Woolson from the author. Geneva, Oct. 16th, 1888."[17]

The only other clues are to be found in their letters to Boott. "[Y]our 'ears must have burned' a good deal lately," James wrote to him on the twenty-ninth, "for you have been a daily theme of conversation with me for the past ten days, with Fenimore. That excellent and obliging woman is plying her pen hard on the other side of this lake and I am doing the same on this one." (Her deadline for the serial met, however, Woolson was probably taking a break from writing.) Their hotels were a mile apart, a distance quickly traversed by boat. Every evening they met for dinner, over which she repeated, without him minding, the details of their friends' final months at Bellosguardo. James particularly enjoyed discussing Lizzie "with one who had entered so much into her life in so short a time." Woolson wrote to Boott that it was James who "talked a great deal of Lizzie; and of you." Either way,

James relived with Woolson the emotionally draining events of the past six months. Sensing the depth of her sorrow, he was "particularly good-natured." (He wasn't always. As she told Boott in a later letter, James "is very changeable as to mood" and "sometimes depressed." How well they understood each other in their moods.) While James looked back fondly on the "golden days," as he called them, of Bellosguardo, Woolson realized that "he meant a time before I even knew the place." She had arrived too late.[18] Such an Arcadia, of which she had caught only the twilight, was now forever beyond her reach.

James had told Alice he would be gone only "a few weeks," but his stay in Geneva stretched into November, making Alice peevish. She knew now of his rendezvous with Woolson and resented having to share her brother's attention. "Henry is somewhere on the continent flirting with Constance," she complained to William. When Alice protested to Henry, he told her "he thought it a 'mild excess.'"[19]

Near the end of November, Woolson and James left Geneva. Back in the Villa Brichieri, Woolson shut herself up to work on the book revisions of the new novel, except during her receiving day, when she typically received upwards of sixty-five calls. Eleanor Poynter helped her entertain the crowds, who "came early and remained late, drank quarts of tea and ate platefuls of cake." Although it was exhausting, Clara insisted that she enjoyed "the bringing up to see her of every distinguished stranger that came to Florence."[20]

Such noisy gatherings were trying for Woolson, however. She longed for conversation with one particular friend. Just then it was the retired Cornell professor Daniel Willard Fiske, whom she had known since her return to Florence in 1886. She invited him to dinner and assured him no one would be there but herself. She was feeling lonely, as she had written to Boott about this time. No wonder she was growing ever fonder of this bookish bachelor, nine years her senior, who sent her gifts—books, maple sugar, fruit, roses, and a coffee set from Egypt. He was just the kind of "simple and trustful, ardent [and] generous" person who appealed to her, a suitable, although temporary, substitute for Boott and James.[21]

Otherwise, she was completely absorbed in her work. As she

explained to Fiske, it was hardly a fib when her servants told callers she was out because she was "indeed out . . . as far away as Lake Superior, where certain tiresome people, of no consequence, are at present disporting themselves, & dragging me with them."[22] Even though her new novel was set in America, she didn't leave Bellosguardo entirely behind. *Jupiter Lights* was full of the baby Francis and Frank and Lizzie, into whose lives she had so completely entered.

JUPITER LIGHTS

Just before the new novel began its run in *Harper's*, Woolson published two stories there that prepared readers for the longer work they would soon encounter. "A Pink Villa," set in Sorrento, where Woolson had spent the winter of 1882, so closely mirrors Lizzie Boott and Frank Duveneck's romance that Francis suspected the rough, manly David Rod was modeled on Frank. Woolson strongly objected: "All I can say is—'Never in the World.' . . . I never describe persons I know. That is, not in a way which could be detected by those who are not writers themselves." Nonetheless, the basic situation resembles that of Lizzie and Frank. The young American woman Eva was raised on the European model by one parent, her mother, who has kept her secluded from the world. She is supposed to marry a Belgian count, but instead falls in love with David Rod, who is seeking Italian laborers for his sugar plantation in Florida (a nod to Constance's old flame Zeph Spalding, then growing sugar in Hawaii). Eva's mother is as bewildered as Boott was by his daughter's fascination for a man so out of place in their cosmopolitan world. In the end, however, Eva's mother has to accept their marriage. As a friend of the family comments, "She won't mind being poor . . . she won't mind anything with *him*. It is one of those sudden, overwhelming loves that one sometimes sees."[23]

"Neptune's Shore," set in Salerno and Paestum, which Woolson visited during her stay in Sorrento, looks at the dark side of such overpowering love. It is, in fact, her most disturbing story, foreshadowing the dark themes of *Jupiter Lights*. A jealous lover becomes possessive and threatening as the object of his affection, a young, free-spirited widow, pulls away from him. His pitiable mother has spent her life watching him as if he were a ticking time bomb. When he finally goes off, he attempts to murder the man who has replaced him in the widow's affections and then kills himself, creating a shocking dissonance with the bucolic setting filled with sojourning expatriates. Glimpses of such violence in Woolson's past—Lawson Carter's and her brother's suicides—suggest where such themes, which reemerge in her novel, may have come from.

Jupiter Lights began its nine-month run in *Harper's* in January 1889. It was, she told Sam, "different from my other stories, because shorter, & full of action, with almost no description." She distanced herself from James in this novel, turning away from the analytical mode of *East Angels* and experimenting again with form, with the same focus on intense, troubling emotions. Instead of pausing and looking closely, as she had done in *East Angels*, she whisks the reader along on a wave of emotion, immersing the reader in the story, as if in real life. However, the absence of analysis by the narrator also left Woolson open to criticism. For she tackled, without comment, matters then only whispered about, such as alcoholism and domestic abuse. *Jupiter Lights* has been called a strange and melodramatic book, but it is also her bleakest and most impassioned one, a reflection of the desperate gloom enveloping her.[24] It was as if Woolson had unleashed the emotions Margaret Harold had so tightly controlled in *East Angels*. The result is Woolson's least Victorian novel as it points toward the eruptions of desire and rage that would become one of modernism's hallmarks.

The main character, Eve Bruce, is a version of Eva from "A Pink Villa." She shares her initials with Elizabeth Boott and was, like her, brought up by her father, her mother having died when she was a baby. After her father's death, Eve follows her brother, Jack, to England (as Alice James had followed Henry after their father's death). When the Civil War erupts, Jack returns to America to fight and after the war marries a southern girl, Cicely, devastating Eve. Jack has little idea of "the exclusiveness, the jealousy of her affection" (an echo of Alice's attachment to her brothers).[25] Shortly after becoming a father, Jack dies of yellow fever. As the novel opens, Eve arrives on an island off Georgia, determined to retrieve the child, also named Jack, from Cicely, who has remarried. The new husband is off in South America.

The little boy, now two years old, answers a deep maternal need in Eve, who asks for him "hungrily." He seems to be a composite of Constance's godson Francis Duveneck and Sam's two boys, whom Woolson longed to see and shower with kisses. Eve is unsuccessful in getting Cicely to give her the baby. She had assumed that Cicely's love for her new husband superseded her devotion to the child, but Cicely corrects her: "It's the strangest thing in the world about a child. When it comes, you think you don't care about it—little red thing!—that you love your husband a million times more, as of course in many ways you do." (When Lizzie had her baby, James wrote to his aunt, while living under Woolson's roof, that he looked like "a little red worm," adding, "Lizzie will plainly be much more of a wife than a mother.") Cicely continues, "But a new feeling comes too, a feeling that's like no other; it takes possession of you whether you want it to or not; it's stronger than anything else—than life or death. You would let yourself be cut to pieces, burned alive, for your *child*."[26]

The dominant subject of *Jupiter Lights* is not mother-love, however, but women's love of men. With this novel Woolson ignored James's criticism of her emphasis on the love story, writing her most unabashed romance, which is also, not by coincidence, her darkest book. When Eve, who has never loved anyone outside of her family, meets Paul, the half-brother of Cicely's new husband, she falls deeply, abjectly in love. The resemblance between Paul Tennant and Frank Duveneck is striking: "broad-shouldered; not graceful like Ferdie [his half-brother], but powerful. His neck was rather short; the lower part of his face was strong and firm." He has thick blond hair as well. Also from the nation's interior (a Lake Superior mining town), Paul is described as speaking roughly, and, when he discovers that he loves Eve in return, his tenacity in pursuing her is reminiscent of Frank's persistence toward Lizzie. His "masterful" way with women and "despotic" form of love render Eve powerless. She suddenly understands everything "she had always despised—pettiness, jealousy, impossible hopes, disgrace, shame." Should he even grow to hate her, she realizes, she would be happy simply to be near him and fold his shirts.[27] This is not the idealized romance of so much popular fiction of the day but a starkly realist portrayal of the degradation love can lead to.

What makes *Jupiter Lights* remarkable among Woolson's works is that she allowed her heroine not only to love deeply but also to express her feelings—verbally and physically. Eve tells an unsuspecting Paul, who doesn't "understand riddles," "I think you understand mine." He takes her insinuation lightly at first, but to her it is a decisive moment: "She had said it. She had been seized with a sudden wild desire to make an end of it, to put it into words." Later, when he takes her in his arms, she does not resist but resolves, "For one day, for one hour, let me have it, have it all!" This is the closest Woolson ever came to portraying the consummation of her characters' passion.[28]

Boott was rather shocked by Woolson's portrayal of Eve—not because she gives herself to her lover, which he may have missed, but because she makes her feelings known to Paul. Woolson responded, "All you say of 'Jupiter Lights,' is extremely interesting to me. I dare say many people might maintain that Eve's betrayal of her love was unusual and extraordinary. Because many people maintain that only the proper, or the guarded, exists; we are all banded together to say so." However, she insisted, "In my fiction I never say anything which is not absolutely true (it is only in real life that I resort to fiction); so you may divine that I know more than one Eve."[29]

In tribute to Lizzie, Woolson also set the culminating scene of Eve's romance in the Villa Castellani. Paul has pursued Eve to Italy, where she has taken refuge in a villa on an Italian hilltop. Its "blank yellow walls are long, pierced irregularly by large windows, which are covered with iron cages; massive doors open upon a square court-yard within," a fair description of the villa in which Lizzie had grown up. Eve has run away from Paul, convinced that their marriage could never be happy because she was responsible for his beloved half-brother's death. She had considered suicide but instead decided to seclude herself in a convent, preventing Paul from a life of misery but also herself from loving and serving someone who despised her. The final lines of the novel show Paul, who has discovered that his brother died of other causes, knocking over several men and women who try to keep him away from Eve with "the violence of a boor."[30] Finally he finds Eve and takes her in his arms, a true dictator in love.

The physical force Paul employs mars the seemingly happy ending (at least for today's readers), not least because violence against women has been a major theme of the book. Cicely's new husband, Ferdinand, Paul's half-brother, attacks her and Jack when he is drunk. He has left a long purple scar on Cicely's breast and has broken the boy's arm. Woolson's portrayal of Ferdinand's great remorse and Cicely's continued love for him, including her conviction that he will not hurt them again, is so eerily accurate, in light of what we know today about abusive relationships, that it would seem Woolson had witnessed one up close. The most likely candidate is the marriage of her friend Jane Carter. In 1888, when Woolson was still in the early stages of her novel, Jane died, freeing her to portray more directly than ever before the trauma that had ended only with Lawson Carter's suicide in 1869, the year in which Woolson set the novel. And just as Woolson has Eve return to Lizzie's home, so does Cicely visit Cleveland, Jane's former home, on her way to stay with Paul on the shores of Lake Superior in the wake of Ferdie's latest, most violent assault.

Ferdie's attacks are not merely the result of drunkenness. He is described as afflicted by hereditary illness, a type of insanity. When he descends into madness, he is delusional. Cicely tells Eve, "When he gets that way he does not know us; he thinks we are enemies, and he thinks it is his duty to attack us."[31] During the breakdown that led up to Lawson Carter's suicide at the offices of the Woolson stove factory, he was also described as delusional. Yet everyone was surprised by his violent act. He may have been a lot like Ferdie, who is similarly able to hide his affliction from most of those around him. Woolson allows her readers to see how intensely attractive and endearing a man could be yet also be a kind of monster who turns on those he loves. James's friend Robert Louis Stevenson had published *Strange*

Case of Dr. Jekyll and Mr. Hyde in 1886. Whether or not Woolson read the novel, hers shares some of its concerns. But *Jupiter Lights* is not an allegory. Her portrayal of madness is meant to be entirely realistic.

Eve (before she meets Paul) is horrified by the way Cicely welcomes Ferdie back without suspicion. "To love any man so submissively was weakness, but to love as Cicely loved, that was degradation!" Eve looks in the mirror and "revolt[s], dumbly, against the injustice of all the ages, past, present, and to come, toward women."[32] Of course, she then goes on to fall into the same trap, one that seems to be impossible for women to escape. There is the same compulsion and lack of free will that marked Zola's novels and those of the American literary naturalists still to come.

One night, when Ferdie attacks Cicely and Jack with a knife, believing they are trying to harm his real wife and child, Eve helps them escape and shoots him. He eventually dies, not from his wounds but from alcohol poisoning. Cicely is barely able to live without him, even when she learns of his infidelities. It wasn't he who attacked her or was unfaithful to her, she reasons; it was the illness.

In the end, the nightmarish side of Woolson's romance overrides whatever pleasure the modern-day reader may be able to derive from Eve's ultimate union with Paul. Contemporary readers may have felt differently. Ten years later, a reader gushed in the *New York Times* about the scene in which Paul forces his way into the convent, adding, "Miss Woolson was a woman who knew what kind of a man other women like."[33] Perhaps she did. But she wasn't merely trying to satisfy her female readers' appetite for domineering lovers. *Jupiter Lights* is a stark, proto-naturalist portrait of what she viewed as women's greatest weakness: their susceptibility to self-abnegating love. She knew that dissecting it would make her less of an artist in the eyes of James and other male critics. But, as she told Boott, she never lied in her fiction. Her highest aim was to tell the truth of women's lives, to look under the masks of acquiescent, idealized femininity that they wore. While other writers of the period portrayed the selfless love of women, they did not bother to examine the fierceness of a woman's passion or the self-immolation it could lead to.

LEAVING BELLOSGUARDO

One night in January 1889, five months after Francis, Frank, and the baby had moved away, Constance laid aside the book revisions of *Jupiter Lights* to welcome Clara and Clare, who had come to live in the ground-floor apartment of the Villa Brichieri. They were greeted by Constance, Angelo, two maids, and a little dachshund named Pax who lived at the Villa Montauto and had become a frequent visitor. The three women stayed up long into the night, catching up in front of the fire.

Constance introduced the "two Claras," as she often called them, to her widening social circle, including Lady Hobart at Hawthorne's Villa Montauto, Dr. Baldwin and his family, and Miss Horner. They went out every afternoon making calls. Woolson also threw a party with a buffet and dancing, with Clara serving as the primary hostess and financier. One hundred fifty people came, among them "Countesses & Counts & Marquises," filling up five large rooms of the house. As Clara, Clare, and forty others danced downstairs until late into the evening, Constance received guests upstairs in her much quieter drawing room. All of the socializing during the Claras' visit forced Woolson to hurriedly finish up the book version of *Jupiter Lights*, writing through the nights until she saw the sun rise, to the great detriment of her health and nerves.[34]

Although Woolson had renewed her lease on the villa for a third year, she soon began to speak of giving it up. James wondered why, unless she was thinking of returning to Florida. Eleanor Washington's widower wrote to her nearly every week to fill her in on the property he was overseeing for her there. His son Harry was in Florence and gave her an excellent report of the orange groves planted for her on the land she called "East Angels." Worrisome accounts came to her, however, of how Standard Oil magnate Henry Flagler had built in St. Augustine two grand hotels with five hundred rooms, dozens of stained-glass windows from Louis Tiffany, and everything from spas and tennis courts to a casino and a bowling alley. Flagler was drawing wealthy northern socialites in droves to his "Newport of the South." Woolson worried that her dream of a peaceful home there had been spoiled.[35]

Nevertheless, Woolson still didn't have the money to return to Florida. Nor, as it turned out, did she have enough to keep up with her household expenses in Italy, which she estimated as anywhere between a half and a quarter of what they would be in the United States. Her letters to Sam that year are full of queries about the American bonds whose interest she relied on. In her letters to Boott she gave other reasons for planning to leave Bellosguardo: "I might go into all the pros & cons. But I won't; I will simply say 'Why did you leave the scene?' You surely can't expect me to stay here without you!" Although she knew at least five hundred people in Florence, those who meant the most to her were gone. As the first anniversary of Lizzie's death approached, she told Boott she would think of him with tender sympathy on that day. In reply to his query about whether she had felt Lizzie's presence, she admitted that she often talked to her and sensed her listening.[36]

As spring approached, Woolson began to get restless. She fantasized about running off to Venice without telling anyone. "I should like a month of quiet; & no visiting list; no 'calls' to make," she reported to Boott. Frank Duveneck was back in Europe and urged her to come to Paris for the Exposition, or World's Fair, promising "to do everything" for her and take her to see the pictures. Eleanor Poynter wanted her to go with her to Tours, France, "and see all the old Châteaux." But Constance's eyes began to turn farther afield, to Algiers and Egypt. Her interest had been piqued by the Egyptian treasures of Daniel Willard Fiske. "If I could but go!" she wrote to him. For now she would have to content herself with the Egyptian coffee cups he had given her, which she used every day, imagining she was in Cairo.[37]

In June, Constance fled to Venice with her niece Kate. She hired two gondoliers to take her far out into the lagoons, where she visited shrines, church ruins, and monasteries on the distant islands, returning by moonlight, never tiring "of the exquisite dreamy beauty, & silence, of the fairy water streets." She knew so many of the local residents already that she wasn't lonely. She had previously met Ariana Curtis in Florence and soon became a frequent guest at her magnificent Palazzo Barbaro. She decided that Ariana and Daniel Curtis, also close friends of James, were among the most enjoyable people she had ever known. She began to dream of renting an apartment in Venice. "To have put a few years of Venice into one's life," she wrote her old friend Stedman, "will be to have wrestled so much from darkness."[38]

That last word is one of the few tangible signs of her depression. As later letters reveal, she was by then unable to eat, sleep, read, or enjoy anything. Most distressingly, she found her money problems spiraling out of control. She was working as hard as she could, but it wasn't enough to sustain her financially. She started drawing on her capital, selling two of her bonds for $2,000, making her question how long she could continue to support herself.[39]

One day late in July, shortly after her return to Bellosguardo, she received a letter from Sam announcing that he was sending her enough money to stabilize her finances—an astounding $15,000. Sam could afford it. He had become quite rich in his father's coal mining company. As she explained to him days later, after she had composed herself enough to write, "I could not believe that I had read aright, and went over the words again. And then, when I realized what you meant, tears came, and the happiest feeling that I have known for years. . . . I am afraid I had become almost discouraged, Sam. I had got behind. . . . The feeling was rapidly taking possession of me—'It's of no use!' A feeling of hopelessness for the future."[40]

The tone of her letter to Sam and other clues suggest that Woolson had grown suicidal. During the time of her troubles at Bellosguardo, she read *The Teaching of Epictetus*, the Greek Stoic philosopher. Many of the pages discussing his views on suicide have been torn out of her copy, perhaps to conceal marginalia revealing her state of mind. But evidence remains, such as the following passage, which she marked with double wavy lines in both margins, indicating its great significance: "And when it may be, that the necessary things are no longer supplied, that is the signal for retreat: the door is opened, and God saith to thee, *Depart*." In the notes section, she also marked the following with darker lines: "This phrase of the 'open door' occurs frequently in Epictetus, usually when, as here, he is telling the average nonphilosophic man that it is unmanly to complain of a life which he can at any time relinquish. The philosopher has no need of such exhortation, for he does not complain, and as for death, is content to wait God's time. But the Stoics taught that the arrival of this time might be indicated by some disaster or affliction which rendered a natural and wholesome life impossible." Then Woolson marked the final sentence with two lines in the margin: "Self-destruction was in such cases permissible, and is recorded to have been adopted by several leaders of the Stoics, generally when old age had begun to render them a burden to their friends."[41]

Woolson's greatest fear was losing her independence. As her niece Clare would later write, "[S]he was very proud and did not wish to be a burden on anyone." Her ability to support herself by her writing "was a great source of pride." Worries about money had stalked her ever since her father's death, but when they grew severe, as they had at Bellosguardo, her thoughts turned to escape. Some of that despair made its way into *Jupiter Lights* when Eve contemplates suicide. She asks herself, "[I]s it wrong to try to die?" But recalling her own father's stoicism, Woolson wrote, "The stern Puritan blood of her father in her answered, 'One must not give up until one has exhausted every atom of one's strength in the contest.'"[42]

More than anything, it was Sam's material aid that gave her the courage to carry on. "I feel inspired to take hold anew," she told him. She would leave the villa at the end of the year, live more closely within her means, and start saving again for the future. "The hopelessness has gone, and that is everything. For we cannot really live without hope."[43] Sam's money would allow her to pay off her debts and move out of the villa, recover from the year's work by traveling (with Clara's assistance as well), and then start over someplace new.

Nonetheless, she lamented leaving Bellosguardo, where she still felt Lizzie's presence. She also feared losing her last tie to Boott. Her solitary evenings were spent playing the piano and singing his songs "Thou and I" and "Through the Long Days," which are about longing for absent loved ones. Meanwhile, happy news arrived from the Harpers, who, as *Jupiter Lights* neared the end of its serial run, informed Constance that it was "considered 'the strongest thing'" she had written. She was hearing the same thing from her literary friends.[44]

On September 6, finally free of the book proofs for *Jupiter Lights*, exhausted and sick of even the sight of a pen, she boarded a train for England. Once there, she rested for a month in Richmond, a bucolic community just outside of London. She slept peacefully and walked six or eight miles a day through the parks surrounding the village and visited Kew Gardens, Windsor Castle, and Hampton Court. She rowed on the Thames, feeling health return to her body and mind with each stroke of the oars. Occasionally, she went to town to visit James, finding him healthy and in good spirits. She was amazed at his productivity. In a letter to Boott, she expressed her concern that he was doing too much, echoing his earlier worries about her. She wished he could take a break from writing as she had.[45]

In December, while she was back in Italy to pack up the Villa Brichieri, *Jupiter Lights* was published in book form. Although Woolson was again cut off from the reviews, the Harpers told her "no novel of recent years has been more favorably received." One paper proclaimed that the "vigorous and romantic composition" went far "to confirm the judgment, already pretty well made, that Miss Woolson is among the few greatest women who write fiction." The novel "evinces much power . . . and a vigor of style most remarkable," declared another magazine. It was "one of the strongest tales ever written by an American." The *New York Herald* thought Woolson was "without an equal in portraying the nature and emotions of women." English audiences were as pleased as ever with her work. The *Spectator* compared *Jupiter Lights* favorably to *Anne*, "one of the best novels that America has produced for the last quarter of a century," and the *Athenaeum* thought the novel would not disappoint English readers, who have come to expect "a powerful and romantic story" from Woolson.[46]

The critical tone taken toward her work returned, however, in some of the usual quarters. The *Atlantic*'s Horace Scudder understood the book's theme—"Woman's love is absolute abandonment of self"—but disliked what he described as "a network of emotional torture." He felt the book threatened a "sane, wholesome" view of life. A religious periodical compared *Jupiter Lights* to French novels and determined that "there is something shameless and offensive in the way in which Miss Woolson conceives and describes her women. . . . Certainly these headstrong creatures, overmastered by passion for men who may be drunkards, licentious, unfaithful, cruel, despotic . . . are not types of sentiment which has ever been recognized as Christian."[47]

Someone made a point of sending Woolson a copy of the *New York Evening Post* containing a brutal attack upon *Jupiter Lights*. As the paper was under the same management as *The Nation*, it appeared there as well. It began, "Miss Woolson must have been dominated by an evil spirit" when she wrote the book. "It is more easy to believe that she was 'possessed' than that she deliberately chose to write a long novel about the stupid and obstinate attachment of a silly woman for a man who, every few months, became insanely drunk, beat her, turned her out of doors, and tried to kill both her and her child. . . . All of this is sheer romantic nonsense." Woolson no longer cared what the critics had to say, but she was bothered by the feeling that this review "<u>may</u> come— in spirit—from Mr Howells, who, strange to say, has turned from a friend to an enemy. He is powerful; & he is on the spot; & he dislikes with a vengeance! When he does dislike. It is the one painful spot in my literary life, because I used to like him so much, & trust him."[48]

The Harpers were satisfied with the positive reviews and the novel's modest sales of 6,000 copies. They wanted a new novel as soon as Woolson could produce one, but it would be a while before she was ready to start writing again. She was on her way to "the lands of the Arabian Nights and the realms of my childhood's dreams."[49]

PART FIVE

The Final Years

1890–1894

"I feel like another person—so broadened in mind by an actual look into the strange life of the East."

—CONSTANCE FENIMORE WOOLSON

"When suffering becomes too great, we are always at liberty to leave life altogether."

—CONSTANCE FENIMORE WOOLSON

13

To Cairo and Back

IN THE third week of December 1889, Constance left Bellosguardo for good and began her journey on the express train down the Adriatic coast of Italy. With the cerulean sea running along outside, the talk inside was of her fellow passengers' travel plans. Their casual references to Cairo, Ceylon, and Java were like "the shining balls of a juggler" hanging in the air.[1] Listening and watching, she began scribbling in a notebook the impressions that would eventually become two articles for *Harper's* magazine.

The Benedicts were waiting for her in southern Italy, where they took a ship bound for the Greek island of Corfu. The next morning, Constance looked out to see blue sky, purple mountains, and the red sails of a fishing boat, all overhung by a golden atmosphere. When they arrived in Greece, the light and colors astounded her—violet fields, a sapphire sea, and "salmon, . . . ochre, saffron, and cinnamon brown" hues.[2]

They spent eleven days in Corfu, including Christmas, exchanging presents in their rooms and attending an English church service packed with sailors and soldiers. From Corfu, they rather boldly sailed

Constance's sister Clara and her niece Clare, now twenty-one years old, were Constance's travel companions to Corfu, Athens, Egypt, and the Holy Land. (From *Voices Out of the Past*, vol. 1 of *Five Generations (1785–1923)*)

without male protection on a small steamer through the Ionian Sea. Constance recalled "everything poetical & classical [she] had ever read, from Homer to Childe Harold," and delighted in the "picturesque effects of the Greek & Albanian peasants on board, & their remarkable costumes & luggage."[3]

Their adventure turned threatening, however, when they approached Patras late at night and were greeted by a mob of Greek men, some of them armed with pistols, competing to secure their luggage. One even grabbed Constance by the arm and tried to drag her toward another hotel. They were finally rescued by their landlord. Upon their departure from Patras, as they attempted to board a train bound for Athens, they were greeted by a crowd of irate boatmen protesting the new railway. A policeman was thankfully on hand to shield them. It unnerved them to discover that women were not "accorded, without question, a first place," as they were in the United States and Europe.[4]

Athens quickly erased the memories of Patras. The Acropolis and the Parthenon were the most beautiful sights of Constance's life thus far. But she was eager to push farther. They decided to sail for Alexandria and then travel to Cairo. Constance never expected to be able to make such a trip, but Sam's money and Clara's offer to pay for her voyages to and from Cairo made it possible.[5]

When they landed at Alexandria, Constance was captivated by her first encounter with Arabs. She explained to her friend and editor Henry Mills Alden, "I knew they were there, before I saw them; but there was no realization of them in my mind. Now, I can picture to myself also the swarms of humanity in India and China. And as I was greatly struck by the intelligence & dignity of the oriental character, I can't look down upon them as I used to,—from a superior Anglo-Saxon standpoint. That is the trouble of traveling widely over the world, and living for years in foreign countries; one inevitably loses one's old standards, and comfortable fixed prejudices and opinions."[6]

As soon as they arrived in Cairo, they found rooms at the Continental. (The more popular Shepheard's Hotel was full following the arrival of Henry Morton Stanley, fresh from his exploration of Africa.) Achmed, a "charming boy in his lovely silk suit," waited on them and escorted them on their expeditions, beginning with the sites recommended by Daniel Willard Fiske, whose notes were their constant companion.[7]

Unfortunately, it poured for two days as soon as they arrived and was colder than they expected. The lack of cheery fires turned their rooms into dank cells. Clara was especially unhappy, fearing she had contracted malaria. Constance was for once undeterred by the cold. She told Sam, "I do'nt know what Clara has been writing to Cleveland on the subject of 'Cairo.' But I, at least, am fascinated & charmed." The trip restored her health and, more importantly, her enthusiasm for life. She felt "twenty years younger," she wrote to Sam just before her fiftieth birthday. While Clara wanted to cut their trip short, Constance began to contemplate staying on by herself. Her sister was dumbfounded, saying that if she were left there alone, she would "become a howling dervish in a day."[8]

Before her sister and niece's departure, the three took excursions to the Sphinx and the Pyramids, where they had their picture taken, Constance appearing fat and happy on her donkey. She refused to ride a camel, and even donkeys were a source of terror for her. They also took a short trip up the Nile to the temple ruins and their tombs. The silver and reddish-gold colors of the desert and the caravan of camels reminded her of images from the Bible. They discovered on these trips relics more ancient than any they seen had seen in Greece, including a mummy over 5,700 years old.[9]

After the Nile, they joined some American friends for a hurried, ten-day tour through the Holy Land. They sailed from Port Said to Jaffa, then traveled to Jerusalem, a nearly full moon illuminating the treeless landscape. Constance was captivated by the Church of the Holy Sepulchre in Jerusalem, the supposed site of Jesus's crucifixion and burial, as large and ornate as Saint Mark's in Venice. A very large group of Russian peasant pilgrims, who had walked most of the way from their homeland, impressed the three women from Cleveland with their intense devotion, kneeling down to kiss the stones, tears running down their faces. In contrast, Constance and the two Claras rushed through the attractions, rising at four or five in the morn-

Constance, Clare, and Clara (left to right) on their trip to the Pyramids.
(The Western Reserve Historical Society)

ing so as to make it to Jericho, Jordan, and Bethlehem before mother and daughter sailed back to Europe. In order to make the trip, poor Connie had to endure three days on horseback. "Do'nt ask me how I arrived," she wrote to Sam, "but think of [explorer] Lady Hester Stanhope." At the end of their journey, they felt as if "part of our being has remained still in the 19th century, while another part of it, has seemed, in some unaccountable way, walking about in the bible days."[10]

ALONE IN CAIRO

With the Benedicts gone, Constance returned to Cairo and quickly found herself at the center of the large expatriate community there. Europeans had long had a strong presence in the region due to the strategic location of the Suez Canal. Since 1882, the British had occupied Egypt in the face of opposition by nationalist forces. During Constance's stay in 1890, the British were attempting to modernize Egypt's economy and political system, but anticolonial resistance remained strong.

Unlike earlier in Florence, Woolson was the feted literary lion, with no one else's shadow to hide in. The American consul Eugene Schuyler visited her daily, bearing flowers or books as tokens of his fondness. She had met him and his wife in Florence as friends of Professor Fiske. A career diplomat, he was also the author of a series of essays on Russian history and literature for *Scribner's Magazine* as well as the first English translator of Turgenev and Tolstoy. He hated Egypt, he told Woolson, but he loved spending time with her and talking about writing. Her literary views were a revelation to him. "She has quite set me up," he wrote to a correspondent. "She cares not about plot, but only for the way things are done, and she puts my little stories way, way up, next to the French, for *facture* [workmanship]. Now she wants me to write a play, and has left me a lot of French ones to read and profit by." Woolson later wrote to Hay, "His whole interest was in his new idea of writing fiction, & upon that he would talk for hours." After he died of malaria, three months later, she realized that she was one of the last Americans who had spent much time with him.[11]

Another daily companion in Cairo was James Peirce, a Harvard professor of mathematics. Although their relationship, which would continue beyond Cairo, seems to have been based primarily on their shared fascination with "the Orient," Peirce also shared many associates with Henry James, including Peirce's brother, the philosopher Charles Sanders Peirce, and two close friends: Thomas Sergeant Perry, who had visited Constance in Florence, and Edmund Gosse.

The German archeologist Emile Brugsch Bey was a frequent companion as well. He thrilled her with the story of his famous discovery of the pharaohs' mummies at Deir el-Bahri: how he descended the shaft into a chamber that had been hidden for three centuries and there saw names on the coffins—among them Ramses the Great—that so astounded him he had to be pulled back up to keep from fainting. He also shared with her his agitation over the success of the English Egyptologist Amelia B. Edwards's lecture tour in the United States. Constance sensed his incredulity "that women could be very profound scholars in anything," and although she didn't agree, she feared it would "take several generations of study and training before our . . . women can equal our men."[12]

The popular Scottish novelist Margaret Oliphant also made an impression on Constance, although they were not close. She wrote to Sam, "I listened to her, (& secretly studied her) very intently; I was curious to find out the secret of the amount of work she produces; she has written about forty novels, & still turns them out at the rate of two or three each year!" In actuality, Oliphant had already written at least eighty novels. For a slow, deliberate writer like Woolson, such an output was inconceivable. Oliphant's secret, she discovered, was a team of people—maid, niece, and son—who relieved her of every conceivable task outside of her writing, even putting on her bonnet and shoes. Oliphant also gathered her impressions quickly, breezing through the Holy Land in a mere two weeks in preparation to write a book about the region. By contrast, Constance stayed in Cairo for two and a half months and felt only barely qualified to "risk some slight 'impressions.'" She was certainly "not a Mrs Oliphant!" she told Sam.[13]

The notes Constance gathered during her stay in Cairo would have made a long book, but the Harpers wanted her to write another novel. In the two-part essay she wrote instead, "Cairo in 1890," she appears curious and remarkably nonjudgmental about the strikingly different modes of life she encountered. Constance ventured far beyond the expatriate and colonial community in her research. For instance, she made it her special mission, as she rode through the narrow streets of Cairo on a donkey, to follow the minarets and hunt down mosques unmentioned by the guidebooks. One day she stumbled upon a small mosque that had never been visited by Western tourists and had no slippers to cover her "unsanctified shoes." Her request to enter was met with a fierce glare, but when she made an offering to the blind, who were considered sacred, the mats were rolled up, "the three or four Muslims present withdrew to the door, and the unbeliever was allowed to enter." Once inside, she reveled in the stunning marble, mosaics, and gilded inscriptions.[14] On her way out, she noticed that a line of blind men had gathered by the door.

The religious piety of Muslims made a great impression on Constance. She noted on the face of one praying man "a more concentrated expression of devotion" than she had ever seen. From the window of her hotel, she observed a plasterer who stopped his work to wash, kneel toward Mecca, and pray. In a letter to Alden she described the impact of Egypt on her religious views. In response to his declaration that Christianity was not the only sanctified religion, she enthused, "When one has been in Egypt—the jumping-off place of history—one comes to believe in ages and ages of human existence; one loses one's way, & all one's old standards and measuring lines. One cannot come back to one's beliefs, & it is exasperating to be asked to come back."[15]

Constance regretted that she rarely had the opportunity to engage Egyptians personally. One day, as she visited the Gizeh Museum, home to the treasures of Deir el-Bahri, she was intrigued by a group of women watched over by eunuchs; they turned out to be the harem of the minister for foreign affairs. She observed them closely, meticulously noting every detail of their appearance, including plump feet stuffed into preposterously high-heeled French slippers. For some time she stood next to one of them, a girl of about fourteen, as they examined together the jewelry of Queen Ahhotpu. She felt a connection to the girl and "our sister in vanity of three thousand five hundred years ago." As their faces came close together, the girl's eyes rose to meet hers, and Constance longed to be able talk to her in her own language.[16]

Everywhere she went in Cairo, she was accompanied by her guide and interpreter. As a Western woman, she was exempt from the strict rules regarding the seclusion of women. She noted that the locals, who "consider all strangers more or less mad," did not object to her prying eyes. When she had the opportunity to go inside a building housing local university students, she and her companion moved from room to room, peering inside at men praying, washing, playing chess. One young man smiled back at them and bowed.[17]

Constance was also a frequent visitor at El Azhar University of Cairo, where instruction was grounded in the Koran. She learned as much as she could about the curriculum and customs of the students. The persistence of medieval rituals deeply interested her; she described the university as "a living relic, a survival in the nineteenth century of the university of the fourteenth and fifteenth." The fatalist in her predicted that it would not survive much longer, however, in the face of Western expansion. The romantic side of her lamented the loss of old traditions in the face of so-called modern progress. She was horrified, for instance, by the Western hotel at the foot of the pyramids, where guests played lawn tennis in the shadow of the ancient tombs.[18]

Nonetheless, Woolson was very much a product of her age's aestheticism, which coveted the oriental splendors of Egyptian architecture, tapestries, and mosaics. For her readers she cataloged the sensory delights of the bazaars: "the sumptuousness of the prayer carpets, the gold embroideries, the gleaming silks, the Oriental brass-work with sentences from the Koran, the ivory, the ostrich plumes, . . . the turquoises and pearls . . . [and] the far-penetrating mystic sweetness" of the perfumes. A particularly popular souvenir was the scarab, an ancient amulet in the shape of a beetle that signified renewal and resurrection. Constance left Cairo with three of them, as well as a bronze figure of a praying Arab, given to her by Clara.[19]

But Woolson did not simply satisfy her readers' aesthetic desires. She also invited them to look beyond their own customs and beliefs and follow the local men who waited on tourists like themselves into the cafés where they loafed, sipping coffee and smoking pipes. Their behavior might seem decadent to American and English eyes, but it was probably the only sustenance the poor men had all day. Woolson strived to understand Egyptian men's custom of a daily rest in cafés, baths, or the streets from their perspective, quoting lines from the *Rubaiyat of Omar Khayyam* by the twelfth-century Persian poet:

> I sent my soul through the invisible,
>> Some letter of that after-life to spell;
> And by-and-by my soul returned to me,
>> And answered, "I myself am heaven and hell!"

Such was the motto of the coffeehouse where one heard the poem recited in Arabic. She reflected, "[F]or if the heaven or hell of each

"An Arab Café."
(From "Cairo in 1890," *Mentone, Cairo, and Corfu*)

person is simply the condition of his own mind, then if he is able every day to reduce his mind, even for a half-hour only, to a happy tranquility which has forgotten all its troubles, has he not gained that amount of paradise?"[20]

Lest her readers miss her larger point, Woolson concludes "Cairo in 1890" with an argument against "the habit of judging the East from the standpoint of one's home customs." The hurried traveler does not have the time to do anything but "observ[e] from the outside alone, which is sure to be founded upon misapprehension." By staying for a while, as she had done in the American South and as she did in Cairo, one becomes "familiar with their traditions, their temperament, their history, and, above all, with the language which they speak." What she found there filled her with wonder. "The East is the land of mystery. If one cares for it at all, one loves it; there is no half-way." She felt a kinship, even, with Egypt that she expressed in a letter to Hay: "[A]t last I know my own land; it is Egypt. There must be Egyptian blood in me somehow."[21]

Constance's impressions from her trip would remain vivid for quite some time. Months later she wrote to Dr. Baldwin of "the great winter of my life. Nothing has ever so much impressed me as Egypt; even now I am still excited about it. I feel like another person—so broadened in mind by an actual look into the strange life of the East." Referring to her adventures, James called her, in a letter to Boott, "our modern Fenimore."[22]

DEADLY DULL CHELTENHAM

Constance sailed from Egypt for England on April 19, 1890. She withdrew into herself and spoke to no one on board. Her only companion was the recently published book *God in His World* by Henry Mills Alden. It was a lengthy argument for the presence of a Christian God in the modern world and a harbinger of the coming social gospel movement that sought to counter laissez-faire capitalism with the creation of a more perfect society. For Constance it had a more personal message. It broadened the spiritual quest that had begun on her trip to the East and would continue for the rest of her life.

Ultimately, she found it difficult to accept Alden's perfect faith that God's purpose would ultimately be revealed, that all of this world's sufferings were part of His plan. "The trouble with me," she confessed,

> is that I am constantly knocked down—as it were—by a horror of the cruelties of life; did you ever see a small insect, trying to climb a wall, and always, sooner or later, falling to the floor—only to begin again? That is I. If the cruelties do not happen to me personally (though many of them have happened, and continue to do so), they happen to some one within my sight; and then down I go again mentally, overwhelmed by the view of so much dreadful, & helpless, & often innocent (or comparatively innocent), suffering. I ca'nt get over it.

It seems her time in the East had been merely a reprieve. The old killing griefs were returning. Next to a passage in Alden's book that read

"The ultimate and only possible blessedness must be the extinction of existence," she wrote simply, "yes."[23]

Overall, however, Alden's book lifted her up when so much of contemporary literature confined itself to the colorless, ordinary life of the day. She found the book full of beautiful maxims. The line "In loving one another, we find God" she found lovely and true. Love was, she confessed, "almost the only real pleasure one can have in this existence."[24]

On arrival in England, Constance settled in the spa town of Cheltenham. Three hours from London and located between the cathedral towns of Gloucester and Worcester, Cheltenham promised healthy air, low prices, and few diversions. She found a second-floor apartment on the Promenade Terrace, a grand, tree-lined boulevard. As soon as she unpacked, she began to write for nine hours a day to "exorcise the ghosts of Cairo and Corfu," shaping the notes of her impressions into two articles.[25]

The seclusion and quiet of Cheltenham soon became tiresome. She pined for company. In July, Boott made a short visit while she was in the midst of feverish work, but he was soon on his way to the Continent. If she had known he would leave so quickly, she would have dropped everything, she complained to him. In September, Dr. Baldwin took the train from London, where he was staying with James, who had recently returned from Italy. Woolson relished recounting her adventures to him. James came for a visit the following week. In a letter to Boott, Woolson indicated that James seemed well but anxious about Alice, who had had another breakdown. Woolson tried to cheer him up. They took the train to Worcester and enjoyed the summer-like weather. As they sat on a bench next to the Severn River and looked up at the towering cathedral, they talked about his trip to Italy, where he had visited Bellosguardo for the first time since Lizzie's death. To Baldwin James wrote, "Miss Woolson, who seemed in very good care, regaled me with anecdotes of your visit, all calculated to make me try to walk in your footsteps & be not less remunerative a guest. I thought her refuge pleasant & comfortable enough for a time; but only for a time. And I left her more than ever struck with her capacity for solitude & concentration."[26]

These visits did little to allay her loneliness. Only two days after James's departure, Constance asked Katharine Loring for a visit of two or three days. She may actually have been fishing for an invitation to London, knowing that Alice's poor health would keep Katharine close to her. Alice and Katharine had been intimate companions since 1879. Alice was greatly dependent on her care and love, but the illnesses of Katharine's consumptive sister had often pulled her away from Alice's side. Beginning in 1890, Katharine was able to live with Alice full time in what many have called a Boston marriage. Katharine had been a teacher and was a staunch advocate of women's education, the kind of protofeminist Henry had mocked in *The Bostonians*. Shortly after penning her letter to Katharine, Constance went to London, no doubt for a visit with her friends. That fall Professor Peirce also came from London to dine with her and to talk about Egypt, while Eleanor Poynter, who was in London for the winter, came for ten days. They talked of Boott and played his songs on the piano. In November, when Alice was doing better, Katharine was finally able to come. Constance felt "ten years younger" after her visit.[27]

Most of the time, however, Constance's companions were books. She riled herself up with Ruskin, whose pedantry she had grown to hate, and made her way through some popular books by authors such as Edna Lyall and Marie Corelli, which she found "very edifying." Her reading also included the correspondence of Wagner and Liszt, lives of Charles Darwin and Muhammad, Schopenhauer's *The World as Will and Idea*, and Rudyard Kipling's Eastern stories. She became particularly absorbed in reading reports from the London-based Psychical Research Society, which investigated paranormal phenomena. During his visit, Professor Peirce dismissed them as illusions, but she was more willing to side with the society's advocates, which included William James. At a meeting of the society in late October, Henry read his brother's account of a medium who had helped him and his wife contact their deceased son. In 1894, William would become the society's president. Telepathy particularly interested Constance. She confessed to Boott, "I sometimes almost believe I have a power of some sort; but I don't know what sort.—Such odd things now & then happen. It may be nothing but a vivid imagination, & easily roused sympathy."[28] It may also have been an increasing eagerness to connect with a world beyond this one.

In spite of Cheltenham's dullness, it served its purpose. The writing was going well. She wrote to Boott in September, "The way to be tranquil is to produce (for a writer, or for any artist). If he (or she) does his work well, that is sufficient; or ought to be. I have laid out several pieces of work, & I have enough to occupy me for two years. I feel very hopeful, & all is going smoothly." Her aching wrist was still a bother, though. She feared she had worn it out and wished she could dictate to a typist, but she didn't believe she could ever adjust to that method of composition.[29]

In October she received news of the death of her brother-in-law, Samuel L. Mather, severing one of the last remaining links to her American past. To his son Sam she wrote, "The tie that bound me to him was (with the one exception of Clara) the oldest I had left." Samuel had "remained a real brother" to her, even though her sister Georgiana, his wife, had died thirty-seven years earlier. She was glad to learn that he had received the note she had sent telling him she had "always loved him dearly." Samuel had presciently written to her the previous summer that he feared he would never see her again because she was now "wedded to Europe."[30] So she seemed to be. Yet she still talked of going back to see Sam and Flora and their boys, now joined by a little girl whom they had named Constance, after her. Constance was overcome with the tribute and yearned more than ever for at least a brief visit to what had once been her home.

HIBERNATING

As the season turned to winter, Constance's contentment evaporated. James, unaware of her growing discontent, assumed she was happily tucked away with her writing, but the frigid weather and increasing darkness were taking their toll. By Christmas, she complained that daylight lasted for only three hours a day. She bought a new copy of

Dickens's *A Christmas Carol*, which reminded her of past celebrations when her family lived in Cleveland. Declining an invitation to London, she stayed home with her "plum pudding as large as a tea-cup" and the ghosts of Christmases past.[31]

As the new year arrived and the freezing weather continued, Constance could no longer hide her low spirits. She wrote to Sam, "[L]et the air grow really cold, and down I go toward the gates of death." Her rooms were warm and her throat was fine, but she felt lifeless and depressed. She thought of getting a dog to keep her company. She missed Pax, the dachshund from Bellosguardo, and lingered over the latest photo of the Mather children, writing to Sam and Flora that family "is the best thing in life; it's the only thing worth living for; this is the sincere belief—& the result of the observations—of one who has never had it!"[32]

While the bitter wind blew outside, Constance lived on her memories, writing a new story, "Dorothy," set at the Villa Castellani and Villa Montauto. It was her "farewell to Bellosguardo," filled with American and British exiles wandering up the hill from Florence for entertainment in the evenings. An unusually high number of widows and older unmarried women find in the art, scenery, and society of Florence compensations for their solo lives in exile. "For the detached American ladies, who haven't yet come to calling themselves old— for the cultivated superfluous and the intelligent remainders—there is nothing like Europe!" one character declares.[33]

Constance put something of herself into an older, single British woman, Felicia, who takes long, aimless walks simply to wear herself out, and sings Francis Boott's "Through the Long Days" with deep emotion, which she struggles to hide from the assembled guests. Felicia meanders home to her lonely apartment in Florence while the man she loves, Alan Mackenzie, celebrates his marriage to a "flighty little creature," nineteen-year-old Dorothy.[34]

To everyone's surprise, Dorothy is not as shallow as she seems. Only Mrs. Charlotte Tracy, a widow of fifty who is a keen observer of others' concealed feelings, sees the grief underneath her stoic exterior when Alan dies suddenly of Roman fever. Everyone else assumes

Dorothy was too young to love deeply and looks forward to her excellent "career" now that she has inherited his money. But Dorothy shows signs of restlessness and melancholy, singing "Through the Long Days" in a soft, low voice.[35]

Like Alice James, Dorothy has simply lost the will to live. When she confesses her deep unhappiness, her stepmother sends for the doctor. He can find nothing to treat. All he can do is sedate her. "Has science no resources for such a case?" Dorothy's friends ask him. But just as Alice James had found, Victorian medical science had no understanding of the relationship between the mind and the body and the power of grief to kill. After Dorothy dies, the women are furious that "[t]he doctors did not tell us." But, the narrator concludes, "the doctors did not know."[36]

Woolson assured Boott that the story was "wholly fiction," not about anyone he knew, but based on a young woman she had known in the United States who had similarly wasted away and died of grief after the loss of her older, wealthy husband.[37] That may be. Yet "Dorothy" also expresses Constance's own grief over losing Boott and her life at Bellosguardo, which had come rushing back to her during the introspective months at Cheltenham. She would never fully recover from the loss.

Constance also began to look even farther back to other losses, writing to Sam of her father and their trips to Zoar and the Tuscawaras Valley in Ohio and summers on Mackinac Island. Her thoughts also returned to Zeph Spalding, whom she had heard was in Italy with his family. She revealed to her nephew that she had once "cared" for the colonel, but she held no ill will. She saw now that her feelings had not been deep; they had only been aroused by the excitement of the war. She was happy for him in his good fortune.[38]

About this time, James reentered Woolson's life. Her trip to the East and his to Italy had kept them apart for most of 1890, and since his return they had seen each other only once as they were both preoccupied with work. With the opening of his play *The American*, their friendship strengthened. After the premiere in Southport, on January 3, 1891, he stopped in Cheltenham on his way back to London to share with Woolson the story of his "splendid success."[39]

A few days later, Woolson met James and Katharine Loring in Stratford-upon-Avon for a performance of *The American*. She knew the play well, having read it "act by act, as it was written." Unfortunately, however, she was unable to hear a single line of dialogue. Her deafness made her feel, in the packed theater, more alone than ever. Only when Boott pressed her on the details of the performance did she relate to him the demoralizing experience in the most revealing letter to have survived on how her hearing loss was plunging her into a silent world. "Yes, I went over to Stratford," she wrote. "I did'nt speak of it, because, while there, & for a good while afterwards, I was, at heart, greatly depressed. To be sitting between K. Loring and H.J., to be unable to hear either a word they were saying, or a word that was uttered on the stage, was hard." Her father's old lesson of fortitude failed her. "Generally, I do not mind the hardships of my lot in life much," she explained, "having been prepared for them very carefully by dear father, who was himself always brave and cheerful." She expected no response from Boott about it. "What ca'nt be cured, must be endured. And endured in silence." Only to him did she reveal her belief, echoing Epictetus, that "[w]hen suffering becomes too great, we are always at liberty to leave life altogether."[40]

What Boott wrote in return has not survived. In her next letter she thanked him for his sympathetic words. "[Y]ou know how to say the things that comfort me. . . . In the ten years I have spent abroad, no one has said so much. . . . [P]erhaps they think I do not need that sort of thing. They are much mistaken." Others understandably missed signs of her depression, which she carefully concealed. Her father had taught her "that a person who was bitter, depressed, downhearted, one or all, became at last unsupportable; a burden to everybody." She dreaded being a millstone around anyone's neck and so carefully hid her despair from James and Loring. They had enough to worry about with Alice, who had seemed to be "in a dying condition for months," which was "a great depression" to her brother.[41]

James's letters to Boott suggest Woolson was successful at putting on a brave face. He wrote in March, "I mustn't forget to tell you that Fenimore seems to have 'take[n] root' in the deadly Cheltenham. It helps her write lively novels. She tests well her staying power; & seems on the whole hearty enough." Meanwhile, she told Boott that she and James lived in two very different worlds now. "With his enjoyment of the world and of society, you may imagine what he thinks of my life in Cheltenham! He comes down here once in a while, looks at the place, looks at me, shakes his head, & departs. I think a month here would really kill him."[42]

In the midst of much talk about James's hopes of striking it rich in the theater—"the thirst for gold that is pushing me down this dishonorable path," as he described it to a friend—Woolson began to receive insistent letters from a newspaper syndicate that was paying Frances Hodgson Burnett $5,000 a year for all she could write. Requests also came from two other syndicates, and the agent of another planned to visit her to make his case in person. She let him know he was not welcome. Everything she could write must go to the Harpers, to whom she continued to feel indebted.[43] Her loyalty would cost her dearly, however.

Such liberal offers and news of others' prosperity—including the $10,000 Howells had earned from a syndicate for one novel—renewed her anxiety about her own financial situation. Her letters to Sam are filled with her worries and questions about her investments. She began to foresee a time when she would not be able to write anymore and wanted to begin putting aside money for her retirement. The youthfulness she had felt in Cairo was gone. When Boott complained to her of feeling his age, she responded pitifully, "But I'm older. There is nothing on earth so old as an old maid." Her goal was to live frugally enough so that she could invest the money earned by her writing over the next five or ten years. The plan required her to produce a considerable amount. It was, she had told Sam, "Now or never!"[44]

When the weather improved, Constance began taking walks in the countryside again and writing witty letters about the peculiar things she discovered, such as the tombstone that read, "Dear wife & children, pray Agree; / Quarrel no more. Then follow me." She fancied the man writing his own epitaph in a house "where missiles were flying about!" "All is well here," she told Sam in February. The discomforts of the winter had passed and she was working away in her "stodgy fairly-comfortable English sitting room" with a "gray English air outside."[45]

In May, Clara, Clare, and Kate returned to Europe and carried her off on excursions through southwestern England and Wales. James joined them for a day trip to Berkeley Castle near the Welsh border. Although her relatives tried to pull her away to Germany or Vienna, she felt that England, where it was easy to rent an apartment with a cook to provide private meals, was the best place for her to work. She dreaded most of all the common tables that were customary on the continent.[46]

After her visitors left, Constance made a quick trip to Oxford in early July and rediscovered her fascination with its fairy-tale atmosphere. Here was a place both bucolic and invigorating that might prove to be the perfect place to write her next novel.

14

Oxford

By the end of July 1891, Constance had settled into temporary rooms in Oxford on Beaumont Street near the Ashmolean Museum. One Sunday, soon after she unpacked, Dr. Baldwin came up from London to see her. Much of their talk was surely of Alice James. Baldwin had just seen her, at Constance's suggestion, and diagnosed the tumor recently discovered in her breast as cancerous. Alice seemed relieved by the diagnosis, glad finally to have a reason to die. Acknowledging "her intense horror of life," as Henry called it, those near to her could not be entirely pained by the news.[1]

Henry, who was recuperating from a bad case of influenza in Ireland, was grateful to Baldwin and glad to hear of his visit to Woolson, writing, "[E]njoy Oxford freely & sweetly, & as the most hospitable woman in the world will help you to do." At the end of the letter he added, "Will you kindly mention to Miss Woolson that I hope to stop & have a look at her on my way back to London? Therefore leave half a bottle of wine & the middle-age of a sofa cushion." He expressed to Boott his delight at her choice of residence. He thought it "a very right & good place for her." He didn't mention the fact that it was much closer to London, and to him—a quick hour by train. He didn't know about Woolson's "Bellosguardo story," he told Boott ("Dorothy" had not yet been published), but he would insist she send him a copy. He predicted that there would soon be "a good deal to show" for her "lonely industry" over the past year.[2]

Soon Constance found rooms for the summer in a charming house for students just outside the gates of Oriel College, in the heart of old Oxford. She could see Corpus Christi and the Canterbury Gate to Christ Church from her windows. A sweet little bulldog named Oriel Bill, a resident of the house, visited her every evening and came along on her walks through the colleges' gardens and meadows. A few years later the *English Illustrated Magazine* published an interview with Oriel Bill, in which he boasted, "I've distinguished acquaintances; one of the most intimate is a niece of Fenimore Cooper's, Miss Fenimore Woolson; she's putting me into a book just now." She often fed him and allowed him to nap before her fire.[3]

Oxford suited Constance perfectly. She could row on the Isis and Cherwell Rivers, where the presence of other women plying the oars made her feel less conspicuous. The town's pastoral meadows and gardens gave her the peaceful landscapes she craved. Its history and architecture, not to mention its monastic atmosphere, appealed to the scholar in her. Although two women's colleges had been founded in 1879, as the students began to return she realized how much the university town was "given over entirely to men and their belongings."[4] Nonetheless, she felt strangely at home among the students, Oxford providing the proper setting for her own solitary work.

With the start of winter term in October, Constance found comfortable rooms in a Regency-era townhouse at 15 Beaumont Street, two doors from her first residence. Her flat on the top floor had a sitting room, dining room (with meals provided), bedroom, and small trunk room. Once she was settled in such agreeable lodgings, "all cheerful, and with big English coal fires," she was content, writing to Sam, "I think I am in the right niche at last."[5]

After spending her days at her writing desk, she wandered the countryside, if the weather permitted, searching for the sites mentioned in two of her favorite Matthew Arnold poems, "The Scholar Gipsy" and "Thyrsis." Then she would stop on her way home at Christ Church Cathedral for evensong, admiring the students in their angel-like white robes and sitting next to the organ to hear its thunderous chords. After walking home through the foggy streets she made tea in her Japanese teapot and wrote letters by the fire.[6]

Oxford's nearness to London also meant that she saw "more of life and the world," and she soon found herself within James's crowded orbit. When his play *The American* had its London premiere on September 26, she was in the audience, seated among the playwright's friends and other distinguished guests. William James, in London to say goodbye to his dying sister, was also there. Constance was pleased to get a look at him, but they did not have a chance to talk in the crowded theater. She sat with Loring on one side and Henry's friend, Wolcott Balestier, on the other. Balestier had just coauthored a novel with Rudyard Kipling and was a literary agent helping to bring American authors to a European audience. He was particularly kind to Woolson, pointing out the celebrities—John Singer Sargent, George Du Maurier, and others. Woolson did her best to fit in with the "splendor on all sides." Presumably she again had difficulty hearing, but nonetheless she thought the play "a great success." Reviews were mixed, however, and it wasn't until the Prince of Wales made his appearance and James revised the play that ticket sales picked up. Woolson was loyal throughout. She attended at least five performances, causing James to exclaim to Baldwin, "[T] here's friendship for you!"[7]

The evening after the opening of the play, Woolson finally had the chance to meet William properly, presumably while she was visiting Alice or Henry. Even though he was only there for ten days, William also came to see her on the eve of his departure for America. Henry had not written much to William about Constance over the years, so it was probably Alice who conveyed to William and/or his wife her significance in their brother's life. Constance wrote afterward that she thought William "perfectly delightful; so kind; so agreeable; so witty, so sympathetic." She now wanted to read his book, *The Principles of Psychology*, published the year before.[8]

Her trips to London and her new acquaintances reignited Constance's desire for social interaction. In an effort to more fully engage with the world, she began to investigate some of the new hearing devices on the market. The most dramatic claims were being made for artificial eardrums, partly made of gold and tucked out of sight inside the ear canal. She decided to give them a try. Although the device was not expected to show results for six months to three years, she began to notice improvement very quickly. She was able to "hear a good deal" of an opera she saw in London with Clara and Clare, who were in England for a brief stay before returning home for the winter.[9]

Back in Oxford, Constance received a call from Margaret Louisa Woods, wife of the president of Trinity College and the author of a well-received novel, *A Village Tragedy*, published in 1888. Woods, who was fifteen years younger than Woolson, was a friend of Rhoda Broughton's and sought her out in hopes of finding a kindred spirit and mentor. Others would also be seeking her out, Woods informed Woolson, who wasn't sure whether to be delighted or chagrined. "I like it, & I do'nt like it!" she explained to Boott. "I was born sociable & hospitable, & I ca'nt eradicate the traits. Yet I need all my time for other employments," namely writing.[10]

About this time Woolson also received a visit from Wolcott Balestier, who had been reading her works. He wanted to get to know the woman who "knew enough of the undercurrent of common American life" to create a "slangy, unpoetical, tobacco-chewing" male character in *Jupiter Lights*, the type of plain American he said most women writers avoided. He also wanted to publish the book in the English Library series, which he had started with William Heinemann. Other writers in the series included James, Howells, Kipling, Robert Louis Stevenson, and Mary Wilkins Freeman. Woolson was flattered by the attention. When Balestier died suddenly of typhoid fever in Germany a few months later, James was distraught and Woolson lost a potential ally in the literary world. Nonetheless, both *Jupiter Lights* and *Anne* were published in the English Library series.[11]

AN INFERNAL WINTER

Around Christmastime, James came up to see Woolson and reported to Baldwin in Florence, "[S]he clings to her antique Oxford & is very busy & contented, seemingly, & void of any offense save that of writing hours & hours on end & bringing on that horrid complaint in her arm & shoulder. But of this, she is incurable."[12] She had little choice, of course, if she was to save money for the future.

As 1892 dawned, the idyll of Oxford turned into a nightmare. The Russian influenza pandemic was reaching the peak of its devastation in England. James had been ill with the flu the previous summer. Now the whole country seemed to be enveloped in a sinister black fog. "England has been like one continuous funeral," she wrote to Baldwin. The death on January 14 of the Duke of Clarence, son of the Prince of Wales and second in line to the throne, dispirited all of England. Constance likened the epidemic to "one of the Plagues of the Middle Ages." Oxford was hit particularly hard. In January, the weekly death toll from the flu rose into the double digits. The start of term was postponed "for the first time in living memory."[13]

In early January, Constance fell very ill—not from influenza, she insisted, but from a cold that left her with a great pain in her head that a local doctor called "neurotic." In other words, he thought it was in her mind. She thought her artificial eardrums were the culprits. The pain was "simply infernal," she told Baldwin, whom she wished was nearby. One night, she thought she "should be mad, or dead, before morning." As the stabbing sensation in her head receded, an unrelenting earache took its place and lasted at least four weeks. At times it felt like a knife was being thrust into her ear. There seemed to be "a slow gathering in the inner ear," first on one side, then the other.[14] She probably had acute ear infections.

In those days before antibiotics, narcotics were the only available treatment. She didn't think she could tolerate the pain much longer. She used a steaming kettle and linseed poultices to help clear her congestion, but they weren't much help. She was descending again into hopelessness. Only relentless attempts at reading and taking sleeping draughts sustained her. Such medications were usually derived from opium. Knowing how addictive they were, she asked Baldwin if he could send her a prescription for one that wasn't harmful.[15]

Constance was hardly in a state to receive visitors, but her friend Eleanor Poynter came up from London against her wishes. Poynter found the curtains closed and Constance lying on the sofa with her head wrapped up, unable to hear or talk due to the pain. Poynter proved herself a true friend and wrote on a slate to communicate. That afternoon a telegram from Henry James arrived with news of Rudyard Kipling's sudden marriage (against his family's wishes) to Balestier's sister. Woolson shared it with Poynter, who was related to Kipling and wrote on the slate, "I am flabbergasted!"[16]

During Constance's long illness, her landlady, Mrs. Phillips, became her friend and nurse. She kept the fire going, even creeping into Constance's room at night. Mrs. Phillips had "a great admiration for literature" and said she felt privileged to be able to help Constance complete her book. Knowing that such care was hard to find, Constance decided to stay in Oxford until her novel was finished.[17]

Nonetheless, she yearned more than ever for a home of her own. She wrote to Boott that she wished they and his family could have lived on at Bellosguardo. She imagined him composing songs and going to Paris every year and Frank and Lizzie painting, while the baby grew up "a beautiful Florentine" and she happily lived out her days at the Villa Brichieri with the little dog Pax.[18]

The pain in her ears, which lasted for six weeks, was, she told Boott, "very depressing. . . . But there is worse suffering all about me & I must not complain too much. Alice James, for instance; hers is one long martyrdom." From her deathbed Alice continued to send Constance clever missives, in spite of her growing pain. "If she had any health, what a brilliant woman she would have been," she mused. Although none of their final correspondence has survived, it is clear they had a great admiration for each other to the end.[19]

After spending most of her adulthood in pain and wanting her life

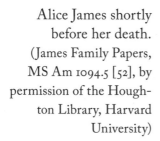

Alice James shortly before her death. (James Family Papers, MS Am 1094.5 [52], by permission of the Houghton Library, Harvard University)

to end, Alice James died on March 6, 1892. The final lines in her diary were about Loring reading to her Woolson's story "Dorothy," which had appeared in that month's *Harper's*.[20] It was an appropriate way for Constance and Alice to say farewell to each other, given the story's themes. They both understood what the doctors did not.

Constance was glad to learn that Alice's suffering had ended, convinced that she had found her way to a better place. She, however, remained in this world, fighting to keep body and mind intact. With the failure of her experiment with artificial eardrums, she feared she would have to resign herself to silence and the small group of friends likely to make an effort to talk into her ear trumpet. Henry, who would always take the trouble, came to see Constance a week after Alice's funeral to tell her about his sister's final days. Constance must have been particularly interested in the dream Alice had shortly before her death of Lizzie Boott and another friend from their Cambridge days heading out to sea in a boat and looking back at her.[21]

Sometime before she died, Alice left a touching final message for Constance. Its contents are a mystery, but it was sensitive enough that

Constance later regretted mentioning it to Sam during his brief visit to her in Oxford the following year. She had spoken without thinking "whether it was safe or not, wise or not, prudent or not." The message very likely concerned her and Henry's relationship. At least one of his biographers believes that Alice's message was intended to "resign her brother to Fenimore's care. Expert in grief, infinite in charity, Fenimore might take on the 'griefs, or aches or disappointments' of her brother's life."[22] Given Constance's discomfort about revealing the message to Sam, it seems quite possible that Alice had given her blessing for some kind of union between Constance and Henry. She might have wished to bring them together, hoping they could find the support and comfort she and Katharine had found in each other.

The hole Alice's death left in Henry's life would not be filled easily. After the funeral he wrote to Boott that "she contributed constantly, infinitely to the interest, the consolation, as it were, in disappointment and depression, of my own existence."[23] After Alice's death and Constance's recovery, Henry's visits to Oxford became more frequent. They had reached a new stage in their friendship, but it remained to be seen what form it would take.

COLLABORATION IN ART AND LIFE

Henry often came up to Oxford for dinner in May, while the Benedicts were visiting. Constance brought her sister and niece to garden and tea parties at Trinity and Balliol Colleges as well as to the races, or "Eights," during Boat Week, when they were invited to sit on the Trinity barge. They spent much time with Margaret Woods, who invited Constance to meet the novelist Mrs. Humphry Ward, who was also a friend of James's. Mrs. Ward had "an estate in Surrey, with a park & deer" that she had purchased with the earnings of one novel, *Robert Elsmere*, which Woolson thought a rather poor book.[24]

Constance was growing weary of working so hard and not being able to afford an apartment in Venice or a cottage in Florida. Her investments were bringing in about $500 per year (about $13,000 in today's money). Her royalties in 1890, after the publication of *Jupiter Lights*, had been about $560; in 1891, about $220. Her plans of saving for retirement had not materialized over the past two winters. She had not been able to get by on the interest her bonds earned in order to invest her earnings, as she had hoped. Moreover, she was already a year late turning in the manuscript of her new novel. She needed an infusion of cash that only serial rights would bring. Finally, the Harpers sent her an advance that would enable her to complete her novel "with a mind freed from anxiety."[25]

Woolson's painstaking method of writing her books and her desire to stay with Harper & Brothers were putting her at a tremendous disadvantage in the increasingly diversified literary marketplace. And she resented watching others—like Ward, Oliphant, or Howells—thrive within it. Earlier that year she had complained to Boott, "To have a hunger for fame is one of the greatest of miseries. And especially for the artist, whether painter, sculptor, poet, author, or musician. And yet how can we help feeling it, when we are neglected, especially when those who are (artistically speaking) less worthy, reap the richest harvests, while we are left with nothing! An artist, of course, ought to find happiness in his art; his soul should live in a serene empyrean, far above the madding (and ignorant) crowd. But it isn't always easy to do this!"[26] No doubt she and James had been commiserating. For years he had been frustrated by the poor sales of his books. Although he was much more prolific than Woolson, producing potboilers alongside his more serious work, he also lived more lavishly than she did. The theater was not turning out to be the gold mine he had hoped for, but he hadn't given up on it yet. The tug between his desires for greatness *and* monetary success—his fury, in fact, over not being able to have both—was the leitmotif of his career. Constance was more than sympathetic. She had not been able to duplicate the success of *Anne*, nor had she tried. She had been after a more elusive prey: artistic achievement, which required a patient labor not conducive to high productivity.

After the departure of Clara and Clare, Constance fell into her old routine, rising at six, working for eight hours, walking for three hours through the countryside, then dining and going to bed. She left letters unanswered and tried to avoid visitors. In July, Boott came to see her. She downplayed the significance of it to Sam, mentioning only that her friend from Bellosguardo was now over eighty.[27] No other record of their visit has survived. It was the last time they would meet in person.

In June 1892, in the midst of her novel writing, Woolson also published a new story, which she may have written earlier. That she dusted it off now is no surprise. "In Sloane Street," her only story set in England, seems to probe the thorny question of what she meant to James and what role she could play in his life, obliquely approaching the possibility that art might be better created in some kind of collaboration rather than in solitude. After Alice's death, that possibility seemed to virtually hover in the air.

James had first considered this question after staying with Woolson at Bellosguardo in 1887. Upon his return to London, he had written "The Lesson of the Master," which was published in 1888, when Woolson was hard at work on *Jupiter Lights*. She may not have read it, in fact, until it was published in book form in February 1892. In the story an older, successful male writer advises a protégée against marrying because it would mean, as it had in his own case, the death of serious ambition. A married man must write for money to satisfy his wife's social and material ambitions. When the young writer meets a woman who appears capable of inspiring rather than inhibiting his art, the "master," who believes no woman can truly sympathize with a man's work, convinces him she would be more concerned for her children's comforts and advantages than for the realization of his great idea. An artist must be, above all, free, he counsels. Ironically, when the older writer is later widowed, he turns around and marries the sympathetic young woman. The young writer feels duped, and the question of whether or not the former "master" will again become a great writer now that he is married to the right woman is left open at the end of the story.

It was as if James himself could not decide. For he had found in Woolson precisely the kind of woman capable of a "full interchange" of ideas about art and literature. Like his hero, he must have felt that "[h]e couldn't get used to her interest in the arts he cared for: it seemed too good to be real—it was so unlikely an adventure to tumble into such a well of sympathy." Constance wrote to Sam in 1889 that it was "dangerous to ask a writer of novels about novels! He may swamp you with the ocean of his words. The truth is, that, to a writer, the subject is so vast,—really his whole life's interest—that if he is to tell you what he really thinks, he will almost never get through. He can go on for days. This is the reason, I think, why writers like to be with writers, painters with painters, & so on; the subject of their art is to them really inexhaustible, & they never tire of it."[28] She was speaking of herself and, surely, James, who had noticed as early as 1883, during their first days together in London, how carefully she listened and how much she understood. What a rarity such comprehension was, he had written to Howells.

Woolson's "In Sloane Street" harkens back to that earlier time, the winter of 1883–1884, when she lived in Sloane Street in London and was receiving frequent visits from James for the first time. It portrays the consequences of a male writer's choice to marry a beauty who cares nothing for his work instead of a close friend who supports and comprehends his art, who in fact has the potential to be a co-creator. The story can be read as a response to "The Lesson of the Master," written from the intelligent woman's point of view. It may also be Woolson's suggestion to James of what he would lose if he chose a simple wife. However, she published it in *Harper's Bazar,* a women's magazine, where James was unlikely to see it.[29]

The protagonist of "In Sloane Street" is the American spinster Gertrude Remington, "[a] tall thin woman," bookish, stiff, and straight, with her hair pulled tightly back—no wonder "all men are afraid of her," another character remarks. She has accompanied the Moore family abroad, having been a friend of the husband, Philip, since childhood. He is a well-regarded writer who has difficulty supporting his family in the manner his "little . . . golden haired, blue-eyed" wife, Amy, would wish. She cares nothing for her husband's literary career, while Gertrude reads every word he writes and is his "chief incense burner." She wants to discuss his works, but he dislikes being dragged back to them after he has already moved on, something Woolson did to both James and Stedman. Philip goes so far as to profess that he would like Gertrude much better if she "had never read a word of them."[30]

Philip's disregard for Gertrude's attention is palpable. He has, moreover, little interest in the minds of women. He insists, in a conversation about George Eliot, to whose grave Gertrude is planning a visit, that "[w]omen can't write. And they ought not to try." When Gertrude presses him he admits, "Children's stories—yes; they can write for children, and for young girls, extremely well. And they can write little sketches and episodes if they will confine themselves rigidly to the things they thoroughly know, such as love stories, and so forth. But the great questions of life, the important matters, they cannot render in the least." Women, he concludes, are too ignorant of life to write anything of value. Noticing the surprise on Gertrude's face, he says, "You need not be troubled, you have never tried." She assents but hesitates before saying, "My ambition is all for other people"— him, of course.[31]

As the story progresses, it becomes clear that Gertrude could have been a writer herself. She is an avid and serious reader, defending the analytical novel against the more entertaining types that Amy prefers. She reads French literature, of which Amy also complains, and is currently reading the journals of Marie Bashkirtseff, which caused a sensation when they were published in English in 1888 for their frank self-exposure of a young artist who possessed the egotism of a Napoleon and the artistic ambitions of a Henry James. (In one entry Bashkirtseff wrote, "Outside of my art . . . outside of this passion . . . there is nothing, or only the most atrocious existence.") Amy is horrified not only that a young woman has recorded such thoughts but that she has had them at all. Gertrude admits that it may be abnormal to write them down, especially for publication, but that the ideas themselves seem to her perfectly normal. Imagine, she tells Amy, "[i]f some invisible power should reproduce with exact truthfulness each one of our secret thoughts, do you think we should come out of it so infinitely better than Marie Bashkirtseff?"[32] Gertrude, it seems, has her own secret thoughts, although she doesn't show them, repressing her jealousy of both Amy (for her marriage) and Philip (for his career), as well as her anger at Philip for choosing such a vapid woman over herself.

At the end of the story, after a scare in which one of the Moore children is believed to have been injured in the Underground, Philip embraces Amy and pets her like a child. He gives in to her demands for a more social life in Washington, which will necessitate their return to the United States and his writing for popularity rather than esteem. He is finally ready to accept offers from the syndicates that have been hounding him. "You would not wish to see him descend to a lower grade of work, would you?" Gertrude had naively asked Amy, who responds that to her a "higher grade" would be providing "a nice home in Washington." A novel has value to her when it is easy to read and amusing. Why can't he simply write more of this kind of novel, which sells by the tens of thousands? Gertrude is baffled by her simplicity. "It isn't purely mechanical work, you know," she responds. Gertrude knows as well as if she were the writer herself. In the final lines of the story, we learn that Gertrude, now home in America, "does not keep a diary" but that she has jotted down a note in her almanac about the Moores moving to Washington.[33]

Gertrude is an obviously autobiographical character—she dresses plainly, hates Ruskin, yearns for the pine barrens of Florida, and is a keen observer of character. She is also an image of the superfluous, discarded spinster Woolson feared she had become. She resented the superiority of married women who looked down on spinsters, as Amy does, calling them "queer" and "prudish" because of their inexperience.[34] She felt excluded from the unique bonds of spouses and children that everyone but she—and James—seemed to have. Gertrude, however, is forty-two and more closely resembles Woolson at that age, when she had lived in Sloane Street. Now, at fifty-two, Woolson faced another kind of superfluity—old age. Although hardly old, she had begun to fear the inevitable decline that she believed was fast approaching.

The publication of "In Sloane Street" three months after Alice's death suggests that Woolson wondered what it would be like to find a home not only in James's work but also in his life, for he had not married the sweet American wife she had thought he would. She was glad not to have been marginalized, as Gertrude was, but "In Sloane Street" still contains traces of the rejection she felt. She never got over feeling that she was undesirable as a woman, that men preferred the Amys of the world over the Gertrudes like her. What she didn't realize, it seems, is that James's lack of attraction to her was something altogether different. He was as good at hiding his desire for men as she was at hiding her desire to be loved.

We cannot know definitively Constance's and Henry's true feelings for each other. About this time, he told a friend who had remarked about his large circle of friends and acquaintances that he had "but <u>five real</u> friends, and she is one of them!" referring to Constance. Several of his biographers believe that he loved her—"in his way," writes one; "without loving her as a woman," writes another. She was his "other self," yet another has suggested.[35] She undoubtedly loved him as well, but her feelings for him had always been mixed with anxieties about ambition and art, as well as fears of losing her independence and identity. As she felt more vulnerable—in finances and in health—she may have begun to feel less ambivalent about the prospect of a union with him. Still committed to her art, she was nonetheless unsure how much longer she could continue to write. If she ever desired a life with James, she may have now when marriage would have seemed less threatening and more stabilizing. Rather than meaning the death of the artist, it could have signaled a rebirth of sorts, a merging of minds that would have allowed her to unite her ambitions with his, as so many wives of "great men" had done. In fact, Alice's message could have planted that seed in her mind.

Henry may have considered the possibility himself, especially if Alice also shared her message with him. He cared deeply for Constance and marriage could have provided a cover for his sexuality, as it did for many gay men of the time. He also was struggling just then with own fears of having failed to achieve greatness. Like Dencombe in his story "The Middle Years," which James wrote in the coming year, he seemed to be convinced that "[h]e should never again, as at one or two great moments of the past, be better than himself." He feared most of all being deprived of his second chance.[36] That Woolson could help James achieve that must have at least vaguely occurred to him.

However, other serious obstacles also stood in the way. He was wedded to England while she was increasingly anxious to return to Italy. Two horrific winters had cured her of her attachment to England, and she never talked of settling there. The fact also remained that James was still wary of intimacies that could siphon off his creative energies. A wife had always seemed to him a burden rather than a help. Woolson's fierce pride and independence would prevent her from even intimating an interest in marriage. Instead, they began to speak about collaborating on a play.[37] That plan would never come to fruition. Yet they had both come closer to collaboration in life or art than they ever would again.

HORACE CHASE

Finishing her novel proved to be a herculean task. The physical toll of writing was beginning to leave its mark. Woolson's hand wouldn't always do what her brain commanded, and the whole right side of her body felt "distorted." She could sometimes continue writing by holding the pen between different fingers. Such complications were common among writers. Within a few years James would employ a typist to take dictation, the method by which he wrote all of his later works. Woolson didn't think she could ever learn to write that way, but she did begin to employ others to copy her final drafts.[38]

Woolson realized that her laborious writing process was unusual. "I take my work hard," she wrote to Sam. "But we must all do as we can, & the only way I can write at all, is to do my very best. Something in me makes me take these enormous pains." Even as she felt the pressure to earn greater sums for her writing, she seemed less concerned with sales and more with craft. Fiction as an art form interested her immensely. She had no desire to sell out or write hastily. She increasingly set her sights on posterity. For her new novel, she moved well beyond James and his influences, looking to her contemporaries who were gaining recognition and copying ideas and mottoes into a notebook to guide her as she was planning and writing:

> The plot must be a riddle, so as to excite curiosity. My idea is that there should be a riddle; and exciting adventures. And growth of at least several of the characters, so that we will not be sure beforehand what they will do. An intense realism of description, & dramatic action like Kipling. Places described very & intensely actually—like some of Hardy. And there shall be nobility! . . . "One must either move sympathy, stir imagination, or raise hope." I will do all 3. . . . "Style alone will never confer fame. One must place one's self in accord with the permanent emotions of the whole race." . . . Have all the scenes as distinctly American as S. Jewett, & Miss Wilkins. . . . like [Mary] Murfree, but more realistic.

Kipling had made a great impression on her, as had Mary Wilkins (not yet Freeman), whose stories she thought "masterpieces." But she found them as yet rather "limited, . . . always the same local New England dialect, & country-people; principally old maids. But of their kind; I think them inimitable."[39]

Although Woolson wanted her book *Horace Chase*, which began its run in *Harper's* in January 1893, to be "intensely modern," for the setting she looked back twenty years to the time she had spent in Asheville and St. Augustine, when both towns were on the verge of development. Inspired by Henry Flagler's transformation of St. Augustine into a fashionable resort, she wrote a Gilded Age novel whose main character was the driving force of the modern era—the American businessman. Horace Chase, she told Alden, was "a careful study from actual life." She had observed plenty of such men growing up in Cleveland and later in Europe as they conquered the Old World with their new wealth. But she didn't want the novel named after him. She had always thought it presumptuous for women to claim to know "the masculine mind" well enough to call their novels *Adam Bede* or

Robert Elsmere. The Harpers had suggested *For Better, For Worse*, but the title had already been used, so they went back to *Horace Chase*. Woolson was mortified.[40]

In spite of her objections, it is not surprising that she chose a man as her central character, considering that she had written many stories from a male character's point of view. She may have been spurred on by Wolcott Balestier's praise of her portrayal of a minor male character in *Jupiter Lights*. Like him, Horace is a rather rough type, a prototypical self-made man, relatively uneducated but hardly illiterate. A "daring, keen, man of business," he enjoys the chase for money as much as the wealth itself. He has made his fortune many times over, first in baking soda, then in a silver mine (as the geologist Clarence King had), in lumber, and in an unspecified speculation in California.[41] Always on the lookout for new opportunities, Horace is drawn to Asheville, which he envisions as a future Swiss-style mountain resort or an American Baden-Baden with its nearby sulfur springs. Ironically, the development of the resort and the building of the railroad threaten the very wilderness that is the site's main attraction.

As a counterpart to Horace, Woolson included a man unfit for business. Jared Franklin is her most fully realized portrait of her brother, Charlie. Loved above his sisters by their mother, he fails at every enterprise and is so broken in body and spirit that he dies before his fortieth birthday. In his final days, he suffers from a "brain-fever" that leaves him ranting madly. In a scene reminiscent of Ferdie's rampage in *Jupiter Lights*, Jared climbs onto a roof in an apparent suicide attempt but is rescued by Horace. Nonetheless, Jared dies of fever within a few days.[42]

Jared's mother, Mrs. Franklin, resembles Hannah in many ways, and shows how much Constance was reflecting on the past during her lonely months in Cheltenham and Oxford. Details from her life with her mother make their way into the book, such as how she and Clara pretended Hannah was the grandmother of their dog, Pete Trone, Esq., who also appears. Mrs. Franklin's daughters—Dolly and Ruth—also tease their mother with a refrain modified from one that Connie and Clara chanted to their mother.[43]

Mrs. Franklin is plagued by financial worries, which disappear when Ruth marries Horace Chase, having fallen for his wealth. She is the feminine half of the Gilded Age's excess, with "no conception of life . . . as a lesson in self-control." She is the intellectual woman's foil: her "sweet, pure, physical womanhood . . . had not been refined away by over-development of the mental powers." She had a "great charm," to be sure, but the lack of "more masculine qualities [such as] stoical fortitude and courage" have left her vulnerable. This time, rather than allow the shallow beauty to simply triumph over her plainer, more intellectual counterpart, Woolson complicates her character by giving her the broken heart her more sensitive heroines usually suffer. When she falls in love with Chase's young partner, Walter, and discovers that her love is not returned, she becomes desperate and loses the will to live. In the end, she confesses her adulterous intentions to her husband, who forgives her and thus also proves himself to be a more complex character and a more noble man than most believed him to be. The heart of the novel, for Woolson, lay in Horace's final words to Ruth: "Have I been so faultless myself that I have any right to judge *you*?" Just then his "rugged face . . . was striking in its beauty; its mixture of sorrow, honesty, and grandeur."[44]

In contrast to Ruth, Woolson's portrait of the younger sister, Dolly, evokes Alice James and herself. Like Alice, Dolly suffers from an unknown malady. When a conventional woman waxes on about the "*privilege* of being a good wife," Dolly bursts out, "Privilege?" She possesses the observant eye and mind of a writer and writes poetry, but not seriously. Dolly explains to Horace, "I think in elegies as a general thing, and I make sonnets as I dress. Epics are nothing to me, and I turn off triplets in no time. But I don't publish, Mr. Chase, because I don't want to be called a *minor* poet."[45] Woolson had felt the same way. Dolly is also socially isolated by her infirmity, staying home while others go out or sitting in the corner while others dance.

One might wonder why, in her most modern novel, Woolson chose to incapacitate her most intellectually capable female character. However, all around Woolson were Dollies—women whose talents lay fallow, whose bodies were broken, who were ashamed of their uselessness. If she was well, Dolly says, she would work, as she hates being a burden. "Nobody stops to think how dreary it is to be always a care," she says, in words that seem to come straight from the lips of Alice James. Dolly is also not appreciated by men, as Alice felt she was not. One young man grows impatient with her "clever talk." Although he "was interested in clever men[,] in women he admired other qualities."[46] As a reflection of Alice, Dolly was also an image of what Woolson feared becoming as her health deteriorated.

Woolson did include one progressive female character, the sculptor Maud Muriel Mackintosh, who smokes a pipe and strikes terror in the hearts of ordinary men. After being kissed by a man for sport, she declares that men's kisses "are *very far indeed* from being what is described. There is nothing in them. Nothing whatever!" She cares not for men's good opinion or protection and instead plays the role of protector to the spinster Billy Breeze. There is something in Maud of Katharine Loring, who was perceived by the Jameses as possessing a masculine vigor and as replacing the role of a man in Alice's life. Maud pronounces that female suffrage is most certainly coming, if not in their generation, then in the next one, a view shared by Loring. Maud is, however, broadly drawn, not only in her masculinity and feminism but also in her aesthetics. She is a realist of the strictest type, searching out the ordinary instead of the beautiful. The other villagers in Asheville find her art ridiculous for its lack of pleasing subjects, but she stands up for realism: "Prettiness is the exception, not the rule. . . . I prefer to model the usual, the average; for in that direction, and in that only, lies truth."[47] Although Woolson herself had begun her career in a similar vein, she ridicules in Maud the elevation of the ugly that she saw in so much of modern literature. Maud's failing is that she cannot look beyond the surface of the ordinary to find its inner beauty.

Nonetheless, Maud is one of the few happy spinsters in Woolson's body of work. Not merely content with her lot, she has actively sought out the company of women over that of men. The humor Woolson expends on this wooden character, however, suggests she did not entirely sympathize with her. Men's derision toward such women is reflected in her depiction of Maud. (James had made his discomfort with protofeminist lesbians clear in his portrayal of Olive Chancellor in his 1886 *The Bostonians*.) Sadly, Woolson did not choose to uncover Maud's inner beauty. She was interested in the ways some women were beginning to actively reject the feminine standard against which she had always measured herself, but she was never able to escape the powerful hold it had on her.

In *Horace Chase* Woolson tried to realize her highest ideal of where the modern novel should go. In her notebooks, she had written, "While I describe as accurately as 'Story of a Country Town' [an 1883 novel by Edgar Watson Howe], I must not be dreary—like . . . Zola." Her sincerest belief was expressed in a quote (somewhat altered) from Emerson's "Poetry and Imagination": "When we think of the really great statues, poems, pictures, music—we find . . . that they present a noble portion of the human soul. Artists may be satisfied with perfect specimens of a craftsman's skill, independent of his theme; but the mass of men will not be satisfied. Art exists for humanity."[48]

Nonetheless, *Horace Chase* lacks the psychological depth of *East Angels* and the emotional power of *Jupiter Lights*. It is a novel very much of its time, so convincingly does it portray the types and tensions of its era. In spite of Woolson's desire to secure a lasting fame with this novel, its realism is time-bound rather than transcendent, reminding one more of Howells's novels than the best works of Eliot, James, and Woolson herself. It seems that her choice of a central male character kept her at a distance and unable to create with a sure hand the kind of convincing, immediate portraits she had made of Anne Douglas, Madame Carroll, Margaret Harold, and Eve Bruce. It was almost as if she could no longer delve into the emotional depths her earlier novels had plumbed and expect to emerge once again.

SAYING GOODBYE

As 1893 dawned, Woolson went to London to see James, who was feeling depressed and suffering from gout (he could hardly walk). Within a few days she was also ill, having developed a bad cold. She sat by the fire, "enveloped in linseed," while vapor from the kettle filled the room. It was another unusually cold winter in England, yet she lingered on, anxious to finish her work on *Horace Chase*.[49]

In the middle of March, with two more parts yet to complete of the novel, now in serialization, her health was barely holding up. She wasn't any worse, she guessed, than she had been at the end of her last two novels. But the doctor had put her "on a modified form of rest-cure," meaning, "I write, but I do absolutely nothing else. And I go to bed at <u>six</u> p.m., & rise at 9 a.m.—Then I have very nourishing food; & quinine, phosphorus, & iron." In a letter to Boott, who was feeling that his own death was not far off, she wrote, "Don't talk of 'going.' I shall very likely go before you do." When Jane Carter's daughter Grace had recently visited her in Oxford, she bluntly told Constance, "I never saw any one so changed. You look like death."[50] Constance did not appreciate her frankness.

Meanwhile, she began to plan for her departure to Venice and was surprised to find that she could still feel the joy of anticipation. If she could not return to the East, then Venice was the next best thing. She had realized after her time in Cairo why she loved Venice so much—it was "the oriental color."[51]

Venice began to look more and more like the key to her future happiness—and survival. Her friends Daniel and Ariana Curtis were helping her look for an apartment and would be nearby, if she were to fall ill. The climate would suit her so much better than England's, and she thought it a perfect place to work. She expected to put together a collection of her Italian stories and imagined that writing a novel in Venice would be easier than it had been in England. She was also eager to get her things out of storage in Florence, to have a home again. She longed to see the writing table Boott had given her, as well as the other items associated with their time at Bellosguardo.[52]

The one drawback was that by moving to Italy she would be leaving James behind. She explained to Sam, "You will see that in all this, I am giving up the being near my kind friend, Mr James. . . .

But Mr J. will come to Italy every year, and perhaps we can write that play after all."[53]

The first week of May, Constance mailed off the last pages of *Horace Chase* to the Harpers and was proud to report to Sam that English publishers were battling over the English rights to the book. Meanwhile, she had packed up her books and few belongings and said goodbye to her dear landlady and other friends. One was a dog named Colin, to whom she had become quite attached. He was "the most wonderful dog I have ever seen," she wrote to his owner. "I do'nt wonder you love him. He is a person. I am sure he has a soul."[54]

Before leaving for Venice, Constance saw a dentist in London. While there she fell seriously ill with a fever but had no other symptoms. The doctor who was called at four in the morning diagnosed her illness as influenza, her first attack of the disease that continued to plague England. The bout left her even weaker than before, and the long journey to Venice still lay ahead. She hoped that once it was over she would finally regain her strength.[55]

James was not in London but in Lucerne with William and other family members. On her way to Venice, Constance stopped over for four days in Paris, where they met. He took her to the theater and showed her his favorite galleries, as he had done thirteen years earlier in Florence.[56] James planned to visit Venice periodically and told her he might even get an apartment there. Theirs would once again be a long-distance friendship. After three years of relative nearness the loss would be significant. They could only assure each other that their separation would be brief.

15

The Riddle of Existence

EARLIER, CONSTANCE had called Venice her "Xanadu" and wondered "whether the end of the riddle of my existence may not be, after all, to live here, & die here." Now she was determined to see if that were true. By the end of May, she had settled in temporarily at the Casa Biondetti. She had four rooms, five windows that commanded a spectacular view up and down the Grand Canal, and access to the roof. As she stood above the water-laced city, catching the sea breezes and watching boats slide into the canals, she felt rejuvenated.[1]

Her afternoons throughout the summer and fall were spent floating out to the islands beyond Venice, often in the company of friends, filling her notebook with observations and thinking she might one day write a short book about the lagoons. She jotted notes about the boats and their picturesque sails. She noted the varying cargo of grapes, melons, fish, or great bunches of flowers, depending on the season. She admired the men leaning into their oars, "very graceful, outlined against the low sky." Everywhere she looked were artists and their easels, floating by in gondolas or sitting on church steps. As she passed the island of San Clemente, home to an insane asylum, she could hear the women's cries: "*O, mamma mia, mamma mia!*" or "My dear Mother will come and take me out. . . . Yes—she *will!* she *will!*"[2]

For these excursions Woolson had her own gondolier, who was referred to her by the wife of John Symonds. She had resided above the family in the Palazzo Gritti-Swift in 1883. The art historian, who died in April 1893, had lived a double life, conducting a love affair with his strikingly handsome gondolier, Angelo Fusato. Mrs. Symonds was probably eager to be rid of the gondolier. Although James was aware of the affair, it is not clear whether Woolson was as well. She was delighted with Angelo, who knew "every out-of-the-way fresco and bit of carving, and interesting church, not only in Venice, but for ten miles around." Gondoliers also acted as servants, so Angelo also brought in wood, polished shoes, did the shopping, and waited at table.[3]

As Woolson had expected, Venetian society suited her. She had known the Curtises and Katherine de Kay Bronson and her daughter, Edith, since 1883. Lady Layard, whom she had also met then, was soon an equally valued friend. Lord Layard was a British archeologist who had carried out excavations at Nimrud and Ninevah and retired to Venice with his much younger wife, Enid. Dr. Baldwin was also in Venice, staying with the Bronsons. Harry Washington, son of her old St. Augustine friend Eleanor, lived across the canal from Woolson. One day, seeing the Stars and Stripes waving from his balcony and realizing she had forgotten it was the Fourth of July, she sent Angelo out to find a flag. Her circle of friends also led to invitations to Ca' Rezzonico, the magnificent palazzo restored by the artist Pen Browning, son of Robert and Elizabeth. She had heard the rumors of Pen's affair with his beautiful housekeeper and model. "Let us hope they are not true," she gossiped to Boott.[4]

Knowing that her rooms were only temporary, Constance could not fully rest. She was "so disheartened at the thought of all the labor that must be gone through before a new place is any where near comfortable,—that it seems as if, after I am settled this time, I shall never have the strength or courage to move again."[5]

A GATHERING GLOOM

That summer, as she explored the city James had once described as "the most beautiful of tombs," Constance's thoughts turned ever more to those she had lost. She became fascinated with a book called *The Law of Psychic Phenomena* (1893), about telepathy, hypnotism, and communicating with the dead. It described many instances of spirits making contact with the living and argued that the subconscious minds of living persons could communicate telepathically. Her deafness may have made such a possibility appealing, but it is interesting that Woolson, whose writings often concerned themselves with the pressures on women to conceal their thoughts and feelings, was so drawn to the idea of speechless communication. She gave Dolly, in *Horace Chase*, the ability to read others' thoughts and had long felt herself capable of intuiting the suppressed longings and griefs of others. This intuition was at the heart of her literary work, and it is what made her such a powerful writer. Yet her interest in telepathy also suggests an almost desperate wish to be read by others. She had become a master at hiding her own secret thoughts, so as not to burden others with her pain. She was, James would later write, like an invalid who puts flowerpots in the windows, allowing most people to saunter by and see only their joyful color, missing the suffering inside.[6] Very few could see past the amiable mask she wore during these last months of her life.

In August Constance confided to her niece Kate, "I have been a good deal depressed in spirit all summer, but no one knows it, for I do'nt let it be seen." The one person she did let glimpse her state of mind was Dr. Baldwin. She empathized with his dark moods. His "grim & desperate will to be resolute" gave her courage to face the blackness that descended upon her as well. When he came to Venice in July, she sought out as many visits with him as she could, inviting him to tea and for gondola rides. As they floated, the two friends combined her version of a water cure with his form of talking therapy. William James's wife believed that during the previous winter he had cured her husband, at least temporarily, of his dark despair by empathizing with him. This was not the "talking cure" or psychoanalysis that Freud and others were then developing.[7] Baldwin's method was basically stoical commiseration. Although comforting, it did not relieve Woolson's suffering.

She sensed a limit to Baldwin's or anyone's understanding of her troubles, explaining to him, "There is no use in our advising other people; for we do not know all the circumstances of their lives; there are always some which they do not (perhaps cannot) tell. Each heart knows its own griefs, or aches, or disappointments, & my own heart knows mine."[8] She did not confide in Boott, as she had before; in fact, she did not write to him at all that summer, although she had received a letter from him in May. And she very likely did not confide in James either, as nothing in his letters to Boott or Baldwin betrays any concern about her. She was inside the cocoon of the depressive, shrouded in an armor no one could penetrate.

Baldwin was rather progressive in taking his patients' moods seriously, but he could not see her compounding sense of hopelessness. Instead, he believed that low spirits were often caused by physical illness. After he had returned to Florence, Woolson explained away her depression by claiming that "part of it is the result of the influenza; another, is the constant work." At the time, the flu virus was widely believed to attack the brain and cause, in the words of one medical dictionary, "nervous exhaustion," "psychical derangement," and "psychoses" that could occur long after fever had subsided. Influenza was also listed in many cases as the cause of suicide. Henry James complained after a severe bout of the flu in 1894 that "[i]t's grotesque how weak & demoralized & depressed the merest brush of the pestilence can make one."[9]

Through the summer, Woolson labored over the book proofs of *Horace Chase*. She rose at four thirty in the morning and worked until nine thirty, when she had her breakfast and dressed, and then worked again until four o'clock. Her late afternoons were spent bathing at the Lido or on excursions in the lagoon. After dinner at seven thirty, she spent the rest of the evening floating through the canals with

Angelo at the helm. She was working almost eleven hours a day. "I am impelled by something stronger than myself to do the very best, absolutely the very best, I can," she explained. However, as James had once said, the effort added fresh nails to her coffin. Her friends began to notice how haggard she appeared and urged her to go somewhere warm for the winter. Instead, she concealed herself from their worried looks and made plans to remain in town.[10]

CASA SEMITECOLO

As her time at the Casa Biondetti wound down, Constance found a new apartment. For forty dollars a month, she rented the top two floors of the Casa Semitecolo, a modest and to her unromantic palazzo near where the Grand Canal opens into the lagoon. She could look across the canal to the golden mosaic façade of the Gritti-Swift. Although the fourteenth-century palace was plainer than some Venetian palazzos, John Ruskin had singled it out on his 1849 tour of the Grand Canal and made detailed drawings of it, noting the windows as "the nearest approximation of a perfect Gothic form which occurs characteristically at Venice."[11]

Constance was looking forward to "going to housekeeping again," she wrote to Boott in her last surviving letter to him, dated September 9, 1893, just before she moved into the apartment.[12] She had Angelo stock up on costly wood, which had to be shipped into the city, so that she could heat her rooms comfortably. She also sent for her things stored away in Florence, in spite of the great expense. When they arrived, she had around her once again the reminders of her old life. As she sat at Boott's desk or in the Browning chair from Duveneck, looking at his etchings of Venice and her favorite Ricciardo Meacci painting, "The Garden of the Hesperides," her sorrow at her great loss—and theirs—crept back in.[13] She had a semblance of a home again, but it reminded her too much of the home she had lost.

Meanwhile, Woolson continued to expect a visit from James, but he kept pushing it further into the future. He had told her that he

The Casa Semitecolo, Woolson's final home,
located near the mouth of the Grand Canal.
(From *Constance Fenimore Woolson*, vol. 2 of *Five Generations (1785–1923)*)

dreamed of having his own apartment in Venice one day, exciting
Ariana Curtis's hopes that he was thinking of moving there, but he
corrected her. He could only "*live* in London," he explained. Woolson
may also have misinterpreted his intentions, but she could not have
expected that he would move away from England. We don't know
what he was writing to Woolson, but his noncommittal attitude about

when he would come must have disappointed her. At the same time, she was sounding rather noncommittal about staying in Europe. She received two letters that fall from one of her Cooper cousins that made her seriously consider "packing all [her] things next spring & sailing by the Italian line for N.Y.," although she feared the severe winters and higher cost of living. When James heard of the plan, he expressed his displeasure, writing to Ariana Curtis, "I shall do my best to prove to Miss Woolson that Venice is better than Cooperstown. I am very glad to hear that she has at last a roof of her own. The having it, I am sure, will do much to anchor her." [14] Promising to visit was another way to anchor her in Europe, for if she left it altogether, he might never see her again. Nonetheless, a visit from him was nowhere on the horizon.

Woolson was also feeling let down by the Casa Semitecolo. She discovered that the front rooms with a view of the Grand Canal would have no sun in the winter, leaving them frigid. But there was one new bright spot in her life. She bought a five-week-old Pomeranian Spitz from Dalmatian sailors, who called him the Moor because of his black fur. So she named him Othello, or Tello for short. Her delight in him was immense. It was nice finally to have "some one who is glad to see me when I come in," she told Sam. However, he was a rambunctious puppy and "full of tricks. He steals my shoes & stockings, & scampers & dances about like a mad creature." Tello slept in a basket next to her bed, and while she sat and wrote at Boott's desk, he bit the buttons on her boots. He was an incorrigible chewer. Once she looked up from reading a letter to see Tello walking off with a silk cushion, larger than himself, that had been a present from James. [15]

Although her rent was very low, Constance continued to worry about money. The opulence of her friends' grand palaces intensified her dissatisfaction with her own humble surroundings. The Layards' Ca' Capello had a suite of rooms mentioned in the Venice guidebooks that was adorned with works by Vittore Carpaccio and Giovanni and Gentile Bellini, as well as a painting by Cima di Conigliano that Ruskin had declared the best he had ever seen. (Their collection now resides in the National Gallery in London.) The Curtises' Palazzo Barbaro was really two joined palaces and was widely regarded as the most beautiful on the Grand Canal. James described it as "all marbles and frescoes and portraits of the Doges." Woolson admitted to Sam that "the constant atmosphere of wealth sometimes becomes oppressive."[16]

Despite the cheap cost of living, Constance felt poorer in Venice than she had anywhere else. She was terrified about falling into debt as she had at Bellosguardo. She wrote to Sam in November, "I am beginning to be haunted by the fear that my reserve fund at the Bank here is not large enough to leave me free from immediate care." She asked him to sell one of her bonds, worth $1,000, which she could put in the bank as a safety net. She relied on the interest from her bonds, but having the money near at hand, she told him, "will have much the same effect that a low-hung carriage has upon my nerves: with it, I feel that I can jump out if I become frightened, and the knowing that I can, acts as a tranquilizer; I never do jump, & never want to. Whereas in a high vehicle, I never have one moment's freedom from terror."[17]

One's capital should be stored up for the inevitable frailties of old age, she admitted, but at fifty-three, she felt as if that time was already upon her. "I hope you will not be shocked," she told Sam, "that for a long time my daily prayer has been that I may not live to be old; I mean really old." Putting on a brave face for him, she assured him that she was not "especially sombre just now. On the contrary. I am much more cheerful and serene than I was in England. Venice suits me in many ways, and I think I am going to be happy here."[18] Nonetheless, drawing on her capital was taking a step backward, not forward toward a peaceful old age in a Cooperstown cottage or a house at East Angels.

One of Woolson's final stories, the beautiful yet heartbreaking "A Transplanted Boy," which would appear posthumously, channeled her fears of being alone and penniless in Europe. It portrays an American mother and her adoring son, the thirteen-year-old Maso (short for the Italian Tommaso), who live in a boardinghouse in Pisa, the cheapest place they have found to live. She yearns to return to the United States, but the boy has lost all connection to his home. He doesn't even notice when it is the Fourth of July (as Woolson had not). When the mother falls ill and needs to move north for the sum-

According to her niece Clare Benedict, this is the last
photograph of Woolson, taken shortly before her death.
(From *Constance Fenimore Woolson*, vol. 2 of *Five Generations (1785–1923)*)

mer, the boy insists on staying behind in the care of his tutor. There
is only enough money for one of them to travel. He cares only for
her health, so he hides from her the fact that the tutor has left him
alone and that the bank with their money has failed. He has but one
object: to hide his suffering from his mother. He just barely manages
to survive, accompanied only by his little dog, Mr. Tiber. Upon coming back to his sparse room one evening, Maso finds that the dog has
simply lain down and died. After burying Mr. Tiber, Maso also falls
ill. When his mother is contacted by a friend, she rushes to him from
Paris, exclaiming, "If I could only have known!" In the final lines of
the story, we learn that she is returning with him to the United States
for his health but that it is probably "too late for that."[19] They had

reached a point of no return—to home or to health—which Woolson increasingly felt she was approaching as well.

Unlike Maso in "The Transplanted Boy," Woolson was not on her own. Since June she had visited the Curtises two to three times a week, even as she worked tirelessly on *Horace Chase*. Daniel Curtis's diary also references regular excursions, dinners, and calls they made together. On October 30, however, the Curtises sailed to India for the winter. James worried that "their withdrawal . . . will make the Venice winter rather bare" for her.[20]

Those who stayed in Venice during the winter sought her out, however. She was surprised by their evident pleasure in visiting her in her modest apartment. Their warmth and kindness touched her deeply, yet she also felt self-conscious about the disparity in their circumstances. She occasionally accepted invitations, but only to tea. As she explained to Zina Hulton, wife of the British painter William Stokes Hulton, "I no longer give myself the pleasure of lunching, or dining, with my friends, because conversation with me at the table is necessarily so awkward."[21]

Knowing that she would need a new home when her lease expired on the first of May, Woolson spent much of the winter apartment hunting with Edith Bronson. They toured a series of grand apartments that were inexpensive, but the cost to furnish and heat them would be prohibitive. One small apartment for a pittance—$200 a year—seemed just right: sunny with balconies and the Gothic windows she loved overlooking the Grand Canal. Yet she made no move to take it, remaining undecided about her plans. She could not continue her peripatetic lifestyle, she decided. As she explained to Sam, "I seem to have come to the end of being able to live in other peoples's [*sic*] rooms."[22]

Meanwhile, James further delayed his visit to Venice until the end of the winter, at least.[23] In the spring, Clara and Clare would also be back in Europe, so Constance seems to have simply put off planning for the future.

The news from the United States didn't help. Clara had written to her of the worst economic depression the U.S. had yet experienced.

Throughout 1893, banks had been closing all over the country, and the panic soon spread to Europe. Banks failed at an alarming rate, making Constance wary of putting her thousand dollars from the bond sale in a local depository, although Daniel Curtis assured her it would be safe. In December, she heard of bank failures in Florence and worried about the fate of Baldwin's money there.[24]

All of the bad financial news clouded the pleasant news arriving from her publishers. In England, new editions of her early novels were being planned, as was an edition of *Horace Chase* for the Continental market. The Harpers were also planning a collection of Italian stories as well as a new collection of some of her earlier stories. She was pleased to report to Sam that "there seems to be a good market for my wares." Her publishers also owed her more than one thousand dollars, so she hoped to be able to reinvest the bond money soon.[25]

FATE, THE CONQUEROR

In preparation for the winter, Constance had moved her bedroom, sitting room, and dressing room to the south side of the palazzo, filling up the sunny rooms on the back that faced away from the Grand Canal. She wasn't happy with the arrangement but understood the necessity of it. So far a large, open fireplace and an unsightly plaster Venetian stove were heating the three rooms nicely. Kate had sent her a hundred dollars, which she used to buy feather pillows, a bed, a wardrobe, a bureau, and a little table, which helped brighten up the small, unpleasant bedroom.[26]

She was feeling better, she assured Kate, and was hopeful that she would make it through the winter just fine. She had been warned of Venice's wintry weather, when the city was often shrouded in a freezing, depressing fog. But she bravely insisted that Oxford and Cheltenham had surely been worse. She claimed to feel rested and ready to start writing again soon. She planned to begin a new novel at the New Year, so she warned Kate not to expect many letters then.[27]

It was now getting dark by five o'clock. With so many of her friends gone, she took her excursions in the lagoon alone, rowed by two gondoliers—Angelo and Tito, whom the Curtises had left in her service while they were away. She took long walks with Tello, combing the beaches and fields of the islands for shells and intriguing ruins. With the Curtises' permission, she raided their library and filled her gondola with forty books at a time. Edith Bronson roused Woolson to join her for an evening at the Goldoni Theater. It took some convincing, but she went. On the twelfth, Edith also took her to look at apartments. The next day, Constance walked around St. Mark's Square with Tello as a military band played for the customers sitting outside Florian's and the Quadri Café, drinking coffee and enjoying one of the last pleasant days.[28]

On December 16, she had tea with Katherine and Edith Bronson at Casa Alvisi. The next day, she received a letter from James and wrote one to Dr. Baldwin, declaring that Katherine Bronson had a "genius for kindness." In the afternoon, Angelo and Tito rowed her over to the mainland, "to Terra Firma at Campalto." It was "a strange waterland,—with many channels, & wet meadows covered with brown grass." She felt melancholy at the sight of an old white horse standing alone in a field. On the way home at twilight, she hoped Tito and Angelo would get lost in the thick fog, but they found the pilings and stuck close to them all the way back to Venice and up the Grand Canal. She enjoyed the ghostly atmosphere of the evening as passing boats and stately palazzos suddenly materialized in the mist.[29]

Her last notebook entry, about her trip to the lagoon on Christmas Eve, describes an excursion to the very end of the Lido. It was warm enough that she could leave her fur cloak in the gondola while she walked along the grassy embankment and marveled at the snow-capped Alps in the distance. She even thought she could see the jagged outlines of the Dolomites. She thought about how mountains form the outer edge of the world, slicing through the air as Earth spins through space. "I should like to turn into a peak when I die," she wrote, "to be a beautiful purple mountain, which would please the tired sad eyes of thousands of human beings for ages."[30] It is an arresting image that recalls her lifelong attraction to heights yet anchors her solidly to the earth. As one of the last things she wrote, it also shows how much her mind was occupied with thoughts of not only mortality but also immortality. She hoped to live on, to be remembered, and to inspire future generations.

On Christmas Day the sun shone as Constance, with Tello at her side, walked among the reveling crowds in St. Mark's Square. The cathedral was full to the doors. She bought a Christmas card for Mrs. Phillips in Oxford and made her way back to her rooms, where she finished a letter to Kate and wrote to her old friend Arabella Carter Washburn, with whom she had not corresponded in years. That evening, having declined an invitation to a Christmas party at the Layards, she sat alone by the fire, reading Dickens's *A Christmas Carol* and Milton's "Hymn on the Nativity," once again welcoming the ghosts of Christmases past. She confided to Arabella, "I often think that though I stay abroad, I seem to remember better than any one else." While others had forgotten those who had long since died, she had not. With her mind on meeting them in the future, she explained, "I feel perfectly sure that the next existence will make clear all the mysteries and riddles of this. . . . [I]f at any time you should hear that I have gone, I want you to know beforehand that my end was peace, and even joy at the release."[31]

This somber tone may have crept into the final letter she wrote to James about this time, for he seemed to grow more concerned about her. He wrote to Katherine Bronson, "Do you see anything of my old friend Miss Woolson? I am very fond of her and should be glad if there was any way in which you could be kind to her." He also wrote to Daniel Curtis in India, "I <u>dream</u> of a Venetian spring. I hear from Miss Woolson. . . . If she only didn't think it her bounden duty to 'make plans' she might be happy yet. Speriamo [Let us hope] that she will be—& will at last find the right house." He planned to "interrogate" Edith Bronson about her when she came to London soon.[32]

The reality was that a gloom had settled upon Woolson that she found hard to shake. On New Year's Day, when she was supposed to start writing a new novel, she instead wrote to Alden what can only be described as a farewell note. While letters from Boott, Baldwin, and

James lay unanswered, she penned to her old friend and editor probably the last letter by her own hand. She described walking through Venice after a snowstorm with Tello and administering to the poor of Venice, whose suffering touched her deeply. Most significantly, she shared with Alden her great fear that she might never be able to write again. Both body and spirit had failed her:

> I have given up my broken sword to Fate, the Conqueror. . . . I am finishing up the fringes and edges of my literary work, for I feel that I shall do very little more. Of course, this feeling may change. But at present it has full possession of me; I am profoundly discouraged. . . . If I could go into a convent (where I didn't have to confess, nor rise before daylight for icy matins), I think I could write three or four novels better than any I have yet done. But there are no worldly convents. So I'll write my new effusions on another star, and send them back to you by telepathy.[33]

Not only couldn't she face another move, but she also couldn't face the hard work of writing another novel, standing for most of the day at her desk, writing through the pain that shot through her right side. Without the ability to keep writing, she rapidly ran out of courage to carry on. She felt as if she had reached a dead end, unable to live independently and unwilling to be a burden on anyone. In the coming days, she reached out to no one, asked for no help, and told no one how afraid she had become of running out of money.

On the second of January the weather turned sharply cold. It was windy and snowing and even windier the next day. On the sixth it snowed again. During the first two weeks of the year, Constance was likely homebound, sitting by the fire and receiving the occasional afternoon visitor. Princess Olga of Montenegro had asked Edith to introduce her to the American author, and she and Woolson had developed a fondness for each other. Zina Hulton and the Bronsons were still in town, although Edith would leave for London on the seventeenth.[34]

On the thirteenth of January, Constance braved the weather for a walk through the snow in the public gardens, although her Venetian physician, Dr. Cini, had advised against it. After she came home, she felt ill and went to bed. On the fifteenth, she hired Marie Holas, whom Edith had highly recommended, to help for a few hours a day with her writing and other tasks. Woolson had no fever, only congestion. For the next few days, she was in "very good spirits," according to Holas, and ate better but moaned periodically, saying "that all her life she could not bear the slightest physical pain." She also dictated letters, one of which was to her publishers, directing them to send a copy of the newly published *Horace Chase* to Francis Boott in Cambridge, Massachusetts.[35] She always wanted to know what he thought of her works.

Yet she began to doubt whether she would live to receive Boott's response, a possibility she neither feared nor regretted. In fact, she seemed to welcome it. As soon as she fell ill, Woolson had handed over her money to Holas and asked her to take charge of the household. Quite matter-of-factly, Woolson began to prepare for her death. She wanted to write her will and told Dr. Cini to let her know when her condition worsened so she would have time to do so. She thought it very irresponsible for those who were ill to wait so long that they missed the chance to put their affairs in order. She wanted to provide for Tello and told Holas to have the apartment sealed up after her death until her sister was able to come and retrieve her things. Above all, she made it clear that she was not to be buried in the Protestant Cemetery outside Venice, which she hated. She should only be buried in the Protestant Cemetery in Rome. Holas claimed that Woolson even "threatened me in case I did not tell her relatives what her wishes were to let me have no peace after her death." All of this was said "half joking," but Woolson was in earnest. She spoke calmly, exhibiting no fear of death.[36]

On the morning of January 18, she began to think death was nearer. Sharp pains shot through her stomach and bowels, and she had a fever of 39.3° C (nearly 103° F). Laudanum helped some, and when the doctor arrived he allowed her to have some morphine. By evening, Constance was feeling better and sat up in bed to read letters and the newspaper, but then she worsened again, vomiting "very bilious green stuff," according to Holas. Reports after her death would say she had been suffering from influenza, which was then rampant in Venice. However, her symptoms more likely indicate cholecystitis, or gallbladder inflammation, which could be caused by a blocked gallbladder stone. Other possibilities are bowel obstruction or pancreatitis. All would have been very painful, potentially deadly, and not easily diagnosed at the time. The doctor suspected none of these conditions and, apparently recalling the traditional association of green bile with ill temper, peevishness, and melancholia, asked Woolson "if she had had anything that had troubled her more than usual." She had recently finished a book and was still not herself, she told him. More than that, "there was not a person under the sun that had more cares & troubles than herself."[37]

As Constance lay in bed, doubled over in pain and feeling increasingly weak, all of her feelings of loneliness and self-pity came rushing out. She had a great fear of being ill and all alone in Europe. There was no motherly landlady to care for her, as there had been in Oxford, let alone family she could call on. Jane Carter's daughter Grace was then her nearest relative in Europe. They had remained close since Jane's death. Unfortunately, Grace's sister Mary had inherited her father's mental illness and broken down after the birth of her children. She was being treated at a sanitarium in Munich, and Grace, who had remained single and devoted to her sister, was staying nearby.[38] Not wanting to pull Grace away from Mary, Constance had so far refused to ask for her. Even when Grace grew concerned and offered to come to Venice, Constance declined, telling Holas there was nothing Grace could do.[39]

As her fever subsided, Woolson spoke little and withdrew into herself. She pushed away the ear trumpet when Holas tried to speak to her. She had grown very weak and repeatedly begged the doctor for more laudanum, but he would only give her a small dose, worried that more would risk killing her. She insisted that she was used to higher doses, but he remained firm. The vomiting had not completely abated, but the accompanying pains had lessened considerably. Beginning on the night of the twenty-first, trained nurses from the Sisters of Charity were employed to stay the night when Holas went home. Woolson would not let the nun on duty stay in the room with her, saying that she liked to have the windows open and didn't want the woman to be bothered by the chilly air.[40] This was a pretext, for however much she liked fresh air, she hated the cold. The real reason was surely that she wanted to be alone.

During these days of decreasing symptoms but increasing weakness, Woolson, it seems, had given up on living. She gave Holas the addresses for Clara and Sam in Cleveland and instructed that they should only be cabled in the event of her death, as they would not be able to cross the ocean in time. She apparently never mentioned James or even Dr. Baldwin, who could have easily come up from Florence. However, with Baldwin's recent loss of money in the bank failures, she may have worried about troubling him and pulling him away from his family.[41] As she lay alone in silence, she felt as if she had no claim on anyone. If she was going to die, she would do it as she felt she had lived—on her own.

Woolson also talked more about making a will. Lady Layard had visited her on January 18 and told Constance that all she had to do was write her will in her own hand and sign it. No witnesses were required under Italian law. Yet she felt the need for something more official, which would hold up under American law. She told Holas that when she was ready to make her will, she would have her call the American consul. She had a sample for Holas to use as a model, for she would have to take dictation. But in the coming days, Constance never asked for the consul. In fact, no will was ever found. This more than anything suggests that she did not expect or plan to die imminently. On the evening of the twenty-second, she told Holas to wire Grace to come. She did not say why. She may have wanted Grace's help to settle her affairs. The telegram read, "Am worse. Come. Grand Hotel near my house."[42]

On the morning of the twenty-third, Woolson was feeling better and drank some milk. The vomiting had ceased, and she had no fever, but she was very weak. She felt she could not sleep without "something strong" and warned, "If I sleep today, I shall be quite well tomorrow, but if I don't sleep, I shall be dead." (During her February 1892 illness, she had told Baldwin much the same.) Dr. Cini gave her a small dose of laudanum, which allowed her to sleep a little during the day. In the evening, she was highly anxious and irritable, according to Holas, snapping at her if things were not immediately brought. During the doctor's last visit that evening, she requested "an injection of morphia, which he decidedly refused to do, for he said, she was so weak, she could not bear it, & never awake again. She would die in her sleep, & he would be responsible for her death." Woolson also requested chloral hydrate, another potent sedative, but he would only give her another, less harmful dose of laudanum.[43]

Laudanum was not strong enough to provide the temporary oblivion Woolson needed to make it until morning. Like morphine it contains opium but only one-tenth as much. At that time, both highly addictive drugs were taken for just about any ailment imaginable. If the drugs are used regularly, the body quickly needs more to achieve the same effects. A fatal overdose was a very real possibility with both drugs, and many people committed suicide by overdosing on one or the other. Woolson may have obliquely hoped never to wake up, but preparations for her death were not yet complete. She expected a protracted and possibly quite painful illness. The fact that she needed ever-greater dosages of laudanum to help her sleep may also indicate that she had become acclimated to it through frequent use. Moreover, as a soporific, laudanum and morphine were only partially effective. They induced sleep but were not so good at keeping one asleep. Users often awoke more restless and became "moody, sullen, mercurial of spirits and even suicidal." Alice James, as she was dosed with morphine during her final illness, called it a "treacherous fiend," because it prevented sleep and caused "hideous nervous distress." She wrote that "K[atharine] and I touched bottom more nearly than ever before." Woolson was getting there as well. What happened after she went to bed on the twenty-third cannot be entirely blamed on opiate consumption, but her reliance on it to sleep and its ineffectiveness that night probably contributed to her death.[44]

When a telegram from Grace arrived saying that she was on her way to Venice, Constance responded to the news simply, "Well, well." Before Holas left for the night, she later remembered, the patient "asked me to change her position in the bed, to turn her & put her head on the other side, & so I did, with the help of the servants—I arranged her blankets, her pillows & cushions; she wished the door, windows, shutters, & curtains very well closed so that the slightest ray of light could not pass through—Then as I took the trumpet to speak to her she said 'I am so comfortable please let me alone.'" When Holas left, a twenty-two-year-old nun, Suor Alfonsa, was stationed outside the bedroom door.[45]

Woolson managed to sleep, but not for long. At midnight she woke. Without the diagnosis of a fatal illness and freely administered morphine that had made Alice James's passing bearable, she might have thought about facing an untold period of pain and sleeplessness before her time finally came. While we cannot know what she thought, we do know that she reached for the small, silver-plated bell with her initials that sat beside her bed and rang it. Suor Alfonsa immediately appeared, and Constance asked her to bring a light, perhaps with which to read, and a cup of milk.[46]

When Suor Alfonsa returned, Constance sent her away again. She wanted a certain pink china cup for her milk, she said, and would only drink from that one. The cup was either far away or required washing, giving Constance time to rise from her bed and make her way to the window. She pulled the curtains aside, unfastened the shutters, and opened the window. Moments later, she was falling three stories to the pavement below.[47]

16

Aftershocks

W HEN THE nurse reentered the room and found Constance's
bed empty and the window open, she looked out to see a
white heap in the narrow street. Frantically, she called out to the servants. Angelo, still groggy from sleep, rushed down the stairs. At the
same moment, the doorbell rang. Three men walking in the Calle del
Bastion had come upon what they thought was a pile of snow against
the wall below Constance's window. Upon closer inspection, they discovered the crumpled body of a woman in a white nightdress. When
they picked her up, she moaned and trembled at their touch. They
heard her say something which they thought was the Italian word for
"cold" (*freddo*). They rang the bell at the nearest door, which Angelo
answered. "Give me my mistress," he told them, and carried her up the
three flights of stairs to her room. He laid Woolson, still breathing but
unconscious, on her bed. The closest doctor was found. Her condition
was hopeless, he determined. Dr. Cini soon arrived and examined her,
discovering fractures of the thighbone and spine. There was nothing
to be done. She lived about an hour. When Grace arrived the next
morning, she was devastated by the news. Dr. Cini tried to comfort

her, saying that "he was sure the shock to the head & spine had been instantaneously so great that she felt nothing really afterwards."[1]

Grace and Marie Holas dressed Constance in the white dress she had wanted to be buried in. Grace telegraphed Clara and Sam and made all of the necessary preparations for the consul to seal the apartment until Clara could arrive. She also arranged for Constance's burial at the Protestant Cemetery in Rome. On the afternoon of the twenty-ninth, a short service was performed in the house for the servants, whose devotion to their mistress Grace found touching. That evening, she left with the body for Rome.[2]

Awaiting her were John and Clara Hay, who had been in Italy and read of Constance's death in a newspaper. They wired the consul in Venice, offering their assistance. When they learned that Grace Carter had taken charge, they put themselves at her service. Hay took care of the arrangements at the cemetery, selecting the site of Constance's grave with Dr. Robert Nevin, rector of the American Protestant Church in Rome. They were able to secure a spot on the hill near Shelley's grave and next to that of the sculptor William Wetmore Story's wife. "I am sure it would have been a solace to her sensitive soul when living to have known she was to repose forever in such a place and in such company," Hay wrote to Sam. Hay procured a large cross of camellias, hyacinths, freesia, and white primroses to represent the Mather family. On the day of the funeral, January 31, "The weather was exquisitely beautiful," Hay wrote, "a real Roman day, with sunshine as bright and sky as blue as summer and yet with a lingered tang of winter in the air." Some of Woolson's friends were able to attend the "simple, but profoundly impressive" service: Richard Greenough, Henry Codman Potter (bishop of the Episcopal Diocese of New York and brother of Mrs. Launt Thompson, Constance's old friend from Florence), the artist Elihu Vedder and his wife, and "two strange, English ladies—one of whom came and begged a flower from the wreaths" to send to Eleanor Poynter. Henry James, who had received word of Woolson's death from Clara and dropped everything to prepare for his departure to Italy, was finally too ill and grief-stricken to attend. He asked Hay to save twenty flowers for him. Two days later, Hay returned to her grave to find a wreath bearing the name of Edmund Clarence Stedman.³

The news of Woolson's death spread quickly throughout the United States. Newspapers ran short statements without mention of the cause of death. The Venetian papers, however, ran longer stories based on interviews, reporting her death as a suicide. One concluded, "[S]he lived alone and was referred to as a strange and eccentric woman." The Venetian reports might not have reached the English-speaking world were it not for the Vienna correspondent of the London *Standard*, who wrote, "It is reported from Venice that the American authoress and novelist, Constance Fenimore Woolson, killed herself yesterday by leaping from the window of the house there in which she had been living for the last seven months. Death ensued almost immediately. She had been ill with influenza for only four days, but long before that attack she had shown signs of eccentricity." This paragraph ran in London on the twenty-seventh and was picked up immediately, almost verbatim, by papers all over the United States, many of them running the news on the front page. Some paraphrased it, altering the ending to read, "A seven months attack of influenza left symptoms of insanity."⁴

Woolson's family refused to believe she had jumped. Grace's telegram to Sam, which he released to the papers, read: "AUNT CON-STANCE HAD INFLUENZA NIGHT NURSE LEFT HER FOR SOMETHING NEEDED IN SUDDEN DELIRIUM FELL FROM WINDOW TO STREET PICKED UP IMMEDIATELY LIVED SHORT TIME UNCONSCIOUS WITH NO APPARENT PAIN FACE LOOKED VERY PEACEFUL NO WILL FOUND." Grace's letter of the twenty-seventh elaborated: "What her fancy had been, a sudden desire for air, & the dizzyness of weakness after the effort of getting from the bed—There is no way of saying." As horrible as was the image of her falling three stories to her death, the peaceful expression on her face was the family's greatest solace, convincing them that she had not died violently by her own hand.⁵

Marie Holas seemed to agree with Grace's interpretation. She explained to Sam, "Nothing gave ever to suppose that she had such a sad purpose in her mind, nor can I think she had it, as she sent for Miss Carter, & was going to make her will, that same day." She made a persuasive case. Constance had been so intent on making a will that she had threatened to haunt Dr. Cini if he did not give her ample warning of her imminent decline. Dr. Cini's interpretation of her death, however, was different. He was certain she had taken her own life and that she was trying to get him to do the job for her by demanding chloral hydrate and morphine. (If he had believed that at the time, then why she was left with only a young nurse stationed outside of her room that night is a mystery.) He blamed Dr. Baldwin for not having warned him of her "queer state of mind" when they met earlier that winter.[6] However, neither Holas nor Dr. Cini would have wanted to feel responsible for her death, so their accounts may be biased. Woolson's death may have been a suicide, but likely not as calculated as the doctor believed.

In her final days, she was in a state very much like that described by Kay Redfield Jamison in her study of suicide: "In short, when people are suicidal, their thinking is paralyzed, their options appear spare or nonexistent, their mood is despairing, and hopelessness permeates their entire mental domain. The future cannot be separated from the present, and the present is painful beyond solace."[7] Constance's earlier bouts with depression and suicidal thoughts, her rationalization of suicide in her letter to Francis Boott and in the margins of her book of Epictetus's teachings, as well as her state of mind in her final months leave little doubt that she had thought of taking her own life.

Her letters show that she had given up on being able to write and support herself. She was too weak to tolerate the dosage of opiates that would help her sleep through the night. She had endured months of financial worries and declining health, not to mention sleeplessness and great pain. Yet her final decision appears to have been an impulsive one. She may have been unable to restrain the longing for death that had been with her since her youth. Death was not terrible to her. It would mean, at last, peace.[8]

HER PRINCIPAL MOURNER

When Clara first received the news of her sister's death, she cabled James in London to let him know and to ask him to rush to Venice to attend to the necessary matters. He was, in her eyes, more or less family. The shock of Constance's death hit him like "a bolt out of the blue." He immediately made preparations to leave but soon received another cable informing him that Grace Carter was already there. He seemed relieved but also felt usurped. In his first letter to Grace, on January 26, he pleaded with her for information. "I write you in the midst of much bewilderment & uncertainty. . . . I am so utterly in the dark about everything that I am reduced to mere conjecture & supposition as to what has taken place & as to <u>how</u> Miss Woolson died. I had not even heard a word of her being ill." This is what puzzled and angered him. Woolson had never told him she was unwell. As he would write to Baldwin on the same day, "To me it is all ghastly amazement and distress. . . . Hadn't she sent for *you*? I have a dismal, dreadful image of her being alone and unfriended at the last."[9]

When the news of Woolson's suicide was reported in the London *Standard* the next day, James's bewilderment turned to horrible certainty. Unlike her family, he was immediately convinced of the accuracy of the reports and collapsed from the devastating blow. Traveling to Rome for the funeral was now impossible. All he could do was write letters to just about everyone he knew about her death. Once so secretive about their friendship, he poured out his grief to anyone who would listen. A New York newspaper three years later would call him Woolson's "principal mourner," and in many ways he was.[10]

Woolson's choice to be alone at the end was inconceivable to James. He wrote to Baldwin a week later, "Miss Woolson's evident determination not to send for you seems to me insane—just as her silence to me does. . . . She kept us both ignorant—with a perversity that was diseased."[11] Underneath his evident willingness to paint Constance as insane, and thus beyond his ability to help her, is also the sting of rejection and immense anger and guilt at not being able to prevent her death.

The final image of their friendship, then, is one of James left behind—left in the dark, in fact, about his friend's deepest thoughts and feelings. Sixteen years later, when he in turn would suffer a severe depression and teetered toward suicide, he would not shut out his closest friends. After a visit to him, Edith Wharton wrote movingly to their mutual friend Morton Fullerton about the shock of his self-revelation: "I, who have always seen him so serene, so completely the master of his wonderful emotional instrument—who thought of him . . . as so sensitive to human contacts & yet so *secure* from them; I could hardly believe it was the same James who cried out to me in his fear, his despair, his craving for the 'cessation of consciousness,' & all his unspeakable loneliness & need of comfort, & inability to be comforted!"[12] By contrast, Woolson's inner anguish at the end—her buried life—remained hers alone.

Yet by taking her own life she had made her pain vociferously apparent. James could not, at first, reconcile this outward declaration with the woman he had known. He explained to Boott, "The event seems to me absolutely to demand the hypothesis of sudden *dementia*." He also wrote to Hay of "some misery of insomnia pushed to nervous momentary frenzy." He wrote to Katherine Bronson, "this publicity of misery, this outward horror and *chiasso* [uproar] round her death, was the thing in the world most alien to her and most inconceivable of her—therefore, to my mind, most conclusive as to her having undergone some violent cerebral derangement." Alice James, who had thought much about suicide, would have understood it differently. As she once wrote in her diary, "It's bad that it [suicide] is so untidy, there is no denying that, for one bespatters one's friends morally as well as physically, taking them so much more into one's secret than they want to be taken."[13] Rather than admit he now understood her secret pain, James looked instead for evidence of sudden mental instability.

However, James also remembered his friend's tendency toward depression, suggesting that he began to understand the persistent nature of her condition. At the time, he used the same phrase—"victim of chronic melancholia"—with slight variation, in letters to three people. Two months after Woolson's death, he explained to his brother William that she had a "predisposition which sprang in its turn from a constitutional, an essentially, tragic and latently insane *difficulty in living*." He also believed that her melancholy was caused by having been "so shut up to solitude by her extreme deafness."[14]

He could not understand, however, what particular reason, save her deafness, she had for being so miserable: "[S]he was free, independent, successful—very successful indeed as a writer—and *liked*, peculiarly, by people who knew her." He seems unaware of her worries about money, her fears about being able to write another novel, her difficulties sleeping and dealing with pain, and her growing conviction that she would never be able to find a permanent home and to retire. Undoubtedly, these circumstances exacerbated an underlying predisposition to severe depression. But by focusing on what he called "the fact that a beneficent providence had elaborately constructed her to suffer," James tried to absolve himself from responsibility. For if her collapse had been caused by her circumstances, he might have been able to ameliorate them.[15] He also reduced her life to one of endless pain and suffering, overlooking her great capacity for joy in her friends as well as children, dogs, art, literature, landscape, and nature. Although her depression may have consumed her in the end, it did not define her life.

James may have wondered if the loss of his company when she moved to Italy contributed to her depression. That she experienced their separation as a great loss is very probable. Although she had many friends and acquaintances, she was close to few people. In these last years, she seemed to be most attached to him, Boott, and Baldwin. However, the separation from James alone was not sufficient to plunge Woolson into such deep darkness.[16] Their separation may have revived the pain of many losses over the course of her life, most linked to her loss of a stable home. In the final months of her life she seemed to be wandering almost aimlessly in search of a place to call home, which she grew increasingly convinced she would not be able to afford.

By the time the Benedicts came in April to unseal Constance's apartment, James was ready to confront with them the ghost of his dead friend. He even stayed in her old rooms at the Casa Biondetti. At her apartment in the Casa Semitecolo, every book and pen lay just where Constance had left them. There were some papers—finished manuscripts of the Italian stories to be collected, which were ready for the Harpers, and unanswered letters. Those that James had written to her were returned to him. He also was given as mementos the Meacci painting and some of her books, among which he chose her copies of *Anne* and *Rodman the Keeper* with her notations.[17]

It took a month for the Benedict women to empty the apartment. James's role appears to have been largely supportive. As Clara described it, James "came every day to see and help us—we could not have gone through it without him. Clare and I did all the personal packing ourselves; a box of pictures and a trunk to be sent to the Mathers, a large box to Mrs. Phillips, and little things to Miss Poynter, Dr. Baldwin, Mrs. Curtis and Miss Bronson. . . . We worked every day until tea time, when Mr. James would come and we would go out in the gondola for two hours; and then, almost every night, he would dine with us."[18] The little dog, Tello, was a source of much concern. They ultimately put him in the gondolier Tito's care until they were able to return for him.

There was also a death mask, whose origin is unknown. Those who attended to Woolson's body after her death must have felt that the family would want a last look at her. Perhaps they also believed that, as a famous author, she needed to be memorialized in this way. However, the Benedicts and James found it morbid and must have realized that the woman who so resented the circulation of her image in life would not want it preserved in death. Clara took on the painful responsibility of destroying the mask herself.[19]

The question of what to do with some of Woolson's papers and her dresses must have vexed them, for it appears that James may have been asked to dispose of them. Many years later, Zina Hulton, Constance's friend from Venice, reported that James told her "that when he had sorted out a few manuscripts of hers which were complete, there remained a great mass of works & commencements & other worthless fragments. After thinking the question over, he decided to destroy all these by drowning them in the lagoon. So he went far out in a gondola & committed them to the water where it was really deep." The image is eerily reminiscent of the narrator of "'Miss Grief'" burying Aaronna's works with her. However, many scraps and notes were saved, which Clare would publish decades later. A much older James also reportedly told a young girl the story about being charged with drowning in a Venetian lagoon a famous woman's dresses, which rose like black balloons all around him and would not go down without a struggle, a fitting metaphor for the way her memory continued to haunt his imagination in the years to come.[20] This story may or may not be true. In any case, there is no evidence that James destroyed anyhing without Clara's permission.

The Benedicts were forever grateful to James for helping them through those trying weeks in Venice, and they remained friends with him for the rest of their lives. They corresponded often, and the two women visited "Cousin Henry" whenever they passed through England on their way to the Continent, which they continued to visit regularly until the First World War broke out.

Before leaving Italy, James went to Rome to attend to a matter for Clara concerning the grave and "largely just to stand beside that grave 5 minutes myself," he wrote to Baldwin. Years later, he wrote to Clare of standing again at "that very particular spot—below the grey wall, the cypresses and the time-silvered Pyramid. It is tremendously, inexhaustibly touching—its effect never fails to overwhelm."[21]

Even after returning to England, during the fall of 1894, James was still seeking out places associated with Woolson. While visiting some friends in Oxford, he stayed in Woolson's rooms at 15 Beaumont St. "[D]istressing as it was to enter the house," he wrote to Clare, it was a moving experience to meet and commiserate with Mrs. Phillips, her devoted landlady. Woolson just the year before had been drawn to the idea that "houses in which persons have lived, become after a time, permeated with their thoughts." She must have shared this theory with James, for he seemed to hope to communicate with her one last time.

While staying in her rooms, he conceived of a story titled "The Altar of the Dead": "I imagine a man whose noble and beautiful religion is the worship of the Dead," he wrote in his notebooks. "He cherishes for the silent, for the patient, the unreproaching dead, a tenderness in which all his private need of something, not of this world, to cherish, to be pious to, to make the object of a donation, finds a sacred, and almost a secret, expression. He is struck with the way they are forgotten, are unhallowed—unhonoured, neglected, shoved out of sight."[22]

In the coming years, James would write many more works that scholars have suspected were inspired at least in part by his complicated friendship with Woolson. The most fully realized is "The Beast in the Jungle," published nine years after her death. He took as the germ of his story an idea in Woolson's notebooks, which he read during those weeks cleaning out the Casa Semitecolo: "To imagine a man spending his life looking for and waiting for his 'splendid moment.' . . . But the moment never comes."[23] James's tale, a kind of posthumous collaboration, was a tribute not only to the memory of his friend but also to her conception of literature. It is one of his most moving tales precisely because it acknowledges the power of a great love, something she first encouraged him to do in his writing over twenty years earlier.

The story centers on John Marcher, who spends his life waiting for something prodigious to happen to him. He is convinced that it will alter his life irrevocably, but he has no conception of what it will be. The one person he tells his secret to is May Bartram, a woman of great sympathy, who at first wonders if what he describes might be "falling in love." He says he has loved but that it hasn't been "overwhelming." She responds, just as Woolson would have, "Then it hasn't been love."[24]

Over the ensuing years, the two become very close and Marcher realizes that he should marry her, but he decides that he can't ask a woman to share in his obsession, to make her watch with him through the years for what waited for him "like a crouching beast in a jungle." This is, however, precisely what May does. He feels great relief in being able to share his secret life with her and realizes that she looks out with him from the mask he wears for the world. She shares intimately in his thoughts and views, just as Woolson did in James's, but in the process she hides herself: "Beneath *her* forms as well detachment has learned to sit, and behavior had become for her, in the social sense, a false account of herself. There was but one account of her that would have been true all the while and that she could give straight to nobody, least of all to John Marcher."[25] This account, we are led to believe, is that she loves him. He remains, however, obtuse, looking anywhere else for his great moment but at her. She finally tells him that she has realized he will never know his fate because he is blind to it. What James realized in the years after Woolson's death was that Woolson had seen him but that he had not seen her. Like May, she "was a sphinx." Moreover, he realized that her powers of perception had been in some regards more penetrating than his. Women, John Marcher comes to believe, "made things out, where people were concerned, that the people often couldn't have made out for themselves. Their nerves, their sensibility, their imagination, were conductors and revealers."[26] James had come to appreciate Woolson's great empathy, it seems, as a woman and as a writer.

As May lies fatally ill and John contemplates her death, he feels "abandoned" and wonders if their long waiting hasn't been in vain. She tells him, "The door isn't shut. The door's open. . . . It's never too late."[27] When she is finally dying he feels cruelly locked out: "[A]ccess to her chamber of pain, rigidly guarded, was almost wholly forbidden him." He realizes that the "stupidest fourth cousin" has more right to be near her than he does, just as James must have felt when Grace Carter, a distant relation, was the person upon whom Woolson called in her final hours. John reflects, "A woman might have been, as it were, everything to him, and it might yet present him in no connexion that any one seemed held to recognise." His last recourse is to visit her grave, but he is unable to penetrate the mystery of death—"no palest light broke."[28]

A year later, however, when Marcher returns to May's grave, he finds there his past as well as her continued attendance, watching and waiting with him still. Thus begins a ritual of visiting her grave that is interrupted one day by a face "with an expression like the cut of a blade." It was that of another mourner, a man who presented "the image of a scarred passion." Then it suddenly flashes upon Marcher: "No passion had ever touched him, for this is what passion meant; he had survived and maundered and pined, but where had been *his* deep ravage? . . . He had seen *outside* of his life, not learned it within, the way a woman was mourned when she had been loved for herself." He had "missed" it after all, the great thing that was to happen to him—"*she* was what he had missed." Now, he discovers that his true fate was to be the man "to whom nothing on earth was to have happened." If he had "love[d] her, . . . he would have lived. *She* had lived—who could say now with what passion?—since she had loved him for himself; whereas he had never thought of her (ah how it hugely glared at him!) but in the chill of his egotism and the light of her use." The story ends with John Marcher throwing himself onto her tomb to avoid the "lurking Beast" then about to lunge at him.[29]

Angel of Grief, sculpted by William Wetmore Story, on Evelyn Story's grave near Woolson's in the Non-Catholic Cemetery in Rome.
It inspired the final scene in "The Beast of the Jungle."
(Photograph by the author)

The articulate silence of Woolson's life and death had finally spoken to James. What she taught him was that to love deeply was the great thing, the only thing perhaps. Without it, one has not really lived at all. Even though Woolson expertly veiled her deeper feelings, which surely were a kind of love, she had lived nonetheless. Now he had to carry on with the sinking feeling that he had not.

Six years after her death, James reflected on his good fortune, living in Rye, England, where he enjoyed financial independence and the comfort of owning his own home, conditions which enabled him to return to writing the novels that would secure his reputation as the "Master." After a visit from Grace Carter, he wrote to her, "You give me great pleasure—more than I can say—by expressing to me your sense of our common memory of, & common affection for, our C. F. W. But how <u>she</u> (in spite of Venetian lures & spells of illusions) would have liked <u>this</u> particular little corner of England, & perhaps found peace in it."[30] He couldn't help but imagine her there as well, living in the atmosphere of settled tranquility she had craved.

Two years before his own death, he was thinking of her still. On January 29, 1914, he miswrote the year as 1894. It was twenty years since her death, almost to the day.[31]

EPILOGUE

Remembrance

W OOLSON'S STORIES and novels were a tremendous critical and popular success in the late nineteenth century. Yet they were summarily dismissed as Victorian in the early twentieth century and then as not sufficiently feminist in the late twentieth. The fate of Woolson's lasting reputation also was not helped by the fact that she died at the age of fifty-three, just as a new era was dawning. Unlike James, she did not have the chance to reinvent herself as a modernist. Nor did she have the opportunity to win the national awards that would be instituted after the turn of the century, such as the Pulitzer Prize, won by her successors Edith Wharton and Willa Cather. She belonged to an earlier generation that was soon forgotten, buried under the epithets of "sentimental" or "local color." Even Wharton and Cather, whose successes owe much to Woolson's pioneering career, appear to have been oblivious to her. As early as 1906, only twelve years after her death, a reader wrote to the *New York Times*, "Miss Woolson has done too much for America and Americans to be forgotten and ignored."[1] Yet she was.

One person who could have ensured she was not did little to promote her memory—James. He continued to draw inspiration from her life and death for his fiction, as in *The Wings of the Dove*, published in 1902. Yet he never paid tribute to Woolson's literary achievements, as he had done when she was alive with the essay in *Partial Portraits*. Had he posthumously acknowledged her contributions to literature, her star might not have faded as quickly as it did.

The obituaries and assessments of Woolson's career immediately following her death gave no indication that she was a writer who would soon be forgotten. She was ranked at or near the head of American fiction writers and was often considered the best of America's living women writers because she had proven herself in the genres of the short story and the novel. Frequently referred to as a hard worker and true artist, she was deemed to have gained not only the momentary praise of the masses but also the more selective opinion of the critics. Many predicted that her works would receive a permanent place in the roll of America's great writers. In an interview that ran in the *New York Tribune*, Edmund Clarence Stedman compared her to Jane Austen and the Brontës, calling her "one of the leading women in the American literature of the century."[2]

Tributes to Woolson's art in Great Britain were also numerous. The Glasgow *Herald* lamented, "Miss Woolson's death is a distinct loss to American literature, and indeed to the list of novelists who have compelled the attention of the English-speaking race all over the world." *The Illustrated London News* classed her with Sarah Orne Jewett and Mary Wilkins Freeman but lamented that her "reputation was so recent," at least in England.[3]

Americans had no such excuse—they had known her for at least twenty years as "one of the first in America to bring the short story to its present excellence," in the words of Charles Dudley Warner, novelist and collaborator with Mark Twain. Warner paid one of the greatest tributes to Woolson, declaring that her death was "deplored by the entire literary fraternity of this country." Perfectly capturing the essence of her achievement, he wrote, "She was a sympathetic

[and] refined observer, entering sufficiently into the analytic mode of the time, but she had the courage to deal with the passions, and life as it is."[4]

When *Horace Chase* was published in book form, shortly after Woolson's death, reviewers considered the novel in light of her career. It proved, wrote the *Atlantic*, that "there was still power in the writer for a long continuance of good work; that it was done by a person who had mastered much of the technique of her art." Most agreed that it showed no falling off of conscientiousness in her work. The Cleveland *Plain Dealer* believed, "In no one of her previous novels has there been greater evidence of deep thought and careful workmanship." Some viewed Horace Chase as "the strongest character she has ever depicted." Overall, the reviews were positive as concerns the novel's craftsmanship but divided once again on questions of its morality and portrayal of female characters, whom some found inappropriate models for contemporary womanhood.[5]

Yet news of her supposed suicide and references in the early notices of her death to her "eccentricity," a code word for insanity, complicated posthumous reactions to Woolson and her work. Her family's counterattack seems to have had some effect, and the Harpers came out in force to defend the reputation of one of their foremost writers. Nonetheless, the rumors of suicide and insanity settled themselves into the collective psyche. There is not a sympathetic word to be found in any of the newspaper and magazine obituaries for the idea that she had taken her own life. An aura of tragic sensitivity had not yet formed around the image of the suicidal artist. In the late nineteenth century, before the world wars, suicide was viewed as a symptom of a diseased mind rather than a consequence of a flawed world. More recently, the suicide, particularly the female suicide, has been viewed as the victim of an oppressive society. As Woolson was recuperated by feminist scholars, her life and death were often aligned with what some have called the head-in-the-oven school of women writers. However, I agree with Phyllis Rose that there should be "less emphasis on despair, more on resilience in the literary history of women."[6] If we allow the purported fact of Woolson's suicide to overshadow her life and work, we fail to appreciate the complexity of her experience and the significance of her literary accomplishments.

Perhaps more damaging to Woolson's literary reputation was the fact that conditions generally were not favorable for a woman writer who wrote passionately about the hunger for love and the restraints of the Victorian era. Woolson died in a time of shifting literary tastes. Naturalism, with its emphasis on the gritty side of existence, was just then coming into vogue. But it was the growing disdain for sincerity and emotion in life generally that hurt her reputation most. During her lifetime, Woolson had noticed a growing suspicion of earnestness. After her death, her sister Clara summed up the post–World War I era: "It's the fashion (terribly increased by the war) to scorn emotions of love or 'feelings'—all must be joking and slang. . . . I occasionally overhear—I sometimes read in letters—things between lovers and husbands and wives that make me feel perfectly thankful to have lived in an earlier period, when each word or line of love was treasured, and each look precious forever." In 1929, the critic John Hervey held up Woolson's *For the Major* as "one of the little masterpieces of American fiction" because of "its perfect sincerity and exquisite sympathy." He was one of the few who lamented the satiric turn in literature and yearned for characters portrayed without "a jeer, a sneer, or a jibe."[7] Woolson sided with sincerity and passion, and it cost her the appreciation of most later critics and readers.

We think of the Victorian era as a time of repressed feelings, but the post-Victorian world showed a much greater contempt for expressions of emotion, labeling them sentimental and associating them with an inferior sphere of popular women writers. The split between high/male and low/female literary spheres was already taking shape when Woolson began her career. She had tried to avoid being classified with other women writers because of this perception and had to a large extent succeeded in distinguishing herself as a writer and not simply a woman writer. But as the desire to consolidate a select, all-male canon of American literature took hold, she and every other nineteenth-century female writer of merit was pushed to the sidelines and virtually erased from the literary map.[8]

In the early decades of the twentieth century, influential literary critics who were invested in a broader literary history, such as Fred Lewis Pattee, John Dwight Kern, and Lyon Richardson, championed Woolson.[9] Yet the gender divide persisted, with Howells and James crowned as American realists and Jewett and Freeman as the leaders of the so-called minor school of women's regionalism. Woolson's work fell into the chasm between, defying easy classification. She had been hailed alongside James and Howells, but there was no room for a female voice in the male literary movement of realism. And she had helped to pioneer an American literary regionalism that examined the lives of men as much as the lives of women, so her work did not fit the all-female construction of that movement.

As feminist critics reclaimed women writers in the late twentieth century, Woolson again did not fit the mold. Her relationships with male writers, her stories written from a male perspective, and her gender- and genre-blurring writing generally made her less attractive to the majority of feminist critics, who more easily reclaimed Jewett, Freeman, and Kate Chopin. There was still no camp to put her in and apparently no room for a writer who defied the existing categories, although that is beginning to change as critics become less invested in gender divides.

The one context in which Woolson's work and life have been most frequently understood is that of her friendship with Henry James, which has been both a blessing and a curse. Without her association with one of the foremost writers of the late nineteenth and early twentieth centuries, she might have been completely forgotten; however, the Master has cast over her a long shadow. It was James's biographer, Leon Edel, who reintroduced her to a general readership in the 1960s. However, despite having written to her niece Clare about his great respect for her and his desire to write a biography of Woolson after he was finished with James, he portrayed her in print as "prosy and banal, a journey-woman of letters," claiming that James's choice to bestow "upon work as regional and 'magazineish' as hers the discriminating literary taste which he had hitherto reserved for the leading European writers of fiction, or upon figures such as Hawthorne or even Howells, strikes one today as curious." In spite of James's respect for her, Edel diminished Woolson's work as "minute—and cluttered," calling her an "ardent devotee of 'local color.'"[10] Edel's disparagement provoked the defense of a small but potent group of feminist scholars, many of whom discovered Woolson through their study of James. In the 1980s and '90s they published groundbreaking studies of her work and were successful in having some of her work republished, including getting "'Miss Grief'" into college anthologies. Joan Weimer's collection, *Women Artists, Women Exiles: "Miss Grief" and Other Stories*, in the influential American Women Writers series published by Rutgers University Press, put Woolson back on the literary map, but confusion over where exactly she belonged again relegated her to the margins, and it has long since gone out of print.[11]

Regardless of the seemingly eternal critical debates about which writing is most respected or how to categorize writers, Woolson wanted simply to be remembered. That is why she refused to be buried in Venice's Protestant Cemetery—on a remote and rarely visited island in the lagoon—and insisted instead on burial in the Protestant Cemetery in Rome among what is estimated to be the densest collection of famous people in a single cemetery. After her funeral, John Hay wrote to Sam Mather, "I am glad to think this fine genius and noble woman is to rest in such surroundings till the day of judgment. She is worthy company for the best and brightest that sleep around her, though Shelley and Keats are among them. Her grave will be a shrine for the intelligence of the world for many a year to come."[12] And for many years it was. Listed in Baedeker's, it was the site of many a devotion by visitors who left flowers on her grave, along with those of other famous British and Americans.

Today, one climbs up a sloping hill to reach a simple tomb of marble coping inscribed "Constance Fenimore Woolson 1894." A plain Celtic cross lies atop a bed of violets. Percy Bysshe Shelley's grave is nearby, as is the grave of the sculptor William Wetmore Story and his wife.

Woolson's grave in the Non-Catholic Cemetery (as it is called today) in Rome. Pansies, a flower of remembrance, bestowed by the author on All Souls Day, 2012. (Photograph by the author)

Clara summed up the beauty and serenity of the place: "This cemetery is the only joyous cemetery I know of—there, the flowers always bloom, the birds always sing. . . . When I think of our cold snowy cemeteries at home, I wish that all I loved rested just there—where Connie sleeps."[13] When Clara died in Venice in 1923, she was buried in the Rome cemetery as well, as was her daughter, Clare, in 1961.

The spot retains its peacefulness, a walled oasis on the outskirts of Rome that attracts scores of visitors each day seeking out its tranquil beauty and making pilgrimages to the graves of Shelley, Keats, and the Italian communist leader Antonio Gramsci. While Gramsci's

grave lies covered with offerings—books, flowers, stones, and notes—
Woolson's is no longer disturbed by tributes of remembrance. Yet her
presence is palpable under the soaring cypress trees and in the shadow
of the ancient Pyramid of Cestius, a place where the living still come
by the thousands each year to remember the dead.

Acknowledgments

T HIS BOOK would not have been possible without the ground-
work laid by the scholars of the Constance Fenimore Woolson
Society, especially Sharon Dean's years-long effort that resulted in
The Complete Letters of Constance Fenimore Woolson. I am enormously
grateful for her willingness to share the manuscript before publication and for her support throughout the research and writing of this
book. The work of Joan Weimer, Cheryl Torsney, Victoria Brehm,
and Lyndall Gordon was also essential to providing me a gateway into
Woolson's life and work.

Funding for this project came from the Office of Research at the
University of New Orleans, which provided a Creative Endeavor
Opportunity Grant in summer 2011; the National Endowment for
the Humanities, which granted me a fellowship for the calendar year
2012; the English Department at the University of New Orleans,
which supplemented the NEH fellowship; and the Louisiana Board
of Regents, which provided an ATLAS (Awards to Louisiana Artists
and Scholars) Grant for a teaching reduction in spring 2013 and travel
funds to conduct research in Europe.

My immense thanks to the Department of English at the University of New Orleans, particularly the chair of English, Peter Schock,
for providing funding for research assistants and for supporting my
work in the few ways left to an underfunded department in a univer-

sity suffering repeated, draconian budget cuts. The following students provided invaluable assistance in the research and production of this book: Megan Cian, Chance Sweat, Coleen Muir, Kimberly Clouse, and Erin Henley. The amazing students in two graduate seminars—"Henry James and the Women Who Influenced Him" and "Writing Lives"—pushed me to think further about the Woolson-James relationship and writing the lives of women of the past.

I am grateful to Sharon Dean, John Pearson, Sharon M. Harris, and Robert D. Richardson for writing letters of recommendation for grant applications; to Cheryl Torsney, Keith O'Brien, Stephanie Stanley, Kate Stewart, Catherine Michna, Molly Mitchell, Patricia Henley, and Miki Pfeffer for feedback on the book proposal and/or chapters of the manuscript; and to Beverly Rude for invaluable editorial assistance throughout. Michael Gorra, Pierre Walker, and Sharon Dean graciously read and commented on the entire manuscript. Any errors that remain are my own.

In collecting the primary research materials for this book, I have incurred many debts. The greatest one I owe to Micha Grudin, who transcribed for me the twenty-two letters Woolson wrote to Francis Boott, now in possession of the descendants of Francis Boott Duveneck. My thanks as well to Carol Osborne for putting me in touch with Micha. I am grateful to the Interlibrary Loan staff at the University of New Orleans, particularly Janet Crane; Hilary Dorsch Wong at the Kroch Library at Cornell University; Dr. Richard Virr, Head and Curator of Manuscripts at McLennan Library, Rare Books and Special Collections Division, McGill University; Darla Moore and Wenxian Zhang at the Archives of Olin Library at Rollins College, Florida; Ann Sindelar and the staff of the Western Reserve Historical Society; Greg Zacharias and Rosalind Parr at the Center for Henry James Studies; Mark Boarman at the Thompson Library at Ohio State University; Jonathan Matthews, Assistant Site Director of Old Cahawba; Marylou Bradley and RuthAnne Jackson at the Kaua'i Historical Society; and John McClintock, archivist at The Albany Academies.

I am also grateful to the following individuals for helping me to locate important sources. Connie Anderson, great-great-niece of Constance Fenimore Woolson, scanned pages of the Mather family scrapbook. Lyndall Gordon helped me locate letters by Woolson. Gary Woolson generously donated many books related to Woolson, after Hurricane Katrina claimed my home library, and shared his genealogical research as well as the death record of Charles Woolson Jr. Edoarda Grego shared with me her translations of Venetian newspaper accounts of Woolson's death. Sharon Harris generously aided me in searching periodical databases to which I did not have access at my institution. Rosella Mamoli Zorzi provided valuable information on the Casa Semitecolo in Venice. Pierre Walker shared proofs of *The Complete Letters of Henry James, 1878–1880*, volume 2, before their publication in 2015 by the University of Nebraska Press. Wayne Franklin and Rochelle Johnson shared letters relating to the Woolson family that they found in the course of their research on James Fenimore Cooper and Susan Fenimore Cooper, respectively. Janet Crane and Jeanne Pavy helped me to scan illustrations. Stella Gray and her granddaughter Ivy Gray-Klein photographed letters written by Clare Benedict.

I am also grateful to the many who helped make my trip to Europe to follow in Woolson's footsteps a success. In Florence, Caroline Burton Michahelles, invited me for lunch at the Villa Brichieri-Colombi and delighted me with her hospitality. I am grateful to Stephanie McCoy, who is writing a novel about Woolson, for putting me in touch with Ms. Michahelles and providing travel advice generally. In Venice, Rosella Mamoli Zorzi gave me a tour of the Grand Canal and showed me landmarks important to Woolson; she also showed me some fragments of Woolson letters at the Biblioteca Nazionale Marciana. In Rome, Amanda Thursfield, director of the Non-Catholic Cemetery, was a wonderful guide and dinner companion. In Oxford, Dr. Robert Tobin, the chaplain of Oriel College, helped me identify Woolson's home outside the gates of the college and discussed the High Church movement in the Anglican Church over tea; Dr. Peter Groves, parish priest of St. Mary Magdalen, gave me a thorough tour of Woolson's home in Beaumont Street, where he now lives; and Lyndall Gordon invited me to lunch at St. Hilda's College, Oxford University, where we had a wonderful talk about all things Woolson.

Family and friends also offered their assistance with childcare over the years, giving me the gift of time in which to write. I want to particularly thank my mother, Beverly Rude, and my good friend Catherine Michna, who were more than generous.

I am immensely grateful to my agent, Barbara Braun, for having faith in this project and finding such a splendid home for it. To my editor at Norton, Amy Cherry, I owe more than I can say, from her championing of the project to her invaluable advice on the manuscript, and ultimately her belief in both me and Woolson. I can't imagine a better editor to have worked with on this project so close to my heart. Remy Cawley, editorial assistant at Norton, was a dream to work with. She answered my never-ending queries about manuscript preparation and production so promptly and patiently that she deserves some kind of award. Nancy Green did a tremendous job copyediting, saving me from many errors.

Paul, Emma, Merlin, and Fritzie, you are "my true country, my real home." Thank you for providing the love and ballast in my life that I wish Woolson could have had in hers.

Notes

The following abbreviations are used in the notes.

PEOPLE

ACW	Arabella Carter Washburn
CFW	Constance Fenimore Woolson
CRB	Clare Rathbone Benedict, CFW's niece
CWB	Clara Woolson Benedict, CFW's sister
ECS	Edmund Clarence Stedman
FB	Francis Boott
HJ	Henry James
HW	Hannah Pomeroy Woolson, CFW's mother
JH	John Hay
KM	Katharine Mather, CFW's niece
PHH	Paul Hamilton Hayne
SM	Samuel Mather, CFW's nephew
WDH	William Dean Howells
WWB	Dr. William Wilberforce Baldwin

WORKS

Benedict I	Clare Benedict, ed., *Voices Out of the Past*, vol. 1 of *Five Generations (1785–1923)* (London: Ellis, 1929).
Benedict II	Clare Benedict, ed., *Constance Fenimore Woolson*, vol. 2 of *Five Generations (1785–1923)*, 2nd ed. (London: Ellis, 1932).
Benedict III	Clare Benedict, ed., *The Benedicts Abroad*, vol. 3 of *Five Generations (1785–1923)* (London: Ellis, 1930).
CL	*The Complete Letters of Constance Fenimore Woolson*, ed. Sharon

L. Dean (Gainesville: University Press of Florida, 2012).

Harper's   *Harper's New Monthly Magazine.*

HJL   *Henry James Letters*, 4 vols., ed. Leon Edel (Cambridge, MA: The Belknap Press of Harvard University Press, 1974–1984).

REPOSITORIES

BHS   The Loring Collection, Beverly Historical Society, Beverly, MA.

Brown   The John Hay Collection, John Hay Library, Brown University, Providence, RI.

Columbia   Edmund Clarence Stedman Papers, Rare Book & Manuscript Library, Columbia University in the City of New York.

Cornell   Daniel Willard Fiske Papers, Rare and Manuscript Collections, The Carl A. Kroch Library, Cornell University, Ithaca, NY. (The cited letters are undated. I have provided the appropriate years whenever possible.)

Dartmouth   Curtis Family Papers, Rauner Special Collections Library, Dartmouth College, Hanover, NH.

Houghton   Houghton Library, Harvard University, Cambridge, MA.

McGill   Edel Papers, McLennan Library, Rare Books and Special Collections Division, McGill University, Montreal, Canada.

Pierpont Morgan   William Wilberforce Baldwin Collection, Pierpont Morgan Library, New York, NY.

Rollins   The Clare Benedict Collection of Constance Fenimore Woolson, Department of College Archives and Special Collections, Olin Library, Rollins College, Winter Park, FL.

University of Basel   English Department, University of Basel, Switzerland.

UVA   The Papers of Henry James, Albert and Shirley Small Special Collections Library, University of Virginia, Charlottesville, VA.

WRHS   Western Reserve Historical Society, Cleveland, OH.

A full bibliography of CFW's publications as well as criticism on her work can be found at http://constancefenimorewoolson.wordpress.com/.

PROLOGUE: *Portraits*

1. Examples are too numerous to mention. Sheldon M. Novick's comment in a footnote to his retelling of the story of HJ's drowning of CFW's dresses in *Henry James: The Mature Master* (New York: Random House, 2007), 554, indicates its pervasiveness: "I have not found confirmation of this improbable story, but as it has become canonical I include it here."

2. Copy of *The Portrait of a Lady* at University of Basel. CFW to Flora Payne [Whitney], [1863/1864?], CL, 2.

3. HJ, *The Portrait of a Lady* (1881; rev. ed. 1908; New York: W. W. Norton, 1995), 64.
4. CFW to HJ, Feb. 12, [1882], CL, 188. The latter is CFW's description of Isabel.
5. HJ, *The Portrait of a Lady*, 362.
6. CFW to HJ, Feb. 12, [1882], CL, 190.

CHAPTER 1: *A Daughter's Country*

1. Clara, who would be born after Constance, wrote that their mother "never could talk about those days," Benedict I, 42.
2. Benedict I, 42.
3. Benedict I, 164. Benedict III, 11.
4. CFW to O. F. R. Waite, Aug. 15, 1892, CL, 485.
5. CFW, "Charles Jarvis Woolson," Benedict I, 94–101. Maurice Joblin, *Cleveland Past and Present: Its Representative Men* (Cleveland, OH: Maurice Joblin, 1869), 400–402. CFW to JH, Dec. 26, [1885], CL, 304.
6. O. F. R. Waite, *History of the Town of Claremont, New Hampshire* (Manchester, NH: John B. Clarke Company, 1895), 498–99. CFW to ECS, July 23, [1876], CL, 74. Benedict I, 127. CFW, "The Bones of Our Ancestors," *Harper's* 47 (Sept. 1873): 535–43.
7. Richard Cooper to James Fenimore Cooper, Aug. 2, 1831, *Correspondence of James Fenimore Cooper*, ed. James Fenimore Cooper (grandson), vol. 1 (New Haven: Yale University Press, 1922), 236.
8. "We have never had any likeness of him which was satisfactory," CFW wrote to O. F. R. Waite, Aug. 15, 1892, CL, 484. "Death of Chas. J. Woolson," *The Daily Cleveland Herald*, Aug. 6, 1869. Charles Jarvis Woolson to Richard Cooper, Apr. 5, 1847, Cooper family. Benedict I, 100, 107.
9. Alan Taylor, *William Cooper's Town: Power and Persuasion on the Frontier of the Early American Republic* (New York: Vintage, 1996), 151.
10. Wayne Franklin, *James Fenimore Cooper: The Early Years* (New Haven: Yale University Press, 2007), 315–16, 330–34.
11. James Fenimore Cooper to HW, Apr. 19, 1840, *The Letters and Journals of James Fenimore Cooper*, ed. James Beard, vol. 4 (Cambridge, MA: The Belknap Press of Harvard University Press, 1968), 29–30.
12. Fenimore was CFW's great-grandmother's maiden name. James added it to his name legally in 1826, having promised his mother to carry on the name, which would have otherwise died out.
13. Taylor, *William Cooper's Town*, 375. Benedict I, 17.
14. Taylor, *William Cooper's Town*, 301, 304–5, 308.
15. Hannah Pomeroy [Woolson] to William Cooper, Oct. 18, 1828, James Fenimore Cooper Collection, Beinecke Rare Books and Manuscript Library, Yale University.
16. Ibid.
17. Benedict I, 158–60, 148–49.
18. The 1850 census shows three Irish servants living in the Woolson household, and

the 1860 census two German "domestics." CFW was "carefully instructed" in domestic arts, she wrote to Katharine Loring, Sept. 19, [1890], CL, 420.

19. Benedict I, 161. Benedict III, 215, 511. CWB to KM, July 26, 1905, typescript, Mather Family Papers, WRHS.

20. Levi Crosby Turner, "Auto-Biographic," Diaries of Levi Crosby Turner, Research Library, New York State Historical Association, Cooperstown, NY.

21. Turner, "Auto-Biographic," 18. Charles Jarvis Woolson to Richard Cooper, Mar. 15, 1847, Cooper family. CFW, "Charles Jarvis Woolson," Benedict I, 98.

22. HW, Journal, Benedict I, 167–214.

23. Benedict I, 42; ellipses in original. Cornelia E. L. May, "Constance Fenimore Woolson," unpublished manuscript, courtesy of Connie Anderson, great-great-niece of CFW.

24. CFW to JH, Dec. 26, [1885], CL, 303. Notes in CFW's copy of James Russell Lowell, *My Study Windows* (Boston: Houghton, 1886), 19, Rollins. CFW to SM, Feb. 27, [1889], CL, 367. CFW, "Round by Propeller," *Harper's* 45 (Sept. 1872): 520.

25. CFW, "The South Shore of Lake Erie," *Picturesque America; or, The Land We Live In*, vol. 1 (New York: D. Appleton, 1876), 526. Anthony Trollope, *North America* (New York: Harper & Brothers, 1862), 158. John Fiske quoted in William Ganson Rose, *Cleveland: The Making of a City* (Cleveland: World, 1950), 304. May, "Constance Fenimore Woolson."

26. Joblin, *Cleveland Past and Present*, 385. George Quartus Pomeroy made Jarvis an "innocent victim of a long series of frauds and deceptions," according to "Forgery, &c.," *The Cleveland Herald*, May 5, 1845. Charles Jarvis Woolson to Richard Fenimore Cooper, July 31, 1851, Cooper Family.

27. CFW, "Charles Jarvis Woolson," Benedict I, 97. CFW to H. H. Boyesen, Aug. 9, [1881?], CL, 171.

28. Oliver Payne, the brother of her friend Flora Payne; Zephaniah Swift Spalding; and Samuel Livingston Mather.

CHAPTER 2: *Lessons in Literature, Life, and Death*

1. Benedict I, 165–66. "Died," *The Cleveland Herald*, Jan. 31, 1846.

2. Benedict I, 166.

3. Benedict II, 16. Quotes from Hannah in Benedict I, 166.

4. Mrs. W. A. Ingham, *Women of Cleveland and Their Work, Philanthropic, Educational, Literary, Medical and Artistic* (Cleveland: W. A. Ingham, 1893), 270. Benedict I, 64.

5. Benedict II, xiv. CRB to Leon Edel, July 23, [1953], McGill. CFW to Harriet Benedict Sherman, [1881?], CL, 180. Ingham, *Women of Cleveland and Their Work*, 271. "Constance Fenimore Woolson: Her Early Cleveland Days, Her Home There and Her Friends," *New York Herald*, Nov. 10, 1889, p. 11. The close friend interviewed was probably Arabella Carter.

6. CFW to Mary Gale Carter Clarke, July 24, [1884], CL, 284.

7. Benedict II, xv. "Constance Fenimore Woolson: Her Early Cleveland Days."

Sarah D. Hobart, "Constance Fenimore Woolson," *The Advance* 18 (Oct. 18, 1883): 684.

8. Benedict II, xv. CFW to KM, Dec. 27, [1892], CL, 494. CFW to ECS, Sept. 28, [1874], CL, 18. CFW to PHH, All-Saints Day, [1875], CL, 54.

9. The parlor's description is taken from Anne March [CFW], *The Old Stone House* (Boston: D. Lothrop, 1873), 64. She used her family's home, the former Irad Kelley mansion on Euclid Avenue, as a model, according to J. H. A. Bone, "With and Without Glasses," Feb. 11, 1894, p. 8, and Cornelia E. L. May, "Constance Fenimore Woolson," unpublished manuscript, courtesy of Connie Anderson, great-great-niece of CFW. C. A. Urann, *Centennial History of Cleveland* (Cleveland, 1896), 62–63. CFW, "The Editor's Sanctum," ch. 3, *The Old Stone House*.

10. George Pomeroy Keese, "Constance Fenimore Woolson," *The Freeman's Journal* (Cooperstown, NY), Feb. 1, 1894, p. 3. Georgiana's poem, Benedict I, 75. Hannah's journal, Benedict I, 167–214. Georgiana's journal, Benedict I, 78–84.

11. "Constance Fenimore Woolson: Her Early Cleveland Days."

12. "Notices of Publications Received," *The Ohio Cultivator* (Columbus) 9 (April 15, 1855): 120. Grannis quoted in Edward A. Roberts, *Official Report of the Centennial Celebration of the Founding of Cleveland and the Settlement of the Western Reserve* (Cleveland: Cleveland Printing & Publishing Co., 1896), 185. "Mrs. Arey's Poems," *Western Literary Messenger* 24 (May 1855): 122.

13. "Editorial Notes—American Literature," *Putnam's Monthly Magazine* 3 (Feb. 1854): 222. Hawthorne quoted in the Introduction to *Selected Letters of Nathaniel Hawthorne*, ed. Joel Myerson (Columbus: Ohio State University Press, 2002), xv.

14. Woolson family volume of *Harper's* in Clare Benedict Collection, WRHS. Mrs. C. S. Hall, "Memories of Miss Jane Porter," *Harper's* 1 (Sept. 1850): 433.

15. CFW to ECS, July 23, [1876], CL, 74. CFW, *The Old Stone House*, 378.

16. Benedict I, 97. CFW to SM, Jan. 21, 1891, CL, 441. Ingham, *Women of Cleveland and Their Work*, 271.

17. Benedict I, 67. CFW, *The Old Stone House*, 163.

18. C. Jarvis Woolson to W. H. Averell, Benedict I, 67.

19. C. Jarvis Woolson to Richard Fenimore Cooper, July 31, 1851, Cooper Family. Georgiana Woolson Mather to Mrs. Thomas Mather, Aug. 30, 1851, Mather Family Papers, WRHS.

20. Typo in obituary of Rev. Lawson Carter, *New York Times*, July 16, 1868. HW, "A Ghost Story," Benedict I, 220. See also Emma Woolson Carter to "Louisa," Mar. 15, 1852, Benedict I, 68–69.

21. Benedict I, 68. CFW to "Louisa," n.d., CL, 1. Although Sharon Dean dates this letter in the 1840s, it must have been written when Emma came home after her husband's death. Sheila M. Rothman, *Living in the Shadow of Death: Tuberculosis and the Social Experience of Illness in American History* (New York: Basic Books, 1994).

22. Susan Sontag, *Illness as Metaphor and AIDS and Its Metaphors* (New York: Picador, 2011), 31–33. Rothman, *Living in the Shadow of Death*, 16–17.

23. Terry S. Reynolds, *Iron Will: Cleveland Cliffs and the Mining of Iron Ore, 1847–2006* (Detroit: Wayne State University Press, 2011), 4. Hannah Peabody Chandler Woolson to CFW, n.d., CL, 565. Benedict I, 71.

24. Poem in Mather Family Papers, WRHS. Georgiana Woolson Mather to Samuel Livingston Mather, July 3, 1853, Benedict I, 85–87. Benedict I, 71.
25. Rothman, *Living in the Shadow of Death*, 107.
26. CFW to SM, Feb. 24, [1877?], CL, 89.
27. Charles Jarvis Woolson to Richard Fenimore Cooper, Feb. 13, 1846, and Mar. 5, 1850, Cooper Family. Clara's description of her mother is in the thinly veiled portrait of Mrs. Barstow in her pseudonymous novel, Agnes Phelps, *One Year at Boarding-School* (Boston: Loring, 1873), 10.
28. Michael J. McTighe, *A Measure of Success: Protestants and Public Culture in Antebellum Cleveland* (Albany: State University of New York Press, 1994), 30. CFW, *The Old Stone House*, 230–31.
29. "Constance Fenimore Woolson: Her Early Cleveland Days."
30. CFW, *The Old Stone House*, 211–12, 38.
31. CFW to Samuel Mather, Oct. 31, 1890, CL, 425. CFW to FB, Mar. 4, [1889], Duveneck Family.
32. Mark S. Schantz, *Awaiting the Heavenly Country: The Civil War and America's Culture of Death* (Ithaca, NY: Cornell University Press, 2008), 39.
33. CFW, *The Old Stone House*, 254.

CHAPTER 3: *Turning Points*

1. Letter to the Editor, "Rockwell St. School Examinations, &c.," *The Cleveland Herald*, Mar. 17, 1853.
2. Mrs. A. W. Fairbanks, ed., *Emma Willard and Her Pupils; or, Fifty Years of Troy Female Seminary, 1822–1872* (New York: Mrs. Russell Sage, 1898), 92. *Circular and Catalogue of the Albany Female Academy. 1848* (Albany, NY: Joel Munsell, 1848). Anne Firor Scott, "The Ever-Widening Circle: The Diffusion of Feminist Values from the Troy Female Seminary, 1822–1872," *History of Education Quarterly* 19, no. 1 (Spring 1979): 3–25.
3. *First Annual Catalogue of the Cleveland Female Seminary, Cleveland, Ohio 1854–1855* (Cleveland: Sanford & Hayward's, 1855), 15. CFW to Katharine Loring, Sept. 19, [1890], CL, 421. CFW to Linda Guilford, [1891], CL, 464.
4. CFW to Katharine Loring, Sept. 19, [1890], CL, 421.
5. Linda T. Guilford, "The Teacher's Disappointments," *The Ohio Educational Monthly. A Journal of School and Home Education*, new ser., vol. 1 (1860): 200. Linda Thayer Guilford, *The Story of a Cleveland School, From 1848 to 1881* (Cambridge, MA: John Wilson and Son, 1890), 74.
6. CFW to Linda Guilford, Mar. 1, [1887] and [1891], CL, 336, 464. Guilford, *The Story of a Cleveland School*, 76–77.
7. Guilford, *The Story of a Cleveland School*, 77–78. CFW to PHH, [April 17, 1876], CL, 67. CFW to Linda Guilford, Mar. 1, [1887], CL, 336.
8. CFW to William Whitney, Feb. 25, [1893], CL, 502.
9. Eugenia Kaledin, *The Education of Mrs. Henry Adams*, 2nd ed. (Amherst: University of Massachusetts Press, 1994), 37–44.
10. Julia Gardiner quoted in Van R. Baker, ed., *The Websters: Letters of an American Army Family in Peace and War, 1836–1853* (Kent, OH: The Kent State Univer-

sity Press, 2000), 13. CFW, *Anne* (New York: Harper & Brothers, 1882), 151, 157. CFW used Madame Chegaray's as the model for Madame Moreau's school in *Anne*.

11. CFW to Hjalmar Hjorth Boyesen, Aug. 9, [1881?], CL, 171. CFW to PHH, All-Saints Day, [1875], CL, 56.

12. CFW, "The Bones of Our Ancestors," *Harper's* 47 (Sept. 1873): 535–43. CFW, *Anne*, 154, 155.

13. CFW, *Anne*, 157. Benedict I, 292.

14. Benedict I, 292.

15. Benedict III, 518.

16. CFW to Flora Payne, [1863/64], CL, 2.

17. David Van Tassel, *"Behind Bayonets": The Civil War in Northern Ohio* (Kent, OH: The Kent State University Press, 2006), 19, 28–32. The Woolsons lived at 288 Prospect St., and Lucy Bagby at 151. "Mr. Lincoln's Reception," *Cleveland Morning Leader*, Feb. 14, 1861, p. 1.

18. CFW, *Anne*, 353–54.

19. CFW to SM, Jan. 21, 1891, CL, 441.

20. CFW, "The Ancient City," pt. 1, *Harper's* 50 (Dec. 1874): 9.

21. Anne March [CFW], *The Old Stone House* (Boston: D. Lothrop, 1873), 139.

22. Sebastian Hubert Lukasik, "Military Service, Combat, and American Identity in the Progressive Era" (PhD diss., Duke University, 2008), 84. *Annals of Cleveland*, vol. 44, 1861 (Cleveland: WPA Project, 1938), 131. CFW to SM, Dec. 10, 1893, CL, 535.

23. David Stephen Heidler and Jeanne T. Heidler, eds., *Encyclopedia of the American Civil War: A Political, Social, and Military History* (New York: W. W. Norton, 2002), 1744. CFW to PHH, July 23, [1875], CL, 48. "The March of the Seventh—Letter from a Cleveland Boy," *Cleveland Morning Leader*, May 4, 1861, p. 2.

24. CFW to SM, Jan. 21, 1891, CL, 441. CFW, "A Flower of the Snow," *The Galaxy* 27 (Jan. 1874): 77, 78. In a letter to SM, Dec. 10, 1893, CL, 535, CFW indicated that she and Zeph had planned to marry. She imagined that if they met again each would think, "Great heavens—what an escape I had!"

25. CFW to ECS, Oct. 1, [1876], Columbia. Concert program in *The (Cleveland) Plain Dealer*, Sept. 21, 1861, p. 3. CFW to ECS, July 8, [1877], CL, 94. Mary Clark Brayton and Ellen F. Terry, *Our Acre and Its Harvest: Historical Sketch of the Soldiers' Aid Society of Northern Ohio* (Cleveland: Fairbanks, Benedict, 1869), 285. CFW, "A Merry Christmas," *Harper's* 44 (Jan. 1872): 234.

26. "Major Zeph Swift Spalding," *The Daily Cleveland Herald*, Oct. 11, 1862. "A Terrible Scene," *The (Cleveland) Plain Dealer*, Nov. 4, 1862, p. 3. CFW, "A Merry Christmas," 235, 234. Report of Lieut. Col. Zephaniah S. Spalding, *Official Records of the Union and Confederate Armies, 1861–1865*, ser. 1, vol. 17, pt. 1, 572–75, Ancestry.com.

27. CFW, "A Merry Christmas," 235. Jessee Hawes, *Cahaba: A Story of Captive Boys in Blue* (New York: Burr, 1888), 14–16. Rufus Spalding, who became a U.S. congressman, later reported on his son's experience to the House of Representatives: "Mr. Spalding and the Million Dollar Resolution," *The Daily Cleveland Herald*, Mar. 25, 1867.

28. CFW to Hamilton Mabie, June 18, [1883], CL, 258. CFW to PHH, July 23,

[1875], CL, 48. J. Henry Harper, *The House of Harper* (New York: Harper & Brothers, 1912), 226.

29. Sandol Stoddard, "Biography of Col. Spalding," Earl Arruda Papers, Kauai Historical Society. "Leasing of Abandoned Plantations," *Nashville Daily Union*, Mar. 9, 1864, p. 1. Robert Tracy McKenzie, *One South or Many?: Plantation Belt and Upcountry in Civil War–Era Tennessee* (Cambridge: Cambridge University Press, 1994), 94. CFW to SM, Dec. 10, [1893], CL, 535.

30. I was unable to verify Zeph's whereabouts from the end of the war until 1867, but his wartime leasing of plantations and his later post as a cotton planter in Hawaii strongly suggest he had gone south. Lawrence N. Powell, *New Masters: Northern Planters During the Civil War and Reconstruction* (New York: Fordham University Press, 1998), 145–46. Cheryl Torsney, "Zephaniah Swift Spalding: Constance Fenimore Woolson's Cipher," in Kathleen Diffley, ed., *Witness to Reconstruction: Constance Fenimore Woolson and the Postbellum South, 1873–1894* (Jackson: University Press of Mississippi, 2011), 114–15.

31. CFW signed herself "Miss Constance Woolson, spinster" on a letter published in the *Cleveland Herald* on Feb. 2, 1869.

32. CWB, fragment of letter, no recipient, n.d., Clare Benedict Collection, WRHS. Benedict III, 615, 621.

33. CFW, "Cicely's Christmas," *Appletons' Journal* 6 (Dec. 30, 1871): 758. CFW, "Wilhelmina," *Atlantic Monthly* 35 (Jan. 1875): 44–55. Torsney, "Zephaniah Swift Spalding," 124.

34. CFW, "Hepzibah's Story," in Robert Gingras, "'Hepzibah's Story': An Unpublished Work by Constance Fenimore Woolson," *Resources for American Literary Study* 10 (Spring 1980): 33–46. The manuscript of this story, previously in the archives at Rollins College, has been lost. Gingras explains that the address 131 St. Clair Street was written on the manuscript, indicating that it was written between 1871 and 1873, when Constance lived there.

35. CFW to SM, Dec. 10, 1893, CL, 535.

36. CFW, "Heliotrope," *Harper's* 47 (July 1873): 274. CFW, "The Lady of Little Fishing," *Atlantic Monthly* 34 (Sept. 1874): 303. CFW to SM, Jan. 21, 1891, CL, 441.

37. CFW to Flora Payne, [1863/64], CL, 2. "Mrs. William C. Whitney," *Harper's Weekly* 37 (Feb. 18, 1893): 148. Flora Payne's letters to William C. Whitney, typed excerpts, in William C. Whitney Papers, Library of Congress.

38. CFW to ACW, n.d., CL, 3.

39. Ibid. The only surviving record of the marriage is in their son Philip Carter Washburn's application to the Sons of the American Revolution, Ancestry.com. CFW to Jane Carter, Jan. 13, [1888], CL, 352.

40. "Criminal," *The Daily Cleveland Herald*, Mar. 31, 1869. "Suicide," *The (Cleveland) Plain Dealer*, Mar. 31, 1869, p. 3.

41. Benedict I, 110. CFW to unknown recipient, Aug. 24, 1871, CL, 6–7.

42. "Death of Chas. J. Woolson," *The Daily Cleveland Herald*, Aug. 6, 1869. Mrs. W. A. Ingham, *Women of Cleveland and Their Work* (Cleveland: W. A. Ingham, 1893), 272.

43. CFW to SM, Oct. 31, [1890], CL, 425.

44. CFW to JH, Dec. 26, [1885], CL, 304. CFW, *For the Major* (New York: Harper & Brothers, 1883), 73.

CHAPTER 4: *False Starts*

1. CFW's first three publications were on these topics. CFW, "An October Idyl," *Harper's* 41 (1870): 907.
2. J. H. A. Bone, "With and Without Glasses," *The (Cleveland) Plain Dealer* (Feb. 4, 1894), p. 8. G.P.K. [George Pomeroy Keese], "Constance Fenimore Woolson," *The Freeman's Journal* (Cooperstown, NY), Feb. 1, 1894, p. 3.
3. "Co-Partnership Notice," *The Cleveland Daily Herald*, Aug. 12, 1870. "Real Estate Transfers," *The Cleveland Daily Herald*, Aug. 29, 1870. "A Successful Author's Advice," *The Ladies' Home Journal* 13 (Aug. 1896): 12. CFW to Elizabeth Mather, Dec. 4, [1874], CL, 23.
4. William F. G. Shanks, "Woman's Work and Wages," *Harper's* 37 (Sept. 1868): 548. According to Marian J. Morton, *Women in Cleveland: An Illustrated History* (Bloomington: Indiana University Press, 1995), 58, female teachers earned $659/year in 1875.
5. Shanks, "Woman's Work and Wages," 548. "Editor's Easy Chair" (July 1867); S. E. Wallace, "Another Weak-Minded Woman" (Nov. 1867); Elizabeth Stuart Phelps, "What Shall They Do?" (Sept. 1867), all reprinted in Anne E. Boyd, *Wielding the Pen: Writings on Authorship by American Women of the Nineteenth Century* (Baltimore: Johns Hopkins University Press, 2009), 228–42.
6. Bone, "With and Without Glasses," p. 8.
7. Ibid.
8. Eugene Exman, *The House of Harper: The Making of a Modern Publisher* (1967; New York: Harper, 2010), 78. Bone, "With and Without Glasses," p. 8.
9. CFW, "An October Idyl," *Harper's* 41 (1870), 907, 911. *Idyl* is misspelled. CFW to ACW, n.d., CL, 4.
10. CFW, "The Haunted Lake," *Harper's* 44 (Dec. 1871): 21, 23, 26.
11. CFW to Edward Everett Hale, Dec. 1, 1871, CL, 8.
12. See letters from Samuel L. Mather to SM, July 12, 1870, and July 23, 1870, Mather Family Papers, WRHS.
13. HJ, *The Portrait of a Lady* (1881, rev. ed. 1908; New York: W. W. Norton, 1995), 88. Gary Scharnhorst, "James and Kate Field," *Henry James Review* 22, no. 2 (2001): 200–206.
14. CFW, "New York," *The Daily Cleveland Herald*, Jan. 10, 1871. CFW, "Gotham," *Supplement to the Daily Cleveland Herald*, Jan. 14, 1871.
15. CFW's letters from Nov. 1870 through early Feb. 1871 are headed with the address No. 49 W. 32nd St. See CL, 5. Mark D. Hirsch, *William C. Whitney: Modern Warwick* (New York: Dodd, Mead, 1948), 47. CFW, "Gotham."
16. CFW to ACW, n.d., CL, 549.
17. CFW, "Gotham." CFW to ACW, n.d., CL, 549. CFW, "New York."
18. CFW, "Gotham."
19. HJ, *The Portrait of a Lady*, 114. CFW to PHH, All-Saints Day, [1875], CL, 57.
20. CFW, "A Merry Christmas," *Harper's* 44 (Jan. 1872): 231–36. CFW, "Cicely's Christmas," *Appletons' Journal* 6 (Dec. 30, 1871): 758.
21. CFW to ACW, [1870/71], CL, 4.
22. "The New Hamburg Disaster," *Harper's Weekly* (Feb. 25, 1871). CFW to WWB, Oct. 5, [1890], CL, 422.

23. *"Thy Will Be Done": George S. Benedict*, privately printed, Clare Benedict Collection, WRHS, 81, 19–21.

24. CFW to Harriet Benedict Sherman, n.d., CL, 560. CFW, "Hepzibah's Story," in Robert Gingras, "'Hepzibah's Story': An Unpublished Work by Constance Fenimore Woolson," *Resources for American Literary Study* 10 (Spring 1980): 45. CFW, "The Flower of the Snow," *The Galaxy* 27 (January 1874): 81, 83.

25. CFW to Harriet Benedict Sherman, n.d., CL, 560. J. H. A. Bone, "With and Without Glasses," p. 8. "A Day of Mystery," *Appletons' Journal* 6 (Sept. 9, 1871): 290–93. Benedict III, 622. *W. S. Robison and Co.'s Cleveland Directory, 1871–1872* (Cleveland: W. S. Robison, 1871), 479.

26. Estimate of CFW's earnings based on typical rates of pay provided by Frank Luther Mott, *A History of American Magazines*, vol. 3 (Cambridge, MA: The Belknap Press of Harvard University Press, 1957), 13–14. Mott posits "$2,000 as a minimum income for moderate comfort" in the period from 1865 to 1885. Bone, "With and Without Glasses," p. 8. A note inside a copy of Agnes Phelps [CWB], *One Year at Our Boarding-School* (Boston: Loring, 1873) in the Clare Benedict Collection at the WRHS explains the circumstances of its production, including the fact that it was published "without remuneration."

27. CFW to Linda Guilford, [1891], CL, 464.

28. CFW to SM, Apr. 11, [1891], CL, 448. Susan Coolidge [Sarah Woolsey], *What Katy Did* (Boston: Roberts Brothers, 1892), 35–36. CFW to Mary Mapes Dodge, Sept. 13, [1888?], CL, 359.

29. Hannah called it "a stirring account of 'the boys' pranks," referring to Sam Mather, Charlie Woolson, and the Carter boys. HW to SM, May 15, 1874, Mather Family Papers, WRHS.

30. "Book Notices," *The Youth's Companion* 46 (Mar. 27, 1873): 103. *New York Mail* quoted in "There Are Two Kinds of Juvenile Books," *The Cleveland Morning Daily Herald*, July 9, 1873.

31. CFW quoted in Bone, "With and Without Glasses," p. 8. According to "Our Youth," *The Cleveland Daily Herald*, June 14, 1873, CFW also wrote a serial called "Along the Slowgo" for a Cleveland children's magazine, *Our Youth*, which I have not been able to locate.

32. "One Year at Our Boarding-School," *North American and United States Gazette* (Philadelphia), Dec. 25, 1873, p. 1. Phelps [CWB], *One Year at Our Boarding-School*.

33. CFW to Linda Guilford, [1891], CL, 464. On the lack of American women writers' recognition as serious artists before Woolson's generation, see Anne E. Boyd, *Writing for Immortality: Women and the Emergence of High Literary Culture in America* (Baltimore: Johns Hopkins University Press, 2004).

CHAPTER 5: *Departures*

1. CFW to unknown recipient, Aug. 24, 1871, CL, 6–7. CFW to R. R. Bowker, May 31, 1873, CL, 10.

2. Reviews quoted in "We fancy the story of 'Solomon,' . . . " *The Daily Cleveland Herald*, Sept. 23, 1873. CFW to WDH, Oct. 27, [1873?], CL, 11. CFW to Thomas

Bailey Aldrich, June 30, [1882], CL, 203. "The Absence of Women at the Whittier Dinner," *New York Evening Post*, reprinted in the *Boston Daily Advertiser*, Dec. 28, 1877, p. 2.

3. CFW to ACW, [1874?], CL, 26. CFW to Miss Farnian, Apr. 17, 1875, CL, 33.
4. CFW to WDH, Oct. 27, [1873?], CL, 11.
5. CFW, "Round by Propeller," *Harper's* 45 (Sept. 1872): 522. "Literary," *Appletons' Journal* 13 (Apr. 3, 1875): 438.
6. CFW to WDH, June 28, [1875], CL, 43. "Ballast Island" prefigures themes in Margaret Wilkins Freeman's "New England Nun" (1891) and Sarah Orne Jewett's *The Country of the Pointed Firs* (1896).
7. CFW to ECS, Sept. 28, [1874], CL, 18. CFW to Henry Mills Alden, Feb. 5, [1881], CL, 161.
8. WDH, *Their Wedding Journey, Atlantic Monthly* 28 (Sept. 1871): 354–55. Review of *Their Wedding Journey, North American Review* 114 (Apr. 1872): 444. Benedict II, 97.
9. George Eliot, *Adam Bede* (1859; Toronto: Broadview, 2005), 241–42, 239.
10. CFW to Roberts Brothers, Nov. 12, [1870], CL, 4. George Sand, *The Devil's Pool*, trans. Andrew Brown (1846; London: Hesperus Classics, 2005), 6, 7, 8. CFW, "Mottoes, Maxims, Reflections," Rollins; quote from Paul Bourget. Clara Benedict, fragment inside a copy of *For the Major*, Clare Benedict Collection, WRHS.
11. CFW, "Solomon," in *Castle Nowhere* (Boston: J. R. Osgood, 1875), 238, 265.
12. CFW to ACW, [1876?], CL, 87.
13. CFW to WDH, June 28, [1875], CL, 44.
14. CFW to SM, Apr. 25, [1875], CL, 34. CFW to ECS, Apr. 13, [1874], CL, 11–12. CFW to ECS, Sept. 7, [1874], CL, 16.
15. "The Magazines for September," *The Nation* 19 (Sept. 3, 1874): 157. WDH, "Recent Literature," *Atlantic Monthly* 35 (June 1875): 737.
16. Samuel Clemens to Olivia Langdon Clemens, Apr. 26, 1873, Hartford, CT. Online at TheMarkTwainProject.org (MS: CU-MARK, UCCL 00909). Bryant Morey French concluded Warner probably borrowed from CFW's "Weighed in the Balance" (June 1872). See *Mark Twain and the Gilded Age: The Book That Named an Era* (Dallas: Southern Methodist University Press, 1965), 295.
17. CFW to James R. Osgood, Oct. 22, [1874], CL, 19. CFW, "St. Clair Flats," in *Castle Nowhere*, 306, 332, 348. WDH, "Recent Literature," 737.
18. CFW to WDH, June 28, [1875], CL, 43. Sharon Dean, *Constance Fenimore Woolson: Homeward Bound* (Knoxville: University of Tennessee Press, 1995), 17. CFW to ECS, Jan. 20, [1875], CL, 30.
19. CFW to WDH, June 28, [1875], CL, 43. WDH, "Recent Literature," *Atlantic Monthly* 35 (June 1875): 736, 737. CFW to WDH, June 28, [1875], CL, 43.
20. CFW to ACW, [1875], CL, 87.
21. "Literary," *Appletons' Journal*, 439. "Fiction in a New Field," *New York Tribune*, Mar. 6, 1875, p. 8.
22. Samuel L. Mather to SM, Dec. 21, 1872, Mather Family Papers, WRHS.
23. HW to Mrs. Samuel L. Mather, Nov. 19, 1873, Rollins. SM to Samuel L. Mather, Oct. 22, 1873, Mather Family Papers, WRHS. CFW, "A Letter from Miss Woolson," *The Cleveland Daily Herald*, Dec. 18, 1873.

24. Harriet Beecher Stowe, *Palmetto Leaves* (Boston: James R. Osgood, 1873), 213.

25. CFW, "A Letter from Miss Woolson." HW to SM, Jan. 3, 1874, Mather Family Papers, WRHS.

26. Today Hospital Street is called Aviles Street, and the Fatio House is the Ximenez-Fatio House Museum. CFW, "The Ancient City," pt. 1, *Harper's* 50 (Dec. 1874): 6. HW to SM, Jan. 3, 1874, Mather Family Papers, WRHS.

27. HW to SM, Jan. 3, 1874, Mather Family Papers, WRHS. CFW to ACW, n.d., CL, 25.

28. CFW, "Ferns," unpublished poem in Cheryl B. Torsney, "Fern Leaves from Connie's Portfolio," *Constance Fenimore Woolson's Nineteenth Century: Essays*, ed. Victoria Brehm (Detroit: Wayne State University Press, 2001), 185. CFW, "The French Broad," *Harper's* 50 (Apr. 1875): 623. CFW to ECS, July 23, [1876], CL, 74.

29. CFW to SM, Feb. 27, [1889], CL, 366. CFW, "Pine-Barrens," *Harper's* 50 (Dec. 1874): 66.

30. CFW, "The Ancient City," pt. 1, 18, 22.

31. Ibid., 18.

32. Ibid., 7. CFW, "Felipa," *Rodman the Keeper: Southern Sketches* (1880; repr., New York: AMS Press, 1971), 209.

33. The term "Boston marriages," referring to relationships between women who lived together as a married couple, was widely used after the publication of HJ's *The Bostonians* in 1886. CFW, "Contributors' Club," *Atlantic Monthly* 42 (Oct. 1878): 503. Some have seen in such literary portrayals in "Felipa," *Anne*, and *Horace Chase* the suggestion that CFW herself had homosexual desires. See Kristen Comment, "The Lesbian 'Impossibilities' of Miss Grief's 'Armor,'" *Constance Fenimore Woolson's Nineteenth Century: Essays*, 207–8. This is possible, although I have found no concrete evidence to support the idea.

34. CFW, "The Ancient City," pt. 1, 14; pt. 2, *Harper's* 50 (Jan. 1875): 172. CFW, "King David," in *Rodman the Keeper*, 274.

35. Quoted in Robert J. Scholnick, *Edmund Clarence Stedman* (New York: G. K. Hall, 1977), 5.

36. Laura Stedman and George M. Gould, *Life and Letters of Edmund Clarence Stedman*, vol. 1 (New York: Moffat, Yard, 1901), 504. "Constance Fenimore Woolson. Her Work and Personality," *New York Tribune* (Jan. 28, 1894), p. 14.

37. CFW to ECS, Dec. 12, [1875], CL, 84. Sharon Dean dates this letter as 1876, but internal evidence indicates it was written in 1875.

38. CFW, "The Ancient City," pt. 2, 179, 180. CFW to ECS, Apr. 13, [1874], CL, 11. CFW to ECS, Sept. 7, [1874], CL, 16. ECS to CFW, Sept. 2, 1889, CL, 569.

39. CFW to ECS, Sept. 28, [1874], CL, 17. CFW to ECS, Sept. 30, [1877], CL, 101.

40. CFW to ECS, Jan. 20, [1875], CL, 28.

41. CFW to ECS, Dec. 12, [1875], CL, 83.

42. Page 114 of CFW's copy of *Victorian Poets*, in Clare Benedict Collection, WRHS.

43. CFW to ECS, July 23, [1876], CL, 72.

44. CFW to ECS, Sept. 28, [1874], CL, 18. CFW to R. R. Bowker, Jan. 19, [1875], CL, 27.

45. CFW to PHH, May Day, 1875, CL, 36. CFW to ECS, July 23, [1876], CL, 73. Excerpts of reviews on the back page of *Two Women: 1862. A Poem*, by CFW

(New York: D. Appleton, 1877). Review of *Two Women: 1862, The Independent* 29 (June 21, 1877), 9.

46. Page 121 of CFW's copy of *Victorian Poets*, in Clare Benedict Collection, WRHS.

47. See Jay Hubbell, "Some New Letters of Constance Fenimore Woolson," *The New England Quarterly* 14 (Dec. 1941): 715–35; quotes from Hayne on 716–17.

48. CFW to PHH, Feb. 13, [1876], CL, 64. CFW to PHH, [Apr. 17, 1876], CL, 66–67.

49. CFW to PHH, Aug. 26, [1875], CL, 50. CFW to ECS, Sept. 28, [1874], CL, 17.

50. CFW to ECS, July 23, [1876], CL, 73.

51. CFW to ECS, Jan. 20, [1875], CL, 30. Patricia A. Cunningham, *Reforming Women's Fashions, 1850–1920: Politics, Health, and Art* (Kent, OH: The Kent State University Press, 2003), 76–78. CFW to ECS, July 23, [1875], CL, 75. CFW to ACW, [1876?], CL, 86.

52. CFW to ACW, [1876?], CL, 86.

CHAPTER 6: *Dark Places*

1. CFW to ECS, [Sept. 6, 1874], CL, 16. CFW, "In the South," *The Daily Cleveland Herald*, Oct. 7, 1874. CFW, "The French Broad," *Harper's* 50 (Apr. 1875): 618–19. HW to unidentified recipient, May 28, [1874], Benedict I, 250.

2. CFW to Elizabeth Gwinn Mather, Dec. 4, [1874], CL, 21. CFW, *Horace Chase* (New York: Harper & Brothers, 1894), 17.

3. CFW to SM, Apr. 25, [1875], CL, 34. CFW, "Up the Ashley and Cooper," *Harper's* 52 (Dec. 1875): 1–24.

4. CFW to PHH, Aug. 26, [1875], CL, 49–50. CFW to PHH, Sept. 12, [1875], CL, 51. CWB to KM, 1921, Benedict III, 223. CFW wrote a long poem she never published that was inspired by the trip: "Gettysburg, 1876," Benedict III, 224–25.

5. CFW to PHH, Sept. 12, [1875], CL, 51–52. CFW to ECS, Oct. 1, [1876], Columbia. CFW to PHH, July 23, [1875], CL, 48.

6. CFW to PHH, Sept. 12, [1875], CL, 52. CFW to PHH, All-Saints Day, [1875], CL, 53.

7. CFW to ECS, Dec. 2, [1875], CL, 82. Dean dates this letter 1876, but internal evidence suggests 1875. CFW to PHH, Jan. 16, [1876], CL, 62.

8. CFW to ACW, undated fragment, CL, 561. It is possible that CFW suffered from manic depression. Her intense work habits and frequent travels may be evidence of manic episodes. Clinical symptoms of depression outlined by the American Psychiatric Association in Michael B. First et al., *DSM-IV-TR Guidebook: The Essential Companion to the Diagnostic and Statistical Manual of Mental Disorders, 4th ed., Text Revision* (Arlington, VA: American Psychiatric Publishing, 2004), 187. Jean Strouse, *Alice James: A Biography* (Boston: Houghton Mifflin, 1980), 184. CFW to ECS, July 23, [1876], 73–74. My understanding of CFW's approach to her depression has been informed by Sarah Berry, who has generously shared with me the draft of an article she is writing on the subject.

9. CFW to ACW, undated fragment, CL, 561. CFW to Mary Gale Carter Clarke, Feb. 25, [1887], CL, 335. CFW to WWB, June 16, [1893], CL, 514.

10. Review of *Rodman the Keeper*, *The Eclectic Magazine of Foreign Literature* 31 (May 1880): 635. HJ, "Miss Woolson," in *Partial Portraits* (1888); reprinted in *The American Essays of Henry James*, ed. Leon Edel (Princeton, NJ: Princeton University Press, 1989), 164.

11. "Recent Fiction," *New York Times*, June 11, 1880. CFW to Barnett Phillips, Aug. 6, [1881?], CL, 177. CFW to ECS, July 23, [1876], CL, 75.

12. CFW to WDH, June 28, [1875], CL 42.

13. CFW to ECS, Oct. 1, [1876], Columbia.

14. CFW, "In the South," *The Daily Cleveland Herald*, Oct. 7, 1874. Although many have assumed the cemetery in "Rodman" was modeled on Andersonville, there is no evidence CFW ever visited there. CFW, "Rodman the Keeper," in *Rodman the Keeper: Southern Sketches* (1880; repr., New York: AMS Press, 1971), 40.

15. Review of *Rodman the Keeper*, *Christian Union* 21 (Apr. 14, 1880), 350. The religious family magazine, edited by Henry Ward Beecher, published the fiction of Mark Twain, Harriet Beecher Stowe, Rose Terry Cooke, Edward Eggleston, and others. CFW to SM, Feb. 24, [1877], CL 91. CFW to ECS, Sept. 16, [1877], 100–101.

16. CFW to PHH, [Apr. 17, 1876], CL, 67.

17. CFW to PHH, Sept. 10, [1876], CL, 76.

18. CFW to ECS, July 23, [1876], CL, 71.

19. CFW to SM, n.d., CL, 548. CFW to PHH, [Nov. 1, 1875], CL, 54.

20. CFW to SM, Jan. 30, [1877?], CL, 88. CFW to SM, Feb. 24, [1877?], CL, 90. HW to SM, Jan. 3, 1874, Mather Family Papers, WRHS. No letters from Charlie have survived.

21. CFW to SM, Feb. 24, [1877?], CL, 90.

22. The common co-occurrence of migraines and manic depression (bipolar disorder) is discussed in Birk Engmann, "Bipolar Affective Disorder and Migraine," *Case Reports in Medicine* (2012), Article ID 389851. http://www.hindawi.com/crim/medicine/2012/389851/. CFW to SM, Jan. 25, [1880], CL, 124.

23. CFW to ECS, May 27, [1877], CL, 92. CFW to ECS, Sept. 16, [1877], CL, 100.

24. CFW to SM, May 20, [1892], CL, 476. CFW to ECS, June 10, [1877], CL, 92.

25. CFW to ECS, Sept. 11, [1877], CL, 96–97. CFW to ECS, Sept. 30, [1877], CL, 101–2.

26. HW to SM, Dec. 23, 1877, Mather Family Papers, WRHS. CFW dated her letters from Hibernia, Clay County, Florida, which she said was an island in the St. Johns River. She must have meant Hibernia Plantation on Fleming Island, just north of Green Cove Springs.

27. CFW to Jane Averell Carter, 1883, CL, 267. "Constance Fenimore Woolson: Her Early Cleveland Days, Her Home There and Her Friends," *New York Herald*, Nov. 10, 1889, p. 11.

28. CFW to PHH, Jan. 16, [1876], CL, 62–63. CFW to ECS, Dec. 12, [1875], CL, 83. Sharon Dean dates the letter 1876, but internal evidence indicates it was written in 1875. CFW Notebooks, Benedict II, 96.

29. CFW, "Contributors' Club," *Atlantic Monthly* 45 (Sept. 1877): 365, 366; 40 (Nov. 1877): 617; 42 (July 1878): 116.

30. HJ, "Mr. and Mrs. Fields," in *The American Essays of Henry James*, 278. In the three

years leading up to *Anne*'s run, novels in *Harper's* were serialized for between six months (HJ's *Washington Square*) and thirteen months (Thomas Hardy's *The Return of the Native*).

31. CFW, *Anne*, 2, 3. CFW to KM, Dec. 27, [1892], CL, 492.
32. CFW, *Anne*, 91, 472, 348, 380.
33. CFW, Notebooks, Benedict II, 103. CFW, *Anne*, 318, 361.
34. According to J. H. A. Bone, "With and Without Glasses," *The (Cleveland) Plain Dealer*, Feb. 11, 1894, p. 8, CFW wrote to him about *Anne*: "The end as I wrote it was very different. I changed it to suit my mother. I am not quite satisfied with it."
35. CFW to ECS, May 5, [1878], CL, 106. CFW to ECS, Jan. 15, [1879], CL, 109.
36. CFW to ECS, Jan. 15, [1879], CL, 109. HW to Mathers, Dec. 1878, Benedict I, 255.
37. Benedict I, 255.
38. CWB to Kate Mather, n.d., Benedict III, 613–14.
39. CFW to PHH, Feb. 16, [1880], CL, 126. CFW to ECS, Mar. 14, [1879], CL, 110.
40. CFW, "Mrs. Edward Pinckney," *Christian Union* 20 (Aug. 6, 1879), 106, 107.
41. CFW to Jane Averell Carter, [1880], CL, 147.

CHAPTER 7: *The Old World at Last*

1. CFW to KM, Dec. 22, 1879, CL, 118.
2. CFW to PHH, All-Saints Day, [1875], CL, 58.
3. "Hearing with One's Teeth," *New York Times*, Nov. 22, 1879. CFW to SM, Dec. 8, [1879], CL, 116.
4. CFW to KM, Dec. 22, 1879, CL, 118–19. CFW to PHH, Feb. 16, [1880], CL, 125.
5. CFW to SM, Dec. 8, [1879], CL, 114. CFW to SM, Mar. 20, [1880], CL, 129. CFW to SM, Apr. 13, [1880], CL, 131.
6. CFW to SM, Jan. 25, [1880], CL, 124. CFW to PHH, Feb. 16, [1880], CL, 126.
7. CFW to SM, Jan. 25, [1880], CL, 123. See also CFW to KM, Feb. 23, 1880, CL, 126–27.
8. CFW to SM, Mar. 20, [1880], CL, 127–28. CFW to PHH, Feb. 16, [1880], CL, 126. CFW to Harriet Benedict Sherman, [1881?], CL, 180.
9. CFW, "'Miss Grief,'" in *Stories by American Authors*, vol. 4 (New York: Charles Scribner's Sons, 1884), 7, 9, 13, 19.
10. Ibid., 21.
11. Ibid., 34.
12. CFW to PHH, July 23, [1875], CL, 49. CFW to PHH, Sept. 12, [1875], CL, 52. CFW to PHH, Jan. 16, [1876], CL, 61. CFW to PHH, Feb. 13, [1876], CL, 63. *Roderick Hudson* ran in the *Atlantic Monthly* Jan.–Dec. 1875 ; *The American* ran June 1876–May 1877; and "Daniel Deronda: A Conversation," appeared in Dec. 1876. WDH, "Recent Literature," *Atlantic Monthly* 35 (Apr. 1875): 490.
13. CFW, "'Miss Grief,'" 6. CFW and HJ would meet in April 1880. As magazine issues appeared in the month preceding their actual date, the May issue of *Lippincott's* would have hit the shelves in April. I discuss these issues more fully

in Anne E. Boyd, "Anticipating James, Anticipating Grief: Constance Fenimore Woolson's 'Miss Grief,'" in *Constance Fenimore Woolson's Nineteenth Century: Essays*, ed. Victoria Brehm (Detroit: Wayne State University Press, 2001), 192–93.

14. Leon Edel, *Henry James, A Life* (New York: Harper & Row, 1985), 177. JH, "Contributors' Club," *Atlantic Monthly* 43 (March 1879): 399–400.

15. CFW to SM, Dec. 8, [1879], CL, 117. CFW uses the first person plural, indicating she and Clara, and perhaps Clare, called on him together.

16. CFW to PHH, July 23, [1875], CL, 47.

17. CFW, "'Miss Grief,'" 37.

18. Review of *Two Women: 1862, Appletons' Journal* 2 (June 1877), 570–71. A clipping of the review is pasted into CFW's copy of *Two Women* at Rollins, with the name "E. L. Burlingame" in CFW's hand. CFW to R. R. Bowker, June 19, [1875?], CL, 27.

19. CFW to ECS, May 5, [1878], CL, 105. CFW, "'Miss Grief,'" 23.

20. CFW to HJ, Feb. 12, [1882], CL, 185–86. Richard Grant White, "Recent Fiction," *North American Review* 128 (Jan. 1879): 104. We can't know whether Woolson read this review, but she was an avid reader of criticism. CFW, "'Miss Grief,'" 23.

21. CFW, "Contributors' Club," *Atlantic Monthly* 43 (Jan. 1879): 106, 107.

22. CFW, "Contributors' Club," *Atlantic Monthly* 43 (Feb. 1879): 259. HJ, "The Art of Fiction," in *Partial Portraits* (1888; London: Macmillan, 1894), 394.

23. CFW to SM, Mar. 20, [1880], CL, 130. CFW, "At Mentone," *Mentone, Cairo, and Corfu* (New York: Harper & Brothers, 1896), 79. CFW to Samuel L. Mather, May 12, 1880, CL, 137. CFW to Mary Crowell, [Spring 1880], CL, 134.

24. CFW to SM, Mar. 20, [1880], CL, 128.

25. CFW to Mary Crowell, [Spring 1880], CL, 134.

26. CWB indicates they met HJ at the Casa Molini. See Benedict III, 588.

27. HJ to WDH, Apr. 18, [1880], HJL2, 285. As Lyndall Gordon has written, CFW's "restlessness fitted his evolving idea of Isabel Archer, who travelled like a thirsty person draining cup after cup. Independent, new to Europe, full of impressions, Miss Woolson provided a complementary model for his Americana." *A Private Life of Henry James: Two Women and His Art* (New York: W. W. Norton, 1998), 162.

28. HJ to Catharine Walsh, May 3, [1880], Houghton, MS Am 1094.1330. HJ to Alice James, Apr. 25, [1880], HJL2, 288.

29. CFW to unidentified recipient, CL, 136. HJ, "Italy Revisited. 1877," in *Portraits of Places* (Boston: Osgood, 1884), 57. CFW to SM, June 8, [1880], CL, 139.

30. CFW to Mary Crowell, [Spring 1880], CL, 135, 134.

31. Leon Edel compared HJ's ease with CFW to that he felt with his mother or sister. See Leon Edel, *Henry James, 1870–1881: The Conquest of London* (Philadelphia: J. B. Lippincott, 1962), 415. I rely on Edel periodically, as HJ's foremost biographer, to flesh out HJ's personality and whereabouts, although his portrait of CFW and her relationship to HJ is deeply flawed. HJ to William James, June 28, [1877], HJL2, 119. Edmund Gosse, in *Aspects and Impressions* (London: Cassell, 1922), 27, describes HJ as "grave, extremely courteous, but a little formal and frightened." CFW to SM, June 8, [1880], CL, 139. CFW to Mary Crowell, [Spring 1880], CL, 134.

32. CFW to unidentified recipient, CL, 136. Stammering mentioned by CRB in an interview with "D.H.L.," Sept. 7, 1952, McGill.
33. CFW, "A Florentine Experiment," *Atlantic Monthly* 46 (Oct. 1880): 509.
34. Ibid. 523, 524.
35. CFW to Henry Mills Alden, Feb. 5, [1881], CL, 161, 160.
36. CFW to Samuel L. Mather, [Aug. 28, 1880], CL, 147. CFW to Henry Mills Alden, Feb. 5, [1881], CL, 161. CFW to Henry Mills Alden, Aug. 23, [1881?], CL, 179.
37. CFW to Henry Mills Alden, Feb. 5, [1881], CL, 160–61.
38. CFW to SM, Dec. 19, [1880], CL, 156.

CHAPTER 8: *The Artist's Life*

1. CFW to KM, June 21, 1880, CL, 143–44.
2. CFW to SM, July 6, [1880], CL, 145. CFW to SM, Aug. 28, [1880], CL, 146.
3. Review of *Rodman the Keeper: Southern Sketches, Spectator* 53 (June 19, 1880), 24. CFW to SM, July 6, [1880], CL, 145–46.
4. "Editors' Table," *Appletons' Journal* 9 (July 1880): 95–96. "Southern Sketches," *The Literary World* 3 (July 1880): 223. Review of *Rodman the Keeper, Harper's* 61 (June 1880): 152.
5. Thomas Sergeant Perry, "Some Recent Novels," *Atlantic Monthly* 46 (July 1880), 125.
6. CFW to SM, Dec. 19, [1880], CL, 156. CFW to SM, Oct. [1880], CL, 150.
7. CFW to KM, Jan. 16, 1881, CL, 159. CFW to Henry Mills Alden, Apr. 8, [1881], CL, 162–63. CFW to Henry Mills Alden, Feb. 5, [1881], CL, 160.
8. CFW to Henry Mills Alden, Apr. 8, [1881], CL, 162.
9. CFW to KM, Easter Even, 1881, CL, 165. CFW's copy of Karl Baedeker's *Italie Centrale* (in French) (1881) is at Rollins. CFW, "The Roman May, and a Walk," *The Christian Union*, reprinted in Benedict II, 251.
10. Percy Bysshe Shelley, *Adonais: An Elegy on the Death of John Keats* (1821). CFW to J. H. A. Bone, Mar. 18, 1881, in "With and Without Glasses," *The (Cleveland) Plain Dealer*, Feb. 11, 1894, p. 8.
11. CFW to ECS, [Aug. 11, 1881], CL 172–73. CFW to KM, Easter Even, 1881, CL, 165. CFW to HJ, May 7, [1883], CL, 252. CFW to HJ, Feb. 12, [1882], CL, 187–88.
12. CFW, "The Roman May, and a Walk," 249–50. HJ, *The Portrait of a Lady*, 629.
13. CFW to ECS, [Aug. 11, 1881], CL, 172. CFW to ECS, Aug. 4, [1882], CL, 204.
14. CFW, "The Street of the Hyacinth," in *The Front Yard and Other Italian Stories* (New York: Harper & Brothers, 1895), 141.
15. Ibid., 157.
16. Ibid., 183, 193.
17. CFW to ECS, Aug. 4, [1882], CL, 205.
18. CFW to HJ, Aug. 30, [1882], CL, 211–12. CFW to HJ, Feb. 23, [1882], CL, 191. HJ to Grace Norton, Nov. 7, [1880], HJL2, 314.
19. CFW, "At the Château of Corinne," in *Dorothy and Other Italian Stories* (New York: Harper & Brothers, 1896), 262.

20. Madame de Staël, *Corrine, or Italy*, trans. Avriel H. Goldberger (New Brunswick, NJ: Rutgers University Press, 1986), 90, 301.

21. CFW, "At the Château of Corinne," 267, 268, 240.

22. HJ, "Felix Holt, The Radical," *The Nation* 3 (Aug. 16, 1866): 128. HJ, "George Sand," *The Galaxy* 24 (July 1877): 59. "His views of American women writers had a tone ranging from condescension to outrage," writes Alfred Habegger in *Henry James and the "Woman Business"* (Cambridge: Cambridge University Press, 1989), 9.

23. CFW to HJ, Feb. 12, [1882], CL, 188.

24. "Literary Notes," *The Critic* 1 (Jan. 29, 1881): 7.

25. Harper & Brothers to CFW, Feb. 22, 1882, in J. Henry Harper, *The House of Harper* (New York: Harper & Brothers, 1912), 484–85. Contract in "Archives of Harper and Brothers, 1817–1914," microfilm (Cambridge: Chadwyck-Healey, 1980), Butler Library, Columbia University, reel 2, vol. 4, p. 301.

26. CFW to HJ, Aug. 30, [1882], CL, 211. HJ had a similarly dispiriting effect on other writers as well. Robert Louis Stevenson wrote to him of the "despair" he felt after reading his work. He felt "a lout and slouch of the first water" compared to HJ. Quoted in Edel, *The Middle Years, 1882–1895* (Philadelphia: J. B. Lippincott, 1962), 125.

27. *Atlantic*'s circulation in Ellery Sedgwick, *A History of the Atlantic Monthly, 1857–1909: Yankee Humanism at High Tide and Ebb* (Amherst: University of Massachusetts Press, 1994), 127. *Harper*'s circulation in Frank Luther Mott, *A History of American Magazines*, vol. 3 (Cambridge, MA: The Belknap Press of Harvard University Press, 1938), 6. Sales figures for *Portrait* in Michael Gorra, *The Portrait of a Novel: Henry James and the Making of an American Masterpiece* (New York: Liveright, 2012), 239. Sales figures for *Anne* in Rayburn Moore, *Constance Fenimore Woolson* (New York: Twayne, 1963), 159.

28. *Literary World* and *Critic* quoted in Kevin J. Hayes, ed., *Henry James: The Contemporary Reviews* (Cambridge: Cambridge University Press, 1996), 132, 126. CFW to HJ, Feb. 12, [1882], CL, 186–88.

29. CFW to HJ, Feb. 12, [1882], CL, 190.

30. "Miss Woolson's 'Anne,'" *The Century* 24 (Aug. 1882): 636.

31. "Recent American Fiction," *Atlantic Monthly* 50 (July 1882): 111–12. Review of *Anne*, *Californian* 6 (Sept. 1882): 287. Others quoted in a Harper & Brothers advertisement that ran nationally and was reprinted in the back of *For the Major* (Harper & Brothers, 1883).

32. *New York Tribune* quoted in Harper & Brothers advertisement. "The Native Element in American Fiction," *The Century* 26 (July 1883): 364.

33. Quoted in Harper, *The House of Harper*, 484.

34. CFW to HJ, May 24, [1883], CL, 256.

35. CFW to Thomas Bailey Aldrich, June 30, [1882], CL, 203.

36. ECS to CFW, Nov. 12, 1882, CL, 567.

37. ECS to CFW, Nov. 12, [1882], CL, 567–68.

38. CFW to HJ, May 24, [1883], CL, 255–56.

39. CFW to HJ, Aug. 30, [1882], CL, 207.

40. CFW to HJ, Aug. 30, [1882], CL, 206–7. HJ, *The Complete Notebooks of Henry James*, eds. Leon Edel and Lyall H. Powers (New York: Oxford University Press, 1987), 220.

41. Benedict III, 495. CFW to HJ, Aug. 30, [1882], CL, 207.
42. CFW to Hamilton Wright Mabie, June 18, [1883], CL, 258. CFW to ECS, Apr. 30, [1883], CL, 240.
43. "Recent Fiction," *Overland Monthly* 11 (Aug. 1883): 212. The *Boston Globe* quoted in a Harper & Brothers advertisement that ran nationally and in the back of most of her subsequent books. "New Publications," *New York Times*, June 16, 1883, p. 3. Review of *For the Major*, *The Independent* 35 (Aug. 2, 1883): 11. Sales figures in Moore, *Constance Fenimore Woolson*, 159.
44. CFW, *For the Major*, 159, 162.
45. Ibid., 188.
46. CFW, "At the Château of Corinne," 270.
47. HJ, *The Portrait of a Lady* (1881; rev. ed. 1908; New York: W. W. Norton, 1995), 357.
48. CFW to HJ, Feb. 12, [1882], CL, 185. Inscribed copy of *The Portrait of a Lady* at the University of Basel.

CHAPTER 9: *The Expatriate's Life*

1. CFW to HJ, Aug. 30, [1882], CL, 208.
2. CFW to ECS and Flora Mather, Sept. 18, [1882], CL, 215.
3. CFW to KM, Dec. 10, [1882], CL, 154. Sharon Dean dates this letter as 1880, but internal evidence suggests 1882.
4. JH, "Clarence King," *Address of John Hay* (New York: The Century, 1906), 348. HJ quoted in Robert Wilson, *The Explorer King: Adventure, Science, and the Great Diamond Hoax—Clarence King in the Old West* (Shoemaker and Hoard, 2007), 15.
5. King quoted in Martha A. Sandweiss, *Passing Strange: A Gilded Age Tale of Love and Deception Across the Color Line* (New York: Penguin, 2009), 124. Sandweiss extensively documents King's secret marriage.
6. CFW to SM, Dec. 10, [1893], CL, 534. JH quoted in Patricia O'Toole, *The Five of Hearts: An Intimate Portrait of Henry Adams and His Friends, 1880–1918* (New York: Simon & Schuster, 1990), 114.
7. CFW to SM, Jan. 31, [1883], CL, 222.
8. CFW to KM, [Dec. 10, 1882], CL, 154, 155.
9. CFW to Clara Stone Hay, Jan. 8, [1883], CL, 220. CFW to HJ, May 7, [1883], CL, 249.
10. CFW to SM, Jan. 31, [1883], CL, 222.
11. HJ quoted in Leon Edel, *Henry James: The Middle Years, 1882–1895* (Philadelphia: J. B. Lippincott, 1962), 115. CFW to HJ, May 7, [1883], CL, 249.
12. CFW to SM, Jan. 31, [1883], CL, 223, 224.
13. CFW to Elizabeth Gwinn Mather, Apr. 25, 1883, CL, 236. CFW to SM, Jan. 31, [1883], CL, 222.
14. CFW to SM, Jan. 31, [1883], CL, 223. CFW to SM, July 18, [1881], CL, 169.
15. CFW to HJ, May 7, [1883], CL, 246.
16. Ibid., 252.
17. Ibid., 252, 247.
18. Ibid., CL, 251. CFW to HJ, May 24, [1883], CL, 256–57. Without HJ's half

of the correspondence, his biographers have tended to assume that her deep affection for him was one-sided. However, CFW was much too sensitive to pursue a friendship that was unreciprocated. That he was capable of tremendous affection is evidenced by his letters to Grace Norton; see Leon Edel's multivolume collection of letters as well as the letters in *Dear Munificent Friends: Henry James's Letters to Four Women*, ed. Susan E. Gunter (Ann Arbor: University of Michigan Press, 1999). As Gunter explains in her introduction, "his letters to these women were warmly human" rather than "withdrawn," as HJ has often been portrayed (11).

19. CFW to Winifred Howells, May 11, 1883, CL, 253.
20. Rebecca L. Tabber, *Letters of a Family: Clarke Family Relations 1822 to 1889* (master's thesis, SUNY-Oneonta, 1997), 26–28, copy at Research Library, New York State Historical Association, Cooperstown, NY. CFW to Mary Gayle Carter, Sept. 5, [1883], CL, 265.
21. "Register of Deaths, September 1877 to January 1888," book 1, Health Department, City of Los Angeles, Los Angeles County Records Office. The record was found by Sandra Woolson. I am grateful to Gary Woolson for providing me with the information.
22. CFW to SM, July 6, [1880], CL, 145. See deed dated May 26, 1882, and "Daily Real Estate Record" in Mather Family Papers, WRHS. CFW to SM, Jan. 10, [1883], CL, 224.
23. CFW to SM, Jan. 16, [1884], CL, 269.
24. Ibid.
25. CFW to SM, Jan. 16, [1884], CL, 269, 270. CFW to Jane Averell Carter, [1883?], CL, 268.
26. CFW to Jane Averell Carter, [1883?], CL, 268. HJ to Grace Norton, Jan. 19, [1884], HJL3, 20. CFW to SM, Jan. 16, [1884], CL, 270.
27. HJ to Lizzie Boott, Oct. 14, 1883, HJL3, 10. HJ to WDH, Feb. 21, 1884, HJL3, 28. CFW to SM, Jan. 16, [1884], CL, 270. French Ensor Chadwick to JH, Jan. 20, 1884, Brown.
28. CFW to SM, Jan. 16, [1884], CL, 270.
29. CFW to JH, Jan. 27, [1884], CL, 274. Leon Edel, "Search for an Anchorage," HJL3, 3.
30. HJ to Grace Norton, July 28, [1883], HJL2, 424.
31. CFW to SM, Jan. 20, [1884], CL, 272. JH to SM, May 10, 1884, Mather Family Papers, WRHS. CFW to JH, Jan. 27, [1884], CL, 275.
32. HJ to WDH, Feb. 21, 1884, HJL3, 29. HJ to Mrs. Humphry Ward, Dec. 9, [1884], HJL3, 59.
33. CFW to JH, [June 1884?], CL, 279. CFW to JH, [May 1884?], CL, 280. CFW to Mrs. Howells, July 15, [1884], CL, 283.
34. CFW to Harriet Benedict Sherman, Mar. 29, 1884, CL, 277.
35. CFW to Mrs. Howells, July 15, [1884], CL, 283. HJ to Elizabeth Boott, [June 2], 1884, HJL3, 44.
36. HJ to Francis Parkman, Aug. 24, [1884], HJL3, 48. CFW to SM, Sept. 14, [1884], CL, 286.
37. CFW to KM, [Oct. 21, 1884], CL, 288.

38. Ibid., 289.

39. Account in CFW's handwriting in the margins of her copy of Ralph Waldo Emerson's *English Traits* (Boston: Houghton, 1886), 262, Rollins.

40. "Miss Woolson's Stories," *Harper's Bazar* 19 (Nov. 20, 1896): 758. "Archives of Harper and Brothers, 1817–1914," microfilm (Cambridge: Chadwyck-Healey, 1980), Butler Library, Columbia University, Aug. 1883 and Apr. 1885, reel 33, F1. CFW to JH, Apr. 29, [1885], CL, 297. Unfortunately, the agreement for the serial rights of *East Angels* has not survived. For her next novel, *Jupiter Lights*, she received $3,500, presumably the new price. See agreement in "Archives of Harper and Brothers, 1817–1914," Oct. 15, 1889, reel 2, vol. 5.

41. Michael Gorra, *Portrait of a Novel: Henry James and the Making of an American Masterpiece* (New York: Liveright, 2012), 244. Georgia Krieger, "*East Angels*: Constance Fenimore Woolson's Revision of Henry James's *The Portrait of a Lady*," *Legacy* 22 (2005): 18–29. Geraldine Murphy, "Northeast Angels: Henry James in Woolson's Florida," in *Witness to Reconstruction: Constance Fenimore Woolson and the Postbellum South, 1873–1894*, ed. Kathleen Diffley (Jackson: University Press of Mississippi, 2011), 232–48.

42. HJ, "Miss Woolson," in *Partial Portraits* (1888); reprinted in *The American Essays of Henry James*, ed. Leon Edel (Princeton, NJ: Princeton University Press, 1989), 170. Gorra discusses James's exploration of "the drama of the interior life" in *Portrait of a Novel*, xvi. Frances Hodgson Burnett, *Through One Administration* (Boston: J. Loring, 1883), 55, 64.

43. CFW to HJ, Feb. 12, [1882], CL, 190. CFW, *East Angels*, 346.

44. CFW, *East Angels*, 498, 549, 551.

45. CFW to JH, Dec. 26, [1885], CL, 305. CFW to SM, Mar. 14, [1893], CL, 506. She describes here her process for writing each of her novels. CFW to KM, July 2, 1893, CL, 517.

46. CFW, "Mottoes, Maxims, Reflections," Rollins. "On the Writing of Novels," *The Critic* 221 (Mar. 24, 1888): 139.

47. CFW, *East Angels*, 551. CFW to Elinor Howells, [Summer 1883?], CL, 296. Although Sharon Dean dates this letter [1884?], it appears to belong with those she wrote during the summer after they had been together in Italy. CFW to JH, Jan. 27, [1884], CL, 275. CFW to JH, [June 1884?], CL, 280.

48. CFW to JH, Dec. 26, [1885], CL, 304.

49. CFW to Emily Vernon Clark, n.d., CL, 550–51.

50. CFW to Mary Gale Carter, Oct. 14, [1885], CL, 299.

51. CFW to Samuel L. Mather, [Feb. 23, 1886], CL, 307. CFW to Katharine Loring, Oct. 9, [1886?], CL, 316. J. Burney Yeo, *Climate and Health Resorts* (London: Chapman and Hall, 1885), 635.

52. Copy of *The Bostonians* inscribed "Constance Fenimore Woolson from Henry James. London Feb. 20th 1886," University of Basel.

53. Alice and William James quoted in Jean Strouse, *Alice James: A Biography* (Boston: Houghton Mifflin, 1980), 238.

54. Strouse, *Alice James*, 259. Alice James quoted in Strouse, *Alice James*, 185, 259. CFW, undated fragments, BHS. The references to "your brother," who is suffering from jaundice in Venice, indicates that the letter was written to Alice James in April 1887.

55. HJ quoted in Natalie Dykstra, *Clover Adams: A Gilded and Heartbreaking Life* (Boston: Houghton Mifflin, 2012), xiii. CFW to JH, Dec. 26, [1885], CL, 302. HJ to Lizzie Boott, Jan. 7, [1886], HJL3, 107.

56. CFW to Samuel L. Mather, [Feb. 23, 1886], CL, 307.

CHAPTER 10: *Home Found*

1. CFW to KM, Apr. 30, 1886, CL, 311, 312.

2. Ibid., 312.

3. CFW to JH, July 30, [1886], CL, 314. HJ to J. R. Osgood, Apr. 18, [1885], HJL3, 77.

4. CFW to JH, July 30, [1886], CL, 314. Linda Simon, "Diagnosing the Physician: Patients' Evaluation of Nineteenth Century Medical Therapeutics," in *Revue Angliciste de l'Université de la Réunion, Alizes/Trade Winds* (Automne 2003); http://laboratoires.univ-reunion.fr/oracle/documents/352.html.

5. CFW to KM, Apr. 30, 1886, CL, 312.

6. HJ to FB, May 25, [1886], HJL3, 119–20.

7. CFW always referred to "Miss Greenough" without reference to her first name. I have been able to identify her as Louisa from Nathalia Wright's "Henry James and the Greenough Data," *American Quarterly* 10, no. 3 (1958): 338–43. Her brother Henry had married Francis Boott's sister, and Lizzie grew up with many Greenough cousins. See Carol M. Osborne, "Lizzie Boott at Bellosguardo," in *The Italian Presence in American Art, 1860–1920*, ed. Irma B. Jaffe (Bronx, NY: Fordham University Press, 1992), 189. CFW to SM, Nov. 14, [1886], CL, 321. CFW to FB, Feb. 7, [1890], Duveneck Family. CFW to JH, July 30, [1886], CL, 313.

8. CFW to Katharine Loring, Oct. 9, [1886?], CL, 316.

9. CFW to ECS, Feb. 24, [1887], CL, 332. I use CFW's name for the villa, Brichieri, although it was also known as the Villa Brichieri-Colombi.

10. CFW to SM, Mar. 18, [1886], CL, 308. CFW to SM, Nov. 14, [1886], CL, 321–22.

11. CFW to SM, Nov. 14, [1886], CL, 322.

12. HJ called her "Fenimore" only in letters to Francis and Lizzie Boott. It is possible the name was a kind of joke between them because of Louisa Greenough's fascination with her illustrious ancestry. HJ to Lizzie Boott, Oct. 18, [1886], HJL3, 136, 135. HJ to FB, Nov. 26, [1886], HJL3, 138.

13. HJ to FB, Nov. 4, [1886], Houghton. MS Am 1094. HJ to FB, Aug. 15, [1886], HJL3, 130. HJ to FB, Nov. 26, [1886], HJL3, 138.

14. CFW to FB, Jan. 9, [1891], and CFW to FB, Sept. 17, [1890], Duveneck Family.

15. HJ to Alice Howe Gibbens James, Apr. 24, 1887, Houghton, Ms Am 1237.16. CFW's letters to FB, Duveneck Family.

16. The poem reads:
   French <u>constancy</u>; a <u>marsh</u>; & "I" beyond
   Nor "I" alone. Still "<u>more</u>," yet not the whole
   Only in part a name, which, to complete
   Some think can only be a <u>cooper</u>'s rôle.

No, rather the embroiderer's. So let
A skillful hand produce the tambour-frame,
Set the <u>wools on</u>, & end with them the name,
A name they'll ne'er dishonor. Far from that!
They'll add to it, increase its world-wide fame.

FB, "Constance Fenimore Woolson," taped into a copy of Benedict II in the Clare Benedict Collection, WRHS. Another version of the poem appears in Benedict II, 301.

17. Josephine W. Duveneck, *Frank Duveneck: Painter-Teacher* (San Francisco: John Howell-Books, 1970), ch. 9.

18. Duveneck, *Frank Duveneck,* ch. 10; quote from William James, 112.

19. Osborne, "Lizzie Boott at Bellosguardo," 191–95.

20. Duveneck, *Frank Duveneck,* ch. 10; quote from Lizzie Boott, 115. Osborne, "Lizzie Boott at Bellosguardo," 195.

21. CRB to Leon Edel, July 23, [1953], McGill. CFW to FB, Mar. 4, [1889], Duveneck Family. HJ quoted in Mahonri Sharp Young, "The Two Worlds of Frank Duveneck," *American Art Journal* 1 (Spring 1969), 94. CFW to SM, Nov. 14, [1886], CL, 324.

22. Young, "The Two Worlds," 99. HJ to Henrietta Reubell, Mar. 11, [1886], HJL3, 117.

23. CFW to FB, Sept. 15, [1888], Duveneck Family. CFW to Flora Stone Mather, n.d., CL, 555.

24. HJ to FB, Nov. 26, [1886], HJL3, 138. Copy of *The Princess Casamassima* at University of Basel.

25. HJ to Mr. and Mrs. William James, Dec. 23, [1886], HJL3, 151. CFW to Mary Gayle Carter Clarke, Feb. 25, [1887], CL, 335. HJ to JH, Dec. 24, [1886], Brown. The letter is also printed in HJL3, where Edel has transcribed the phrase as "a prospect on our part" (153).

26. Rayburn Moore, *Constance Fenimore Woolson* (New York: Twayne, 1963), 159.

27. WDH, "Editor's Study," *Harper's* 73 (Aug. 1886): 477–78.

28. CFW to JH, July 30, [1886], CL, 313.

29. Susan Goodman and Carl Dawson, *William Dean Howells: A Writer's Life* (Berkeley: University of California Press, 2005), 272. CFW to JH, Feb. 23, [1887], CL, 330.

30. "Our Monthly Gossip," *Lippincott's* 38 (Nov. 1886): 548–50. "Mr. Howells on 'East Angels,'" *Christian Union* 34 (July 29, 1886): 7. "Our Monthly Gossip," *Lippincott's* 39 (Jan. 1887): 179. WDH, "Editor's Study," *Harper's* 79 (June 1889): 153.

31. "A Romance of Florida," *New York Times,* June 6, 1886, p. 5. "East Angels," *The Literary World* 24 (July 1886): 243. "Recent Fiction," *The Independent* 38 (Aug. 26, 1886): 10. "East Angels," *The Critic* 6 (Sep. 4, 1886), 111. "Divorce," *Church Review* 48 (Oct. 1886), 393. "Recent Novels," *The Nation* 11 (Nov. 1886): 396. Horace Scudder, "Recent Novels by Women," *Atlantic Monthly* 59 (Feb. 1887): 268.

32. CFW to SM, Mar. 31, [1887], CL, 339. CFW to ECS, Feb. 24, [1887], CL, 331, 332.

33. CFW to Mary Gayle Carter Clarke, Feb. 25, [1887], CL, 334. Elizabeth Barrett Browning, *Aurora Leigh and Other Poems* (New York: James Miller, 1866), Sev-

enth Book, 255–56. Barrett Browning visited the villa only once but was so taken with the view that she had her heroine Aurora live there.

34. CFW to SM, Mar. 24, [1887], CL, 338.
35. CFW to SM, Mar. 31, [1887], CL, 340. CFW to Harriet Benedict Sherman, [1887], CL, 350.
36. CFW to Mary Gayle Carter Clarke, Feb. 25, [1887], CL, 334.
37. CFW to SM, June 7, [1887], CL, 343. CFW to SM, Jan. 12, [1888], CL, 352.

CHAPTER 11: *Confrère*

1. CFW to JH, Apr. 24, [1883], CL, 223. CFW to HJ, May 7, [1883], CL, 248. The sentence in each is nearly identical.
2. CFW to JH, Apr. 24, [1883], CL, 233.
3. CFW to JH, Dec. 26, [1885], CL, 302–3.
4. CFW to SM, Mar. 18, [1886], CL, 309. CFW to SM, June 7, [1887], CL, 345. The bust now resides at Rollins, where it sits on the mantel in the English faculty lounge and, sadly, has grown discolored with dirt.
5. "Miss Woolson. Something About the Famous Novelist and Former Clevelander," *The Cleveland Plain Dealer*, Feb. 13, 1887, p. 5.
6. The essay was titled "Miss Constance Fenimore Woolson" when it was first published in *Harper's Weekly* but was shortened to "Miss Woolson" when it appeared in *Partial Portraits*. For the sake of consistency, I will use the shorter title, by which it is usually referred.
7. HJ, "William Dean Howells," *Harper's Weekly* 30 (June 19, 1886): 394–95. HJ, "Edwin A. Abbey," *Harper's Weekly* 30 (Dec. 4, 1886): 786–87.
8. HJ, *The Complete Notebooks of Henry James*, eds. Leon Edel and Lyall H. Powers (New York: Oxford University Press, 1987), 40.
9. HJ, "Miss Constance Fenimore Woolson," *Harper's Weekly* 31 (Feb. 12, 1887): 114, 115.
10. Rob Davidson, *The Master and the Dean: The Literary Criticism of Henry James and William Dean Howells* (Columbia: University of Missouri Press, 2005), 145.
11. HJ, "The Death of the Lion" (1893), in *Selected Tales*, ed. John Lyon (New York: Penguin, 2001), 265. HJ, "Miss Constance Fenimore Woolson," 114.
12. Davidson, *The Master and the Dean*, 147. HJ, "Miss Constance Fenimore Woolson," 114.
13. HJ to FB, Mar. 15, [1887], HJL3, 176. He does not mention the nature of CFW's presumed offense, but in the fragment cited below she wrote to Alice about him needing to stay in bed and apparently resisting the advice. Alice James to Alice Howe Gibbens James, Apr. 3, [1887], in *The Death & Letters of Alice James, Selected Correspondence*, ed. Ruth Bernard Yeazell (Boston: Exact Change, 1997), 130. HJ to Alice Howe Gibbens James, Apr. 24, 1887, Houghton, Ms Am 1237.16. An undated fragment of a letter from CFW to Alice James mentions HJ's jaundice and provides a report from Mrs. Wagniere, just returned from Venice to Florence, on his health. The fragment is in BHS.
14. HJ paid no rent this time. See HJ to Alice Howe Gibbens James, Apr. 24, 1887,

Houghton, Ms Am 1237.16. HJ to Emma (Wilkinson) Pertz, [Apr.–May 1887], HJL3, 179. HJ had heard a story in Florence after his previous stay on Bellosguardo that gave him the idea for "The Aspern Papers." He borrowed the name "Tita" for one of the characters from CFW's *Anne*. See Lyndall Gordon, *A Private Life of Henry James: Two Women and His Art* (New York: W. W. Norton, 1998), 212. Gordon also explains that "[i]t has been assumed that the narrator speaks for James when he resists a proposal" from the younger of the two women, "but this has served to prop a biographic premise for which there is no evidence, that Fenimore hunted a husband" (218–19).

15. HJ to Alice Howe Gibbens James, Apr. 24, 1887, Houghton, Ms Am 1237.16. CFW to SM, Apr. 23, [1887], CL, 341. HJ to Edmund Gosse, Apr. 24, [1887], in *Selected Letters of Henry James to Edmund Gosse, 1882–1915: A Literary Friendship*, ed. Rayburn S. Moore (Baton Rouge: Louisiana State University Press, 1988), 46. HJ to Katherine Bronson, quoted in Leon Edel, *Henry James: The Middle Years, 1882–1895* (Philadelphia: J. B. Lippincott, 1962), 216.

16. HJ to William James, May 3, [1887], HJL3, 182–83.

17. CFW to SM, May 15, [1887], CL, 342. CFW to SM, June 7, [1887], CL, 344.

18. "Pen Picture of Mrs. Burnett," *The Richfield Springs (N.Y.) Mercury*, Mar. 27, 1890.

19. CRB to Leon Edel, Nov. 27, 1947, McGill. The lack of evidence has led James's biographers to treat the fact of his living under the same roof with CFW in various ways. Edel, in *Henry James: The Middle Years*, downplayed its significance for James, stressing that his contentment and productivity had to do with his surroundings: "He had discovered, for a time, an Italian paradise" (214). The two probably took "certain of their meals together" but "lived very much as they would have lived had they been housed apart" (217). He speculated that "this pleasant and *méticuleuse* old maid may have nourished fantasies of a closer tie," although HJ was oblivious to her desires (217). Fred Kaplan, in *Henry James: The Imagination of Genius, A Biography* (New York: William Morrow, 1992), saw the arrangement in a different light: "Undoubtedly, he saw Fenimore every day. It was as much of a love affair with a woman as he was ever to have, a daily intimacy that protected daily privacy, that made no physical demands beyond courtesy, no emotional demands beyond friendship" (318). HJ to Grace Norton, Oct. 17, 1882, quoted in Tara Knapp, "Epistolary Fluidity: Privacy and the 'False Code' of Letter Showing," in *Tracing Henry James*, eds. Melanie H. Ross and Greg W. Zacharias (Newcastle upon Tyne, UK: Cambridge Scholars, 2008), 447, 448.

20. CRB to Leon Edel, Nov. 27, 1947, McGill. CWB also discussed her agreement with CFW in a letter to May Harris, Benedict II, 387. CWB to KM, n.d., Benedict III, 607. CFW to HJ, Aug. 30, [1882], CL, 211.

21. CRB to Leon Edel, July 23, [1953], McGill.

22. On the subject of their love for each other, see Kaplan in *Henry James: The Imagination of Genius*, where he writes that CFW was "a woman [HJ] could love without loving her as a woman" (313); and Paul Fisher in *House of Wits: An Intimate Portrait of the James Family* (New York: Macmillan, 2009), who describes HJ's "love" for CFW as another instance of the "love that dare not speak its name,"

comparing it to his unauthorized love for Paul Zhukovsky (521). CFW called HJ "Harry" in a letter to SM, Jan. 2, [1888], CL, 355. She also always called him "Harry" in her letters to Francis Boott; the first that survives is dated Aug. 7, 1888, Duveneck Family.

23. Theodora Bosanquet, *Henry James at Work* (1924), ed. Lyall H. Powers (Ann Arbor: University of Michigan Press, 2006), 48. Wharton quoted in Hermione Lee, *Edith Wharton* (New York: Alfred A. Knopf, 2007), 213.

24. *Poems from Shelley*, ed. Stopford A. Brooke (London: Macmillan, 1880), Non-Catholic Cemetery in Rome, Clare Benedict Library. In the published letters, I was able to find only one contemporary instance of HJ using the word *confrère*, in reference to himself, in a letter to Alphonse Daudet in 1884, HJL3, 46. HJ appears to have used it more liberally later in life. In CRB's letters to Leon Edel at McGill, she always refers to HJ as "Cousin Henry."

25. HJ, "Miss Woolson," *Partial Portraits* (1888), reprinted in *The American Essays of Henry James*, ed. Leon Edel (Princeton, NJ: Princeton University Press, 1989), 162–63. Gordon, in *A Private Life*, also thinks CFW could have requested that HJ cut out the biographical material (213).

26. HJ, "Miss Woolson," 171.

27. CFW, Notebooks, Benedict II, 102–3. In 1887, she was reading Augustine Birrell and James Russell Lowell, who is also mentioned nearby. The story idea about Mrs. B. appears to have been written afterward. See CFW, Notebooks, Benedict II, 107–8.

28. Gordon, in *A Private Life*, 286, describes how in "The Beast in the Jungle" HJ used CFW's story idea, outlined in her notebooks, about a man to whom nothing ever happens.

CHAPTER 12: *Arcadia Lost*

1. CFW to ECS, Feb. 24, [1887], CL, 333. CFW to Linda Guilford, Mar. 1, 1887, CL, 336. CFW to SM, Jan. 22, [1888], CL, 354.

2. CFW's copy of Augustine Birrell's *Obiter Dicta*, 2nd ser., at Rollins; marginalia on p. 229. CFW's copy of *Poems from Shelley* at Non-Catholic Cemetery, Rome. CFW's copy of Margaret Woods's *A Village Tragedy* at Claremont Historical Society, Claremont, NH. CFW to SM, Jan. 22, [1888], CL, 355. CFW to JH, Aug. 6, [1887], CL, 347. CFW to JH, Dec. 20, [1890], CL, 434.

3. HJ to Alice H. James, Apr. 24, 1887, Houghton, Ms Am 1237.16.

4. Elizabeth Boott Duveneck to FB, July 7, [1887], Frank Duveneck and Elizabeth Boott Duveneck Papers, 1851–1972, Smithsonian Institution, Archives of American Art, Washington, DC. CFW to FB, Sept. 11, [1890], Duveneck Family.

5. CFW to JH, Aug. 6, [1887], CL, 348. "Pen Picture of Mrs. Burnett," *The Richfield Springs (NY) Mercury*, Mar. 27, 1890. CFW to SM, Jan. 22, [1888], CL, 355.

6. HJ to Elizabeth Boott, Jan. 29, [1888], Houghton, MS Am 1094.580. The letter is incorrectly marked as [1887?].

7. Josephine W. Duveneck, *Frank Duveneck: Painter-Teacher* (San Francisco: John Howell-Books, 1970), 120. Carol M. Osborne, "Lizzie Boott at Bellosguardo,"

in *The Italian Presence in American Art, 1860–1920*, ed. Irma B. Jaffe (Bronx, NY: Fordham University Press, 1992), 198. Osborne convincingly refutes Jean Strouse's speculation in *Alice James: A Biography* (Boston: Houghton Mifflin, 1980) that Lizzie may have committed suicide, see p. 199 n. 15.

8. HJ to Henrietta Reubell, Apr. 1, 1888, HJL3, 230–31. HJ to FB, May 15, [1888], HJL3, 233. HJ quoted in Fred Kaplan, *Henry James: The Imagination of Genius: A Biography* (New York: William Morrow, 1992), 325. Leon Edel speculates that CFW gave HJ the description. See *Henry James: The Middle Years, 1882–1895* (Philadelphia: J. B. Lippincott, 1962), 248.

9. CRB to Leon Edel, July 23, [1953], McGill. CFW to FB, Sept. 15, [1888], Duveneck Family.

10. HJ to FB, Apr. 3, [1888], HJL3, 232.

11. Duveneck, *Frank Duveneck*, 123–24. CRB to Leon Edel, July 23, [1953], McGill. CFW to FB, Mar. 4, [1889], Duveneck Family.

12. CFW to FB, Aug. 7, [1888], Duveneck Family.

13. CFW to FB, Aug. 7, [1888]; CFW to FB, Mar. 14, [1893], Duveneck Family.

14. CFW to FB, Aug. 7, [1888]; CFW to FB, Sept. 15, [1888]; CFW to FB, Dec. 13, [1888], Duveneck Family.

15. CFW to FB, Sept. 15, [1888], Duveneck Family.

16. HJ to WWB, July 3, [1888], Pierpont Morgan. CFW to SM, Aug. 22, [1888], CL, 358.

17. HJ to FB, Oct. 29, [1888], HJL3, 247. HJ to FB, May 15, [1888], HJL3, 233. CFW's copy of *The Aspern Papers, Louisa Pallant, The Modern Warning* at University of Basel.

18. HJ to FB, Oct. 29, [1888], HJL3, 247, 246. CFW to FB, Dec. 13, [1888]; CFW to FB, Nov. 27, [1889], Duveneck Family.

19. HJ quoted in Edel, *The Middle Years*, 250. Alice James quoted in Strouse, *Alice James*, 259.

20. CWB to May Harris, n.d., Benedict III, 589.

21. CFW to Daniel Willard Fiske, Dec. 4, [1888], Cornell. The undated letters at Cornell mention many gifts. Quote about Fiske in Horatio S. White, "A Sketch of the Life and Labors of Professor Willard Fiske," *The Papers of the Bibliographical Society of America*, vol. 12 (Chicago: University of Chicago Press, 1919), 84.

22. CFW to Daniel Willard Fiske, Dec. 4, [1888], Cornell.

23. CFW to FB, Mar. 4, [1889], Duveneck Family. CFW, "A Pink Villa," *Harper's* 77 (Nov. 1888): 856.

24. CFW to SM, Feb. 27, [1889], CL, 367. Caroline Gebhard, "Romantic Love and Wife-Battering in Constance Fenimore Woolson's *Jupiter Lights*," in *Constance Fenimore Woolson's Nineteenth Century: Essays*, ed. Victoria Brehm (Detroit: Wayne State University Press, 2001), 83–96.

25. CFW, *Jupiter Lights* (New York: Harper & Brothers, 1889), 17.

26. Ibid., 11, 292. CFW to SM, Jan. 16, [1884], CL, 269. HJ quoted in Edel, *The Middle Years*, 208.

27. CFW, *Jupiter Lights*, 142, 234, 163.

28. Ibid., 179, 257.

29. CFW to FB, Feb. 7, [1890], Duveneck Family.

30. CFW, *Jupiter Lights*, 340, 347.
31. Ibid., 79.
32. Ibid., 90.
33. Caroline Halstead Royce, "Remembered Books," *New York Times*, Jan. 28, 1899, p. BR60.
34. CWB to KM, Jan. 27, 1889, Mather Family Papers, WRHS. "In reality, Clara gave [the party]," CFW wrote to SM, Feb. 27, [1889], CL, 365. CFW to WWB, [1889], CL, 363. CFW to Henry Mills Alden, Aug. 23, 1889, CL, 381.
35. HJ to FB, Jan. 18, 1889, HJL3, 249. CFW to SM, Feb. 27, [1889], CL, 366. Edward N. Akin, *Flagler: Rockefeller Partner and Florida Baron* (Kent, OH: The Kent State University Press, 1988), 116.
36. CFW to SM, Jan. 12, [1888], CL, 352. CFW to Mary Mapes Dodge, Sept. 13, [1888?], CL, 360. CFW to FB, Aug. 23, [1889]; CFW to FB, Mar. 4, [1889], Duveneck Family.
37. CFW to FB, Mar. 13, [1889], Duveneck Family. CFW to KM, 1889, CL, 370. CFW to FB, Nov. 27, [1889], Duveneck Family. CFW to Daniel Willard Fiske, May 13, [1889], CL, 369. CFW to Daniel Willard Fiske, Friday, n.d., Cornell.
38. CFW to Daniel Willard Fiske, Friday, n.d., Cornell. (This is a different letter than the one quoted above.) CFW to ECS, Aug. 10, [1889], CL, 377. CFW to SM, July 6, [1889], CL, 373. CFW to WWB, July 13, [1889], CL, 374. CFW to SM, Aug. 13, [1889], CL, 378.
39. CFW to SM, Oct. 16, [1889], CL, 383. CFW to SM, Nov. 4, 1890, CL, 427.
40. CFW to FB, Nov. 27, [1889], Duveneck Family. CFW to SM, Aug. 13, [1889], CL, 378.
41. CFW's copy of *The Teaching of Epictetus* (London: Walter Scott, 1888) is at Rollins. Pages torn out are 55–58, 66–68, and 71–72. Marked passages are on pp. 135 and 200. Someone later tried to erase her markings on p. 200.
42. CRB to Stella Gray, June 22, [1956], in possession of recipient. CFW, *Jupiter Lights*, 307.
43. CFW to SM, Aug. 13, [1889], CL, 378.
44. CFW to FB, Aug. 23, [1889], Duveneck Family. CFW to SM, Aug. 13, 1889, CL, 379. CFW to Henry Mills Alden, Aug. 23, 1889, CL, 380.
45. CFW to Daniel Willard Fiske, Oct. 16, [1889], Cornell. CFW to SM, Oct. 16, [1889], CL, 383. CFW to FB, Nov. 27, [1889], Duveneck Family.
46. CFW to SM, Feb. 25, 1890, CL, 403. "Recent Fiction," *The Independent* 43 (Nov. 28, 1889): 16. Review of *Jupiter Lights*, *The Book Buyer* 6 (Dec. 1, 1889): 453. "Harpers for September," *New York Herald*, Aug. 23, 1899, p. 2. The *Spectator* quoted in a Harper & Brothers advertisement, *New York Herald*, Oct. 30, 1899, p. 7. "Novels of the Week," *The Athenaeum*, no. 3247 (Jan. 18, 1890): 81.
47. Horace Scudder, "Recent American Fiction," *Atlantic Monthly* 65 (Jan. 1890): 127, 128. "Talk About New Books," *Catholic World* 50 (Mar. 1890): 826, 827.
48. CFW to SM, Apr. 17, [1890], CL, 409. "Recent Fiction," *The Nation* (Mar. 13, 1890): 225.
49. CFW to SM, Feb. 25, 1890, CL, 403. Sales figures in Rayburn Moore, *Constance Fenimore Woolson* (New York: Twayne, 1963), 159. CFW to SM, Dec. 8, [1889], CL, 388.

CHAPTER 13: *To Cairo and Back*

1. CFW, "Corfu and the Ionian Sea," in *Mentone, Cairo, and Corfu* (New York: Harper & Brothers, 1896), 284.
2. CFW to SM, Jan. 5, 1890, CL, 392. CFW, "Corfu," 286, 290.
3. CFW to SM, Jan. 5, 1890, CL, 390, 391.
4. CFW to SM, Jan. 5, 1890, CL, 391. CWB to Elizabeth ("Libbie") Gwinn Mather, Jan. 30, 1890, typescript, Mather Family Papers, WRHS. CFW, "Corfu," 355.
5. CFW to Henry Mills Alden, Jan. 17, 1890, CL, 396.
6. CWB to Elizabeth ("Libbie") Gwinn Mather, Jan. 30, 1890, typescript, Mather Family Papers, WRHS. CFW to Henry Mills Alden, Jan. 17, 1890, CL, 396, 397.
7. CFW to Daniel Willard Fiske, Feb. 19, [1890], Cornell.
8. CWB to Elizabeth ("Libbie") Gwinn Mather, Jan. 30, 1890, in typescript, Mather Family Papers, WRHS. CFW to SM, Feb. 25, 1890, CL, 404. CFW to SM, Jan. 31, 1890, CL, 399.
9. CWB to Samuel L. Mather, Mar. 4, 1890, typescript, Mather Family Papers, WRHS. CFW to SM, Feb. 25, 1890, CL, 403. CWB to Elizabeth ("Libbie") Gwinn Mather, Jan. 30, 1890, typescript, Mather Family Papers, WRHS.
10. CFW to SM, Apr. 17, 1890, CL, 406–7. CWB to Samuel L. Mather, Mar. 4, 1890, typescript, Mather Family Papers, WRHS.
11. CFW to Flora Stone Mather, n.d., CL, 553. Eugene Schuyler, *Selected Essays with a Memoir by Evelyn Schuyler Schaeffer* (New York: Charles Scribner's Sons, 1901), 198. CFW to JH, Dec. 20, 1890, CL, 436.
12. CFW to SM, Apr. 17, [1890], CL, 408–9. CFW to Flora Stone Mather, [1890], CL, 438.
13. CFW to SM, Apr. 17, [1890], CL, 408.
14. CFW to KM, June 12, 1890, CL, 415. CFW, "Cairo in 1890," in *Mentone, Cairo, and Corfu*, 158, 160.
15. CFW, "Cairo in 1890," 156, 236–38. CFW to Henry Mills Alden, May 20, [1890], CL, 413–14.
16. CFW, "Cairo in 1890," 177.
17. Ibid., 232, 224, 225.
18. Ibid., 193, 220. CFW's prediction was incorrect; Al-Azhar University in Cairo remains today a center of Islamic learning.
19. Ibid., 276–77. CFW to WWB, Dec. 17, [1893], CL, 542. Praying Arab figurine at Rollins.
20. CFW, "Cairo in 1890," 208, 211.
21. Ibid., 278, 279. CFW to JH, Dec. 20, [1890], CL, 435.
22. CFW to WWB, Aug. 17, [1890], CL, 418. HJ to FB, Apr. 23, 1890, Houghton, MS Am 1094.609.
23. CFW to Henry Mills Alden, May 11, [1890], CL, 411. CFW's copy of *God in His World* in Clare Benedict Collection, WRHS; quoted passage and marginalia on p. 33. Lines in both margins also mark the passage.
24. CFW to Henry Mills Alden, May 11, [1890], CL, 412–13.
25. CFW to Katharine Loring, Sept. 19, [1890], CL, 421. CFW to KM, [June 12, 1890], CL, 415.

26. CFW to FB, Sept. 11 and Sept. 17, [1890], Duveneck Family. HJ speaks of his upcoming "pious pilgrimage" to Bellosguardo in HJ to FB, Apr. 23, 1890, Houghton, MS Am 1094.609. He stayed with Baldwin in Florence in July. HJ to WWB, Sept. 29, [1890], Pierpont Morgan. CFW told WWB that HJ spent "two days" with her; Oct. 5, [1890], CL, 423. He most likely stayed at the Queen's Hotel up the street or in the apartment below her; both are mentioned in letters to other visitors.

27. CFW to Katharine Loring, Sept. 19, [1890], CL, 421. CFW to WWB, Oct. 5, [1890], CL, 423. CFW to FB, Nov. 23, [1890], Duveneck Family.

28. CFW to Katharine Loring, Sept. 19, [1890], CL, 422. William James's report in *Proceedings of the Society for Psychical Research*, vol. 6 (London: Kegan Paul, Trench, Trübner, 1890), 660. CFW to JH, Dec. 20, [1890], CL, 437. CFW to FB, Jan. 9, [1890], Duveneck Family.

29. CFW to FB, Sept. 17, [1890], Duveneck Family. CFW to FB, Nov. 23, [1890], Duveneck Family. CFW to SM, Nov. 4, 1890, CL, 428.

30. CFW to SM, Oct. 31, [1890], CL, 425. CFW to SM, Oct. 9, [1890], CL, 424.

31. HJ to FB, Dec. 19, 1890, Houghton, MS Am 1094.611. CFW to SM, Dec. 15, [1890], CL, 431. England has eight hours of daily sunlight during December; CFW must be exaggerating for effect or referring to the grayness of the days.

32. CFW to FB, Jan. 9, [1891], Duveneck Family. CFW to SM, Jan. 21, 1891, CL, 439.

33. CFW to FB, May 2, [1891], Duveneck Family. CFW, "Dorothy," *Harper's* 84 (Mar. 1892): 562.

34. Ibid., 563.

35. Ibid., 566, 570.

36. Ibid., 574, 575.

37. CFW to FB, Feb. 28, [1892], Duveneck Family.

38. CFW to SM, Jan. 21, 1891, CL, 442, 441.

39. HJ to Alice James and Katharine Loring, [Jan. 4, 1891], HJL3, 320.

40. CFW to FB, Feb. 28, [1891], Duveneck Family.

41. CFW to FB, May 2, [1891], Duveneck Family. CFW to FB, Feb. 28, [1891], Duveneck Family. CFW to WWB, Jan. 25, [1891], CL, 444.

42. HJ to FB, Mar. 24, [1891], Houghton, MS Am 1094.612. CFW to FB, Feb. 28, [1891], Duveneck Family.

43. HJ quoted in Leon Edel, *Henry James: The Middle Years, 1882–1895* (Philadelphia: J. B. Lippincott, 1962), 287. CFW to SM, Jan. 21, 1891, CL, 442.

44. CFW to FB, Nov. 23, [1890], Duveneck Family. CFW to SM, Nov. 4, 1890, CL, 427.

45. CFW to FB, Feb. 28, [1891], Duveneck Family. CFW to SM, Feb. 23, [1891], CL, 447.

46. CFW to FB, May 2, [1891], Duveneck Family. See also KM to SM, May 29, 1891, Mather Family Papers, WRHS. CRB to Leon Edel, Jan. 29, 1948, McGill. This comment was in response to Edel's question about whether CFW stayed in England to be near HJ. His nearness, she insisted, was but one benefit of living in England.

CHAPTER 14: *Oxford*

1. Jean Strouse, *Alice James: A Biography* (Boston: Houghton Mifflin, 1980), 305; quote from HJ on p. 306.
2. HJ to WWB, [July 25, 1891], Pierpont Morgan. HJ to FB, July 29, [1891], Houghton, MS Am 1094.615.
3. James D. Symon, "Oriel Bill," *English Illustrated Magazine* 11 (Feb. 1894): 455–56.
4. CFW to FB, Nov. 21, [1891], Duveneck Family.
5. CFW to Flora Stone Mather, [1891], CL, 462. CFW to SM, Oct. 16, [1891], CL, 459.
6. CFW to Flora Stone Mather, [1891], CL, 461–62.
7. CFW to SM, Oct. 16, [1891], CL, 459. CFW to FB, Nov. 21, [1891], Duveneck Family. CFW to KM, Oct. 20, 1891, CL, 460. Premiere described in Leon Edel, *Henry James: The Middle Years, 1882–1895* (Philadelphia: J. B. Lippincott, 1962), 297–99; and Fred Kaplan, *Henry James: The Imagination of Genius: A Biography* (New York: William Morrow, 1992), 344–45. HJ to WWB, Oct. 19, 1891, in Philip Horne, ed., *Henry James: A Life in Letters* (New York: Viking, 1999), 242.
8. CFW to FB, Nov. 21, [1891], Duveneck Family.
9. CFW to Linda Thayer Guilford, [1891], CL, 465. CFW to FB, Nov. 21, [1891], Duveneck Family.
10. CFW to FB, Nov. 21, [1891], Duveneck Family.
11. CFW to SM, Jan. 9, [1893], CL, 499–500. On the English Library series, see Clement Vollmer, *The American Novel in Germany, 1871–1913* (Philadelphia: International Printing, 1918), 26–27.
12. HJ to WWB, Dec. 29, 1891, Pierpont Morgan.
13. CFW to WWB, Feb. 5, [1892], CL, 467. CFW to FB, Feb. 21, [1892], Duveneck Family. "Statistics of the Influenza Epidemic," *The British Medical Journal* 1 (Jan. 23, 1892): 190.
14. CFW to WWB, Feb. 5 and Feb. 6, [1892], CL, 467, 469. CFW to SM, Feb, 8, [1892], CL, 470.
15. CFW to WWB, Feb. 6, [1892], CL, 468, 469. CFW to SM, Feb, 8, [1892], CL, 470.
16. CFW to SM, May 20, [1892], CL, 476.
17. CRB to Leon Edel, Jan. 29, 1948, McGill. CFW to SM, Nov. 24, [1892], CL, 492. CFW to SM, [Jan. 1893], CL, 496.
18. CFW to FB, Feb. 21, [1892], Duveneck Family.
19. CFW to FB, Feb. 21, [1892], Duveneck Family. CFW to WWB, Feb. 6, [1892], CL, 469. Only a small fragment of a letter survives, in BHS, written by CFW and addressed, I believe, to Alice James. It was written when HJ had jaundice in Venice in 1887.
20. Strouse, *Alice James*, 312.
21. CFW to SM, May 20, [1892], CL, 476. HJ to FB, Mar. 9, [1892], HJL3, 382.
22. CFW to SM, Apr. 29, [1893], CL, 512. Lyndall Gordon, *A Private Life of Henry James: Two Women and His Art* (New York: W. W. Norton, 1998), 249. Edel also acknowledges the possibility that the message was about their relationship but doesn't examine it further. See *The Middle Years*, 318.
23. HJ to FB, Mar. 9, [1892], HJL3, 381.

24. Benedict III, 605. CFW to SM, July 15, [1892], CL, 482.

25. CFW to SM, Jan. 21, [1892], CL, 466. CFW to SM, Feb. 15, [1892], CL, 473. "Archives of Harper and Brothers, 1817–1914," microfilm (Cambridge: Chadwyck-Healey, 1980), Butler Library, Columbia University, reel 34 F2. CFW to Henry Mills Alden, June 30, [1892], CL, 480.

26. CFW to FB, Feb. 21, [1892], Duveneck Family.

27. CFW to SM, Oct. 14, [1892], CL, 488. There are no surviving letters from CFW to FB from between April 1892 and January 1893.

28. HJ, "The Lesson of the Master," in *Selected Tales* (New York: Penguin, 2001), 145. CFW to SM, Feb. 27, [1889], CL, 364.

29. This is the only story CFW published in *Harper's Bazar*, and there is no conceivable reason why Alden would not have wanted the story for *Harper's*. She had published in *Harper's* only twice since *Jupiter Lights* finished its run in September 1889.

30. CFW, "In Sloane Street," *Harper's Bazar* 25 (June 11, 1892): 474.

31. Ibid., 474.

32. Gordon, in *A Private Life*, believes Gertrude is a secret writer (251). Marie Bashkirtseff, *The Journal of Marie Bashkirtseff*, vol. 2 (London: Cassell, 1890), 103–4. CFW, "In Sloane Street," 475.

33. CFW, "In Sloane Street," 475, 477.

34. Ibid., 475.

35. Sheldon M. Novick, *Henry James: The Mature Master* (New York: Random House, 2007), 204. Kaplan, *The Imagination of Genius*, 313. Gordon, *A Private Life*, 198. HJ quoted in CRB to Leon Edel, July 23, [1953], McGill.

36. HJ, "The Middle Years," in *Tales of Henry James* (New York: W. W. Norton, 2003), 211.

37. CFW to SM, Apr. 29, [1893], CL, 512.

38. CFW to KM, Dec. 27, [1892], CL, 493. CFW to SM, May 20, [1892], CL, 477. CFW to SM, Nov. 4, 1890, CL, 428. CFW to SM, Jan. 9, [1893], CL, 498.

39. CFW to SM, Mar. 14, [1893], CL, 506. CFW, "Mottoes, Maxims, Reflections," Rollins. CFW to FB, Mar. 4, [1889], Duveneck Family.

40. CFW to Henry Mills Alden, June 30, [1892], CL, 481, 480.

41. CFW to SM, Jan. 9, [1892], CL, 498, 499.

42. CFW, *Horace Chase* (New York: Harper & Brothers, 1894), 283.

43. See CFW to KM, Dec. 27, [1892], CL, 493. The chant appears on pp. 4–5 of *Horace Chase*.

44. CFW, *Horace Chase*, 255, 340–41, 419. CFW to Henry Mills Alden, June 30, [1892?], CL, 481.

45. CFW, *Horace Chase*, 212, 9, 30–31.

46. Ibid., 160, 175.

47. Ibid., 80–81, 18.

48. CFW, "Mottoes, Maxims, Reflections," Rollins.

49. CFW to SM, Jan. 9, [1893], CL, 500. CFW to FB, Jan. 9, [1893], Duveneck Family.

50. CFW to SM, Mar. 14, [1893], CL, 505. CFW to FB, Mar. 14, [1893], Duveneck Family.

51. CFW to unknown recipient, 1893, CL, 510. CFW to KM, June 12, 1890, CL, 415.
52. CFW to SM, Apr. 29, [1893], CL, 512. CFW to FB, Mar. 14, [1893], Duveneck Family.
53. CFW to SM, Apr. 29, [1893], CL, 512.
54. CFW to Rebekah Owen, May 9, [1893], CL, 513.
55. CFW to WWB, June 16, [1893], CL, 513. CFW to KM, July 2, 1893, CL, 517.
56. CFW to WWB, June 16, [1893], CL, 515.

CHAPTER 15: *The Riddle of Existence*

1. CFW to Winifred Howells, May 11, 1883, CL, 253. CFW to HJ, May 7, 1883, CL, 246. CFW to Flora Mather, July 1, 1893, CL, 516. The Casa Biondetti is near the Peggy Guggenheim Museum.
2. CFW, "Lagoons," Benedict II, 393–99. Ellipses in original.
3. CFW to Flora Mather, July 1, 1893, CL, 516.
4. CFW to FB, Sept. 9, [1893], Duveneck Family.
5. CFW to KM, July 2, 1893, CL, 517–18.
6. HJ, "The Grand Canal," [Nov. 1892], in *Italian Hours* (New York: Penguin, 1992), 33. CFW to WWB, July 20, [1893], CL, 518. HJ to William James, Mar. 24, [1894], HJL3, 470.
7. CFW to KM, Aug. 20, 1893, CL, 520. CFW to WWB, June 16, [1893], CL, 514. Linda Simon, "Diagnosing the Physician: Patients' Evaluation of Nineteenth Century Medical Therapeutics," in *Revue Angliciste de l'Université de la Réunion, Alizes/Trade Winds* (Automne 2003), http://laboratoires.univ-reunion.fr/oracle/documents/352.html. Sigmund Freud, "The Origin and Development of Psychoanalysis" (1901), in *From Madness to Mental Health: Psychiatric Disorder and Its Treatment in Western Civilization*, ed. Greg Eghigian (New Brunswick, NJ: Rutgers University Press, 2010), 207–23.
8. CFW to WWB, June 16, [1893], CL, 514.
9. Simon, in "Diagnosing the Physician," writes, "Baldwin, unlike other physicians, affirmed his patients' experience that depression and fatigue often resulted from organic illness, and that pain, whatever its cause, was real." CFW to KM, Aug. 20, 1893, CL, 520. Daniel Tuke, *A Dictionary of Psychological Medicine*, vol. 1 (Philadelphia: Blakiston, 1892), 688. Some medical scientists continue to look for a link between influenza and depression; see Olaoluwa Okusaga et al., "Association of Seropositivity for Influenza and Coronaviruses with History of Mood Disorders and Suicide Attempts," *Journal of Affective Disorders* 130 (2011): 220–25. F. B. Smith, "The Russian Influenza in the United Kingdom, 1889–1894," *Social History of Medicine* 8, no. 1 (1995): 71. HJ to Ariana Curtis, [June 21, 1894], Dartmouth.
10. CFW to KM, Aug. 20, 1893, CL, 520. CFW to SM, Oct. 31, [1893], CL, 526. CFW to unknown recipient, Oct. 14, [1893], CL, 524.
11. CFW to KM, Aug. 20, 1893, CL, 521. Ruskin quoted in Stephen Kite, *Building Ruskin's Italy: Watching Architecture* (Farnham, UK: Ashgate, 2012), 115. Ruskin's drawings and notes of the Palazzo Orio, as it was then called, are on p. 112.
12. CFW to FB, Sept. 9, [1893], Duveneck Family.

13. The painting by Ricciardo Meacci today hangs in Lamb House, Rye, England, the final home of HJ. He had originally given CFW the painting and CWB gave it back to him after her death. Although CWB later asked for it back, the painting was returned to Lamb House, presumably after CWB's death. The painting as well as notes pasted on the back, one in CFW's hand, are viewable at http://www.nationaltrustcollections.org.uk/object/204158.

14. HJ to Ariana Curtis, July 14, [1893], HJL3, 420. CFW to SM, Dec. 21, [1893], CL, 544. HJ to Ariana Curtis, Sept. 19, [1893], quoted in Leon Edel, *Henry James: The Middle Years, 1882–1895* (Philadelphia: J. B. Lippincott, 1962), 348.

15. CFW to CRB, Dec. 3, [1893], CL, 533. CFW to SM, Oct. 31, [1893], CL, 527.

16. Julian Norwich, *Paradise of Cities: Venice in the 19th Century* (New York: Doubleday, 2003), 247–48. HJ quoted in Rosella Mamoli Zorzi, Introduction, *Letters from the Palazzo Barbaro* by Henry James (London: Pushkin Press, 1998), 25. CFW to SM, Dec. 21, [1893], CL, 543.

17. CFW to SM, Nov. 20, 1893, CL, 528–29.

18. Ibid., 529.

19. CFW, "A Transplanted Boy," in *Dorothy and Other Italian Stories* (New York: Harper & Brothers, 1896), 120, 121.

20. Unpublished Curtis diary for 1893, private collection. HJ to FB, Oct. 21, 1893, HJL3, 37.

21. CFW to SM, Nov. 20, 1893, CL, 529. CFW to Zina Hulton, Nov. 15, [1893], Hulton Papers, Bodleian Library, Oxford University.

22. CFW to KM, Dec. 13, [1893], CL, 539. CFW to SM, Nov. 20, 1893, CL, 528.

23. HJ to WWB, Nov. 10, 1893, Pierpont Morgan.

24. CFW to SM, Nov. 23, [1893], CL, 530. CFW to SM, Dec. 10, [1893], CL, 534.

25. CFW to SM, Dec. 20, [1893], CL, 543.

26. CFW to KM, Dec. 13, [1893], 537–38.

27. Ibid., 536, 538.

28. CFW to WWB, Dec. 17, [1893], CL, 541. CFW to KM, Dec. 13, [1893], 537.

29. CFW to WWB, Dec. 17, [1893], CL, 541. CFW, Notebook, Rollins.

30. CFW, "Reflections," Rollins. This is written on a scrap of paper, presumably from a different notebook than that in which she kept her notes on the lagoons. The passage is also printed in Benedict II, 411, with some slight modification. It does not end with a period, and, in fact, it may have continued on another page that has not survived.

31. CFW to KM, Dec. 25, [1893], CL, 540. CFW to ACW, Dec. 25, [1893], CL, 545; ellipses in original.

32. HJ to Katherine Bronson, Dec. 31, 1893, quoted in Edel, *The Middle Years*, 356. HJ to Daniel Curtis, Dec. 27, 1893, Dartmouth.

33. Henry Mills Alden, "Constance Fenimore Woolson," *Harper's Weekly* 38 (Feb. 3, 1894): 113.

34. CFW to KM, Dec. 25, [1894], CL, 440. Lady Layard's Journal, *The Brownings: A Research Guide*, http://www.browningguide.org/browningcircle.php. CFW to SM, Dec. 21, [1893], CL, 544. Lady Layard's Journal makes many mentions of Zina Hulton, the Bronsons, and the princess, whom she calls Olga, during these first weeks of the new year. Olga would later report to Lady Layard what she learned of CFW's death.

35. Dr. Cini is identified as "head physician of the hospital" in an article about Woolson's death, "The Suicide of an American Lady," *Il Gazzettino* (Venice), Jan. 25, 1894. Lyndall Gordon, in *A Private Life of Henry James: Two Women and His Art* (New York: W. W. Norton, 1998), spells his name Chene, as it would be pronounced, which is how Grace Carter, who did not know him, spelled it. Lady Layard, who knew him well, spelled it Cini. Marie Holas to SM, Jan. 31, 1894, CL, 571. Grace Carter to SM, Jan. 27, 1894, Mather Family Papers, WRHS. This letter is incorrectly dated as [2-4-1894]. The correct date appears at the end of the letter, after the signature. CFW to Harper & Brothers, Jan. 17, 1894, CL, 546.
36. Grace Carter to SM, Jan. 27, 1894, Mather Family Papers, WRHS. Marie Holas to SM, Jan. 31, 1894, CL, 572.
37. Grace Carter to SM, Jan. 27, 1894, Mather Family Papers, WRHS. Marie Holas to SM, Jan. 31, 1894, CL, 572. CFW's words reported by Holas. CFW's vomiting has been interpreted by Gordon, in *A Private Life*, as evidence that she was trying to poison herself "under the cover of supposed flu," 273–74. However, the presence of fever indicates illness, and the fact that CFW left no will shows a lack of premeditation to kill herself. Lady Layard recorded in her journal on Jan. 19, [1984], "There is a great deal of influenza about." Associations of green bile with ill temper, etc., in the entry for *bile*, in the Oxford English Dictionary, 2nd ed. (1989). Possible causes of CFW's symptoms identified in Joan Weimer, *Back Talk: Teaching Lost Selves to Speak* (New York: Random House, 1994), 264, and independently confirmed in discussion with Dr. Eva Lizer.
38. CFW to KM, Dec. 13, [1893], CL, 537.
39. Marie Holas to SM, Jan. 31, 1894, CL, 573.
40. Grace Carter to SM, Jan. 27, 1894, Mather Family Papers, WRHS. Marie Holas to SM, Jan. 31, 1894, CL, 573.
41. HJ to WWB, Jan. 26 [1894], HJL3, 457.
42. My reading of CFW's final days differs from that of Gordon, in *A Private Life*, who sees CFW as calmly preparing for and planning her suicide over many days (274–76). Lady Layard's Journal, Jan. 28, [1984]. Marie Holas to SM, Jan. 31, 1894, CL, 573. Grace Carter to SM, Jan. 27, 1894, Mather Family Papers, WRHS.
43. Marie Holas to SM, Jan. 31, 1894, CL, 573. Grace Carter to SM, Jan. 27, 1894, Mather Family Papers, WRHS. Lady Layard's Journal, Mar. 7, [1894].
44. Martin Booth, *Opium: A History* (New York: Thomas Dunne, St. Martin's Press, 1996), 49. Alethea Hayter, *Opium and the Romantic Imagination* (Berkeley: University of California Press, 1968), 57–59. Jean Strouse, *Alice James: A Biography* (Boston: Houghton Mifflin, 1980), 308.
45. Marie Holas to SM, Jan. 31, 1894, CL, 573. "The Suicide of an American Lady," *Il Gazzettino* (Venice), Jan. 25, 1894, translated by Edoarda Grego.
46. Alice James, *The Diary of Alice James*, ed. Leon Edel (Boston: Northeastern University Press, 1999), 232. Grace Carter to SM, Jan. 27, 1894, Mather Family Papers, WRHS. Marie Holas to SM, Jan. 31, 1894, CL, 574. CFW's bell is at Rollins.
47. Grace Carter to SM, Jan. 27, 1894, Mather Family Papers, WRHS. Marie Holas to SM, Jan. 31, 1894, CL, 574. According to Lady Layard's Journal, Jan. 28 [1894], CFW requested a cup that was holding flowers and would thus require washing. No one knows for sure what happened after the nurse left the room. There are

conflicting accounts of the window she may have jumped or fallen from. Gordon, in *A Private Life*, correctly identifies the room as "overlooking the *calle*" but indicates that the sill of CFW's bedroom window was too high for her to have fallen out of it accidentally (276). However, Rosella Mamoli Zorzi has taken for me pictures of the windows in what must have been Woolson's bedroom, as it is the only room facing the calle that was then in existence. (An addition was made in the twentieth century.) These pictures show that the sills were about two feet above the floor, indicating that CFW easily could have fallen out of one of the windows. In fact, today there are bars over the bottom portion of the windows to prevent anyone from falling or jumping out of them again. In any event, because no one was in the room with CFW and no description of the windows as they were then has survived, we cannot definitively know if she fell or jumped deliberately.

CHAPTER 16: *Aftershocks*

1. "The Suicide of an American Lady," *Il Gazzettino* (Venice), Jan. 25, 1894, and "Suicide," *La Gazzetta di Venezia*, Jan. 25, 1894, both translated by Edoarda Grego. "Miss Woolson's Fate," *The Buffalo (NY) Express*, Feb. 16, 1894, a translation by Kate Field of a Jan. 25 story in the paper *La Venezia*. Grace Carter to SM, Jan. 27, 1894, Mather Family Papers, WRHS.
2. Grace Carter to SM, Jan. 27, 1894, Mather Family Papers, WRHS.
3. JH to SM, Jan. 31, 1894; Clara Hay to Flora Stone Mather, Jan. 31, 1894; JH to SM, Mar. 2, 1894, Mather Family Papers, WRHS.
4. For initial U.S. reports, see, as a sampling: "A Favorite Writer Dead," *Kansas City Star*, Jan. 25, 1894, p. 3; "Death of Constance F. Woolson," *New York Times*, Jan. 25, 1894, p. 2; "Mrs. [*sic*] Woolson, the Novelist, Dead," *Philadelphia Inquirer*, Jan. 26, 1894, p. 1. In Venice, the following stories ran: "The Suicide of an American Lady," *Il Gazzettino* (Venice), Jan. 25, 1894, and "Suicide," *La Gazzetta di Venezia*, Jan. 25, 1894; quote from the latter, translated by Edoarda Grego. "Suicide of a Lady Novelist," *The Standard* (London), Jan. 27, 1894, p. 5. For reprints of this report in the United States, see, as a sampling: "Says Miss Woolson Was a Suicide," *New York Times*, Jan. 27, 1894, p. 8; "Miss Woolson Committed Suicide," *The Sun* (Baltimore), Jan. 27, 1894, p. 1; "Suicide of an American Authoress," *Omaha Daily Bee*, Jan. 27, 1894, p. 1; and "Jumped from a Window," *Idaho Daily Statesman*, Jan. 27, 1894, p. 1.
5. Grace Carter to SM, Jan. 27, 1894, Mather Family Papers, WRHS. Telegram, presumably from Grace (not signed), presumably to SM (addressed to Mather Hotel, Windsor, NY), microform, Constance Fenimore Woolson Papers, WRHS. Only a few papers ran the story; see, for instance: "MISS WOOLSON NOT A SUICIDE: She Fell from Her Window While Wandering About in Delirium," *New York Times*, Jan. 28, 1894, p. 3; *The Freeman's Journal* (Cooperstown), Feb. 1, 1894, p. 3; "Not a Case of Suicide," (New Orleans) *Times-Picayune*, Jan. 29, 1894, p. 10; "Prominent Personals," *Vermont Phoenix*, Feb. 9, 1894, p. 3. R. J. Nevin to Anna Grace Carter, Feb. 7, 1894, Henry James Papers, University of Virginia.

6. Marie Holas to SM, Jan. 31, 1894, CL, 574. Lady Layard's Journal, Mar. 7 and Apr. 3, [1894].

7. Kay Redfield Jamison, *Night Falls Fast: Understanding Suicide* (New York: Alfred A. Knopf, 1999), 93.

8. "Death is not terrible to me," CFW wrote to HJ, Feb. 23, [1882], CL, 191. "To me it is only a release; & if, at any time, you should hear that I had died, always be sure that I was quite willing, & even glad, to go." Jamison explains in *Night Falls Fast* that many suicides are neither simply "long-considered" or sudden but "both: a brash moment of action taken during a span of settled and suicidal hopelessness" (198).

9. HJ to Anna Grace Carter, Jan. 26, [1894], Henry James Papers, UVA, 6251 (Box 2:73). HJ to WWB, Jan. 26, [1894], HJL3, 457.

10. Some of HJ's letters in which he discusses CFW's death can be found in HJL3, 457–71. Lyndall Gordon discusses the letters HJ wrote in *A Private Life of Henry James: Two Women and His Art* (New York: W. W. Norton, 1998), 279–80. Clipping from the *New York Herald* in Mather family scrapbook. Much else in this article, which suggests that HJ remained unmarried because his heart was buried in CFW's grave, is erroneous. But it is interesting that the family kept the clipping. It was one of the few verifications in print of their close tie. I have been unable to locate the original.

11. HJ to WWB, Feb. 2, 1894, HJL3, 464.

12. Quoted in Hermione Lee, *Edith Wharton* (New York: Alfred A. Knopf, 2007), 213.

13. HJ to FB, Jan. 31, [1894], HJL3, 463. HJ to JH, Jan. 28, 1894, John Hay Collection, Brown. HJ to Katherine de Kay Bronson, Feb. 2, 1894, HJL3, 465–66. Alice James, *The Diary of Alice James*, ed. Leon Edel (Boston: Northeastern University Press, 1999), 52.

14. HJ to FB, Jan. 31, [1894], HJL3, 463; HJ to WWB, Feb. 2, 1894, HJL3, 464; HJ to Katherine de Kay Bronson, Feb. 2, 1894, HJL3, 465. HJ to William James, Mar, 24, [1894], HJL3, 470.

15. HJ to Katherine de Kay Bronson, HJL3, 467.

16. Leon Edel posed the question in *The Middle Years, 1882–1895* (Philadelphia: J. B. Lippincott, 1962): "Had her act been a partial consequence of frustration—of frustrated love for Henry?" (363). More recently, Gordon, in *A Private Life*, has imagined James asking, "What if Fenimore had killed herself because of him?" (289). But there is no evidence that she killed herself because of unrequited love for HJ or separation from HJ.

17. CRB to Leon Edel, Nov. 27, 1947, McGill. Edel, *The Middle Years*, 367–68.

18. Benedict III, 4–5; ellipses in original.

19. CWB to SM, May 2, [1894], Mather Family Papers, WRHS.

20. Zina Hulton, "Fifty Years in Venice," typescript, p. 130, Hulton Papers, Bodleian Library, Oxford University. Scraps and notes from CFW published in Benedict II. Anecdote by Mercede Huntington, "Recollections of Henry James in His Later Years," a transcription of interviews done by the BBC in 1956, Houghton, MS Eng 1213.4(20).

21. HJ to WWB, [May 27, 1894], Pierpont Morgan. HJ to CRB, Sept. 13, [1907], HJL4, 460.

22. Benedict III, 4. CFW to WWB, July 20, [1893], CL, 518. HJ, *The Complete Note-books of Henry James*, eds. Leon Edel and Lyall H. Powers (New York: Oxford University Press, 1987), 98.
23. Benedict II, 144–45.
24. HJ, "The Beast in the Jungle," in *Selected Tales* (New York: Penguin, 2001), 432.
25. Ibid., 436, 437.
26. Ibid., 443, 445.
27. Ibid., 446, 449.
28. Ibid., 454, 456.
29. Ibid., 459–60, 461.
30. HJ to Grace Carter, June 7, 1900, Henry James Papers, UVA, 6251 (Box 8:83).
31. HJ to unknown recipient, Jan. 29, 1894, Edel Papers, McGill. Note at the end by a researcher indicates that the proper date of the letter is Jan. 29, 1914, and another note indicates that this was "the date of Fenimore's death." It was close— Jan. 24 was the real date.

EPILOGUE: *Remembrance*

1. M.H., Letter to Editor, *New York Times Saturday Review of Books*, June 2, 1906, p. BR358.
2. See for instance, "Constance Fenimore Woolson," *Brooklyn Eagle*, Jan. 25, 1894, p. 4; Margaret Sangster, "Constance Fenimore Woolson," *Harper's Bazar* 27 (Feb. 3, 1894): 93; "Constance Fenimore Woolson," *The Critic* 21 (Feb. 3, 1894): 73; "Books and Authors," *The Graphic* (Chicago) (Feb. 10, 1894): 120; and "Editorial," *Godey's Magazine* 128 (Mar. 1894): 366. The Mather family scrapbook contains many more examples in (often unidentified) clippings. ECS quoted in "Constance Fenimore Woolson," *New York Tribune*, Jan. 28, 1894, p. 14.
3. "Our London Correspondence," *Glasgow Herald*, Jan. 30, 1894. *The Illustrated London News*, Feb. 3, 1894, p. 135.
4. Charles Dudley Warner, "Editor's Study," *Harper's* 88 (May 1894): 967.
5. "Comment on New Books," *Atlantic Monthly* 73 (May 1894): 705. "Fiction New and Old," *The (Cleveland) Plain Dealer*, Mar. 11, 1894, p. 4. "Horace Chase," *The Critic* 24 (Apr. 21, 1894): 270. "Recent Fiction," *The Interior* 25 (Apr. 26, 1894): 536.
6. Phyllis Rose, *Woman of Letters: The Life of Virginia Woolf* (New York: Harcourt, 1987), xvi.
7. Benedict III, 603. John Hervey, "Sympathetic Art," *The Saturday Review of Art*, Oct. 12, 1929; reprinted in Benedict II, 559.
8. See Suzanne Clarke, *Sentimental Modernism: Women Writers and the Revolution of the Word* (Bloomington: Indiana University Press, 1991); Anne E. Boyd, *Writing for Immortality: Women and the Emergence of High Literary Culture in America* (Baltimore: Johns Hopkins University Press, 2004).
9. Fred Lewis Pattee, *A History of American Literature Since 1870* (New York: Century, 1915); John Dwight Kern, *Constance Fenimore Woolson: Literary Pioneer* (Philadelphia: University of Pennsylvania Press, 1934); Lyon N. Richardson,

"Constance Fenimore Woolson, 'Novelist Laureate' of America," *South Atlantic Quarterly* 39 (Jan. 1940): 20–36.

10. Leon Edel, *Henry James: The Middle Years, 1882–1895* (Philadelphia: J. B. Lippincott, 1962), 203. See his many letters to Clare Benedict in Edel Papers, McGill. Rayburn Moore's important academic study of CFW was also published at this time: *Constance Fenimore Woolson* (New York, Twayne, 1963).

11. See the work of Victoria Brehm, Cheryl Torsney, and Sharon Dean, among others, as well as Joan Myers Weimer, ed., *Women Artists, Women Exiles: "Miss Grief" and Other Stories* (New Brunswick, NJ: Rutgers University Press, 1988). It was this anthology that first introduced me to CFW when I was a graduate student.

12. JH to SM, Jan. 31, 1894, Mather Family Papers, WRHS.

13. Benedict III, 290.

Index

Page numbers in *italics* refer to illustrations.
Page numbers beginning with 332 refer to endnotes.